Outrageously funny

best describes this mammoth book of wit, parody and satire about poetry and poets.

"Dean Blehert ... is quite simply the finest satiric poet working in America today." — *Satire Magazine*

"Dean Blehert is a radical innovator in contemporary poetry. He has rediscovered pleasure. His poems are – how contrarian – both fun to read and wonderfully perceptive about the follies of modern life. I hope he represents the cutting edge of poetry for the new millennium. But if not, we can console ourselves by rereading him." — Dana Gioia

"What a banquet!! the chapters are incredible – a feast of wit. They are wild and wonderful — incredibly clever!" —Lyn Lifshin

"The [Dylan] Thomas sendup is just a scream... Tears, I assure you. The Vale of Laughter." — John Mella, Editor, *LIGHT*

" I'd rather read Dean Blehert's poetry than my own. He's the me I'd like to be when I grow up." — Larry Gross, Author, *How to Write and Appreciate Poetry*

This book can ruin your life too!

Please, Lord, Make Me a Famous Poet or at Least Less Fat

or Everything You Always Wanted To Know About Poetry, But Were Afraid If You Asked, Someone Would Start Talking About Whatchamajigger Pentameter

or Life In The Pen, by I. M. Bic

(unused sub-titles for sale here)

by Dean "My-Other-Slim-Volume-Won-A-Prestigious-Poetry-Prize" **Blehert**

Illustrated by Pam Coulter "I'm-Really-A-Fine-Artist-And-This-Isn't-The-Sort-Of-Art-I-Normally-Do" **Blehert**

FIRST EDITION

Publisher's Cataloging-in-Publication
(Provided by Quality Books, Inc.)

Blehert, Dean.
    Please, Lord, make me a famous poet or at least less fat, or, Everything you always wanted to know about poetry, but were afraid if you asked, someone would start talking about whatchamajigger pentameter, or Life in the pen, by I.M. BIC / by Dean Blehert ; illustrated by Pam Coulter Blehert. -- 1st ed.
    p. cm.
    Includes index.
    "Unused sub-titles for sale here."
    Preassigned LCCN: 98-96522
    ISBN: 1-892261-03-0
    1. Poetry. 2. Poetry--Humor. 3. Poetics.
I. Blehert, Pam. II. Title.

PN1031.B54 1999   808-1.
                         QBI98-1056

Published in the United States by Words & Pictures East Coast, LLC

Printed in the United States of America

Table of Contents

Previous published books of poems by Dean Blehert (all available from Words &
Pictures East Coast):

Dear Reader or Love Letters From Here to There, Admiral Books, L. A., 1976
The Naked Clowns, Great Western Publishing, L. A., 1982
Poems for Adults and Other Children, Pogment Press, Reston, VA, 1988
I Swear He Was Laughing, Words & Pictures, Irvine, CA, 1996
*No Cats Have Been Maimed or Mutilated During the Making
        of This Book...but Some of Them are Disappointed — DEEPLY
        Disappointed — in Me*, Words & Pictures, Irvine, CA, 1996
and several poetry booklets registered as ISBN FINE — HOW'S U BN?

Words & Pictures East Coast also publishes *Deanotations*, a bi-monthly subscription
poetry letter containing the poems of Dean Blehert, illustrated by Pam Coulter Blehert.
For information on obtaining free sample issues, visit http://www.blehert.com

Many of the poems in this volume (too many to list here) were previously published
in issues of *Deanotations* and I want to thank the editor and publisher (me) for his
generous and enlightened permission to use those poems in this work. The author
and publisher (half of which is the author) are supposed to express grateful apprecia-
tion to other publications in which some of the poems in this work appeared, but
frankly, I think they were lucky to get me, so let me rather congratulate the following
publications which had the good fortune and good sense to publish the poems noted
below:

Advance!, "...So Here We Are"; *Bogg*, "Hunters Wear Bright Colors"; "Asking for
WHO the Bell Tolls"; "This Poem is Biodegradable"; "Dyslexic Poet"; *The Buzz*,
"It's easy to find your own voice"; *Carousel*, "How Poetry is Done" (reprinted in
HWUP, View From the Loft and elsewhere; it perhaps helped sink *Plains Poetry
Review*, which got my permission to reprint it, then went under too soon; in *View
From the Loft*, this poem was printed as a prose article in combination with "Gently,
Schmently — just Go!" and "How To Be A Prestigious Mainstream Twentieth-Century
Academic Poet"); *Creativity Connection*, "NEA Nay-Saying"; *LIGHT*, "Bogged in
Odgen"; "How Grimly They Bare It"; "T. S. Eliot"; "Samuel Johnson"; "James
Boswell" (the last three are limericks); "Le Sonnet La Furie"; "Not Goodbye, but
Good Buy!"; "Big Knell"; "Whose Sleep is This"; *Minimus*, "Angels" (also ap-
peared earlier in *Stroker* and later in the anthology *Voice of Many Waters*); "Right to
Remain"; *Pulpsmith*, "Testing..."; *Reston Review* (since renamed *Edge City Re-
view*), "Form and Duty"; "July Night"; *Satire*, "Urbane Violence"; *View From the
Loft*, "How Poetry is Done" (see *Carousel* listing above); "From" and versions of
some 20 of the aphorisms that precede each chapter in this volume; *Voice of Many
Waters*, "Water From Stone"; "There is a place for Poetry" ("The Hunger Artist");
"Poetry is communication devoutly to bewitched"; "It is easy for me to get con-
fused...."

DEDICATION

For Pam: Thanks for everything, and especially for laughing at *almost* all the right places and doing many other things in the right places. (What's an artist like you doing in a place like this?)

And thanks again, Ron, for many lessons (that did not lessen me) learned about laughter.

Also thanks to all the friends who, like me, have been tragically stricken in the midst of healthy lives with the poetry virus (don't miss the movie of the week on this!) and who have supported me in the endeavors that resulted in this book, but who should not be blamed for any of it...well, maybe they should be. It certainly isn't MY fault. I meant well...

Anyway, special thanks to Russell Salamon and Hilary Tham, who read nearly all of this and made several useful suggestions (more, alas, than I could bring myself to follow in this most self-indulgent of books). Thanks also for help, patience, suggestions, needed applause and all the other good stuff poets can give each other to Miles David Moore, Lyn Lifshin, Shirley Windward, Mel Belin, Doris Brody, Judith McCombs, Celia Brown, Thom The World Poet, Alan & Maggy Graham, Pete Specker, Dick Coanda, Larry Gross, Alice Pero, Ralph Grimes, Peter Ludwin, Charlie Potter, Bill Joyce and many others whose names I've omitted because I'm not sure they'd want to be associated with this dastardly book. But I can thank you, David Ross, because you died in 1994, so you can't object (and I'll bet you **would**). That'll teach you to die!

Those of you I've omitted inadvertently — I'd say "You know who you are," but how many poets know who they are? (Read this book and find out.)

This book is also for Sally, the last (so far) of our cats, who vanished the night I finished the last chapter. Still alive somewhere? Tabby or not tabby? Reader, would you like to have your head scratched? [Flash: One week later she turned up, still purring. Reader, you'll just have to buy a good comb.]

A Rather Forward Introduction

I leave these poems for those who come after me. The poems may distract them so I can escape.

Poetry comes from a Greek word meaning "to make" — because its survival depends upon generations of teachers making us read the stuff.

BUY MY POETRY. Your contribution will help me find loving homes for a few of the thousands of homeless, abused, runaway poems that come to me every day. (I try to help them before they turn to rhyme.)

"Preface" — Your face before you were born, when you had only one hand to clap.[1]

The following collection of parody and satire is aimed primarily at students and lovers of poetry (and I do mean "aimed"), and (to widen the readership slightly) at haters of poetry and also those who are mostly indifferent to poetry. My main purpose in assembling these works is to increase appreciation for poetry, especially MY poetry, by trashing everyone else's poetry so that mine will be the only alternative. (And I'd like to apologize in advance to Matthew Arnold, George Meredith, A. C. Swinburne, Thomas Hardy, Marianne Moore, Philip Larkin, Robert Lowell, Anne Sexton, Robert Creeley and a host of other eminently trashable poets utterly neglected in this book. So little time, so many poets.)

Personally, I can't stand the stuff. That's why I publish only my own poetry. If I published anyone else's, I'd have to read it. My own I just write.

---

[1] Taken from two notorious Zen koans (riddles): What was your face before you were born? What is the sound of one hand clapping? Poets are good at answering these, having, at readings, heard many half-hearted half-claps and, as a result, losing face.

I don't know why anyone would be mucking through these pen-droppings when he or she could be settling back against the pillows (saying "That is not what I meant at all") with a good Elmore Leonard novel or a Louis L'Amour.

You probably think I'm kidding. On a good day, I am.

But I have good reasons to prefer my own work to the other stuff I see: First, I understand my own poems better. Second, other poems are printed in books and magazines for which I must pay retail, whereas my own I get a good deal on — you might say, for a song. Third, when I read my own poems, I get a particularly vivid sense that the author is right here in the room with me. And, fourth, all other poets are "fresh new voices," while I'm just me talking to myself and anyone who listens just as I've been doing forever, it seems. Also, I have a very fine EAR, two, actually, each with a long, plump lobe, each diligently kept wax-free. (The caps of Bic pens serve me well.)

Also, unlike inferior brands, all my poems come with 90-day guarantees. If before 90 days after purchase of this book, any of my poems becomes obsolete or starts to smell overripe, you may return it in exchange for twice as many poems. We also provide lifetime (that is, for the life of the poem) aesthetic support. If you are having difficulty getting one of my poems to work, call our free hotline, and we'll guide you through it. Don't panic if you read a poem and nothing happens. Often it's as simple as "the reader neglected to learn to use a dictionary" or the page is being held upside down. (You should see the word "Introduction" at the beginning of this section. If not, whatever you think I've been saying, I haven't been.)

Here's a poem that summarizes my feelings about my poems:

Let's compare MY poem to poem X! Here's
what readers everywhere are saying:
"I get more pleasure from YOUR poem,
and it doesn't leave me mired in obscure allusions."
"YOUR poem is subtle — and works FAST too."
"I feel great, and YOUR poem doesn't leave me
sick to my stomach." "I can't believe I read
the whole poem!" "I've always been satisfied
with poem X, but let's just see your...SAY!
This IS good. Funnier and deeper too! From now on
I'LL read YOUR poem." *Yes, folks, TODAY 9 out of 10*
readers are reaching for MY poems. Why? Watch
this simple test: Notice how MY poem sharpens perception,
chases the blues and brightens this drab day. NOW watch
a leading brand drop into the day and turn it grayer.
That's because my NEW IMPROVED poem contains
more perception sharpeners, more blues chasers AND
more gray-day brighteners than any other leading brand.
All this PLUS patented despair deepeners to produce
the darkest darks and deepest despairs mortality can bear.
So read MY poems today! The poems written with YOU in mind.

[I guess it's funnier if you hear me do the voices...]

If it were only that simple. Alas, there's no getting around it: If I want you to appreciate MY poems, I'll have to work on your appreciation of PO-ETRY. Hence this book. But let me suggest to you at the outset, by far the fastest and simplest way to increase your own appreciation of any given poet: Recently, talking to a fellow poet, I was complaining about Ezra Pound. This is something I often do. In current poetry, anything could turn into anything, but I have never grasped why every college English student has to be persuaded that the faces on the metro (or their "apparition") resemble petals on a wet black bough. We had a black poodle who would come out of the weeds wet and with varied vegetation adhering to his ears, perhaps petals on a wet black bow-wow.

But I digress. As I was debunking Pound, suddenly it dawned on me! I said to my friend, "You know what would INSTANTLY increase my admiration for Pound's poetry?"

"A Greek-English dictionary? Having to study the original 'Wasteland' before Pound cut it in half?"

"No, what would INSTANTLY increase my admiration for Pound's poetry would be finding in my mail box a letter to me from Ezra Pound, telling me how much he enjoys MY work — or better yet, a rave review of my poems written by Pound in a respected journal."

"But Ezra Pound is long dead."

And there, dear readers, lies the sad urgency of my plight: Merwin, Ashbery, Kunitz, Hass, Dove, Angelou (*et alia*)[2] — if you are reading this (and why not?), YOU still have time. Do NOT let slip this ever-narrowing window-slit of opportunity to increase my appreciation for YOUR work. (Dana Gioia, your stock has risen remarkably!) Reader, if you don't recognize some of these names, this book may be for you. It won't help you recognize the names of current poets, but it will make it impossible for others to make you feel guilty for not recognizing them.

In this immodest volume, you will find answers to the following burning questions:

1. How can you create intense, complex and, most importantly, AC-CEPTABLE modern poetry simply by the judicious, but generous, insertion of two common English words? (Chapter 6)

2. How would Poe, T. S. Eliot, Wordsworth, Chaucer, Whitman, Sylvia Plath and over 40 other distinguished (or is it indistinguishable?) poets have said "You can lead a horse to water, but you can't make him drink"? (Chapter 1)

3. What is the secret formal element of traditional haiku, hitherto unknown outside Japan? (Chapter 5)

---

[2] For anyone reading this book a few years after publication, these folks were all prestigious poets once. Some of them are remembered in your time mainly because they were mentioned in this introduction. No, poets, don't thank me...

4. Why are poets so seldom paid for their poetry? (*passim*)

5. Who invented death and why? (Chapter 10)

6. Can the limerick supplant the critical essay? (Chapter 3)

7. Was Shakespeare gay? Read the just-discovered sonnet, "Shall I compare thee to a guy named Fred" and judge for yourself! (Chapter 2)

8. What resulted when Joyce Kilmer and Alan Ginsberg collaborated? (Chapter 2)

9. Why *thirteen* views of a blackbird? Why not eight or twelve? (Chapter 6)

10. What do Rilke and Roethke have in common? (Chapter 3)

11. What is the cause of the recent surge in drive-by poetry readings? (Chapter 7)

12. How are poetry slams conducted in Baghdad? (Chapter 7)

13. What is a "poetry reading special"? (Chapter 10)

14. Why is there such a long long line outside the bathroom at a poetry reading? (Chapter 7)

15. What is the "Apathetic Fallacy"? (Chapter 8)

16. What do Laurel and Hardy have to do with deconstruction and subtexts? (Chapter 9)

17. What is the link between Lorca and Peter Pan? (Chapter 2)

18. How the hell do you pronounce "triolet" and why should you anyway? (Chapter 4)

...all this and, as Shelley might so aptly have put it, much much more — and presented in the approved scholarly format: Even the footnotes have footnotes!

One often-asked question I have not yet been able to resolve to my own satisfaction (or yours, no doubt) is, precisely what IS the difference between Merrill and Merwin? A partial and unsatisfying answer: One of the two (Merrill) is deceased. Merwin, as of this writing, is alive, albeit academic. (I use words like "albeit", but no college would have me, so I'm only academic *manqué*. So how come I don't wear the academic manqué monkey suit — no tie, no tweed suit with leather patches, etc.?)

I have not dealt much in this book with the "Deconstructionist" critics, nor with the phenomenon known as "LANGUAGE poetry" (which, unlike other poetry, consists of language), because this is primarily a work of parody, and to attempt parody of such esoterica is to write on water with a hose (or some similar implement). (Also, to parody the stuff, I'd have to READ it!) But since so many people come up to me on the streets and ask me, "Dean, what IS Deconstructionist criticism? Is it the opposite of constructive criticism?" — I offer, as a very tentative answer, the following passage from the

Deconstructionist Bible, *Canned Potty Matter*[3] (people will buy anything if you package it right):

> Actually, there is no such phenomenon as criticism, or at least no conceivable definition of such a phenomenon, for one's words here — so to speak — are but an encrustation (defined by the social lint adhering to that stickiness of asserted identity called language) upon the encrustation called criticism, which is, itself, an encrustation upon the attempted spherical or concentric encrustation (spherical to create the illusion of containment of the world it, in fact, constitutes) that we call a poem, whose merely *attempted* sphericality is exposed by the dry, powdery nature of the critical encrustation (coated with only the most refined cultural lint), which enables it to delineate any flaw or discontinuity (or grease-spot) in the orbicularity of the poem in a manner analogous to that whereby fingerprint powder defines a fingerprint; however, the critical powder hardens on contact, becoming, itself, a concentric sphericality containing nothing "we" (if one may so designate these mobile encrustations of socio-historical accidence) can see other than itself, which is, in fact — or should be — an absence of self. Thus, ultimately, the only critique is the poem itself, and the ideal form for a poem is the Klein bottle[4], having neither inside nor outside, but, like the ideal critic, having its anterior protrusion stuck firmly up its posterior intrusion and thereby encrusted with an emulsion best recollected when heavily tranquilized.

I hope this answers or at least silences all your questions on that subject. More succinctly, as Edgar Guest might have remarked, if the Deacon's a lousy driver, when you see the Deacon's truck, shun it.

A final warning: Folks, poetry may *look* like fun, but it is extremely hazardous when attempted by other than skilled professionals, so please don't try these stunts at home.

Thank you for browsing this book. Please purchase a copy if you can and if you want to and if it doesn't violate what is true to your deepest self or

---

[3] An allusion to a very Undeconstructionist article and book, *Can Poetry Matter* by Dana Gioia, though I'm not sure why he wants to can poetry matter. Most poetry, being full of nothing, is already vacuum-packed.

[4] "Klein bottle": Constructed by taking a tapered open-ended tube, bending it and pushing the small end through a hole in the side of the tube, then stretching and attaching the small end to the large end. The result is a surface that looks like a container, but has only one side, no inside or outside — so claim mathematicians, but don't try this at home, kids, because once you've made one, you are automatically both inside it and outside it, which means that, like many mathematicians, you won't know enough to come in out of (or is it out into) the rain.

make either of us less than we are and if your Mom says you may. Or just write. Being a reader is never having to say you're sorry. Apathy, on the other hand, is never having to say. And poverty is never having.[5] So buy this book! I can be had!

Meanwhile, help fight the prose backlash against Affirmative Action for poets: cookbook writers taking publishers to court, claiming they were bumped for poets (reverse discrimination), threats of return to the days of "No Poetry Wanted" signs.

Don't let the Hard-lickin' Romance and Valley of the Dulls crowd return us to those dark days! Write your congressman & insist on fore play fair...I mean fair play for poets! Better Read than Dead! Let us not go back to the days when poets had to "drop in" on patrons around supper time to read a poem and get a free meal. Remember, if you don't buy our books, WE SHALL COME OVER! *POETIC JUSTICE NOW!*

Don't forget to write.

Dean Blehert, 1998

Not written in Southern France, Spain, an island
off the New England coast, a cabin in the Rockies, a
cell in St. Elizabeth's or anywhere else
worth mentioning.

---

[5] And my Nobel Prize for Poetry is never. And everything is. (cf. Karl Marx on the withering away of the dictatorship of the syntax.)

Section 1: A Survey of English Poetry

Chapter 1: On Leading Horses to Water and Driving Poets to Drink

An Ounce of Epigram (Worth a Pound of Ezra)

In school we learn that the only good poet is a dead poet. How nice to have something to look forward to.

What is required of poets? Forgiveness! The poet reads, and the world responds: "I beg your pardon?"

In the good old days most poets were consigned to oblivion. These days even oblivion won't take poets on consignment.

When is a poem **significant?** *When I try to get it and yawn as a* **sign-if-I-can't.**

Some poetry reminds me of weddings: Unlike things united with a solemnity aimed at lastingness (though most metaphors fall apart in the first year), something old, something new, something borrowed, something blue.

We don't live anywhere else, really, than in our art. When we stop creating, we live on scraps of leftover admiration.

The romantic imagination feeds not on common oats, demanding unique corn.[1]

La Brea Tar Pits: Full of mammoths, saber-toothed tigers and other cherished skulls: Spines of out-of-print species. Please teach your children to survive and to remember our poems so that we don't have to write them all over again.

Poets, too, have pornographic fantasies: Modern readers have short attention spans. Anything occupying more than six inches of page-length will not be read. O for the days of hearty <u>Paradise-Lost</u> *and* <u>Iliad</u> *readers who would exclaim, "My, what a long poem you have there!" and "O! It's so hard!"*

A pride of lions, an ecstasy of larks, a preening of starlets, a clutch of fans, a privy of poets, a carping of critics, a quibble of scholars, a scarcity of readers, a courtesy of applause, a reality of silence.

---

[1] The unique corn of romanticism is, of course, the unicorn, which went extinct after being over-hunted by bullfighters-in-training, who would stand in front of cork trees and dare the beasts to charge, then step aside just in time, leaving unicorns stuck, quivering, in trees, hanging there like unwieldy darts. They inspired the inventor of the corkscrew.

Chapter 1
On leading horses to water and driving poets to drink
or the horse-to-liter theme in English Waterature

Horse that follow drink not.
Horse that drink follow not.
    Lao Tse

           Poetry? No — I'm just Horace-ing around.
           Dean

      The horse won't drink
      Cause the vandals stole the handle.
      Bob Dylan

This book will tell you everything you never wanted to know about poetry, the writing and reading thereof, and much less, beginning with this chapter's survey of English poetry. It's not as bad as it sounds: I am easily bored, and I read every word of it with a growing sense of wonder. ("When will it end," I wondered.) (I am the taster of all I purvey.)

But one of the nicest things about being a poet in the late Twentieth Century [for those of you who have just arrived, this is the late Twentieth Century] is that you don't HAVE to know anything about poetry to be a poet these days. It can be done by the numbers (and I don't mean metrical numbers[2]). That's why, instead of going through the subject in chron-illogical order, you can, if you are impatient, skip directly to chapter 6 ("Bone and Blood I Love You"), which jumps right into the subject of how to write state-of-the-art (don't ask!) poems for prestigious poetry journals, so that you don't

---

[2] In the 18th Century, what we now call "metrics" (pertaining to the meter or beat of a poem) was called "numbers." Today it is the poets themselves we call numbers, because they numb us. In fact, promising experiments with recordings of major poets reading their own work shows that these tapes work as well as anaesthetics when used during major surgery — BUT the patients must wear earphones, lest a nurse or surgeon fall asleep face down in an abdominal incision.

have to slumber through hundreds of pages of O THEEs and O THOUs to get down (and I mean DOWN) to the nitty gritty.

For those of you who are still with me: In this chapter we will attempt to stimulate your flat-lining interest in English Poetry by tracing a single theme through the centuries: "You can lead a horse to water, but you can't make him [or her — or him/her...or hem?] drink." A study of the manuscript revisions of several poets shows that first versions of many well-known poems dealt with that theme. For some reason, it has seldom survived to appear in the anthologized versions and has remained, until now, a well-kept secret, possibly because it is simply too dark, too despairing a vision for mere mortals — the utter frustration of trying to feed an old dog who won't swallow or get a cat to understand anything or a teenager, all these are comprehended within the mythic and banal bounds of the horse-to-water scenario or, as it is generally referred to among scholars, the *nonaqueophagus equine paradigm* (or NEP). The impatience of frustrated horse waterers is known as the *nonaqueophagus equine equanimitylessness paradigm* (or NEEP). (The scholar who came up with these useful classifications was honored in the popular song, "Brother, can YOU paradigm!")

Where did it begin? The scholarly trail vanishes into pre-literary antiquity. It is, perhaps, THE fundamental theme. Thus, for example, the very word "literature" derives from "liter," a metric volume of fluid (keep in mind that English poetry was once metric), because so much of our ancient literature (now mostly lost) dealt with the watering of horses. The very word "Poet" comes from a Greek word meaning "to make," and, of course, one of the first things we learn to make is water. When English was the unreadable stuff we call Old Anguish, the first known draft of the epic *Beowulf* began:

Hwaet, we gar-Danum in Geardagum
Hwaetered ourn Horsen sae hwelle sae we Konnen...

[Behold, we spear-Danes in years of yore/watered our horses as well as we could...] and so forth. Of course, it's hard to know just what those cunning ancients were saying (even hard for cunning linguists), since they spoke in cunning kennings (poetic circumlocutions), referring to horses as "long-faced cows," "oat-snuffers," "Neigh-sayers," "Warrior tossers" and "dog meat." (Hey! They were sailors, OK? No horses have been harmed in the making of this chapter, for PETA's sake!)

Getting closer to poets who, at least, could speak English (*somewhat* free of the ignorance of the Dark Ages, though they still couldn't spell worth a damn), we find this theme in an early draft of the famous "Prologue" to Geoffrey Chaucer's *Canterbury Tales,* followed by a translation:

You Can Lead A Horse To Water, But, Oh! You Canterbury Tales!

Whan that Aprille with his shoures soote
The droghte of March hath perced to the roote,
And bathed every veyne in swich licour
Of which vertu engendered is the flour;
Thanne longeth hostler eke to water stedes,
So to the running water them he ledes;
Mekely they follow, but if they'll not drink,
But from the streme rere up and backwards shrink,
He can do naughte but pray. Thus longen folk
To goon on pilgrimages, for if poke
And prodde and begging won't availle, mayhappe
At some shrine dekked with relics — bones and crappe —
The hooly blisful martir hem wille holpe
To make the foolysh stedes the streme to golpe,
For if they wolle not drink, how can they gallop?
At beste they'll go at canter with the taile up,
Then bot a crepe — no rider colde be carried;
Soon they must be — who can't e'en canter — buried!
So off they goon to prayen in Caunterbury
That Criste hem holpen make stedes less countrary.

Translation:

When April with his sweet showers
The drought of March has pierced to the root
and bathed every vein in such liquor (nourishing fluid)
From the goodness of which is engendered the flower,
Then also the stable-keeper longs to water steeds
So he leads them to the running water.
Meekly they follow, but if they won't drink,
But from the stream rear up and backwards shrink,
He can do nothing but pray. Thus folks long
To go on pilgrimages, for if poke
And prod and begging won't avail, perhaps
At some shrine decked with relics — bones and crap—
The holy blissful martyr will help them
To make the foolish steeds gulp the stream,
For if they will not drink, how can they gallop?
At best they'll go at a canter with the tail up,
Then but a creep — no rider could be carried;
Soon they must be — who can't even canter — buried!
So off they go to pray in Canterbury
That Christ will help them make steeds less contrary.

And here's the earliest known form of the famous anonymous 15th Century lyric which became "Western wind, when wilt thou blow?/The small rain down can rain./ Christ! If my love were in my arms/ and I in my bed again."

Anonymous 'tang[3] (also recorded as Hey Nonny Mustang)

Western horse, when wilt thou drink?
Thy small brain's past my ken...
Christ! If thou'dst learn to use the sink
So I could sleep in till ten.

Moving right along (skipping nearly two boring centuries), we'll sample poets of the Elizabethan Age. This was a time of strenuous dieting. The Queen herself was known as carroty Bess because of her vegan fanaticism. From its plague of teenage anorexia, the period became known as the Hell-is-a-Be-Thin-Age. It was a time of lean and hungry ambition. Even gentry were starved enough that a little horse meat was a temptation, so it was not a good time for horses to try a poet's patience. Here is Sir Philip Sidney's contribution, the proto-poem of "With how sad steps, O moon, thou climbst the skies":

"Philip" (Philos Hippos): Horse Lover

With how sad steps, O horse, thou nearst the streams!
How silently, and with how wan a snout!
What! may it be that even a horse can pout?
That horses, too, are smitten with such dreams?
Unless one long-with-thirst-acquainted deems
Amiss of love, thou art in rut, thou lout!
I read it in thy longish looks — no doubt!
To me, whose codpiece binds, thy state speaks reams.
Then, tell me as a pal, O horse, I plead:
Are constant studs *persona non grata*?
Are mares averse as wenches to hot melding?
Well, I can sympathize— I'm off my feed.
Still, you had better cease to scorn this wata,
Or else I'll have to send you off for gelding.

from *Astrophel and Stella*

With how sad steps, O Moon, thou climb'st the skies!
How silently, and with how wan a face!
What, may it be that even in heavenly pace

---

[3] 'tang: Middle English for "piece of tail."

6

That busy archer his sharp arrows tries?
Sure, if that long-with-love-acquainted eye
Can judge of love, thou feel'st a lover's grace,
To me, that feel the like, thy state descries.
Then even of fellowship, O Moon, tell me,
Is constant love deemed there but want of wit?
Are beauties there as proud as here they be?
Do they above love to be loved, and yet
Those lovers scorn whom that love doth possess?
Do they call virtue there ungratefulness?

Here is a little-known Shakespeare sonnet on the theme (not an earlier version of any of the better known sonnets — simply a discarded early effort) that hints at the hitherto concealed sexual implications of leading a horse:

Add Age And Mix Well

When after days of arid iron skies,
You seize the reins of equine leadership
To go against that adage hoary and wise,
Your grip as firm as gentle, never a slip,
Then, Lady, there's no doubt that you can lead;
I'd follow you myself to hell or bed!
A horse, be it jaded nag or fiery steed,
Cannot but follow you — unless it's dead —

Even to where frogs croak and rushes teem,
Down to the willowy brink of a chattering stream;
There you can even shove that velvet snout
Into the water — but it may twitch right out!

What though you rail, you cannot make him drink,
Else I have never thought the thought I think!

A more famous Shakespearean passage in *Richard III* tells how Richard lost his final battle because his horse, exhausted from thirst, would not drink, and the more Richard beat the horse in an effort to MAKE him drink, the more stupefied and unresponsive grew the horse. In Richard's immortal words: "Aching! Aching! My horse dumb for aching!"[4] In this next passage, a more mature Shakespeare considers all sides of the aphorism — with excerpts of the later, better known version (the famous Hamlet solo, low-key) following:

---

[4] Richard said, of horse, "A course…" — I mean, of course, "A horse, a horse, my Kingdom for a horse!" Someone misheard him and took his kingdom in exchange for a hearse.

Gelding the So-lily-quy[5]

To drink or not to drink, that is the question;
Whether, thou crowbait, in this bind to suffer
The stings and goadings of my outraged patience,
Or to dip snout into the brook that foams
And ripples round thy hooves: To slurp: To thirst
No more; and by a drink to know you end
The nagging and the thousand tugs and prods
Horseflesh is heir to; 'tis a cool consumption:
Devoutly tongue be swished, to lap; to slurp —
To slurp; perchance to steam; aye, then be rubbed
Down, when, no dearth of slurp, from stream we come,
When I have shoveled hay into thy stall —
O thou'rt behooved to me — show some respect!
Stop acting Hamlety, or "So long, life!"
Why shouldst thou bear these whips and scorns of mine,
When, watered, thou again might fardels[6] bear
and grunt and sweat beneath my weary bulk?
Ah, wilt not even meet my eyes? Damn thine!
We're in bad lands from whence, alas, on foot
No traveler returns, or I'd bury your bod[7]...
Yet though I cannot force thee, nor can'st thou
Avoid my endless stream of eloquence,
And I have oodles more to say to thee
Of the insolence of equines and the spurs
That patient masters to the unworthy take
Who will not do what's meant for their own good —
I shall rave on all day: Listen thou must...
What! Wilt thou drink? But wait! I have not finished...

Excerpts from Hamlet (so you don't have to see the movie):

To be or not to be, that is the question;
Whether 'tis nobler in the mind to suffer

---

[5] "Gelding…": Since it's impossible to improve on Shakespeare, I am only "gilding the lily" of this soliloquy or solo, low-key. That is, Hamlet is babbling to himself, not a horse, in the "final draft." This sort of substitution is how we grow up: First the hero talks to his horse. Then the horse is replaced by a pretty girl. Hamlet is even more grown up. He differs from most adults in that he talks to himself with his mouth *open.*

[6] A "fardel" is a burden — or possibly a very small fart (if from a lady, perhaps a fardelle).

[7] "I'd bury your bod" dimly echoes Shakespeare's "with a bare bodkin" — that is, a naked blade, though it sounds like a cute, diminutive "bod." Perhaps a gay blade. Or maybe those Elizabethans gave their knives pet names.

8

The slings and arrows of outrageous fortune...
...To die, to sleep —
No more — and by a sleep to say we end
The heartbreak and the thousand natural shocks
That flesh is heir to. 'Tis a consummation
Devoutly to be wished. To die, to sleep;
To sleep, perhaps to dream. Aye, there's the rub,
For in that sleep of death what dreams may come,
When we have shuffled off this mortal coil,
Must give us pause. There's the respect
That makes calamity of so long life,
For who would bear the whips & scorn of time...
...who would fardels bear,
To grunt and sweat under a weary life...
...from whose bourn/No traveler returns...
...The insolence of office, and the spurns
That patient merit of th' unworthy takes...

And this introduces another disturbing element of the horse-to-water theme (seen later in Wordsworth, Whitman and others): The more long-winded bards can inflate this poor terse adage only so far before it pops. It better serves the more concise — Ben Jonson, for example ("Drink for me, only, damn your eyes!"[8]) or John Donne (who knew when he was Donne), in this early version of "Death be not Proud" (followed by the better known version):

Dobbin UnDonne

Horse be not proud, though some have called thee
Noble and haughty, for thou art not so;
For those whom thou think'st thou dost overthrow,
Remount, poor horse, nor yet canst thou throw me.
From dogs and ponies, miniatures of thee,
Obedience; then from thee much more must flow.
And where I lead, there surely thou dost go,
Else bit shall bite thee most untenderly.
Thou art slave to whip, reins, harness, spur-shod men,
And dost with straw and dung and horseflies dwell,
And Chevy or Ford can carry us as well,
And smoother than thy gait; why swell'st thou then?
Because I can not make thee drink? Bad actor, ye?
Then horse shall be no more! To the glue factory!

---

[8] An early draft of "Drink to me only with thine eyes..." or "Think of me only with dry eyes" or "Wink to me only with fine thighs." (I have SUCH a bad memory

9

Death, be not proud, though some have called thee
Mighty and dreadful, for thou art not so;
For those whom thou think'st thou dost overthrow
Die not, poor Death, nor yet canst thou kill me.
From rest and sleep, which but thy pictures be,
Much pleasure; then from thee much more must flow,
And soonest our best men with thee do go,
Rest of their bones, and soul's delivery.
Thou art slave to fate, chance, kings, and desperate men,
And dost with poison, war and sickness dwell;
And poppy or charms can make us sleep as well
And better than thy stroke; why swell'st thou then?
One short sleep past, we wake eternally,
And death shall be no more; Death, thou shalt die.

Note: Donne's horse was a dun, so this sonnet tells us of Donne's dun undone.

In this next poem, by George Herbert (famous for poems shaped like an altar and a pair of wings) the frustration is doubled, in that Herbert's rather wobbly "bucket" came to a point before he could reach the final rhyme. Herbert is known for his sweetness of temper, both in his life (as a country clergyman) and in his poems. Here we see that Herbert, too, could throw a tantrum — perhaps hinted at in his famous "The Collar," but nothing there is as raw as what follows, which may explain why the work evaded discovery until recently. Here, then, is "The Bucket":

```
                        (kicking)
                        B  u  c
              e                      k
         h                             e
     T                                  t
                                         by
      Lord, who hath made man to lead a horse   g
      To water  though not  to make him drink     e
      By cursing,  nagging  or brute force,       oR
      Thereby  thou  leadest  man  to think      G_E!
      What Thou  must bear who showest
       Sinners the  only  way  to slake
       Lustful  thirst,   yet  knowest
       Thy jackass  man  will  take
       The   old    forbidden turns
       To   where   thirst  burns
        Endlessly  —  and  yet
        Hourly  Thou  nagst
        Thy   willful   pet
         That      lagst...
          But  fuck  it!
          I've   run
          Out  of
           bu ck
            e t
             !
```

John Milton, on the other hand, is not known for sweetness, and, as the following shows, had to work through some powerful snits before achieving the equanimity of "On my Blindness." Apparently he was better able to put up with blindness than with the indignity of waiting on a stubborn horse. Milton DID have a sense of humor and, in fact, wrote a volume of parodies nearly as hilarious as these, but they are, alas, lost works (see the famous study, *Parodies Lost*), and he is known to us only by his sour, somber surviving works, like the following:

Spam-Soon Agonistes[9]
Or: Son of Spam

When I consider how my day is spent,
With half my morn in this dark world and wide,
Wasted beside this trough, where I abide
Thy whim, thou churlish nag, thy head not bent
To drink or serve thy Master and present
A docile eye — I yearn to tan thy hide!
How long must I stand furious by thy side?[*]
God grant me patience lest, my spleen to vent,
I take His name in vain! Thou wilt not heed
My pleas, nor be cajoled by gifts? Oh damn!
I'll wring thy neck! 'Twill serve thee right! My state
Is kingly. Coursers at my bidding speed
And post from here to town. Drink or be Spam!
For I'm ill-served who only stand and wait.

[*] Alternate line: Know I'll demand dray-labor, drink defied.[10]

On His Blindness

When I consider how my light is spent
Ere half my days in this dark world and wide
And that one talent which is death to hide
Lodged with me useless, though my soul more bent
To serve therewith my Maker and present
My true account, lest He returning chide;
"Doth God exact day-labor, light denied?"

---

[9] Refers to his *Samson Agonistes*, i.e., Samson, Egg on his Toes — Milton's image of Samson after his eyes (like broken eggs) have been put out. Not to be confused with *Simpson Agonistes*, an epic about the courtroom struggles of O. J. Simpson to get his hand into a glove that is too small for it.

[10] A dray is a cart, often horse-drawn. The rest of the time it just stands there.

I fondly ask. But Patience, to prevent
That murmur, soon replies, "God doth not need
Either man's work or his own gifts. Who best
Bear his mild yoke, they serve him best. His state
Is kingly: thousands at his bidding speed,
And post o'er land and ocean without rest;
They also serve who only stand and wait."

Andrew Marvell had to work for Milton. He was his deputy Minister of State — or "Latin Secretary" — under Cromwell. (Imagine today John Milton as Secretary of State, Marvell his deputy! "My Dear Prime Minister, Had we but world enough and time, Your tactful stalling were no crime....") Ministers of State used to be called Latin Secretaries because they conducted all their business in Latin so that their citizens would have no idea what they were up to.

Some of Milton's impatience perhaps rubbed off on the more urbane Marvell, as shown in this early draft of what became, eventually, the classic seduction poem (English clergymen do them so well!), "To His Coy Mistress":

To His Coy Horsie

Had I the patience and the time,
This coyness, horsie, were no crime.
I'd stand idle while you'd waffle —
Spit and chew another chaw full.
You by this purling streamlet's side
Should snort and snuffle — damn your hide! —
While I, beside you, would complain
In fancy verse with sweet refrain.
I'd plead with you to drink for pages
While you swished your tail for ages,
Pretending that you weren't aware
Of any silly human there.
A week or two should go to reason
With you gently, then a season
To cajole with coos and soothing,
Then a year — you brute uncouth thing! —
Fondles having failed and verses,
To pepper you with obscene curses.
For, horsie, you deserve no less —
Deserve all that you'll get, O yes!
But at my back I always hear
Time's winged chariot hurrying near
(Drawn, no doubt, by horses who,

When asked to drink, know what to do),
And yonder all before us lie
Deserts where stubborn horses die
Who have not drunk their fill before
They pass the stream to drink...no more.
Thy bulk shall never more be found
Nor in thy stinky stall shall sound
My scuffling step in dung-caked boots.
A brutal ending comes to brutes:
Dog-food is full of nutrients
From horsies lacking plain horse sense.
The can's a fine and private space
For horsies who won't know their place.
   Now therefore while I yet can hold
My temper in, do what you're told!
My breathing's ragged, knuckles white,
My heart is pounding, teeth clenched tight.
O now, ere one of us expire,
Please drink! O damn thy dam and sire!
You WON'T drink? Fine, you've made my day!
So there, you moron! Birds of prey
Will now your carcass fast devour.
You poor slow chap: feed jackal, flower —
Whate'er I can't convert to dog food,
Glue, fine leather, sausage, hog food...
Thus, though I cannot make my pony
drink, yet he'll make fine baloney.

To His Coy Mistress To Make Much of Time

Had we but world enough and time,
This coyness, Lady, were no crime.
We would sit down, and think which way
To walk, and pass our long love's day.
Thou by Indian Ganges' side
Should'st rubies find: I by the tide
Of Humber would complain. I would
Love you ten years before the flood,
And you should, if you please, refuse
Till the conversion of the Jews;
My vegetable love should grow
Vaster than empires and more slow;
An hundred years should go to praise
Thine eyes, and on thy forehead gaze;
Two hundred to adore each breast,

But thirty thousand to the rest;
An age at least to every part,
And the last age should show your heart.
For, lady, you deserve this state,
Nor would I love at lower rate.
   But at my back I always hear
Time's winged chariot hurrying near,
And yonder all before us lie
Deserts of vast eternity.
Thy beauty shall no more be found,
Nor, in thy marble vault shall sound
My echoing song: then worms shall try
That long preserved virginity,
And your quaint[11] honour turn to dust,
And into ashes all my lust:
The grave's a fine and private place,
But none, I think, do there embrace.
   Now therefore while the youthful hue
Sits on thy skin like morning dew,
And while thy willing soul transpires[12]
At every pore with instant fires,
Now let us sport us while we may,
And now, like amorous birds of prey
Rather at once our time devour,
Than languish in his slow-chapt[13] power.
Let us roll all our strength and all
Our sweetness up into one ball,
And tear our pleasures with rough strife
Thorough[14] the iron gates of life;
Thus, though we cannot make our sun
Stand still, yet we will make him run.

We've already skipped the Cavalier poets[15], known for their cavalier attitudes toward horses and women ("I could not ride thee, horse, so much,/

---

[11] Probably a quadruple pun: "Quaint," when this poem was written, meant elaborately contrived, slightly odd and old-fashioned, quenched or extinguished (queynt) AND (drumroll…) vagina! (an old meaning already in Marvell's day, but lingering like an old acquaintance). All four meanings fit (pardon my diction) and work with each other like a big jazzy chord. Parody fails me!

[12] Transpires here means gives off vapor, or, less delicately, sweats. Is Marvell correct? If you sweat too much, can you exude your soul? More on this at eleven.)

[13] "Slow-chapt" — slowly chewing. Chapt means jawed. Time is slowly chewing us as cud. Since we're cud, says Marvell, let's get cuddly!

[14] A spelling for "through" that (in those days of creative spelling) helped Marvell keep the beat. Modern metric poets envy that old flexible spelling. Damn these spellbinding dictionaries!

[15] A Cavalier is a supporter of Charles I, the king who eventually lost his crown and, unwilling to remove it, lost his head with it after a civil war against Cromwell and

Rode I not on her more"[16]). Cavalier means horseman (and also legman, breastman, etc.). These poets are among the few who (or so they bragged) could lead their horses to it AND make them drink. Sure, horses tried to ignore them ("Stonewall? Do not! Uprisen, mate?...") but a few taps with a metal rod ("With iron bars I rage") soothed the most savage beast[17]. Besides, it ill-befits a parodist to stoop to mockery of men with names like Lovelace and Suckling. Growing up on the playing fields of Eton with names like that, no wonder they gained the firmness of character to tame a sullen pony.

Let us move on, then, to the Age of Reason, the Eighteenth Century, where Alexander Pope, abusing his real or fancied enemies in perfect, venomous couplets, became the master debater. He preferred to ride duns and wrote a long mock-epic, "The Dunciad", about the many duns he had. Here is a short passage that became the core of his "Essay on Man" and led to his great refutation of the philosophy of John Locke, "Rape of the Locke"[18] (Locke argued that horses brought to the river bank could be taught to slake their thirst. This became known as the "bank-slake" theory of education.[19] He also recommended that children not be deprived of their baby blankets until they reached maturity, which is called the "blankets-late" theory of child-raising and strongly influenced Lucy's younger brother, Linus.[20]):

The Rape of the Essay
Or: Who Is Yanking Man's Great Chain Of Being[21]

Presumptuous man! the reason wouldst thou find
Why thou art stonewalled by thy steed's behind,

Parliament. The most noted Cavalier poets were Lovelace and Suckling. The most noted (especially footnoted) Puritan poet (the other side) was Milton. If you were betting on the outcome of a war, would you bet on the side with soldiers named Lovelace and Suckling, or would you choose a sturdy Milton and tough John Bunyan and even stony Marvell (who, like Milton, worked in Cromwell's government)? What's in a name? Answer: A soul (*ame* in French) — an *ame*.

[16] Lovelace wrote "I could not love thee so, my Dear,/Loved I not honor more." (Some would say "honor and off her.")

[17] Referring to "Stone walls do not a prison make,/Nor iron bars a cage." He's right, of course. Stone walls and iron bars don't make a prison cell; rather MEN with stone walls and iron bars make a prison cell. If we outlaw stone walls and iron bars, only outlaws and, perhaps, in-laws will make prison cells. To paraphrase W. H. Auden, demand your right to live in the cell of yourself.

[18] Pope's "Rape of the Lock" is actually a mock-epic romp about the social spat resulting when a flirtatious young fop snips and swipes a lock of hair from a coquette. (He probably put it in his poquette.) Pope's *Dunciad* (that is, a mock epic about dunces, as *Iliad* is an epic about Troy [or Ilia]), mocks many of the poets of his time. What an odd idea! Pope must have been a vicious character!

[19] John Locke's theory is actually "blank slate" (*tabula rasa*), the notion that a child's mind is a blank slate ready to be written upon. (Nice analogy: So having written on the child's mind, is there an eraser we can buy to make corrections?) So if you know anything, says Locke, chalk it up to experience.

[20] Linus, in the "Peanuts" comic strip, clings to his blankety-blank blanket (Lucy's viewpoint). So would you if your older sister were Lucy.

[21] In his *Essay on Man*, Pope writes of "The Great Chain of Being" on which man

How, though just short of angels thou art ranked
On nature's chain, yet thee hath brute outflanked,
And why, though thou can'st lead a horse to water,
Thou can'st not make him drink despite thy hauteur —
Not though thou hast by far the finer brain,
Not though thou thrashest him with nature's chain?
The answers are revealed in reason's light:
Whate're we water, we are what are right.[22]
That is, we are what wat'reth that which is,
Which is what's right?...whatever. So UP HIS!
Know then thyself, presume no horse to scan;
The proper stud farm of mankind is man.

from **Essay on Man**

Presumptuous man! the reason wouldst thou find
Why, formed so weak, so little, and so blind?...

And all the question (wrangle e'er so long)
Is only this, if God has placed him wrong.
Respecting man, whatever wrong we call,
May, must be right, as relative to all...

One truth is clear, Whatever is, is right.

Know then thyself, presume not God to scan;
The proper study of mankind is man.

Pope also argues that if man were more aware than he is, it wouldn't be good for him; for example, with overly sensitive smell, he might "...die of a rose in aromatic pain." Certainly, a sensitivity to smell would not benefit a waterer of horses.

Moving right along, we traverse Gray's "Elegy," where he stands waiting for his horse to do his business while lowing herds (that is, low-flying flocks — low-wing) wind slowly o'er the lea (like many poets, he had a speech impediment — difficulty pronouncing the "v" in "over"). He meditates upon poets who die unknown after wasting their lives tending ungrateful horses and mourns rich flowers that blossom only to be buried in horse

---

ranks between ape and angel, nor should he presume to rise beyond his proper place in nature. This worldview is associated with Deism, rationalism, and Pope-ulism. Today no one reads poems and no one reads essays and no one reads sermons. Pope, with his sermonizing essays in verse, is a triple threat. (The joke's on us: He wrote some hilarious stuff.)

[22] Pope insists that "whatever is is right." I tried to include that phrase, but my word processor won't allow the repetition of "is." It's been picking on me all day...

flops. And of course, there is Samuel Johnson's famous rendition of "You can lead a horse to water, but you can't make him drink": "Why sir, you can lead a horse to water, but you can't make him drink, the scoundrel!"[23]

But all these fellows are relatively polite. None of them really lambaste their horses until we get to the Romantics, who curse like fishwives (a quaint view of the annoyance of female fish when their mates are hooked). That is why William Blake and Robert Burns (who, along with Bach, Brahms, Beethoven and the Beatles, are commonly referred to as the nine B's [counting four Beatles]) are often called "precursors of the Romantic Movement" — because after them came poets who knew how to curse. Blake and Burns don't do so badly themselves, though Burns talks funny and can't spell very well. Here's one of Blake's death poems, or as he called them, "Songs of Expiry Hence"[24]:

The Horsie

Horsie! Horsie! turning tail
From the fountains of the vale,
What immortal hand or whip
Could force thy horsy head to dip?

Of what distant deep or shallow
Dream'st thou that, though thou dost follow
to this stream and in it wallow,
There's no hand can make thee swallow?

And what shoulder, what soft note
Could tug the sinews of thy throat?
And when thy throat gives not a twitch,
What then, thou stubborn son of a bitch!

What the hammer? what the chain?
(In thy anus sleep'th thy brain?)[25]
What the sugar? what red apple
Could persuade thee? Thus I grapple —

And when I throw up my hands,

---

[23] Besides pontificating at the coffeehouse, Johnson *did* write poetry, including his famous poem on the futility of expecting a horse to drink, "On the Vanity of Human Wishes." He says that at first this shocks the rider (who goes "EEK!") — then drives him to drink (since the horse won't). This expectation, therefore, Johnson calls the EEK/wine fallacy, though some call it the EEK/whine fallacy — poets do more whining and dying than wining and dining.

[24] Actually Blake wrote *Songs of Innocence* and *Songs of Experience*, tra la tra la.

[25] Words like "sleep'th" are to be spoken aloud in the voice of Sylvester Puddytat. Don't say them within spitting distance of your audience.

Tired of curses, vain demands,
Dost thou smile thy work to see?
Dost thou who will not drink mock me?

Horsie! Horsie! turning tail
From the fountains of the vale,
Drink right now or thee I'll bury
In a fearful cemetery!

The Tiger

Tiger, Tiger, burning bright
In the forest of the night,
What immortal hand or eye
Framed thy fearful symmetry?

In what distant deeps or skies
Burned that fire within thine eyes?
On what wings dared he aspire?
What the hand dared seize the fire?

And what shoulder, and what art,
Could twist the sinews of thy heart?
When thy heart began to beat,
What dread hand and what dread feet?

What the hammer, what the chain,
Knit thy strength and forged thy brain?
What the anvil? What dread grasp
Dared thy deadly terrors clasp?

When the stars threw down their spears,
And watered heaven with their tears,
Did He smile His work to see?
Did He who made the lamb make thee?

"The Tiger" is usually paired with "The Lamb" (from "Songs of In-No-Sense") in which frustrated Mary "has" a little lamb. As for who "made" the lamb, Blake answers this question in his famous Sheepherder's song, "Climb Every Mutton, Ream Every Ram," in which the hero-shepherd, Homer, mistaking a deer for one of his ewes, exclaims, "D'oh! A deer — a female deer!" This poem is also the source of that popular form of address for shepherds, "Hey, ewes' guys!"[26]

---

[26] "Climb..." was later adapted, in *The Sound of Music* to become "Climb Every Mountain,

Blake also wrote "Mock on! Mock on!" — addressed to Voltaire and Rousseau, but I have taken his advice.

This next poem shows how the horse-to-water theme is woven into several famous Robert Burns works. Just as Shakespeare is generally overrated because he filled his works with famous sayings, so Robert Burns cleverly won praise beyond his deserts by basing many of his poems on popular songs:

Fit To Be Kilt [Wherein may be found the seeds of "My Luve is Like a Red Red Rose," "Auld Lang Syne," "Green Grow the Rashes O," "To a Mousie" and "Flow Gently, Sweet Afton"]

O My mare she has a dead, dead nose,
  That can't tell dung from water;
O where she's led my mare she goes,
  But wi'na drink, the rotter!

Should auld acquaintance be forgot, or
  The hours I've spent my lashes[27] — Ow! —
On thee? Take yet a sip of water
  Ere red red flow the gashes — Ow!

I dreamed of riding her again
  Alang the bonnie brae...[28]
The best laid schemes o' mares and men
  Gang aft agley[29].

Flow gently, sweet Afton, among thy green braes,
Flow gently, sweet river, where my mare delays,
Flow gently, sweet Afton, where nibbled by bream[30]
Lies one who'd not drink from thy murmuring stream.

Dream Every Dream...", while "D'oh!" became "Do." Homer who says "D'oh" can be seen regularly on "The Simpsons." There was a Mary Lamb, and her brother (essayist Thomas Lamb) used the penname Elia (not mocked in an epic called the Eliad) which can be found in every other crossword puzzle. Names have been changed...(a little *Dragnet* music please).

[27] Not eye-lashes or (when drunk) the bonnie "lashes," but lashes of the speakers horsewhip, of course.

[28] That is, along the pretty bank (of a stream). Burns would have called the Boston celtics "keltics" — that says it all.

[29] Go often awry. (Forgive Burns. He's a foreigner.) Or "gang aft agley" COULD mean there's an ugly gang behind us (aft). The problem is that the Scottish had to learn the language from the English while at war with them, and were deafened (mercifully) by their own bagpipes.

[30] Bream: a type of fresh water fish often used to decorate hats — you've heard of hat breams?

from **Green Grow the Rashes**[31]

Green grow the rashes, O;
Green grow the rashes, O;
The sweetest hours that e'er I spend,
Are spent amang the lasses, O!

from **To a Mouse...**

The best laid schemes o' mice and men
gang aft agley...

from **Afton Water**[32]

Flow gently, sweet Afton, among thy green braes,
Flow gently, I'll sing thee a song in thy praise;
My Mary's asleep by thy murmuring stream—
Flow gently, sweet Afton, disturb not her dream.

from **A Red, Red Rose**

O my luve is like a red, red rose,
That's newly sprung in June...

And, lo, we have reached the Romantics (gasp!). Here is William Wordsworth's (the poet known, palindromically as the "drab bard") first stab at "Lines Composed a Few Miles above Tintern Abbey..." (the title alone goes on long enough to be the collected works of a Japanese poet who died young) followed by selected passages of the final version:

Lines Written In Abeyance For A Bay

An hour has passed; sixty minutes, with the length
Of thirty-six hundred seconds! yet I hear
These waters, rolling from their mountain-springs
Untouched by equine tongue, and once again
Do I behold these steep and lofty cliffs
So pleasant to my eye when first I led
You to this stream, but now a slumber has

---

[31] Usually the rashes that grow from hours spent among the lasses are red, not green, but Burns' "rashes" are what we call "rushes" or reeds. Thus, in Burns' dialect, we might say "This poem gives me a terrific rash." If Burns is GOING with the lasses, since "go" is "gang," perhaps the rash is gang-green.

[32] Known to nuclear physicists as "heavy water." Afton water is twice as heavy as quarter-ton water.

My spirit sealed from rude delights[33]: I am
No longer what I was an hour ago
When first I came among these hills — when like
A roe I bounded, like a bounder rode
And led you — as I've mentioned — having hopes
That you would slake your thirst in lonely streams
And leap o'er mountains, but, alas, I see
That your glad animal movements have gone by.
  How often in this long and lonely hour —
Lonely the more for your unbending presence —
Have I dreamed of the din of towns and cities
Where hackneys can be hailed and coaches chartered[34]
And all of man's conveniences be reached
Afoot. I weary of the mountain winds,
The dreary din of glassy cataracts
That merge with gleams of half-extinguished thought,
With many recognitions dim and faint,
Of fish and chips in Piccadilly Circus,
And bawdy wenches leering as I pass,
meandering among the lonely crowd.[35]
  After I'd stood and prodded you five minutes —
I cannot paint what then I was — the fishwife's
curses haunted me like passion; whores
And peddlers, domes and columns, cornices
Were then to me a joy — that time is past,
And all pedestrian joys are now no more,
And all my travels now must go on feet
That plod iambically down the page.[36]
  But not for this grieve I, nor moan nor mourn
Nor murmur (though a moment now long passed
I ached to shove a splinter in thine ass,

---

[33] This passage is from another Wordsworth poem, "A Slumber Did My Spirit Steal." Wordsworth and his readers are always in danger of being mugged by "a slumber."

[34] This reverses Wordsworth, who in the din of towns and cities, dreams of wilder scenes, preferring rural slumber to urban slumbings. He wanted to leave towns and cities and get down to their anagram: cows and nitties (as in gritties). Why, O why are the nitties always so gritty?

[35] Elsewhere he wanders "lonely as a cloud". *The Lonely Crowd* was a pop-sociology best-seller years ago by someone or other. If you know enough to come in out of the rain, you'll be far from the madding cloud.

[36] That is, poetic feet. The unit of meter in a formal poem is the foot, meaning a group of syllables (usually two or three) with a certain pattern of stressed and unstressed syllables where that pattern is repeated regularly throughout each line of the poem (or in some poems, different sections use different patterns). Thus, for example, in the line "And all my travels now must go on feet," the first foot is "and all," where "all" gets more stress (volume, emphasis) than "And." It is "and ALL." That type of foot (unstressed syllable followed by stressed) is called "iambic." This poem, like

21

Make gory all the flowers![37]), for in this hour
I have received abundant recompense
For stifling boredom by the babbling stream,
No company but you, a surly horse,
And clouds of flies you flurry with your tail;
For hearing endlessly against my will
The still sad music of this tone-deaf water,
I feel a presence that sedates me with
The joy of soporific thoughts; a sense
Of something far more deeply deep and dull,
Whose dwelling is the dingy grammar school,
The tomb-like tomes, the lamp-lit dusty texts,
The anthologies, the critical reviews,
The minds of tenure-hungry assistant profs,
A something that rolls on from phrase to phrase
In ceaseless repetition of its themes,
For what's a single word's worth? — but a thousandth
Of a picture; therefore, like this stream,
I've learned to maunder on and on for pages
In this the language of the common man[38],
Lugubriously solemn; nor perchance,
If I were not thus taught, should I the more
Suffer my menial spirits to decay:
For thou art with me here upon the banks
Of this fair river; thou my dearest friend,
My dear, dear friend[39], who, though thou dost not drink,

---

most formal poems in English, uses five iambic feet in each line (with a few minor variations). This is called "iambic pentameter." So the line's beat is (more or less) "and ALL my TRAVels NOW must GO on FEET" (though not all stressed syllables are equal in stress, and not all unstressed syllables are equal in...distress?) Poetry is basically oral, so the traditional poet generally has his foot in his mouth, which may explain why poetry is so serious — there's no room for a tongue in cheek. We suffer from fallen archness. If you're a serious reader, treasure this note and reread it to savor it, since it is the last serious passage for many chapters. Fill up here, last gassy stop before desert.

[37] Refers to "...of splendor in the grass, of glory in the flower..." from "Ode: Intimations of Immortality." As with T. S. Eliot and several other culprits, lines from many of Wordsworth's poems can be interchanged with lines from his other poems with "nobody the wiser." In fact, a great deal of poetry can be studied with nobody the wiser. Now that you know the source of "Splendor in the Grass," see the movie! Natalie would. It starred her (Natalie Wood). Wordsworth, being a poet, didn't get a cent for it.

[38] Wordsworth argued that poetry of the previous century had been written in artificial "poetic diction" and that poetry should be written in the language of the common man. "How you doin', Bill?" "Oh, lugubriously solemn, nor perchance blah blah suffering my menial spirits to decay...." "Right, Bill, got that, got to be movin' on, I have lots of leeches to gather...."

[39] The friend here, noble steed (Wordsworth is the nag!), becomes, in the final

Doth listen patiently to my laments
And memories and fits and dreams and...HEY!
Wake up, you stupid nag! I heard that snore!...

Excerpts from Mr. Wordsworth's version of the poem:

Five years have past; five summers, with the length
O five long winters! and again I hear
These waters, rolling from their mountain-springs
With a soft inland murmur. Once again
Do I behold these steep and lofty cliffs...
[From here on it's mostly every reader for himself: Find an anthology.
Oh well...just a bit more:]
...Though changed, no doubt, from what I was when first
I came among these hills; when like a roe
I bounded o'er the mountains, by the sides...
...And their glad animal movements all gone by...
...yet, oh! how oft — /In darkness and amid...
...And now, with gleams of half-extinguished thought,
With many recognitions dim and faint
And somewhat of a sad perplexity
The picture of the mind revives again:...
...I cannot paint/What then I was. The sounding cataract
Haunted me like a passion: the tall rock...
...that time is past
And all its aching joys are now no more...
...Abundant recompense. For I have learned
To look on nature, not as in the hour
Of thoughtless youth; but hearing oftentimes
The still, sad music of humanity...
... presence that disturbs me with the joy
Of elevated thoughts; a sense sublime
Of something far more deeply interfused
Whose dwelling is the light of setting suns
And the round ocean and the living air,
And the blue sky, and in the mind of man:
...A motion and a spirit that impels...
And rolls through all things...
...Nor perchance
If I were not thus taught, should I the more
Suffer my genial spirits to decay:
For thou art with me here upon the banks

version, the poet's sister, Dorothy, who, put to sleep by his rambling monotone, dreams she is in the Land of Oz, where she finds all that Technicolor a vast relief from her dear brother's endless gray meanderings.

23

Of this fair river, thou my dearest Friend,
My dear, dear Friend; and in thy voice I catch
The language of my former heart...

Wordsworth was so long-winded that his friend, Samuel Taylor Coleridge, fell asleep while listening to Wordsworth read from "Preludes." ("Prelude" means preceding play. For Wordsworth, the play never begins.) While asleep, he dreamed in vivid detail a long poem about Kubla Khan, but was interrupted when, Wordsworth, hearing his snores, violently shook him awake, just as he woke the horse in the first draft of "Tintern Abbey" above. Coleridge, thus awoken, could recall only a fragment of "Kubla Khan," [40] which is just as well, since there were no horses in it. But here are a few fragments from an early draft of Coleridge's "The Rime of the Ancient Mariner," followed by passages from the final version:

From: **Rime of the Ancient Mare**

Minute after minute, minute after minute,
She stands, nor snort nor shiver;
As idle as a painted horse
Before a painted river.

Water, water, everywhere,
And we stand on the brink;
Water, water everywhere,
But this damned nag won't drink!

From: **Rime of the Ancient Mariner**
(no relation to Silas Mariner)

Day after day, day after day,
We stuck, no breath or motion;
As idle as a painted ship
Upon a painted ocean.

Water, water, everywhere,
And all the boards did shrink;
Water, water everywhere,
Nor any drop to drink.

Lord Byron made little use of this theme — like the Cavalier poets, he never met a horse he didn't like. He came closest in the story of the old

---

[40] I lie. For the true story of how Coleridge came to write "Kubla Khan" (then came to, right?), you'll have to read Chapter 3, below. (Coleridge could out-talk Wordsworth.)

knight asleep on his stubborn mare, which begins, "She balks at duty like the knight", but was revised to "She walks in beauty, like the night" after the early version scored poorly when tested on audiences in Oregon and Indiana. (Byron was an early master of public relations and "image." His image inspired me to become a poet: I thought, based on Byron, that if I were a poet, I'd never have to button the top button of my shirt or wear a tie. But if I am awarded a Nobel prize, I'll wear a tie, I promise!)

Shelley, a more futile figure, was much attracted to the horse-to-water theme, and in the following early manuscript may be found the seeds of "To a Sky-Lark," "The Indian Serenade," "Adonais," "When the Lamp is Shattered" and *The Godfather.* And Shelley probably inspired *Wayne's World* with lines like "Sweet tones are remembered NOT." His wife, Mary, wrote a novel called *Frankenstein,* stealing the plot from a popular movie. Dr. Frankenstein makes a man (of sorts) out of spare parts. DID Mary make a man out of Shelley?[41] To cast YOUR vote on this controversial issue, call 1-800-SHELLEY.

Years after writing the following draft, Shelley got so pissed off with his horse's refusal to drink that he chased the horse into the lake, where, getting in over his head, he (Shelley) drowned. To those on shore who heard his cries, his last words sounded like "Percy Bysshe — why did I have to be named Percy Bysshe." (Alas, poor Shelley — not so well he. Alas, poor Bysshe, He's with the fysshe. Alas, poor Percy — He'd prefer Circe.) Parallel passages from the first four titles above follow the draft — and "draft" is very appropriate for Shelley, who liked to write about clouds scudding before the wind and was, generally, a bit of a restless-air-head):

Odor Of An Unseen Presence

Hail to thee, blithe spirit!
 Horse thou never wert —
That at the stream, or near it,
 Farteth thy full fart
In profuse strains of unpremeditated art.

Direr still and direr
 Gut'rally thou stinkest
Loudly like a choirer;
 Thy hooves deep thou sinkest
In mire sour as a still, still not a drop thou drinkest.

---

[41] Actually, he was pretty tough, if windy, but the name suggests shilly-shally and "shall I or shall I not" (some en-shan't-ed evening) and a fragile shell. Then there's "Percy" and "Bysshe." No wonder, having had these names visited upon him, he decided, in school, to write a paper defending Atheism (for which he got expelled).

    You fall upon the swale!
     I'd lift you from the grasses —
    I try! I faint! I fail! —[42]
     Done in by all your gasses:
Your life, like a poem of any dullard ass, now passes.[43]

    When the horse is battered
And lies in the dust quite dead,
    E're his parts are scattered
(For doggies must be fed)
    Then I will remember
He followed where I led
    And gently I'll dismember
Him...and keep the head,

    For when one sleeps in exile
In a soft Italian bed
    And tries to live in high style
With finances deep in red,[44]
    The Italians understand guile
And a horse's bloody head.[45]

From **To a Skylark**

Hail to thee, blithe spirit!
Bird thou never wert —
That from Heaven, or near it
Pourest thy full heart
In profuse strains of unpremeditated art.

Higher still and higher
From the earth thou springest
Like a cloud of fire;
The blue deep thou wingest,
And singing still dost soar, and soaring ever singest.

---

[42] These lines mimic "Oh lift me from the grass! I die, I faint, I fail!" from "The Indian Serenade," considered even by some admirers of Shelley's to be among the silliest lines in English poetry. With amateurs like that around, it just doesn't pay to work hard at being funny.

[43] Refers to Shelley's "Adonais": "Life, like a dome of many-colored glass, /Stains the white radiance of Eternity." Sounds like the 'before' part of a toothpaste commercial.

[44] Shelley plunged into debt, living above his means in Italy. In the basement, his means subsisted on bread and revisions.

[45] This is unfair to Italians, since the creeps who leave a horse's severed head at the foot of someone's bed in *The Godfather* are Sicilians (no relation to the Sissy Lion who goes to see the Wizard).

26

From **When the Lamp is Shattered**

When the lamp is shattered
The light in the dust lies dead —
When the cloud is scattered
The rainbow's glory is shed —
When the lute is broken
Sweet tones are remembered not —
When the lips have spoken
Loved accents are soon forgot...

If Shelley's here, can Keats be far behind? Here (followed by parts of its ultimate version) is "Ode on a Grecian Urn." ("Ultimate version" sounds religious — perhaps describing the Version Mary?) Keats' dad ran a stable, so when young Keats left the horses to try his hand at poetry, his entire life was destabilized, which probably contributed to his early demise. (Wordsworth's demise, on the other hand, was tardy. Some say he was stable; others say he stalled.) Keats himself was probably a poor rider, since he had a big ass. That is, he is reported to have had a lot of Fanny Brawn. (His sweetheart was named Fanny Brawne. I don't know if he had her, but his Fanny was never far from his side. Pretty hip!)

O Dam, Egregious — UUUURGHH!

Thou still unwatered dam of stubbornness,
  Thou filly of impatience and slow time,
Equine Gandhi-ist[46] who canst thus express
  A brute refusal, duller than my rhyme:
Swallowed water's sweet, but that unswallowed
  Sweeter still — or so thou seemst to think,
    Unhappy horse! Unhappy sappy horse!
Therefore, although all servilely thou followed
  Me to this murmuring stream, thou wilt not drink!
    But standst forever panting — I thy chorus!*

* Alternate line: But standst forever panting — Oi! Such tsoris![47]

---

[46] Referring to the horse's nonviolent (passive aggressive?) resistance and to Gandhi's tactic of winning concessions by refusing food and water until he practically disappeared, and one of his disciples cried out "Where's Mahatma?!" and his buddy said "It's on your head, stupid, and I'm not your Ma!".

[47] "Tsoris" is Yiddish for troubles, misery, grief. It rhymes with "chorus" or "dinosaurus," not with "You're a sight for tsoris!"

Ah me, I'm held here! Shall I ever leave
  If I wait for thy whim? Thou standeth there,
So near and yet so far, but I'll not grieve,
  Though ever wilt thou stand — it's just not fair!
This childish, anal snit, cold past oral![48]
  When old age shall this generation waste,
    Thou shalt remain, in midst of other "Whoa!"
Than mine, a foe to man, to whom thou neigh'st
    "Brute, he is rude, rude brute he! — that's the moral:
      Ye lead on earth, and where ye lead I go
      But I won't drink — that's all ye need to know!"

From **Ode on a Grecian Urn**[49]

Thou still unravished bride of quietness,
Thou foster-child of silence and slow time,
Sylvan historian, who canst thus express
A flowery tale more sweetly than our rhyme...
Heard melodies are sweet, but those unheard
Are sweeter; therefore, ye soft pipes, play on...
More happy love! more happy, happy love!
Forever warm and still to be enjoyed,
Forever panting, and forever young...
Fair youth, beneath the trees, thou canst not leave...
When old age shall this generation waste,
Thou shalt remain, in midst of other woe
Than ours, a friend to man, to whom thou sayst,
Beauty is truth, truth beauty,— that is all
Ye know on earth, and all ye need to know.

Walter Savage Landor was once considered a flaming romantic, but lost his reputation by growing old, though never wordsworthwordy. He got his middle name when he showed up at his first brothel, singing out "Walter's of age! Walter's of age!" Here's Landor's very rough draft for "Rose Aylmer" (whose full name was Rose Aylmer Fudd?):

---

[48] Keats calls the urn a "cold pastoral." I passed my orals too, but I never completed the Ph.D. thesis. I wanted to write poetry, and the thesis had to be in prose, and a prose thesis (or prosthesis) is what I'd have needed soon — a replacement (called a "degree") for the abilities to create and imagine, being lost to gangrene as academic pressures cut circulation to the intellect. Getting a thesis accepted is called "passing ones anals."

[49] I wonder, did anyone ever write "Ode On A Madonna?" (Repeat aloud, rapidly.)

Gross Old Mare

Ah, what avails the Arab blood,
  Ah, what the winsome whinny!
What though once fast on sand or mud!
  Gross old mare, you're a ninny!

For, gross old mare, you would not drink,
  Though taken to the trough,
And now, though it's not yet a "stink,"
  You smell distinctly "off."

Rose Aylmer

Ah, what avails the sceptered race,
Ah, what the form divine!
What every virtue, every grace!
  Rose Aylmer, all were thine.

Rose Aylmer, whom these wakeful eyes
May weep, but never see,
A night of memories and of sighs
  I consecrate to thee.

Enough of these tight-assed Englishmen. Now for a spell we'll hang loose with some rude 19th Century American poets. First, Edgar Allen Poe's first draft of what later became "The Raven" ("Once upon a midnight dreary, /while I pondered, weak and weary,/Over many a quaint and curious /volume of forgotten lore..."). This poem (with its insistent rhythms and its "As of someone gently *rapping, rapping* at my chamber door") is the inspiration for Rap, foreseeing which Poe was driven to drink and dissolute death (which further inspired Rap):

If You Can't Beat A Dead Horse, Please Join Him
Or Neigh Naemore

Once upon a morning early,
how my little horse was surly!
Though I led him to a purly stream and nudged him to the shore —
Though I prodded and cajoled him
and I told him and I told him
(O! I wish that I had sold him ere he learned thus to ignore
My implorings) — though I begged him, yet he boldly would ignore;
  Only this and nothing more.

Ah, distinctly I recall it
was late summer in St. Paul[50]; it
Was a sweaty day and squalid — Christ! This meter is a bore!
It won't win me bay or laurel;
Therefore, let's cut to the moral:
For my ancient swaybacked sorrel, though I kicked him aft and fore,
Hollered, "DRINK, you stupid nag!" and pinched and kicked him aft
    and fore,
    He just stood there, nothing more.

How I pinched him and I kicked him,
Yanked his tail and spurred and pricked him!
But he would not drink, damned victim! He just licked his latest sore.
Then that hack of little virtue,
He just collapsed into the dirt — "You
Silly horsie, have I hurt you? That will teach you to ignore!
Will you drink now, little horsie, or continue to ignore?"
    Quoth the horsie, "Nevermore."

Then he perished with a rattle,
But I wouldn't yield the battle,
Pried his lips apart — dumb cattle! — but they stuck in rigor mor-
Tis so I tried intra-venous,
And he bloated up — obscene as
Something else that rhymes with venous, then blew up all the hell
        o'er!
That's my stubborn little sorrel, yes indeed, that's him all o'er!
    All in pieces evermore!

The final draft of this poem changed the horsy to a raven, inspired by a Medieval ballad called "The Three Ravens." This ballad goes as follows: "Nevermore!" "Nevermore!" "Nevermore!" (Get it? THREE ravens?...I guess you had to be there.)

Sorry to expose you to such a sad ending. Here's a much more cheery poet, Henry Wadsworth Life-is-Ernest Longfellow, in a rough draft of "Hiawatha" in which the poet struggles heroically with his chosen form. I wish he'd won. The first seven lines appear unchanged (except the word "pony" in line three becomes "wigwam."):

Hey! Uh...Water? (Just For Whad's Worth)

By the shores of Gitche Gumee,

---

[50] By strange coincidence, **I** was born in St. Paul!

By the shining Big-Sea-Water,[51]
Stood the pony of Nokomis,
Daughter of the moon, Nokomis.
Dark behind it rose the forest,
Rose the black and gloomy pine-trees,
Rose the firs with cones upon them,
Rose the sheds and seedy cabins
With red pickup trucks beside them
Rusting in the fields long fallow,[52]
Rose the fancy new casino
Run by wealthy tribal elders,
Rose...but where was I? The pony!
Yes, let's get back to the pony:
Bright before it beat the water,
Beat the clear and sunny water,
Beat the shining Big-Sea-Water,
Beat the...wait a minute, STOP that!
So this pony that Nokomis
Led to water — it just stood there,
Stood there glazed-eyed and unbending,
Stood there like a wooden Indian —
I mean wooden native Am'rind —
Stood and stared and stomped and shivered,
Stood...now STOP that, damn it! STOP that!
Stop this pointless repetition;
Stop before you drive me batty,
Batty as the little pony —
There, I tricked you neatly that time,
Tricked you as the wily white wolf,
He who, blessed by Manitou,
Father of the sun, Manitou,
Tricked the children of the beaver...
WAIT, what happened to the pony?
Yes, the pony, little pinto —
Many things Nokomis called him,
Names that have no place in poems
That would foster wholesome values,
Names that little Hiawatha

---

[51] "Big-Sea-Water": Lake Shapiro, one of the Great Lakes along with lake Cock-ran (or Urine), Dershowitz (or Michiganer), Simpson (or Eerie) and Lake Endless Trial (or On-Tarry-O!). For the media-intolerant, Shapiro (Superior), Cochran (Huron) and Dershowitz (Michigan) were lawyers in the endless trial of Erie — I mean O. J. Simpson.

[52] "Long fallow" — that is, Longfellow. Why does that silly kids' joke always associate "long fellow" with the *feet*? Probably because "shows it" doesn't rhyme with "poet."

Though she'd taught him every language,
That of every bird and insect
And of beasts their names and secrets,
Yet such things she'd never taught him,
Things not known to the language
Of the fowls, though foul her language,
Things that singed the pony's earlets —
OOH WaEEE! They singed his earlets,[53]
But, to make a long long story,
Long as Hiawatha's childhood,
Long as Cyrano's appendage —
And I will not will not — WILL NOT! —
Mention "fellows" or poetic
"Feet" — I would not be so fell...O!
I've half done it![54] — mentioned one who
Long and desperately struggled:
Like mad Strangelove with his own hand,[55]
So was he caught up and strangled
By this meter that so long fell
O'er[56] and o'er itself like water —
Water, yes, as I was saying,
Of this pony, yes, in brief, though
Led to water, to the shining
Big-Sea Water, by the shores of
Gitche Gumee, to the water
Of... ENOUGH now! Stop it! STOP IT!
This damned pony — there! I've almost,
ALMOST said it — would not drink!

Had enough rhyme and meter? Here he is, Walt Whitman, breaker of horses and forms, in an early draft of "Song of Myself" from *Leaves of Grass* (followed by passages from the final version):

Grassy Leavings

I conduct my horse, and sing my horse,
And what I shall assume my horse shall assume,

---

[53] "Oowa-ee, my little owlet" in the final draft, "Oowa-ee" being Chippewa for "I'll get you!" (Let us return to where I chip away at Longfellow.)

[54] That is, "fell...O!" is half of "Longfellow" — actually two thirds. If we crossed Longfellow with Horatio at the Bridge, we'd get Longfellatio.

[55] "Strangelove" refers to the movie, *Dr. Strangelove*, in which Strangelove's own black-gloved hand tries to strangle him. Strangelove was played by Peter Sellers, and peter sellers are gigolos, which brings us back to Longphalo...

[56] "Long fell O'er," that is, Longfellower — what a coinkidink!

For every atom belonging to my horse as good as belongs to me.
My horse loafs and invites my prod.
I lean and loaf at my ease observing each twitch of horse's ass,
My horse, my brother, drink or do not drink,
For I cannot make you drink,
Nor do you follow me to this rush of cool delight under coercion,
But from comradeship of blood and hunger and muscular preening,
The same sun kindling your eyes and my eyes,
The air I sneeze snuffled up your snout,
Your every neigh my aye,
Perfect, both of us, you in your shuffling, me in my waiting.
Welcome is every flea of you, every scab of your mangy hide,
Not an inch or particle of an inch is vile, and none shall be less
      familiar than the rest.

I have said that the soul is not more than the body,
And I have said that the body is not more than the soul,[57]
And a dead horse is as beautiful as a living horse,
And when you are rigid and glazed-eyed, your stubbornness will be
      perfect in its permanence,
And therefore why should I urge you to imbibe this turbulent
      brew, this fishy elixir, this confluence of dew,
When your horsey farts and grassy droppings are as dear to me as
      your glossy coat,
When your bleeding carcass will be as lovely as now the grace of
      your gallop, the tossing of your mane in the sun,
When your corpse will fester with maggoty life as dear as any of
      thine or mine?

For I am Walt Whitman, lover of disobedient steeds
And I am Walt Whitman, killer of disobedient steeds,
And my loving is not more loving than my killing,
And my killing is not more killing than my loving,
And I will embrace you with my slaying as eagerly as I seize the
      slender stableboy in his smelly leather boots,
And my bullet will strike you with crimson gladness,
And my killing of you will be a perfect killing,
And the last flash of amazement in your eyes as you go down will
      burn me like the stableboy's hot sweaty muscular kiss.

Therefore I swear now by my strong bony freckled finger on the
      trigger of my stiff, pent pistol

---

[57] These two lines (on soul and body) are Whitman's own — parody could not make them sillier. Perhaps "I have said that the driver is not more than the car...."

That I care not whether you choose to drink or choose not to
   drink,
Choose instead to loaf eternally, as ignorant of me as any stone,
Pecked at by vultures and torn by rooting pigs and...
Wait! Don't drink yet! I have but begun!...Cowardly nag!

from **Song of Myself**

I celebrate myself, and sing myself,
And what I assume you shall assume,
For every atom belonging to me as good belongs to you.
I loaf and invite my soul,
I lean and loaf at my ease observing a spear of summer grass...
Welcome is every organ and attribute of me, and of any man hearty
   and clean,
Not an inch nor a particle of an inch is vile, and none shall be less
   familiar than the rest...

Thank you, Walt. Stirring, but messy. Now we'll let Emily Dickinson
tidy up a bit in an early draft that reverberates in "Because I Could not Stop
for Death," "The Train," "The Soul Selects Her Own Society," "I Taste a
Liquor Never Brewed," and "Success is Counted Sweetest." Ms. Dickinson
was better with birds than with horses. Her birds drank freely, knew no force
— she watched one "drink a dew." I doubt she ever led a horse or knew just
what to do. (Oh my, this is, of course, her rhythm — catching, just like flu!
Reader, if you're here, within her range, you'll catch it too.) Her stubborn
horses are, then, no doubt symbolic. She apparently led at least one man to
her "water," but either could not make him drink (so to speak) or would not
allow him to. She probably dismissed this fellow courteously, hiding a tear
or two, then, when he'd gone, broke some crockery or tore some lace, then
went to bed sick (after sweeping up the crockery), recovered gradually, then
wrote some wonderfully cheery poems about lying in the grave. By the way,
I utterly deny the scurrilous theory that she was attacking Longfellow when
she called a snake a "narrow fellow in the grass."

Because He Would Not Stoop To Drink
Or On Dasher![58]

I'd like to see him lap the streams —
And lick the rivers up —
And stop to fill himself at tanks —
And still prodigious sup —[59]

---

[58] Emily Dickinson liked to use dashes. I suppose she had colon trouble. Did she die
in a comma?

[59] These first four lines are only slightly changed from Ms. Dickinson's description of a train.

But the horse selects its own sobriety —
Then shuts its mouth —
Offering stiff contrariety —
Suffering drouth.

Or inebriate of air is he —
And debauchee of dew?
Well quench your fussy thirst with air —
For, Horsey, I am **through!**

Since then 'tis days and days, and yet —
Feels shorter than the hour —
I could not nudge my horse's head —
With my persuasive power.

Success is counted sweetest —
By those who never lead —
He won't suck cess or nectar —
The devil take this steed!

from **The Soul Selects her own Society**

The soul selects her own society,
Then shuts the door.
To her divine majority
Present no more...

from **I Taste a Liquor Never Brewed**

Inebriate of air am I
And debauchee of dew,
Reeling through endless summer days
From inns of molten blue...

from **Because I Could not Stop for Death**

...Since then 'tis centuries, and yet
Feels shorter than the day
I first surmised the horses' heads
Were toward eternity.

from **Success is Counted Sweetest**

Success is counted sweetest
By those who ne'er succeed

To comprehend a nectar
Requires sorest need...

Emily Dickinson's affection for dashes led her to promote them to other poets. In her own famous words: For zingier punctuation use DASH! — the UnColon!

Back to England — to a poet Emily Dickinson admired, Elizabeth Barrett Browning, who, unlike Emily, found a man who could appreciate her either in her poetic persona or as a sensual woman (that is, either "Aurora Lee" "or orally" — and be glad her persona wasn't Anna Lee![60]) , but it was a close call: Robert Browning had to battle her Dad (Grinnan Barrett) for her soul. Her dad appears in the following poem in the guise of a horse's ass:

Barrett, Not Contrite[61]

How do I curse thee? Let me count the ways.
I curse thee to the depth and breadth and height
My shoe can sink into thy steaming shite
While shoving, pleading, moaning my "*Oi Weh*s!"[62]
I curse thee to the treble of thy neighs
When quietly I kneed thee out of spite.
I curse thee freely — not one bit contrite;
I curse thee purely, as a butcher slays.
I curse thee — with such passion Robert tore
Off my old briefs, Ah! — with my childhood's tantrum!
I curse thee, for you stand there — such a bore!—
And will not drink! I curse thee! How I rant, trum-
Peting my hate! Drop dead? — I'll but curse more!
I'll pound you till you burst or till I can't drum!

What She Really Wrote:

How do I love thee? Let me count the ways.
I love thee to the depth and breadth and height
My soul can reach, when feeling out of sight

---

[60] And by God! there IS an Anna Lee: She's the detective heroine of several novels by Lisa Cody. But I have not as yet located a Genita Lee (or Jenita?).

[61] The title conceals Robert Browning's affectionate advice to the poet not to put up with her father's tyranny, but to dedicate herself to her writing: "Bear it not, Cunt: Write!" Though she addresses here her stubborn horse, this is one of the sonnets she dedicated to Robert: "Sonnets to a portly geezer." (Actually, the collection is *Sonnets from the Portuguese*. Browning did get rather portly and red-faced in his later years, which made him an easy mark for those who cared to mock his message of "strive on!" and "the best is yet to be!" Nobody takes a fat man seriously, alas.)

[62] For the Yiddish-challenged, "Oi Wehs!" is pronounced "Oy Vays" and means "Oh Woe." The full expression is *"Oi Weh ist mir!"* or "O woe is me!"

36

For the ends of Being and ideal Grace.
I love thee to the level of everyday's
Most quiet need, by sun and candlelight.
I love thee freely, as men strive for Right;
I love thee purely, as they turn from praise.
I love thee with the passion put to use
In my old griefs, and with my childhood's faith.
I love thee with a love I seemed to lose
With my lost saints — I love thee with the breath,
Smiles, tears, of all my life! — and, if God choose,
I shall but love thee better after death.

It seems we have tackled the aromatic Romantics and emerged Victorian. Here's a rough draft of Alfred Lord Tennyson's "Charge of the Light Brigade," a poem that typifies his aesthetic pronouncement: "Words, idle words, I know not what they mean":

High Tennysion

Half a leg, half a leg,
Half a leg onward[63]
Into the river to drink
I rode my sick horsie.
His not to make reply,
His but to drink or die —
Into the river to drink
I rode, of course, he.

Water to right of him,
Water to left of him,
Water in front of him,
Rock-torn and sundered.
Beat at with heels and whip,
Mutely he stood — the drip!
Stood there and would not drink,
not take the slightest sip!
I sat and wondered
How I had blundered.

---

[63] You might think that "Half a leg" means the water is half-way up the horse's leg, and perhaps it is (go and have a look), but I borrowed this line from my wife, Pam, who says that when she was little, she and her Mom (poet Olivia Williams Coulter) would recite this poem, and they'd always yell out "Half a leg" instead of "Half a league," then laugh. I doubt they ever got through the poem — but then whoever does get to the end of these long Victorian poems?

"Into your jaws," I said,
"Into your mouth so pink,
"Ere my fist turn it red,
"Drink! you sick horsie!
"For if you will not drink,
"I cannot force ye;
"Then I'll go back, but not,
"Not the sick horsie."

from **The Charge of the Light Brigade**

Half a league, half a league,
Half a league onward,
All in the valley of Death
Rode the six hundred.
"Forward the Light Brigade!
Charge for the guns!" he said.
Into the valley of Death
Rode the six hundred.

"Forward, the Light Brigade!"
Was there a man dismayed?
Not though the soldier knew
Someone had blundered.
Theirs not to make reply,
Theirs not to reason why,
Theirs but to do and die.
Into the valley of Death
Rode the six hundred.

Cannon to right of them,
Cannon to left of them,
Cannon in front of them
Volleyed and thundered;
Stormed at with shot and shell,
Boldly they rode and well,
Into the jaws of Death,
Into the mouth of hell
Rode the six hundred.

Flashed all their sabers bare,
Flashed as they turned in air
Sabering the gunners there,
Charging an army, while

All the world wondered.
Plunged in the battery smoke
Right through the line they broke;
Cossack and Russian
Reeled from the saber stroke
Shattered and sundered.
Then they rode back, but not,
Not the six hundred.   [And so forth; Tennyson, at this point, had
only begun to fight.]

Tennyson, depending upon which poetry circles you stumble into, was either a great Victorian poet or a great Victorian writer of unconscious parodies. Those who consider him a great Victorian poet will not likely enjoy having him roughed up by a parodist. For those who read his poems to laugh at them, parodying Tennyson is carrying coals to Newcastle — or plutonium to Hanford? Therefore, parodying him is not very gratifying. But he is one of the most remarkably lop-sided English poets. I can think of no other (not even Wordsworth) who combines so much genius with so miniscule a sense of humor. Even serious academic poets feel an urge to cheer up Tennyson. I don't think he could make a horse drink, but he could make one weep.

Here is a recently discovered fragment from an early draft of Edward Fitzgerald's translation of "The Rubaiyat of Omar Khayyam"[64] (in this case, the rub-you-out of "O Mare, I am..."):

O Mare, I Am About to Rub You Out

A Book of Verses underneath the Bough,
A Jug of Wine, a Loaf of Bread — and Thou
Beside me drinking from the Crystal Stream...
But, Horse, you should have lapped the Stream ere now!

The mare decides; and, having set her Wit
'Gainst yours, nor all your Pleas and such Horseshit
Shall lure her back to drink a single Drop:
She's no more use than, to a Bull, a Tit.

---

[64] Omar Khayyam was a Persian poet of some century or other (I think he was born in one of the *circas*, perhaps three-ringed). "Rubaiyat" is Persian for the quatrains (four-lined rhymed stanzas) that comprise the poem, in which we are advised to eat, drink and be merry, for tomorrow summer vacation ends, and we have to go back to school and memorize stuff like this.

In the finished work, these stanzas became:

A Book of Verses underneath the Bough,
A Jug of Wine, a Loaf of Bread — and Thou
Beside me singing in the Wilderness —
Oh, Wilderness were Paradise enow!

The Moving Finger writes, and, having writ,
Moves on, nor all your Piety nor Wit
Shall lure it back to cancel half a line,
Nor all your Tears wash out a Word of it.

Fitzgerald beat his horse (a bay mare) so fiercely that she became depressed and could not be cheered up, whereupon he said, "Dost thou rue, bay, yet? Oh mark! I am fed up!" Then he had her skinned and made into a tent. (We use pup tents; the Persians used pony tents.)[65]

Now an early draft of Robert Browning's "Last Duchess." Realizing that British gentlemen would never stomach a poem about the senseless killing of a thoroughbred horse, Browning changed it to the far more acceptable poem we all know and love in which the Duke of Ferrara explains why he killed his wife. This poem started a whole sub-genre of poetry, which Browning called "dramatic manure-log" in honor of a disgusting (and *brown*ing) moment with the same horse that inspired the early draft of the poem (which follows), wherein the stallion's promiscuous nickers foreshadow the Duchess's possibly loose knickers[66] that so incense her husband, who is "to the manure born" (no wonder he craves incense):

My Last Stallion or **Too Many Nickers Lead to the Knacker, With a Nick-Knack Paddy-Whack**...[67]

That's my last stallion painted on the wall,
Looking as if he were alive. I call
That piece a wonder, now; a pretty fellow,
Came trotting as quick to whisper as to bellow;
Fine-mettled, sportive — see his fiery eye!

---

[65] "Khayyam" is Persian for tentmaker. He was "Omar the tentmaker." In his country people LIVED in tents, so a lot was at stake.

[66] Nickers are neighs, while knickers are long bloomers that used to be worn as women's underwear, so to defend decency, SAY NEIGH TO LOOSE KNICKERS!

[67] Here nickers (or gentle neighs) lead to knackers (horse butchers, though it could also be a playboy, someone with a knack for knickers) which leads to the silly chorus of an old song ("With a knickknack paddy-whack, give the dog a bone; this old man came marching home"), which leads to the end of this note just in the knick of time.

Would let me lead to water, but when I,
Even I, blessed with my ancient name,
My pride, my etchings and my stable's fame —
When I, I say, all gently bade him drink,
He swerved his head from me. What could I think?
I could have forced his head into the bucket
And held it there until he drank, but fuck it![68]
E'en then would be some stooping, and I choose
Never to be stupid. Sir, to my coos
He nickered, but who cooed without the same
Nicker, so thinking of my age-old name,
I gave commands; then quicker than a wink
All nickers stopped because he would not drink,
And there he stands as if alive. Will't please
You rise. I'll lead you to — no, I but tease:
I will not lead — Nay, we'll go down together
As cozy as two falcons of a feather
To see this steed you offer — is he thirsty?
He'll not refuse a drink, I hope — or durst he?

from **My Last Duchess**

That's my last Duchess painted on the wall,
Looking as if she were alive. I call
That piece a wonder now...
...She had
A heart — how shall I say? — too soon made glad,
Too easily impressed; she liked whate'er
She looked on, and her looks went everywhere.
Sir, 'twas all one! My favor at her breast,
The bough of cherries some officious fool
Broke in the orchard for her...
...She thanked me — good! but thanked
Somehow — I know not how — as if she ranked
My gift of a nine-hundred-years-old-name
With anybody's gift. Who'd stoop to blame...
...and if she let herself be lessoned so, nor plainly set
Her wits to yours, forsooth, and made excuse

---

[68] Genteel readers ("It's my first poem — please be genital!") may prefer to substitute "well" for "bucket" and "Hell" for "fuck it!" If that's not tame enough for them, well fuck it! They can go to Hell in a bucket. (I'm really a very nice person. The words did it!)

— E'en then would be some stooping, and I choose
Never to stoop. Oh sir, she smiled, no doubt,
Whene'er I passed her; but who passed without
Much the same smile? This grew; I gave commands;
Then all smiles stopped together. There she stands
As if alive. Will't please you rise. We'll meet
The company below, then...
...Nay, we'll go
Together down, sir...

Not all Victorians were rough and imperious with their reluctant nags. Matthew Arnold, for example, tried the "We're in this together" gambit in "Dover Beach": "Ah, horse, let us be true/ To one another!" It didn't work — Arnold's equine muse remained incurably dry.

Here's one of Edward Lear's lost limericks. (He'd been indulging in lime rickeys[69] and misplaced it.) Lear is noted for getting off to a good start, then losing interest after line four and repeating line one to end off. Here he tries his damndest to expand his scope:

Leery Leary Limerick

A jolly old burger from Rotter-
Dam led his old mare to the water.
   Though she walked to the brink,
   That old dam would not drink
For the jolly old burger from Rotter-
Damn!

Next, an obscure barrack-room ballad from Rudyard Kipling, that doesn't seem to be the source of any one of his better known poems, though several echo it:

Beast Of White Man's Burden

Hoy! Yer Arab, 'e's a bugger
An' yer pure-breds shy and shrink,
But there hain't no bleedin' fugger
Like an 'orse 'at will not drink.
Yer can wheedle as yer lead 'er,
Yer can stroke an' coo an' wink,

---

[69] A lime rickey (i.e., limericky?) consists of soda, lime and gin — a gent needs his vitamin C.

But yer cannot make 'at bleeder
Of a bloody kaffir[70] drink.

Saber slashes, dumdum[71] smashes;
What they miss, the sergeant mashes.
Soon enough we'll both be ashes,
Dry as dust on my mustaches.
Hoy! The stream is gently rippling,
Leaf-laced sun its surface stippling —
NOW, by CHRIST! I'll have yer tippling,
Or me name hain't Ruddy Kipling!

Drink yer fill — I can't be 'erdin'
Yer to water every hour.
Yer a bloody white man's burden![72]
Won't I show yer 'oo's got power!
What're yer? A snooty shopper?
Drink, yer 'eathen — it ain't sour!
I can civilize yer proper,
Christ'enize yer till yer cower!

Cannon crashes, bayonet gashes;
What they miss, the sergeant mashes.
Soon enough we'll both be ashes,
Dry as dust on my mustaches.
Hoy! The stream is gently rippling,
Leaf-laced sun its surface stippling —
NOW, by CHRIST! I'll have yer tippling,
Or me name hain't Ruddy Kipling!

---

[70] "Kaffir"— a South African native, often a generally derogatory term, though today white South Africans are more polite. Instead of "Kaffir! A drink!" it's "Kaffir a drink, my dear?" Probably the first race problems in Rome occurred because of Julius Caesar, who, Antony says, "…hath brought many kaffirs home to Rome." (Actually "coffers" — having defeated the Germans, Caesar brought home the germs.)

[71] Dumdum: a soft-nosed bullet...or perhaps a blonde bullet? Instead of the drumming of bullets, you could hear the dumdums tomtom.

[72] Kipling's poetry is often associated with the Victorian rationale that England was colonizing the world in order to civilize and Christianize it, a God-given responsibility, the "White Man's Burden," as Kipling calls it in a poem by that name. This idea is much scorned in modern America, where we subvert governments that displease us and run schools to train torturers in order to Make the World Safe for Democracy and Prozac without regard for race (including human), creed or color. (And what a safe world it is!) That's a strident remark, and you might think I'm pissed off at our Government. Not really — I'm more annoyed at a poet as (usually) sharp as Kipling getting ignored by our more-liberal-than-thou generations. "White Man's Burden" is not to be confused with "White Man's Bird," probably the bald ego.

When 'mongst men an 'orses seethin'
Rifle bullets zip — kerPLING!
(An' them ruddy naked 'eathen
Sure can make them bullets sing!),
Then yer drouthy nag is thinking
"Where is Din[73], the ding-a-ling!"
Hoy! Yer shoulda done yer drinking
Where it's only bees 'at sting.

Forty lashes, poxy rashes;
Then what's left, the sergeant mashes.
Soon enough we'll both be ashes,
Dry as dust on my mustaches.
Hoy! The stream is gently rippling,
Leaf-laced sun its surface stippling —
NOW, by CHRIST! I'll have yer tippling,
Or me name hain't Ruddy Kipling!

If't please yer drink, yer spavined 'ighness? —
Mangy bleedin' knock kneed farce!
If yer've got a yen fer dryness,
Soon enough yer'll have much worse,
Parched by gun smoke to the tongue roots,
Dry as any parson's verse!
DRINK! Or BOOTS BOOTS BOOTS BOOTS BOOTS BOOTS[74]
Will be ticklin' yer scrag arse.
BOOTS BOOTS BOOTS BOOTS BOOTS BOOTS BOOTS BOOTS
'Ard as Fuzzy-Wuzzy's[75] arse!

Gun butt bashes — oo's blood splashes
On me shirt? Then yer what trash is!
Soon enough we'll both be ashes,
Dry as dust on my mustaches.
Hoy! The stream is gently rippling,
Leaf-laced sun its surface stippling —
NOW, by CHRIST! I'll have yer tippling,
Or me name hain't Ruddy Kipling!

---

[73] Din: Gunga Din, Kipling's famous water carrier, not related to Din Blehert, whose poems, some say, cannot hold water.
[74] "BOOTS", repeated is the chorus of "Boots." I don't know…it worked for the Victorians.
[75] Fuzzy-Wuzzy: What the Tommies (British soldiers, "thin red line of 'eroes") called Sudanese native warriors. It takes many years of study to learn such things. Poetry is a hard life.

Bah! Yer bay comes up like thunder[76]
An' yer roan's a bloomin' fink,
But their hain't no dimwit dunder-
Head like one 'oo will not drink —
Worse than purse-lipped office 'olders
Which, when cut, bleed printer's ink
On their precious ledger folders;
Worse than Ganges' mucky stink
Where the broody Brahmin moulders
An' the filthy lepers slink;
Worse than 'ag-tongued wives, shrill scolders;
Worse than 'ores which must have mink
On indifferent shruggin' shoulders;
Worse than wenches which can think;
Worse than drunken Irish soldiers
'Oo in maudlin mire sink;
Worse than vengeance that long smoulders
Is an 'orse which will not drink!

See them far artil'ry flashes?
There's the light that all hope dashes.
Soon enough we'll both be ashes,
Dry as dust on my mustaches.
Hoy! The stream is gently rippling,
Leaf-laced sun its surface stippling —
NOW, by CHRIST! I'll 'ave yer tippling,
Or else I'm a wet-arsed stripling,
Not no bloody Ruddy Kipling!

For a poet who is associated with pride in his country, Mr. Kipling couldn't spell any better than Burns.

Here's another medley, a Gerard Manley Hopkins draft that contains the core of, among others, "God's Grandeur" (most of the first two stanzas below), "No Worst, There is None," "The Windhover" (stanza 3, lines 1-4) and "Spring and Fall" (the last line). His strong beat led to a whole class of rap music called "hiphopkins" as performed by groups like The Cute Li'l InScapers[77]:

---

[76] This line refers to "...and the sun comes up like thunder 'cross the bay," a Kipling line from "Road to Mandalay" his famous script for Bob Hope, Bing Crosby and Dorothy Lamour. Wait a minute — maybe it was Crosby's crooning that was called "Fuzzy-Wuzzy" while the Sudanese native warriors were called "Sudan Death" — I can never get these things straight.

[77] "Inscape" is Hopkins' term for the unique selfness of everything in the universe except, possibly, stubborn horses.

Manley Forbearance

The whip is charged with the frenzy of fury.
   It will flick out like lightning if I'm foiled;
   It hurtles to a hissing, in my hand held coiled...
CRACK! Why do you then now not drink — and HURRY!
I coddle you, caress with comb and curry;
   To coax you to take fluid, long I've toiled;
   My brain and blood have boiled, have boiled, have boiled;
If you won't drink, I will — my tongue turns furry.

You'll soon repent — long ere my wrath is spent —
   Not drinking dearest freshness deep down springs!
How readily you followed where I went,
   Then balked — now soon you'll be with deep down things,
For waterless, your shaky shanks all bent,
   You silly one[78], your neck I'll wildly wring

Until you buckle, fall, are galled — and yet,
   My little mare, sheer plodder never more,
I'll feel your fall perforce with fell regret,
   For gashing gold vermillion, smeared with gore,
You'll stain my good garrote — Ah! THERE'S my upset
(Unriddle, Lord, this twisted Jesuit![79]):
It's merely my good mare garrote[80] I mourn for!

---

[78] "Silly one"— (now we get real scholarly) see "sillion" in "Windhover." It means the furrow made by a plow. "Wildly wring" in this same line, refers to a line from "No Worst, There is None": "More pangs will, schooled at forepangs, wilder wring." In other words, when you're sweating in bed and can't sleep and despair of any future because your wife, lover or God is nowhere to be found, no worst (it can't get worse) you think, but there IS no worst, it can ALWAYS get worse, because the latest pang has learned from the previous pang how you can even better torture yourself. I think it's a great poem, but the title still makes me think, "No Wurst, We Have None, but Yes, we Have Some Bananas."

[79] Hopkins converted from Anglican to Roman Catholic at Oxford and became a Jesuit. He was twisty in more ways than his syntax and his sins: Assigned to teach, for example, he graded his papers on a scale of zero to 10, then, feeling this too inexact, made it zero to 100. Then he had a "nervous breakdown" and was removed from teaching. On a scale of one to 1000, his best work rates 1,256,798. (He liked precision.)

[80] Garrote: a device used to strangle. Thus a "mare garrote" would be used to strangle a mare. This mimics the line from "Spring and Fall": "It is Margaret you mourn for." Poets, being suicidal, often live in garrotes.

from **God's Grandeur**

The world is charged with the grandeur of God.
  It will flame out, like shining from shook foil;
  It gathers to a greatness, like the ooze of oil
Crushed. Why do men then now not reck his rod?
Generations have trod, have trod, have trod...

And for all this, nature is never spent;
  There lives the dearest freshness deep down things....

from **The Windhover**

...Brute beauty and valour and act, oh, air, pride, plume, here
  Buckle!...
  No wonder of it: sheer plod makes plow down sillion
Shine, and blue-bleak embers, ah my dear,
  Fall, gall themselves, and gash gold-vermillion.

from **Spring and Fall**

...It is the blight man was born for,
It is Margaret you mourn for.

Note: I haven't quoted the pertinent passages from "No Worst, There is None," because it's the finest poem in the English language, so I assume you all know it by heart (or wherever you keep such things). Quiz on Friday as usual, but don't worry, all life death does end, and even quiz days end in sleep. [Hopkins: "...All/ Life death does end and each day dies with sleep."]

Next, a scrap left behind by A. E. (Alfred Edward) Housman that anticipates "Loveliest of Trees," "To an Athlete Dying Young" (The "garland briefer than a girl's"), and numerous other lyrics about doomed lads (and even a few lasses), some of them doomed by the stroke of a bell *ala* "Tom Dooley," though not necessarily doomed, in those pre-AIDS days, by the other strokes contemplated by this scholarly, dignified, and horny poet. (The lads probably called him "Dad." One wonders how often over the doomed lad loomed Dad.) By the way, his many poems about the "Shropshire Lad" were inspired (and this is based on very recent scholarship) by his failure to seduce a young man. He tried to soften the "lad" by plying him with drink at the local pub. Then he started reciting poetry to the sodden youth. "Shurrup!" said the lad. "Sure, Lad," said the poet, desperate to please. The memory of this conversation ("Shurrup!" "Sure, Lad") tormented the humiliated Housman until he gave it form in "Shropshire Lad," since which it torments only English majors:

On the High Incidence of Heart Failure and Strokes
Among Shropshire Lads

Stubbornest of brutes, old Dobbin now
Still hung, but stupid as a cow,
Just stands upon the daisied brink —
Why, lad, do you refuse to drink?

Now of my threescore years and ten,
Twenty will not come again,
And take from seventy that twenty —
Ample time to score — but PLENTY! —

Lovely lads in garlands brief
To kiss before that darksome thief
Has slipped them from my artful arms
To where rude worms shall taste their charms —

But not much time if it's my fate
To wait and wait and wait and wait
While you won't drink — it's such a waste
Of rosy cheeks — O please make haste!

Sweet lads are dying every minute —
The tomb's the rage! They MUST get in it!
The fevered brow, the gallows tree,
The broken heart — how fast they flee

Beyond where I can reach; how sad
To waste a single slender lad!
Have you no pity, no horse sense?
Each second bears a sweet lad hence!

No longer, therefore, shall I wait:
Drink now before the stroke of eight
Or you'll not hear the stroke of nine
When lads combine their strokes with mine.[81]

---

[81] The strokes here allude to the stroke of the bell in some Tom Dooleyish poem, the stroke that the lad sentenced to hang for killing his beloved will not hear, nor will he again stroke the belle. It's such a sad thing, these hangings of lovercides. I think lovers (if attractive and remorseful) should get one free murder (after all, romance is so upsetting) and only be executed if they do it again.

from **Loveliest of Trees**

Loveliest of trees, the cherry now
Is hung with bloom along the bough,
And stands about the woodland ride
Wearing white for Eastertide.

Now of my threescore years and ten,
Twenty will not come again,
And take from seventy springs a score,
It only leaves me fifty more...

Well, we're up against it. There's no turning back. We're going to have to look at modern poetry. But first, a last nostalgic gasp from that quaint premodern bard, Joyce Kilmer, whose famous "Trees" (honored at great length in another chapter of this very volume) was published in *POETRY* in 1912, just three years before that same distinguished journal (or, in Swedish, urinal) published Eliot's "The Love Song of J. Alfred Prufrock" and the rest used to be history, but now we're not so sure when things became history, which probably hasn't begun yet. Kilmer actually advanced the proverb, asserting that, not only couldn't a poet make a horse drink water, but also only God could MAKE water. Here is Kilmer's rough (if such a word can be applied to this gentler Joyce) draft for "Trees":

Horses

I think that I shall never force
The fluid intake of my horse,
My horse who, rooted as a tree,
Can stand all day — ignoring me,
Whose mane wind-ruffled, tail a'twitch
Are all the parts of the sonovabitch
That move — and he can stand this way,
Rather than hear me and obey,
Through rain and sleet and all the rest,
While on his rump spring robins nest...
Kill-mare I'm called — but cease thy dallyin'
Or I'll rejoyce to kill a stallion!
For it's a no-brainer, leading to water
But making him drink is an only-Godder.

from **Trees**

I think that I shall never see
A poem as lovely as a tree.

A tree whose hungry mouth is prest
Against the earth's sweet flowing breast...

[Wherein the tree looks to God all day; that is, the branches are eyes, though the base of the trunk, per preceding lines, is the mouth; and the tree lifts her leafy arms to pray, so the eyes must be on the arms. And the tree wears a nest of robins in her hair — which hair is also eyed arms. And snow has lain on the tree's bosom, which bosom (as the tree sucks at the earth's bosom — a rather adult nursling) is also the hair that consists of arms with eyes; and finally the tree "intimately lives with rain," which I guess means the tree shacks up with the rain, which suggests that the act of rain falling on a tree is an act of sex, which suggests that those hairy eyed arms are even MORE versatile.[82] And after all this, Kilmer concludes:]

Poems are made by fools like me,
But only God can make a tree.

Given the anatomical mess he describes, I would think that only a committee could design a tree. But perhaps God is a committee. Many have suspected as much. I can hear it now: "Point of order, Dad...." "You're out of order, Son. The Holy Ghost has the floor...."

Oh, we should make mention of homey old Edgar Guest, who said, "You can lead a horse to water, but it takes a heap o' horseshit to make a horsy poem."[83] And here's a bit of anonymous doggerel from Kilmer's generation (hey, if I don't use it here, where can I use it?):

Authorities Aver

You can lead
A fine steed
Or trotter
To water,
But can't make
That accurst
horse slake
his thirst.

Now we come to the great seminal work of modernism, the aforementioned Prufrock. Here we have TWO drafts of that revolutionary poem by

---

[82] These anatomical observations I swiped from an old poetry textbook I can't seem to locate, *Understanding Poetry* by Cleanth Brooks and Robert Penn Warren. (He who Cleanth is next to he who Godth.)

[83] Actually Guest said "It takes a heap o' livin' to make a house a home." If you'd like to do a heap of living in my house, be my Guest. I am much more inclined to live in heaps, mainly of paper.

Thomas Stearns Eliot, a very early and unsatisfactory draft and a later, far more detailed draft, obviously close to the final version, yet still containing as its matrix the horse-to-water theme that mysteriously vanished in the final version, leaving its structure behind, suggesting the "lost-wax" method of creating bronzes, with the horse-to-water theme, here, as in so many of these works, constituting the waxen mold for the final brazen figure. In the final version, Prufrock himself becomes our horse-figure, impatiently urging himself to act, able to lead himself TO the nameless woman, but UNable to force himself to ask the unspecified question (probably the same question Hamlet poses regarding Ophelia: To bed or not to bed her? Hamlet, like Prufrock, delays: "Cool it, Ophelia later, alligator.").

Here is a passage from the earliest version, in which the speaker is a coprophiliac (one who does not poopoo poopoo) recently freed from prison, Eliot's vision of the role of the poet in the Twentieth Century:

The Love Song of a Jail-Freed Poop Freak[84]

Let us go now, you and I,
To where the rich brown water
Slips past suburban yards
Like a dysenteric effluvium.
Let us go, my thoroughly bred horse,
Now, while the evening is stretched out
Across the fields like a black lace stocking
On a thick thigh, and there,
By the murky water, we shall hear
The naiads singing each to each.
Dare I feed you a laxative peach?
By the stream, where minnows come and go,
Burbling of pike, pale and yellow,
You plop a fibrous muffin at my feet,
As I compose a face to meet the feces that I meet.
You sniff the stream and whinny,
"That was not what I meant at all."
O, I was never meant to lead a horse
To water. I do not think
That you will drink for me.

In the later, much more elaborate draft, we see that Eliot incorporates the "Poop Freak" theme in the climactic moment when the horse "drops a soft conclusion" at the speaker's well-laced feet. This scatological theme survives in the final poem in but a few places, for example, "Then how should

---

[84] Thanks to L. A. poet, Dick Coanda, for suggesting "Poop Freak."

I begin/ To spit out all the butt-ends of my days and ways?" and "To have squeezed the universe into a ball/ to roll it towards some overwhelming question" (which evokes a dung beetle rolling his ball of dung toward his nest). Here is Eliot's contribution to Non-aqua-ivorous equinology, best appreciated if you have a copy of "the final draft" open as well (poetry books need exercise just like dogs):

> **The Cerebral-Lobe Song of J. Well-Read Pluperfect Subjunctive**
> or **PRUF: The Magic Drags On**
> or **Summon Chanted Evening: You Will Lead, Estranged, A**
> **Crass and Crudded Roan**
> or   **Met Aphorism, Sanks Just the Same**[85]
>
> by 'Tis Silly — Yet...

Hope? Eh, Gumbah, you leada da horsie tru dissa gate,
fahgeddaboudit, capiche? Am I right, Guido? Datsa RIGHT.
                    Don T. Allegory, from The Good Fodder[86]

Let us go then, you and I —
When the evening hay's spread out, again you shy,
Click impatient teeth, your eyes upon the stable;
Let us go, my thoroughly bred high-strung horse,
Down certain half-deserted trails
(These cluttering details!)
Of restless knights who ride toward one-horse towns
And raw saloons with gals in scarlet gowns;
Trails that follow like a tedious simile
Whose point's perceived but dimile
To lead you with your overweltschmerzed Kvetching[87]...
Oh, do not ask, "What boots it?" —
Hardly any critic hoots it.[88]

---

[85] A take-off on "Met enemy, sank same." It has been argued that "Prufrock" sank the logical use of metaphor ("*Met Aphor*ism,...) — or do you, too, see etherized patients in the evening sky? (If so, you've seen too many episodes of "ER.")

[86] Translation from the Italian: "Ladies, please refrain from stroking that portion of *David*, as it is wearing away at the rate of one inch every century."

[87] A Germanization or Yiddishization of "overwhelming question." "Weltschmerze" is supposed to be profound pain over the sadness of the world, but when it is repeated *ad nauseam* by generations of professors concerned mainly about tenure and fellowships, it becomes the less dignified "Kvetching" or chronic whining.

[88] Actually this take-off on "Oh, do not ask, 'What is it?'/ Let us go and make our visit" is unfair: Lots of critics have sniped at Eliot. They just weren't allowed in our college classrooms back in the '50s and '60s. And for some reason almost NO critics object to one of the silliest tenets of "Modernism": That there's something

In the stream the minnows come and go,
Burbling of pike, pale and yellow.[89]

The yellow fog that gently weights the weary reader's eyes,
Like mellow smoke that stings with catlike feet the reader's eyes,
Wove word cobwebs in the corners of the eyelids,
Lingered upon the fools who think they're wise,
Enchanted them with ghostly numb high-priestly chanting:
    (Chanty chanty chanty)[90]
They slip down in their chairs — a sodden heap,
And seeing that this poem repeats itself for pages,
They sense all poetry's an ageless sleep.

And indeed there will be time
(If you persist in stalling at the water)
For the yellow smoke, unceasing, to repeat,
As endlessly the reader rubs his eyes,
There will be time, there will be time
(In a sort of runic rhyme
To the tintinabulation that so musically[91]...oopsie!
Is it worship under duress
That makes me so digress?) —
As I may have mentioned, there will be time, there will be time
To retie a lace — two feet, the laces at my feet,
To featly lace the laces to the shoes upon my feet,[92]
There will be time to curse you and to wait,
Time for even impotent critics to masturbate,
Yes, time for all the jerks and plays of hands,

---

profound about dissociation, that something that's "unconscious" is more profound than something conscious, that psychoanalysts know more about you than you do and that being illogical equates to transcending logic. Personally, I prefer a pun to a Fraudian slop.

[89] C'mon, go get a copy of "Prufrock"! Don't miss a single complex ironic allusion.

[90] "Chanty" refers both to Eliot's propensity to chant at us (High Churchman that he is) and to the "Shantih" chant in "The Wasteland" which is not the "Shanty in old Shanty Town," but a Sanskrit benediction, but it could also be Prufrock's motto: "Shall I or shantih?"

[91] Here Eliot slips into Poe ("The Bells"), to whom he owes much of his musicality, though he — or at least his academic worshippers — would have been ashamed to say so. Eliot is quite within the tradition of "nevermoring." The next two lines ("worship under duress...," a take-off on "Is it perfume from a dress/ That makes me so digress?") refer to the once monolithic academic insistence on the profundity of Eliot, a reverence enforced upon generations of undergraduate English majors.

[92] Prufrock, of course, wanted "...to prepare a face to meet the faces that you meet." Notice the academic smugness of saying "of course" just before saying something that some of my readers may not know. But that goes without saying.

Time for visions and nocturnal emissions,
And time for all this solemn maundering —
You lift your tail and drop a soft conclusion at my feet:
DattadamyatadayadhVAM[93]
(A Datta overload, Goddamn!
For I'm not one to stand in lieu of loo,[94]
To have your loo goo dumped upon my shoe
Like a loo-goobrious yellow fog — Oh PHOO!)

There will be time,
Time for inversions and perversions and submersions
Time for potations and flotations,
Time for following and wallowing and swallowing,
Time for muzzle nuzzling and guzzling,
Time for imbibitions and inhibitions, for libations and bad vibrations,
Time to fail to wet your whistle 'mid the thistle and the thyme,
Time for me to think and think while you refuse to drink,
Time for you and time for me,
Tea for two and two for tea,
And time yet to imagine disconnections,
A horse or poem in sections and dissections,
And time to wipe from both my shoes your feces,
And time for a hundred learned doctoral theses —
The reader stirs — he has to take a pee.

In the stream the minnows come and go —
Horse, would you prefer a tangelo?

And indeed there will be time...
But you have known these lines already, known them all,
Have known this trick of repetitious loops,
This repetitiousness that lets one move,
Move on in half-steps, one line to the next,
And ever dies with dying fall
As by a shores of Gitcheegumee,
By the shining big sea water,
By the...Whoops![95]

---

[93] Datta, damyata, dayadhvam, three Sanskrit words in "The Wasteland" meaning "Ta ta!", "Damn you too" and "Die hard, bum!"
[94] "Loo" is English slang for bathroom. Thus, if your bird has to go real bad, you sing out, "Skip to the loo, my Darling!" (Or perhaps, "My crumpet"?)
[95] Briefly the poem is haunted by another of Eliot's closet mentors (along with Poe), Longfellow, who, like Eliot, had the trick (or compulsion) (e.g., in "Hiawatha") of beginning each line by repeating half of the preceding line — dragging his poetic feet.

I should have been a pair of shell-rimmed specs
Scuttling on the floor of a saloon.[96]
How can parody scuttle a poet whose poem
Prepares a preface to eat the peaches that one eats?
(They will say, "How his wit is growing thin!")
After all, this is T. S. Eliot: Do I dare
Disturb the universe?
For I have been the eternal Footnote fetishist
who would reunite thinking and passion
 (It's become quite the ultra-mod fashion);
and I have seen the infernal Editor browse my poems and snicker
(Don't you DARE nicker!)
(It made me belch my dandy liquor quicker),
And in short...I felt a Little Gidding,[97]
No kidding.

Yet I dare more than Eliot, for having no Italian,
Yet I proceed, UnDanted,[98] to water my stallion,
Who stands by the stream
All the afternoon and evening in a dream,
Snoring so peacefully.
Should I, after coaxing and cajoling and all that,
While glaring at the yellow streak besmirching my left spat,
Should I have the gumption to exclaim, "Oh dreary drat!"

And would it have been worth it, after all,
After the hay, the oats scattered on the ground
Among the fly-flecked turds, among some talk of Ezra Pound,
Would it have been worth while
(Ezra will know, that wily crocodile!),[99]

---

[96] These two lines were given me by Dick Coanda, the generous fellow mentioned earlier (so I've just wasted a chance to use *Op. Cit.*).

[97] "Little Gidding" (in Punnish or Punese, "a little giddy" or in this chapter, a little Giddy-up!) is the name of one of Eliot's "Four Quartets," a name Eliot took from the name of an estate once owned by poet George Herbert's mentor, whose name was taken from my memory by about 35 years, but it's something like Nicholas Ferrare. A quartet is a small quart, probably of dandy liquor, which is an allusion to Ogden Nash's witty ditty about dandy candy and quicker liquor (quicker for facilitating the lickerish, which is not dandy candy, but an old word for lecherous, which makes it a lewd alewsion).

[98] "UnDanted" — without Dante Alighieri, who provides the epigraph for "Prufrock." Here Don T. Allegory suffices. Dante was a famous Italian comedian (he wrote *The Divine Comedy*). I tried to read it, but it didn't seem funny at all, except the part where someone must have told Satan what he could do with Judas, because that's where Satan has put him.

[99] Ezra Pound promoted Eliot's work and cut "The Wasteland" in half for him. (I'd like to take some pounds off my own waistland.)

To have forced the matter, had a brawl,
Poured bucketfuls far down your gaping maw
And stroked your light brown throat to make you swallow,
Left no Trojan cranny of you hollow—
If one, snuffling later, snorting in the hay,
Should neigh, "That is not what I want at all.
I'm not that sort of horse at all."

And would it, as I may have mentioned previously
(For these phrases circle back upon themselves most deviously),
have been worth it, after all,
Would it have been worth while,
After the years of loathing discreetly my neighbor
From behind my modest desk at Faber and Faber[100]
After the boom in poetry metaphysical[101]
And writing poems so quizzical
That it is impossible to say just what I mean
But as if a tragic slattern threw her curves in patterns quite obscene:
Would it have been... — Christ! No wonder
My horse, no matter how I rage and thunder
(In my quiet ethereally grey well-modulated numbers),
Keeps subsiding into horsy slumbers.
Shall I part your tail behind
With a kick most unkind?
At home my Vivienne[102] grows colder,
Turns to my caress her shoulder —
That is no tit at all.
That is no twat I mount at all.[103]

For I am not one to sin. Can't a Tory[104]
Do aught but wax incantatory?

---

[100] A publishing house where Eliot worked, back when he was fab and they were Faber.

[101] Eliot's critical writings promoted Donne, Herbert and other "Metaphysical" poets, as they were called, perhaps because they never met a physique they didn't like. (At least several described by Donne in his more profane poems suggest that he was more peninsula than island.)

[102] Eliot's first wife, who was, reportedly (how does one do things in a "reported" manner?), both hysterical and frigid and ended her days in a spin-bin after doing her best to give Eliot the tormented life of a poet. What did he do to her? Probably read his poems to her.

[103] These last two lines twist Prufrock's woman's lament: "That is not it at all./ That is not what I meant at all." To those among my readers who feel that my references to "tit" and "twat" demean women, I (me, Dean, not demean) can only say, that is not what I meant at all.

[104] Eliot was a Tory Royalist Anglican—heavily right wing, making his lyrical flights uneven. (That's why politicians go in circles.)

I am no Hamlet to rant a gory
Story...dreadfully sorry.

But it's past time for revision and derision;
I want to get back to my television —
Yet though I preach and blast you, blast and preach,
Before you'll dare to reach
With your huge tongue, dare to breach
The current's dark and rippled silk,
We'll hear the naiads crying each to each
Over — though it's no use — spilt milk.[105]
I have seen them ride the current toward the beach,
The progress of their swell...my uneasy tool...

In the stream the minnows come and go.
Do I dare to give you peach Jell-O?

You sniff the stream and whinny,
"This is not what I meant at all."
O I was never meant to lead a horse
To water. I do not think
That you will drink for me,
you ninny!

We've malingered — as on chamber pot to pee
I've sat and read Italian and French
("T. Eliot" spelled backwards names my bench)
Till Vivienne threw a fit about the stench
With insidious intenti-
-on, poor hysteric wench!
(Oh why am I not Hamlet-like — a mensch!
O some mensch-haunted evening...)[106]

Well then, if you won't drink, my English horse —
And would it have been worth it? Yes, of course!
I'd MAKE you drink if intellectual force

---

[105] Another great theme of rough drafts, e.g., "Say not the weeping over spilt milk naught availeth!" "Say not the struggle nought availeth" is a line from Hugh Arthur Clough, an extremely controversial poet among those who debate whether Clough is tough or Clough doesn't have a clue or Clough made dough...as though! (I like to think of him as Hug Arthur Clug.)

[106] This line is yet another gift from Dick Coanda. Inspired by an early draft of this parody, he decided to play Pound to my Eliot and made many other delightful suggestions, but I took only a few and told him to go write his own parody. I hope I have prodded a parody out of him.

Could teach a horse —

But now we'll mount our dry high horse,
Our high-and-dry-Church, Tory[107] horse, of course,
Whence it behooves us to out-Brit the British,[108]
For Yankee voices make our brute grow skittish,
Whereas it makes us feel quite tinglish (WHEE!)
Pontificating to the English (OUI!)
With *our* editorial *we* from London Town
Till mocking voices fake *us*, and *we* frown.

Meanwhile, back in the U.S.A., Robert Frost (who was actually an English nobleman[109], but did his best to out-American the Americans just to "show" T. S. Eliot that two could play that game) actually kept a real horse or two, barring their escape with fences, for, as he noted, "Good fences make good Neigh bars." He also used lots of rhyme and meter without the proper poetic licenses and got away with it, much to everyone else's chagrin and his own shaggy grin. Here's what Frost adds to the adage when his little horse greatly frostrates him (he's a frost-rate poet):

Stopping By Woods With A Stubborn Horse

Whose woods these are I think I oughter
Know, though I'd not wed his daughter.
But he won't see me stopping here
To watch my horse fill up with water.

My little horse must think it queer
To stop without a farmhouse near
For he won't dip into the lake
Though I cajole him for a year.

He gives his stubborn head a shake
To ask if there is some mistake.
The only other sound's my "[BLEEP-
BLEEPING] NAG!", but he won't slake

---

[107] Eliot was a conservative, or in Britain, a "Tory" (opposed to the Labour party). He hoped, that way, to be able to attract loose women and avoid having unwanted children, knowing that one can, by exhortation, lead a hortatory [whore to Tory], but one can't make her Labour.

[108] Eliot, from Missouri, became the most English of the English, as described in Isaac Walton's biography, The Compleat Anglophile. (Note: Walton wrote *The Compleat Angler*, about fishing, not geometry. I told you even my footnotes have footnotes.)

[109] Your author, Dear Reader, is lying. Frost was born in San Francisco and was more no-bull than noble.

His thirst. The woods are dark and deep.
Shoot him? But then on foot I'd creep
With miles to walk before I'd sleep,
With miles to walk before I'd sleep.

from **Stopping by Woods on a Snowy Evening**

Whose woods these are I think I know.
His house is in the village though;
He will not see me stopping here
To watch his woods fill up with snow.

My little horse must think it queer
To stop without a farmhouse near
Between the woods and frozen lake
The darkest evening of the year....

And so on: It's the harness bells the horse shakes, the only other sound is wind and flake (and it takes a flake to hear one), and the poet would linger (or stay forever?) in the lovely, dark, deep woods, but he has promises to keep and miles to go before he sleeps — times two. A year later the freeway went through, leaving only a decorative fringe of trees on either side, but from the old road, if you wear ear plugs, on a snowy night the woods still look lovely, dark and deep.

For all his plain folksy image, Frost in person is said to have been as frigid as his name, more rime than rhyme, perhaps resulting from his bitterness about horses refusing to drink. That is, he was more horse-fraught than hoarfrost. Brrr! Let's move on to a sunnier soul.

e. e. (Edward Estlin) cummings, like Archie, the cockroach, had trouble reaching the shift key. Not that cummings was at all a cockroach, no, he was just a little shiftless. At a time when revulsion from traditional forms was typically indicated by dispensing with rhyme and meter, cummings managed to retain them (though he failed to "capitalize" on them), yet appear radical by screwing up his typography and mingling, promiscuously, the various parts of speech, including the intimate private parts — which led to yet more cummings. Here is his first draft for "anyone lived in a pretty how town":

Drank His Didn't And Went His Cummings

anyhorse lived in a oney-horse town
(with up so oating many bales down)
spring summer autumn winter
he drank his didn't he led his did

fillies and colts (both little and small)
cared for anyman not at all
they peed their isn't they munched their same
dun roan stalls reins

children guessed (but only a few
and down they forgot as up they grew
autumn winter spring summer)
that no horse loved man mare by mare

some studs mounted their everymares
snorted their shyings and butted their bares
(sleep stand wake and stand) they
neighed their ayes they poohed their whinnies

one day anyhorse died I bet
shot for drinking his didn't though led
went his cummings and came his wents
hooves mane down drain
nouns verbs mundane
bard moons bun-brains

from **Anyone Lived in a Pretty how Town**

anyone lived in a pretty how town
(with up so floating many bells down)
spring summer autumn winter
he sang his didn't he danced his did.

Women and men (both little and small)
cared for anyone not at all
they sowed their isn't they reaped their same
sun moon stars rain

children guessed (but only a few
and down they forgot as up they grew
autumn winter spring summer)
that noone loved him more by more...

someones married their everyones...

one day anyone died I guess...

Women and men (both dong and ding)
summer autumn winter spring

reaped their sowing and went their came
sun moon stars rain

The above poem had a major impact on the world, inspiring the naming of an important character (Princess Summerfallwinterspring) on the TV show that launched a generation, *Howdy Doody*. So, e. e. cummings, how do you like your blue-eyed Buffalo Bob?[110]

Wallace Stevens is the sort of author working for an insurance company who is good to have around if you want to buy insurance from an author, because in the absence of Wallace Stevens, you'd probably have to buy your insurance from that other insurance executive, Franz Kafka, and after a few minutes with Franz Kafka, you'd probably figure, why bother, so it's nice that Wallace Stevens gives us literary types a cheerier, more avuncular presence in the insurance industry. Actually, Kafka had a great sense of humor; he'd probably sell you a policy that pays double if you turn into a giant beetle. But I digress. Like Robert Frost and T. S. Eliot, Wallace Stevens could spell much better than Chaucer, Burns and Kipling, plus he knew how to use the shift key, clearly a competent poet. He liked to contemplate the introduction of messes into orderly scenes, so was attracted to horses, as in his poem, "The Idea of Ordure at Key West."[111] Here's the first draft (all of our horses are "draft" horses) of "Anecdote of the Jar":

Jarring Anecdote

I placed a jar in Tennessee,
And round it was, upon the straw.
It made the slovenly stable yard
Surround that straw.

My thirsty horse walked up to it,
And lolled around, no longer dry.
The jar was round upon the ground
and full — my horse just tossed his mane.

I took dominion all in vain:
The horse with grave disdain
just stared, would not give in and drink —
Like nothing else in Tennessee.[112]

---

[110] In cummings' poem, "Buffalo Bill" (or is it "buffalo bill"?), Bill is called mr. death's "blue-eyed boy." Buffalo Bob Smith was the emcee on Howdy Doody, right, boys and girls?

[111] Actually, "The Idea of Order at Key West." Like many poets, Stevens was on a sacred keywest for a higher order.

[112] Tennessee produces lots of whisky, some in the still of the night, and consumes much of same. I don't know what Tennessee horses drink, but they are notable as being WALKING horses, perhaps because it is unsafe for them to drive, given their drinking habits.

from **Anecdote of the Jar**

I placed a jar in Tennessee,
And round it was, upon a hill.
It made the slovenly wilderness
Surround that hill.

The wilderness rose up to it,
And sprawled around, no longer wild....

And so on — the jar is round and tall, takes dominion everywhere, being "gray and bare" and devoid of birds and bushes "like nothing else in Tennessee." Was it a partially open jar? Was the jar ajar? On this the poem is silent.

Sadly, Stevens was, almost immediately after writing this poem on the scene, picked up for littering, after which his poems were boycotted by the Sierra Club and other environmental groups and labeled "Litterature." In despair, Stevens sold more insurance policies.

Dylan Thomas's life was nearly as adventurous as Wallace Stevens's. I don't know if he ever placed a jar on a hilltop (he probably just pissed right on the hill), but he did drink and wench himself to death. (If he was insured by Stevens's company, he was probably one of Stevens's adventures.) But it's OK, because he was Welsh, and the Welsh are that way — or is that the Irish? He was a terrific reader with a rich resonant voice that could make almost anything sound good, so please add his voice to the following rough draft (one of three in this volume — see chapter 2 for more) of "Do Not Go Gentle into That Good Night" (but the title became another poem: "The force that through the green fuse drives the flower/ Drives my green age") :

The Horse That Drink Refuses Drives Me Nuts! — Drives Me to Rage

Do not, unwatered, turn from that good stream,
Lest burning seize your throat at end of day;
Drink, drink, or else I'll thrash you till you scream!

Wise nags may loll and look askance and scheme
To let the others pull their load; yet they
Do not, unwatered, turn from that good stream.

Good men, kept waiting till the sun's last gleam,
Rage, rage against the stalling of a bay!
Drink, drink, or else I'll thrash you till you scream!

Wild men — who aren't as jovial as they seem —
Would tan your skin for drummer boys to play...
Do NOT, unwatered, turn from that good stream!

Grave men look patient, but they'd gladly ream
You out, if you dared flummox them this way.
Drink, drink, or else I'll thrash you till you scream!

And I — such bother! How you make me steam!
Goddamn you with your shrill pathetic "Neigh!"
Do not, unwatered turn, from that good stream!
Drink, drink, or else I'll thrash you till you scream!

from **Do Not Go Gentle into That Good Night**

Do not go gentle into that good night,
Old age should burn and rave at close of day;
Rage, rage against the dying of the light.

Though wise men at their end know dark is right,
Because their words had forked no lightning they
Do not go gentle into that good night...

[And so on (these "and so ons" proliferate as we get into recent poems where copyright law looms). Stanza three mentions good men's deeds dancing in a bright bay; I think MY use of bay is far less strained. Good men prefer rage, as do wise men, wild men and grave men. How could his dying father resist such logic: Dad, look, EVERYBODY'S doing it! Don't be left out. Rage is all the rage. Be like the wise, good, wild, grave men, (I guess women don't get to rage at death — maybe at life?) Such logic could drive anyone into a rage. ARRRGH!]

...And you, my father, there on the sad height,
Curse, bless, me now with your fierce tears, I pray.
Do not go gentle into that good night.
Rage, rage against the dying of the light.

In its final form, Thomas turns his frustration with his horse into exasperation with his father, who stands "on that sad height" up in the attic peering through the darkness by match-light, in search of the fuse box after the house has gone dark. Young Dylan is spitting mad and can't bear his father's equanimity in the face of the dying of the light (right in the middle of one of Dylan's favorite radio shows!). Neither realize yet that Mr. Thomas failed to pay his power bill. This is when Thomas decided to write only "powerful" poetry.

Whenever one mentions modern poetry, one mentions (right after Eliot and maybe Stevens) W. H. Auden. So I have now mentioned him. Like A. E., T. S. and E. E., W. H. actually had names (Wystan Hugh). Despite converting Wystan Hugh to initials as soon as he could, Auden was homosexual, but perhaps the name Wystan should not be blamed, as Housman was, harmlessly enough, Alfred Edward, while who could find fault with Whitman's Walt? Anyway, they are all dead now, so it's OK. I don't know why all these poets preferred initials to names. I suppose they were men of letters. Here is an early horse-to-water version of Auden's "O Where are You Going" — also the theme of "Musée des Beax Arts" which begins "About suffering they were never wrong" and shows how, as the "torturer horse" scratches its behind on a tree and refuses to drink, a "dreadful martyrdom must run its course" — for it is not easy for a sensitive poet to be patient with a horse. As Yeats put it, describing the stupidity of a horse that would not drink: "How can you know the dun, sir, from the dunce."[113]

O Come Where I Lead You

"O come where I lead you," said stabler to stallion,
"The field's like a cellar where furnaces burn.
Yonder's the streamlet whose liquid will cool us;
I'll teach you to drink it, if horses can learn."

"O drink of this stream," said hostler to horsie
"Your chemistry needs it, um yummy! It's good!
Nutritious, delicious, not scummy — not very...
Just try it, you'll like it! No, really, you should!"

"O do you imagine," said eager to equine,
"That sunlight and air will sustain you all day?
The path of your grazing is pooled with your urine.
It hurts you, not me, when you will not obey."

"I'm coming, I'm coming" — said stallion to stabler,
"Then drink it yourself" — said horsie to hostler,
"But I'd prefer not" — said equine to eager,
As he spat it out, as he spat it out.

---

[113] A take-off on the last line of Yeats' poem, "Among School Children," where, describing an ideal of wholeness in life, he asks, "How can you know the dancer from the dance?" At least that's what's critics claim. I think the line means, "You know the dancer, the one from the dance?" "You mean Alice? Sure, I know her VERY well!" "Huh? How can YOU know the dancer from the dance?" Shouldn't "the dance" be "the dancee?"

from **O Where are You Going**

"O where are you going?" said reader to rider,
"That valley is fatal when furnaces burn,
Yonder's the midden whose odors will madden,
That gap is the grave where the tall return."

"O do you imagine," said fearer to farer...
[that you're search will be successful, given the delays of dusk,
missing the path, etc.]

"O what was that bird," said horror to hearer...
[and do you see those other vague threatening shapes, and, by the way,
what's that spot on your skin?]

"Out of this house" — said rider to reader,
"Yours never will" — said farer to fearer,
"They're looking for you" — said hearer to horror,
As he left them there, as he left them there.

Odd poem for a reader (not rider) to write, though he did go out of his
house to pay his respects, briefly, to the revolution in Spain. He's a jaunty
intellect, Auden, as if Robert Browning were a symphony for orchestra, and
someone were playing him as a trio for xylophone, cello and clarinet.

From Auden to Ogden: For some reason, Ogden Nash don't get no re-
spect, but I place him in this exalted company because, whether or not he
deserves it, all these serious serious bards certainly deserve Ogden Nash:

Gnomic Gnashing at Gneigh-Saying

If you lead your horse to water
And ask him to drink, why he oughter,
But if he won't, you can't make him —
Devil take him! —

For though you can force him to follow,
It's harder to get him to swallow.
Then deed that steed to your daughter or
To the slaughterer.

Hay
Is OK,
And oats
Are the items upon which one dotes,
But water

Beats slaughter
For it's not slaughter — 's laughter
We're after;
So when led to water and asked to drink and you're a horse,
Say, of course!

No one Nash poem derives from the above draft, but the last two lines perhaps foreshadow "When called by a panther,/ Don't anther" (which, during WWII became "When called by a panzer, don't anzer" and is now "When called by a cancer, don't ancer"), and the preceding lines dimly forebode "Candy is dandy, but liquor is quicker." Another humorist of the 20th Century (Dorothy Parker) said something like "You can lead a horticulture, but you can't make her think." Nash is rash, but Parker is darker. Parker is also terser. Nash is a Rambler.[114] Well, they too are both dead. Isn't ANYBODY still alive!

Sylvia Plath certainly should be, but she stuck her head in the oven and turned on the gas. Biographers variously blame her husband, Ted Hughes (poet laureate of England since 1985, but he doesn't get into this chapter because what's the point of parodying somebody that no one has ever read — and who reads a Laureate? He writes about crows), her father (who, in her poems, is a brute) and Sylvia herself, who, after all, knew that her head wasn't a cake. Also, there's the psychiatrist her parents took her to when she was a child who decided that the best way to help a bright unhappy child was to run hundreds of volts of electricity through her brain over and over. That probably helped. Anyway, here is an early draft of her poem "Daddy," in which she exorcises him (here, her horsy) from her life. In the final stanzas she seems to be planning her suicide:

Horsy
or Who Is Sylvia, That All The Swines Pursue Her[115]
And Why Did She Go To Pot?[116] or Beaucoup Boohoo To You Too

You do not do, you do not do
Any more, dark loo
To which I have stuck like a rump
For thirty years, fat and cracked,
Barely daring a fart or a poo.

---

[114] For those too young to remember, the Nash Rambler was a car. What's the matter with you people? More and more of you are getting born too late to know anything!
[115] Referring to Shakespeare's song (from *Two Gentlemen of Verona*), "Who is Sylvia? What is She That All Our Swains Commend Her." Since one meaning of "swain" is lover, this title suggests what Sylvia must be. (Isn't that what YOU say after lovemaking? "Highly commendable, my dear.")
[116] "Go to pot" — since she died with her head in the oven. Or perhaps she was being a critical pan.

Horsy, I have had to kill you.
You died before I had time —
Leaden stupid George Washington face,
Ghastly portrait with one slobbered lip
slick as a disco heel

And a tongue aloll the racing flume
You do not drink, you do not drink
I wanted you pulped to glue
When I stepped in your goo.
Ugh, doodoo.

It stuck like your glue to my shoe.
Ick, ick, ick, ick,
I could hardly speak.
I thought every horsy was you.
And the panting obscene,

An engine, an engine
Chuffing me off like a Jew.
A horse with a Hitler mustache,
A Deutschland Uber Alles leer, who
Ever heard of a horse like you?

The smells of the stable, the soft meadow hues
Are much overrated too.
Standing there waiting like a lump
of cancer to grow, Oi!
I talk like already a Jew.

Oh it was you, just you you you.
Whose are these you's? You know whose,
Or is it Hughes? Is it youse, Hughes,
With your crows, or you, youhoooo,
Dear dead Daddy, boohoo, is it you?

O who who who is Sylvia's who?
I have so many, a whole crew,
But, it's you, horsy,
as I may have mentioned earlier,
It's you, you big booboo, you.

I have always been scared of you,
With your fascist schlong — how it grew!
And the Luftwaffe snot that flew

From your Horst Wessel snout.
Nazi-nag, Nazi-nag, Oh you —

You may ask, you with hoof uncleft,
How can a horse be a Nazi swine?
You stand at the stream, horsy,
And do not drink, nu?[117]
You do this to irk me, you DO TOO!

Why did you follow and not drink
The bucketfuls I drew?
I stomped and screamed for hours,
Five minutes, if you want to know,
Brute heart of a brute like you.

And then to drop dead, become glue
Before I could beat the piss out of you
Broke my pretty red princess heart in two
And crunched it beneath your iron shoe,
But I'll get back at you,

Bloodsucking ghoul, I'll get you,
For I know what I always knew:
I hear your hiss and snort in the flue.
I know you're in there, you,
behind the oven door...BOO!

I'm coming in, I'm coming in,
Head first I'm coming after you,
You and your Auschwitz ovens,
Your 6,000,000 Jews baked in a pie.
Screw you for the slews you slew.

Baker, Baker, bake Mommy's head.
You can't escape me by being dead.
Oh Mommy's a pie, Mommy's a stew,
Mommy's a blood-red worm ragout,
And Mommy's coming in after you.

---

[117] "Nu?" is a Yiddish expression akin to "Well?" (or, in Yiddish, "Vel?"), except the doctor makes you well, while the poet makes you nu? In "Daddy" Plath compares Daddy to a Nazi and herself to the persecuted Jews. And not long after writing it, she gassed herself in an oven. I suppose her death could be called a failure of modernism, since she killed herself to make her metaphor make sense, which modern metaphors aren't supposed to do.

Before they say I do, I do,
The cowboys kiss the girls, not you.
The spirit is breath, and this is a gas.
Horsy, watch your Gestapo ass.
Horsy, horsy, you dog meat, you're through.

Excerpt from **Daddy**

You do not do, you do not do
Any more, black shoe
In which I have lived like a foot
For thirty years, poor and white,
Barely daring to breathe or achoo.

This chapter is getting too long, so you'll have to find the rest of "Daddy" yourself. (Searching for Daddy is very fashionable in literature.) Pop is compared in the poem to a Nazi; the "ick ick ick" of this poem becomes the German "Ich Ich Ich" (I I I — or ayyiyi?); doodoo becomes "Du, Du"; the nursery-rhyme beat and dominance of "oo" rhymes remain, and many of the lines are similar enough to bear out my contention that, poorly concealed behind the "Daddy" mask is the real source of Sylvia's despair — a horse who would not drink.

OK, let's have someone who is (yessiree!) ALIVE even as I write! Lyn Lifshin is the most published poet of our time, "Queen of the Little Magazines." She is incredibly prolific, so it must go without saying that she's not a very good poet, right? Or rather, it SHOULD go without saying, but it gets said all too often, usually by people who are not very prolific, but somehow that doesn't help their poetry much (though it helps their readers — both of them). But to many who have never met Lyn, she seems an old friend. For example, you get your first acceptance and proudly open your copy of this obviously very astute magazine to your poem, in the process noticing a poem by Lyn Lifshin in the same issue. You get your second acceptance in another magazine and notice, in it too, a poem by Lyn Lifshin. And so on for years. You begin to feel you and she are buddies, share the same tastes, please the same editors. It must be Kismet. Then one day you happen to browse through a poetry magazine that does NOT include any of your poems (I know this is a rare experience for poets — which is why many never discover that Lyn isn't their personal good-luck charm — but it does happen) — and there's a poem by Lyn Lifshin. Aha! Quickly you grab another poetry magazine at random — Christ! There she is again. But wait a minute, this is a magazine that features Gay Black Male poets, yet there she is! The light begins to dawn: She's in ALL of them — well, not the ones that publish only academics who are dead white males before their time, but pretty near all.

So, peekaboo, she's here too. She has a whole series of "Madonna" poems. This COULD be one of them:

HORSE MADONNA

[Lyn's Madonna would more likely be hoarse.]

can be led
to it but
not made
to put it
in her
mouth and
swallow

Thank you, Lyn. In the words of Sergeant Pepper, we're getting very near the end. (Did your mind add the little trumpet riff there too?) I've run out of named poets with whom anyone is likely to be familiar enough to enjoy a parody...of?— but I can offer you several TYPES of current poetry and show how they address the horse-to-water question. First, here's a run-of-that-old-mill-stream nameless-forever academic poet, culling microscopic bits of complex self-knowledge by filtering the world through his rueful-at-the-ultimate-futility-of-it-all fine-meshed[118] sieve:

A Purely Academic Question

Foursquare you stand on iron shoes
over the small commotions
of the mirror you won't face.

We came here for a reason,
or so I told myself in the dawn's
gray blur, but now the slant sun
makes fine distinctions between leader
and led, biped and quadruped (a distinction
against which I thought myself
well-armed[119]), follow
and swallow, need and will,
steed and swill.

Your stillness beats like a drum.
Reeds shiver to the beat, blackbirds flit,
grace notes, winking their crushed-berry-

---

[118] As in "Here's another fine mesh you've gotten us into!" — Oliver Hardy.
[119] See how subtle this guy is? Well armed (therefore a biped of the featherless variety) against the biped/quadraped distinction. Now why doesn't "biped" rhyme with "piped?"

crimson flecks.[120] Your stillness throbs
against my skull like a knocking engine.

Twisted and bubble-torn in the ripples
to which you won't touch tongue,
your broken image
could be any old unquenched dream —
the smell too as, hitching your tail,
you punctuate your refusal properly
with a rank, steamy plop.

Each moment enlarges the chorus
of moments croaking the futility
of telling myself I am here for a reason.
I led, you followed; I wait, you...
do you wait? For me? For a reason
to drink? And what is
waiting?

We are ripple-points, eddies in
endless time, purls that were our I's,[121]
small commotions in that mirror we won't
face, you and I, old mare, my
mirror, demurrer.

This poem and the next attempt to capture that Yeatsian core of academic modernism (the mood, not the form): Passionate language used, not to *convey* passion, but as a *substitute* for passion, much as an artificial leg replaces a living leg; and as the artificial leg is *almost* disguised by clothing (all but the give-away woodenness), so this cautious academic numbness is *almost* disguised by the complexities twined modestly about it. Reading these poems is like watching a wooden puppet perform a striptease. Only the clothes are real. Generations of students have been led to it, and all too many have swallowed it, but none have slaked their thirst.

Here's a less gentle academic, someone who wants to make his paradoxes jagged and savage and passionate (but no less complex and evasive) and all that good stuff, but is still, basically, using the tools of poetry (e.g., metaphor, image) less to communicate than to create enough distance be-

---

[120] This guy will be damned before he'll tell you he's talking about a red-winged blackbird. He wants someone else to come along and footnote it like this...well, not exactly like this.

[121] Alluding punningly and cunningly to Ariel's song from *The Tempest*: "Those are pearls that were his eyes." Notice the suggestions of a complex, intensely FELT life, or rather a life that MIGHT be felt if only one weren't quite one, as it were.

tween himself and any emotion to make himself a spectator - poetic technique serving most poets the way television serves nearly everyone else:

Leading But Not Making Is Not Leading

It wasn't always a stream,
a brook, river foaming with
detergent, not that it mattered
to you, your mane ragged with wind,
eyebrows twitching, the grass
mocking your greenless thirst, the stagnancy
of an old saw, old saw grass,
the making of movement, but not of you,
no making you, though you followed
to stream, river, meeting places
of water, air and earth, but not
of man and horse, bodies adjacent but
oceanic distances like unhappy beds
in a sepia haze of dusk, paralysis
of a fading photo, season gone to salad,
the dusk shaped like our
impasse, but there is no
our
there,
where are you
there where you would not take from the water
what its absence had taken from you.

This next poem or barber pole is, I suppose, of the concrete (or kind of cretinous) poetry school. If you don't like it, write a better one. At least this one could be cut into a pattern and made into a good horse blanket:

```
YOUCANLEADAHORSETOWATERBUTYOUCAN'TMAKEHIMDRINK
OUCANLEADAHORSETOWATERBUTYOUCAN'TMAKEHIMDRINKY
UCANLEADAHORSETOWATERBUTYOUCAN'TMAKEHIMDRINKYO
CANLEADAHORSETOWATERBUTYOUCAN'TMAKEHIMDRINKYOU
ANLEADAHORSETOWATERBUTYOUCAN'TMAKEHIMDRINKYOUC
NLEADAHORSETOWATERBUTYOUCAN'TMAKEHIMDRINKYOUCA
LEADAHORSETOWATERBUTYOUCAN'TMAKEHIMDRINKYOUCAN
EADAHORSETOWATERBUTYOUCAN'TMAKEHIMDRINKYOUCANL
ADAHORSETOWATERBUTYOUCAN'TMAKEHIMDRINKYOUCANLE
DAHORSETOWATERBUTYOUCAN'TMAKEHIMDRINKYOUCANLEA
AHORSETOWATERBUTYOUCAN'TMAKEHIMDRINKYOUCANLEAD
HORSETOWATERBUTYOUCAN'TMAKEHIMDRINKYOUCANLEADA
ORSETOWATERBUTYOUCAN'TMAKEHIMDRINKYOUCANLEADAH
RSETOWATERBUTYOUCAN'TMAKEHIMDRINKYOUCANLEADAHO
SETOWATERBUTYOUCAN'TMAKEHIMDRINKYOUCANLEADAHOR
ETOWATERBUTYOUCAN'TMAKEHIMDRINKYOUCANLEADAHORS
TOWATERBUTYOUCAN'TMAKEHIMDRINKYOUCANLEADAHORSE
OWATERBUTYOUCAN'TMAKEHIMDRINKYOUCANLEADAHORSET
WATERBUTYOUCAN'TMAKEHIMDRINKYOUCANLEADAHORSETO
ATERBUTYOUCAN'TMAKEHIMDRINKYOUCANLEADAHORSETOW
TERBUTYOUCAN'TMAKEHIMDRINKYOUCANLEADAHORSETOWA
ERBUTYOUCAN'TMAKEHIMDRINKYOUCANLEADAHORSETOWAT
RBUTYOUCAN'TMAKEHIMDRINKYOUCANLEADAHORSETOWATE
BUTYOUCAN'TMAKEHIMDRINKYOUCANLEADAHORSETOWATER
UTYOUCAN'TMAKEHIMDRINKYOUCANLEADAHORSETOWATERB
TYOUCAN'TMAKEHIMDRINKYOUCANLEADAHORSETOWATERBU
YOUCAN'TMAKEHIMDRINKYOUCANLEADAHORSETOWATERBUT
OUCAN'TMAKEHIMDRINKYOUCANLEADAHORSETOWATERBUTY
UCAN'TMAKEHIMDRINKYOUCANLEADAHORSETOWATERBUTYO
CAN'TMAKEHIMDRINKYOUCANLEADAHORSETOWATERBUTYOU
AN'TMAKEHIMDRINKYOUCANLEADAHORSETOWATERBUTYOUC
N'TMAKEHIMDRINKYOUCANLEADAHORSETOWATERBUTYOUCA
'TMAKEHIMDRINKYOUCANLEADAHORSETOWATERBUTYOUCAN
TMAKEHIMDRINKYOUCANLEADAHORSETOWATERBUTYOUCAN'
MAKEHIMDRINKYOUCANLEADAHORSETOWATERBUTYOUCAN'T
AKEHIMDRINKYOUCANLEADAHORSETOWATERBUTYOUCAN'TM
KEHIMDRINKYOUCANLEADAHORSETOWATERBUTYOUCAN'TMA
EHIMDRINKYOUCANLEADAHORSETOWATERBUTYOUCAN'TMAK
HIMDRINKYOUCANLEADAHORSETOWATERBUTYOUCAN'TMAKE
IMDRINKYOUCANLEADAHORSETOWATERBUTYOUCAN'TMAKEH
MDRINKYOUCANLEADAHORSETOWATERBUTYOUCAN'TMAKEHI
DRINKYOUCANLEADAHORSETOWATERBUTYOUCAN'TMAKEHIM
RINKYOUCANLEADAHORSETOWATERBUTYOUCAN'TMAKEHIMD
INKYOUCANLEADAHORSETOWATERBUTYOUCAN'TMAKEHIMDR
NKYOUCANLEADAHORSETOWATERBUTYOUCAN'TMAKEHIMDRI
KYOUCANLEADAHORSETOWATERBUTYOUCAN'TMAKEHIMDRIN
YOUCANLEADAHORSETOWATERBUTYOUCAN'TMAKEHIMDRINK
```

73

Here's another do-it-yourselfer. It's a lot more difficult to write than it looks, honest! It requires, not only correct spelling, but a mastery of both the space bar and the enter key:

```
        Yo
yo
            u c
    an lea
d a hor

  se t

o      w
ate
    r
            but y
ou can

    ,

  t  m  ake

                        h

            im d
        rink
```

Returning to poetry that uses sentences and communication and other obsolete approaches, here's another voice, a faint echo of e. e. bukowski[122] or an echo of one of the echoes (Several come to mind, poor mind):

to dad whos dead and cant answer

you can lead
a fucking
horse to
water
but you
cant fucking
make him
drink
pa
you sonovabitch

---

[122] The poem combines elements of e. e. cummings and Charles Bukowski. I hope they are happy together. But the nasty language is not really cummings or Bukowski. Bukowski could BE nasty. Others, lacking that vision, have to talk it.

but I
can

easy as
shooting
the pink
sad eyes
   out of
            bunny rabbits
I can do
   it
      every

   time

OK, that touch of Oh-so-stirring foul language ("I am shocked, gentle-men, shocked!" — *Casablanca*) moves us closer to current performance po-etry, for example, the sorts of poems that win poetry slams. Among the rules (mostly unstated, but observable) for most winning slam poems are the fol-lowing:

1. Every phrase must pop with some vivid shock, like Chinese New Years — each line a fire cracker.
2. But no two phrases should connect coherently — dissociation is key (and makes it a lot easier to be vivid).
3. You have to create just the right degree of nonsequiturness (nonsequituricity?) from phrase to phrase, just enough suggested sense to create a surprise. ("Non-sequitur" means that, having joined that sect, you're not going to quit, yet you are not a follower.)
4. It's all got to be monotonically, blood-and-gutsily passionate.
5. Any references to establishments, governments, mother, God, country must be flippant, surreal, nasty and generally reeking of political correctness (e.g., feminist kiss-offs, gay in-your-faceness, Blacker-than-thou). Black poets should read poems about jazz and blues, full of earthy and metallic and sexy imagery and references to real cool nicknames (e.g., "'Trane"). Hispanic poets MUST include lines in Spanish. Almost everything should have a protective veneer of snide. Holocaust images and druggie slang closed high yesterday....
6. Where an abstraction is expected, throw in a trendy specific and vice versa. "I slipped on a Holocaust and skinned my humanity, making me cry blue blazing baby fat."
7. Don't read your poem. Memorize it and perform it. It's a deadly betrayal of poetry to *read* it to an audience. *Never* do that! (Remember how awful it was to have your Mom or Dad read to you when you were a kid....)

There are, no doubt, other rules (e.g., later lines allude to previous lines to counteract the dissociation). Here's a horse-to-water poem that might do well at a slam, especially if you are a sexy Black Hispanic female with no last name and a lot of attitude — must be read loudly, rapidly and emphatically, bouncing off the beats (You can LEAD a HORSE to MOTHer, but/ she BLEEDS like a HUNger, e RUPting...):

Where the Beef Is

You can lead a horse to Mother, but
she bleeds like a hunger, erupting
rancid bubbles — you prick them
and they implode, squealing
PLEASE! My horse is
mooning me, what does he
want from me, where did I
go wrong? I wanted to be a
cowboy, but the job was taken
by a quadriplegic Afro-American lesbian
spotted owl with an NEA grant and terminal AIDS.
They shoot horses, but you can't make
my day. Is endless thirst a disease
or an alternative lifestyle?
My horse wanted to be a cow. Life
is an ass. Mama said, Why can't you be
like Trigger? Daddy laughed like a
scar, his eyelashes and nostril hairs
shaking lose into the soup, then his
eyeballs — PLOP! — and his pipe, he's
losing everything, even my voice,
but can't stop guffawing his guts into
the chicken soup. I'm hungry enough
to eat a reliable source. I wanted
to be an authentic voice, but Mother
made me eat my words. They tasted like
the Department of Health and Human
Services. My horse wants to be a camel.
I'm hungry enough to smoke a horse
or hump a camel or walk a mile[123] for
nine out of ten doctors. If you can't
be a cow, be jerky. You can make a
jerk-off come, but you can't fight
city hall is a real mother you can't be

---

[123] Long ago Camels had the slogan, "I'd walk a mile for a Camel." That's camels — hike it or hump it.

a cowboy or Ronald Reagan, a real
mother, mother, how will I ever
explain? My horse is deeply disappointed
with Life and would demand a refund
if he could fill out Dale Evans[124] in triplicate.
I too am deeply like a cow's bone-hunger, a
camel's blood-thirst, a mother's son.
Life is disappointed with me. Life is
a mother of a different color. You can lead
a life, but your mama can't make water.
Excuse me, I cut myself on Leona Helmsley[125] and
I'm bleeding chicken soup.

On that hell of a note, the sun sets on English and American poetry, a quaint mixture of the very old and the very new, meaning many different things to many different people... (Next week we visit the proud, simple daffodil herders of Western Wordsworth...) But you may have wondered, does this horse-to-water theme occur in the poetry of any non-English-speaking nation? Yes, at least in one, for it is common in Japanese haiku, discussed in more detail in the haiku section of this book. Here, for example, is one of Issa's haiku:[126]

Haiku! You Ah-So!

Frozen stream.
I can lead the horse to water
but not make him drink.

And here is an earlier version of Basho's classic haiku of the frog jumping into the pond to produce a water sound:

Frog in His Throat?

Scummy old pond —
a frog jumps in:
Sound of my horse's YECHHH!

---

[124] Back before Roy Rogers was a fast-food chain (low on the food chain?), he was a singing cowboy star, appearing in movies and on TV with his horse Trigger and his singing-cow-gal wife, Dale Evans. Cowboys were guys hired to take care of cows and ensure that they got to the slaughterers and butchers in good shape — basically gofers for butchers. For some reason, we don't have many movies about the glamour of being a singing butcher. Maybe if butchers wore those hats...

[125] You remember her — the sharp-edged hotel-owning lady who went to jail after a dispute with the IRS.

[126] The plural of "haiku" is a whole lot of them, and they keep getting more plural.

Next, an early version of an Issa classic, which, in its final form, became a poem about the death of his son (A dewdrop world — and yet...and yet...; "dewdrop world" referring to all things passing away quickly as dew vanishes before noon):

Issa Far Far Better Thing I Dew

A dewdrop world —
and yet...and yet...you won't drink,
little horse?

And here's an earlier form of Issa's famous haiku about the mouse drinking from the flood-swollen river:

Issa Tso?

From the river,
spring-swollen, sips a mouse,
but not my damned horse.

What of other cultures? Do poems like these breed in, for example, Pago Pago, Walla Walla or Agar-Agar? (The latter is the culture studied by our Dept. of Agarculture.) The answer to that question is left as an exercise for the reader.

You have now completed a mini-survey of English poetry. Go forth and emulate these poets, and you shall become the poetaster of all you survey! And you'll become, like too much poetry and the emu, "late."

Section 1: A Survey of English Poetry

Chapter 2: Parodies Regained

A Few Edgy Adages

"Important writer": one good enough to become the model for the next generation's bad writers.

Bad poetry is like bad cooking: Just add significance, heat and stir.

"Words fail me," said a poet, failing words.

Poetry is often stilted, as each bard tries to stand tall above the runts of the literate.

Thou shalt not bear false wittiness, nor shalt thou bear false with-it-ness.

"Pen" from penna, a feather. We kill something that flies to make our implement for borrowed flight. (And it requires PLUCK!)

a poet is one who is too busy punctuating silences, dawns and twilights to remember to punctuate sentences

"Darted a look" — I remember that — used to be a metaphor!

Most poetry is environmentally sound, using only recycled words and ideas. My own words are particularly recycled — I've had to eat most of them.

Charging a machine gun — OK, sometimes that's necessary; but what's brave about walking blindly onto a busy freeway? Too many poets use words like "infinity" and "soul" that way. Such words are to be used heroically, against the odds, or not at all and definitely not just because the poet doesn't realize he's stumbled out onto millennia of heavy traffic.

Out of a poem drops with a CLUNK a heavy word — sounded like a "destiny" or "infinity" — but the poem grinds on in first gear, the only one remaining.

Infinity — a word spun of fine silver wire beaded with ice, slippery path for a desperate tight-rope walker over the abyss or for an abysmal poet.

Stock still, stark naked, dead right, 10 p.m. sharp, 10 p.m flat, flat out, bloody well, plum loco, high noon...Welcome to the land of lost metaphors.

It isn't true that recognition comes to a great poet only long after he's dead. Sometimes they kill him right AFTER they recognize him.

Confucius say, artist who use technique as protective shell becomes egg that must be broken to make omelet.

Chapter 2
Parodies Regained

Our poems are plucked from the sky as in huge flocks ideas pass overhead. Sometimes we misfire or shoot down only a few dead leaves, often bring home a wooden sentiment, having mistaken for the real thing one of our own decoys.

Now that you've completed the mini-horse-to-water-survey-of-English-lit course, here's a batch of parodies unconnected by theme. They do share an alphabet, a language, an author (me) and, I hope, a reader (you).

Satire (par-odious) is often confused with parody. They overlap, but parody is more often an affectionate gesture. We always mock the things we love. Or is it we always love the things we kill? But one reader DID ask me, isn't it possible that all these parodies are just sour grapes — my growing cynicism as my own serious poems fall upon deaf ears? I suppose it would be harder for a poem to fall upon someone's ear (deaf or not) if the poet didn't first put the listener to sleep, since a reclined head offers a much larger ear-surface to fall upon. But I digress. My answer to that reader was:

And You Can Put These Words
In Stone — Or In Nickel!

Readers are so finical —
Here I've reached the pinnacle
Of genius bold and uniqual,
Yet with quibbles quite rabbinical
They're finding that I'm "cynical".
I'm NOT — that's unequivocal!
Reader, your case is clinical,
Your ear for irony tinnical,
To think — to *think ME* cynical!

However, satire is all too often acidified by a trace of sour grapes. Some satirists are, indeed, sour grapists:

To a Young Satirist (Whose Youth Goes Harshly On)

He has loosed the leerful fright'ning
Of his terr'ble Swiftian sword;
He is trampling out the vintage
Where his sour grapes are stored.
As he vies to make men silly,
Let us try not to be bored:
Uncouth, he crashes on.

Gory story, we out-grew ya.
Hoary bore, we hardly knew ya.
Sorry mores — what's it to ya?
Half-truth goes marching on!

Can you make a living writing parodies? Palindromically speaking, the
answer is: Parody? Do rap.

But enough about — uh — me. Here are some devious meddlings with
poets who never should have entrusted their delicate devices to my evil ears.
First: another variation on that anonymous 15th Century lyric, (Western Wind,
when wilt thou blow — the small rain down can rain? Christ! If my love
were in my arms and I in my bed again) (Or put the question mark after
"blow" — it works both ways.)

Mid-Evil Earache

Long-winded guest, when wilt thou blow?
The small-talk out is talked.
Christ! If my smile were off my face,
And thou out my door had walked.

Next, a fresh look at Shakespeare's "Shall I compare thee to a summer's
day?" This newly discovered version (with a much tighter rhyme scheme
than his other sonnets, a felicity he was unable to sustain, apparently) may
clarify the much discussed question of Shakespeare's sexual preferences.
The title, which includes an allusion to "apples and oranges," suggests that
certain things are beyond comparison:

Apples And/Or Angels

Shall I compare thee to a guy named Fred?
Less hair hast thou upon thy floppier chest,

Thy calves, thy underarms and all the rest —
Except the ropy stuff atop thy head
(Not more, but merely longer, truth be said),
And densely nestled in thy nether nest —
There art thou more...or less? Which way is best?
I cannot say which is the best in bed —
Ne'er have I bedded Fred; I can but say
That when dark shades have shut the eye of day,
If I must lie with someone — all undressed,
I'd rather bump the baldness of thy breast
Than guzzle booze and burp with hirsute Fred.
If this be error, who'll care when I'm dead?

The next sonnet is a medley, with line one taken from Milton's "On His
Blindness," while the last eight lines toy with the end of Shakespeare's "When
in disgrace with fortune and men's eyes": "Haply [by chance] I think of thee,
and then my state,/ Like to the lark at break of day arising/ From sullen earth,
sings hymns at heaven's gate:/ For thy sweet love remembered such wealth
brings/ That then I scorn to change my state with kings."

Sonnet For Poets Who Write For Themselves Alone

When I consider how my days are spent
Considering how my days are spent, I wonder
If I perchance should rather think to ponder
How first my days were earned or perhaps lent
Me to improve upon by interlarding
Them with fine thoughts like these and thoughts of thought?
Then my thoughts turn to thee — and so they ought
If I'm to do a standard bit of barding —
And then, like to the lark at break of day,
I all alone behold my giddy state:
There's no one list'ning; Why should I not prate
Instead of ponder? Alone, I dare to say
I think I am the one who thinks these things —
But must risk scorn to state my trade with kings!

Next, just a friendly nod to Robert Herrick's "To the Virgins to Make
Much of Time," which begins, "Gather ye rosebuds while ye may,/ Old time
is still a-flying:/ And this same flower that smiles today/ Tomorrow will be
dying." It's a poem that's telling people to hurry, an easy horse-to-water con-
version — TOO easy, for I'm a proud parodist.

Optimize Career Potential While The Sun Shines

Gather ye rosebuds as you may...
But will it enhance your résumé?

Here are three parodies of John Donne's "Holy Sonnets," each followed by Donne's original. One of them, "Death be not Proud," is also among the victims of Horse-to-Water madness.

Don't Let Hard Butter Get Your Goat

Butter your bread, impatient child, for you
As yet but jab, scrape, clot — then slop on jelly,
Little of which shall ever reach your belly,
Dripping, instead, upon your shirt, your shoe
From rents your earnest buttering tore through
In your rough haste to get back to the telly
Before commercial's end — poor loaf, from deli
But this morning bought, whole, fragrant, new...
Worse yet, your gelid butter clumps in chunks,
Some bread bits slabbed and smothered, others bare.
Rather would I, a savage, tear off hunks
To sop up sauce, than taste such shoddy fare!
O thaw thy butter that it gently spread,
Nor gash nor rashly gouge thy willing bread!

How Donne done it:

Batter my heart, three-personed God; for you
As yet but knock, breathe, shine and seek to mend;
That I may rise and stand, o'erthrow me and bend
Your force to break, blow, burn and make me new.
I, like a usurpt town, to another due,
Labor to admit you, but Oh, to no end;
Reason, your viceroy in me, me should defend,
But is captived and proves weak or untrue.
Yet dearly I love you, and would be loved faine,[1]
But am betrothed unto your enemy:
Divorce me, untie, or break me, for I
Except you enthrall me, never shall be free,
Nor ever chaste, except you ravish me.

---

[1] "Faine": fain or gladly, as in "Wouldst fain feign a faint, fair femme?"

Not Goodbye, but Good Buy!

Beth, be not cowed, though swept from bargain table
By swarms of fellow shoppers — if you lose
One blouse, find others; look long ere you choose:
Buy not, poor Beth, 'til you have read the label;
What though raw silk stir jealousy in Mabel
If it won't fit? Buy only what you'll use:
Who shops impatiently, at leisure rues.
Hold thy heart calm and shrewd amidst this Babel.
But no! Eyes glazed — and not with drugs, nor sleep,
Which but the pictures be of shopper's lust,
Deaf to your husband's pleas — in whims thy trust!
No slave art thou to notions of dear and cheap;
Patch not nor dye old frocks, but let them lie:
For Beth shall dye no more; Beth, thou shalt buy.

Note: Bob Dylan later summarized the importance of getting your Christmas shopping done early as follows: He who is not born a busy bee is dizzy buying.[2]

For "Death Be Not Proud," see the Donne section of the horse-to-water chapter. (p. 10).

John Donne Sets The Corset Of Feminism

At the round girth's imagined flatness, TUG!
You strumpet handmaids, and arise, arise
From dress, you numb, braless (infinite tease!)[3]
Soft doves, popped upward by the corset's hug,
You whom rude men dismiss as tit, boob, jug,
You by whom knights, priests, boys with woeful sighs
Claim to be slain, claim once you've filled their eyes,
They've beheld God! OOF! pull those stays...OUCH! UGH!...
But let them loll, girls, and me moon a space,
For if, beyond my boobs, my buns abound,
Unbound, they'll bound — a bun dance of my grace!
Unstay me — why make flat what's jolly round?
Touch me! I'll be unpent! Loose is not lewd![*]
BURN corsets, bras! I'm in a muu-muu mood!

[*] *Variant: Why pinch so tight when looseness is as good?*

---

[2] Actually, "He who is not busy being born is busy dying" from Dylan's Xmas song, "The Dimes, They are A-jangling."
[3] "Infinite tease" — and in fine nineties.

How Donne do'd it, and in valid diction, too, one forbidding morning[4]

At the round earth's imagined corners, blow
Your trumpets, Angels, and arise, arise
From death, you numberless infinities
Of souls, and to your scattered bodies go,
All whom the flood did, and fire shall o'erthrow,
All whom war, dearth, age, agues, tyrannies,
Despair, law, chance hath slain, and you whose eyes
Shall behold God and never taste death's woe.
But let them sleep, Lord, and me mourn a space,
For, if above all these my sins abound,
'Tis late to ask abundance of thy grace
When we are there; here on this lowly ground,
Teach me how to repent; for that's as good
As if thou'dst sealed my pardon, with thy blood.

Thank you, John — we, too, have donne with you.

Apathy

They flee from me who only stand and wait.

That was a one-line collaboration between Sir Thomas Wyatt and John Milton. Wyatt's great poem begins "They flee from me..." (his women). Milton's sonnet on his blindness ends "They also serve who only stand and wait." That sonnet may be found in chapter one. Wyatt is especially known for his encounter with Henry VIII, who, as usual, was gorging himself and burping. Seeing the poet, he said, "Wyatt...URP!" which inspired that great TV theme song, "Wyatt...URP" (brave, courageous and bold...long may his story be told...).

One more shot at Milton's "On His Blindness" (p. 11)— this time the plaintive prayer of a girl afraid to surf (and win the guys) because she can't swim (not one of the swimmin' women):

A Shallow Prayer

"Dear Lord, I cannot swim. My surfer buddies
Mock me, even Joe, who's such a stud — he's
Really rad! But, Damn! My dullsville days

---

[4] Judgment Day, the subject of this sonnet, would qualify as a forbidding morning. A famous Donne poem is entitled "A Valediction Forbidding Mourning." A "valediction" is a goodbye, which shows that my parody of "Death be not Proud" is most aptly titled ("Not Goodbye...").

Are spent in shallows or in catching rays!"
"My child, be patient — <u>some</u>day you'll get laid:
They also surf who only stand and wade."

A few lines that Richard Lovelace might have written, loved he not honor more:

Cellular Studies

Stone walls do not a prism make,
Nor iron bars a gauge.
A scientist in prison seldom
Makes a living wage.

Resolution And Independence
[A Wordsworth title, here borrowed to parody Burns]
Or: Fling Out The Old

Should auld acquaintance be forgot
And never brought to mind?
Nay! I'll remember all that lot
And leave them all behind.

I'll leave them all behind,
And ne'er be taken blind:
I'll spot their unkind mugs afar
And cross the street in time.

Red Itch The Rashes, O

My love is like a red red rose,
Her days spent in a bed;
Her thorns abound, for in her grows
Many a prick, it's said.

Her hair's like petals — falling out;
She sweetly sheds her clothes.
Her reek draws buzzing bugs — no doubt
My love is like a rose.

A nasty Take on Burns' song "A Red Red Rose," which is in chapter one. He who lies with such a woman may well exclaim, later, "It burns!"

Here's one inspired by S. T. Coleridge's lyrical fragment, "Kubla Khan." The title, "Kubla Befrands a Dolly," alludes to an old T.V. show called "Kukla, Fran and Ollie." Fran was a pretty girl, Kukla and Ollie puppets. This has

nothing to do with anything, but I do want to do my bit to keep future genera-
tions of grad. students busy.

Kubla Befrands A Dolly
or: Was His Mount A Bore — Ah?
or: I Think I Khan! I Think I Khan!

Though you'd think one kind word from a glorious emperor would
    turn a maiden's heart to pudding — or at least her
    pudenda,
One word from Kubla Khan woulden'da,
Because Kubla would always put his foot in't,
So the women agreed that Kubla Khan couldn't,
And though he begged and flattered and assailed them with gifts,
    prayers, raves and rants,
He couldn't get into their short thick pants;
But after restoring his courage in taverns measureless to man
(Where ceaselessly from bottles booze for sots with halph a
    scarred liver ran),
He would try again, his pitch getting fulsomer and fulsomer,
Until, though he never heated a single damsel to a full boil, he
    did at last get a damsel with a dull simmer.

Clearly, then, Khan of Xanadu was not a Khan-du sort of guy. In the
preceding poem, "Mount A Bore — Ah?" refers to Coleridge's Mt. Aborah;
the "short thick pants" are actually in the original (but strangely changed in
the process of transplanting them to my poem); "taverns measureless to man"
are "caverns..." ditto; "halph [half] a scarred liver" is a miraculous reincar-
nation of Alph, the sacred river; and the "dull simmer" started out as a dulci-
mer. I hope I have properly insulted the intelligence of those of you (both of
you) who knew all this already.

Now for two variants of the following passage from Coleridge's "Rime
of the Ancient Mariner" (no relationship to Silas Mariner[5]):

Water, water, everywhere,
And all the boards did shrink;
Water, water everywhere,
Nor any drop to drink.

---

[5] Silas Mariner is really Silas Marner, title character of a novel by George Eliot, who
is really Mary Ann Evans, a great English novelist who is really rather boring. Rather,
boring, describes a famous newscaster at work.

Here are the variants (the first of which is wildly incorrect, politically, but be assured that no actual Italians or obese women have been maimed, spindled or mutilated during the making of this book):

Rime of the Ancient Marinara

Who'd wed a wench wide as a mare
Giuseppe could not think:
"O Daughter! Daughter everywhere,
Nor any Wop to Wink!"

On Wishing I Could Hold One With My Eye[6]

Waiters among the tables fare —
Only from ours they shrink:
Waiter, waiter everywhere,
Nor any drop to drink!

Now we turn over a new (or green) leaf, that is, John Greenleaf Whittier, whose old gray head shall not be spared here, alas (he said):

A Whittier Version

Penn, Brigham Young and M.I.T.
Vie for Ben Franklin's library:

The Institute of Tech bids high —
O hear the losing scholars cry:
"The saddest words of Young or Penn
Are these four words: 'MIT might have Ben.' "

A bit strained - doesn't work unless you pronounce it "M - I -T" in line one and "mitt" in line six. Well Damn MIT!

Poe's raven made some shrewd political predictions:

A Gory Tale — Not for the Craven

On a midnight dark and dreary,
While I pondered weak and weary
Over many a quaint and curious column of
    spin-doctored lore —

---

[6] This is how the Ancient Mariner "holds" the wedding guest still long enough to tell the guest his story. An eye, beaming at you, can exert considerable force. In fact, eye-beams are used as girders in building construction.

At last, grown sick of theory,
To an expert I made query:
"Say will '02' be merry for the Democrats once more?"
        Quoth the maven, "Never Gore!"

Here's a lovely Emily Dickinson poem, followed by the destruction...er, deconstruction thereof:

I heard a fly buzz when I died.
The stillness in the room
Was like the stillness in the air
Between the heaves of storm.

The eyes around had wrung them dry,
And breaths were gathering firm
For that last onset when the king
Be witnessed in the room.

I willed my keepsakes, signed away
What portion of me be
Assignable; and then it was
There interposed a fly

With blue uncertain stumbling buzz
Between the light and me;
And then the windows failed; and then
I could not see to see.

That's what Emily said. Here's what I said, feeling the fly deserved equal time:

No Flies on Emily!

I heard a bard die when I buzzed.[7]
The stilling of her yapping
Was like the stilling of the air
Before the swatter's slapping.

My thousand eyes each lit with joy:
"This lady isn't napping!
She'll give my maggots a good home..."
And then two hands came clapping!

---

[7] Wanted: A one-syllable synonym for "bardess." How about "byrd?"

90

I dodged the mourners, zipped away
From hands hot to mishandle;
The thunder fell behind — and then
There interposed a candle

With blue-tinged flickering spear of flame
'Twixt door and me, ungentle.[8]
Then on singed back I twitched and knew
No maggots would I dandle.

A friend suggested an alternate title: "Flies for Miss Emily" — aping Faulkner's story title, "Roses for Miss Emily." Since the fly in my poem "zipped away" until sternly stopped and turned by candle into a brown study, we could say that the candle unzipped a fly, something our Miss Emily, apparently, never did (unzip de doodah). (Did they have zippers then?)

No one seems to read Landor these days, but he's pure gold for a parodist:

Walter's Savage Can-dor (based on "Rose Aylmer")

Ah, what avails the septic tank,
   Ah, what the new flush toilet!
What though it swirl away what's rank
   Ere oily *merde* can soil it!

Ah, what the pebbled window pane
   That greets the foiléd gaper!
Thy lush appointments — all in vain
   Without the toilet paper!

"Rose Aylmer" by Walter Savage Landor, begins "Ah, what avails the sceptered race,/ Ah, what the form divine!" and so on: See page 29.

It was Tennyson who said "'Tis better to have loved and lost than ne'er have loved at all." Of course, what he *really* meant (like any true poet) was, 'Tis better to have loved and lost than to have loved and *not* lost. (Count the poems, folks: It's "lost love is sweeter far" by a landslide!)

Lust is nettles, ashes, dust,
The shame of Adam's fall,
Yet better to have love and lust
Than ne'er have love at all.

---

[8] For a niftier rhyme, the candle interposes "Between my genes and Mendel" but Mendel experimented with fruit flies, not big blue flies. Also with beans, but not human beans.

This next poem is a famous quatrain from Ed Fitzgerald's "Rubaiyat of Omar Khayyam" ("A loaf of bread, a jug of wine and thou...") as it might have been rewritten by Ogden Nash ("Candy is dandy, but liquor is quicker").

Ogden Khayyam

Paradise
Is vera nice,
But a jug of wine, a
Loaf and Thou is fina.

[I wrote a funnier version that includes an ancient early adolescent rhyme ("nothing could be fina than to be in your va..."), but I withhold it out of no-longer-so-common decency.]

Shall we deconstruct Robert Frost? Press the defrost button:

Stopping by Langley* on an Autumn Day

Whose woods these are I think I know.
The sign says "U.S. Government,"
(Both Central and Intelligent)
"NO TRESPASSING". But I must go...
I hope no watcher thinks it strange
To see me pause in spy-glass range
To watch these woods fill up with leaves
Behind which, covertly, who weaves
What woeful webs? My little car
Starts with a jerk. I can't go far
Enough from here, to where the woods
Do not conceal our neighbor hoods,
Where we make promises we keep
And at day's end serenely sleep,
Miles from these men who cannot sleep,
Miles from these men who cannot sleep.

*Wooded home of the CIA

Here's another inspired by the same original (excerpted in the horse-to-water chapter):

Whose Sleep is This?

So much I would do if I could —
The promises that I would keep!

92

I would be slim! I would be good...
The woulds are lovely, dark and deep.

Sleep and responsibilities await, arms akimbo and tapping their feet, but Frost is often tempted to stray into the deep and lovely woods, as in that other famous poem, beginning "Two legs diverged in a mellow mood...."[9]

Please, can I take another little jab at Prufrock — I mean, Eliot — just one?

Feathers Under the Light

Because of the duck,
because of the duck's webbed feet,
because you know the duck's webbed feet
are not for you,
in the long agony of a pudding's pout
sunlight loses its name,
and these eyes that meet your eyes in ducks,
peeking or peeping perilously,[10]
weaving in a waddling way among us
in the room where we come and go,
stalking raspberry Jell-O,
eyes you have known in pigeons,
button you up.

Oh! Just one more, I really mean it this time! — a really little one?

Diet Tribe

In the room the women come and go,
Talking of rye, kale and Jell-O.

Why do Prufrock's women talk only of Michelangelo? Why couldn't they suffer just a teensy from quinsy from shouting about Leonardo Da Vinci?

William Carlos Williams wrote a little poem that is supposed to be a note left in his host's refrigerator explaining that he ate the plums and they were delicious. Would anyone read poems by Bill Williams? Or Bill Bills? W. C.'s (Water closet's?) day job was doctor. His doctor bills were, therefore, Bill Bill's bills. Williams was staunchly against un-American rhyme and meter in our poetry. They required too much care. He preferred to be Carlos. Here's a variation on W. C.'s poem:

---

[9] Frost wrote, of course, about two ROADS diverging in a yellow wood, not a mellow mood. But we Freudians know what he was REALLY thinking of...

[10] When the Chinese shifted their spelling from Peiping to Peking, Peeping duck became Peeking duck. But Tom (Thomas S. Eliot?) still lives in Peiping.

Why the Election is Canceled

Just a note to say that,
finding the bag where you left it
in the fridge, I, to be candid, ate
the candied dates. What's left
is the pits.

If you didn't see the word "candidate" twice in the above poem, please reread. And take two presidential aspirins (aspirants?) and call me in the morning.

Dorothy Parker alleged that men don't make passes at girls who wear glasses. I feel this needs qualification, as it depends on what sort of glasses they are wearing:

On the Goggled Not Being Ogled

Men who don't make passes
At girls who wear glasses
Often commit sexist offenses
Against girls who wear contact lenses
And conduct panty raids
Against cool chicks in shades.
Though teachers with lenses frosted
Are seldom hall-accosted,[11]
Never spake a prince "Nay"
To a dame in *pince nez*;
But the fate of femmes monocled,
Has not been chronocled.

The next 15 poems or so (it's late at night — the number changes with each count) pay tribute to a much maligned poem, "Trees", by Joyce Kilmer (excerpted in the horse-to-water chapter of this book). It's an easy poem to tear apart, but just as political cartoonists loved Ronald Reagan, so any parodist worth his or her salt or saltess must adore Joyce Kilmer (and Edgar Allen Poe, especially "The Raven"). To write badly is easy. To write MEMORA-BLY badly is a gift. The greatest bad poems are, indeed, greatly bad. Try, for

---

[11] Every serious poet needs a Holocaust allusion or two. I shouldn't joke about such things. Even now, a spokesman for the Anti-Defamation League is issuing a statement that starts: "Auschwitz his head!" I can ALMOST get away with this because I'm Jewish. But not quite. To really get away with joking about the Holocaust, you have to have died in it first. Perhaps there are some things that should not be laughed at — that's possible. What's for certain is that people who tell people what can't be laughed at should be laughed at.

example, to write a line as luciously bad as "I think that I shall never see...."
It has that twisty lilt (much like Keats's "When I have fears that I may cease
to be"), that somber modulation of the beat, and yet...and yet... — something
there is in "Trees" that seduces the parodist in me.

First, here is an unnatural liaison of Joyce Kilmer's "Tree's" with Alan
Ginsberg's "Howl" (they alternate lines) — one poem where Mr. Kilmer gets
to have the last word — in fact, the last 4 lines:

There Be Howls In Them Trees

I think that I shall never see
The best minds of my generation destroyed by madness, starving
    hysterical naked ranting Plotinus and Zen disjointedly,
For good minds do not get their kicks
From dragging themselves through the negro streets at dawn
    looking for an angry fix,
Good minds who think it rather trite
To burn for the ancient heavenly connection to the starry dynamo
    in the machinery of night,
For even graduating has
Less pretentiousness than poverty and tatters and, hollow-eyed
    and high, sitting up smoking in the supernatural darkness of
    coldwater flats floating across the tops of cities
    contemplating jazz;
Good minds can end a poem or line,
Not feeling impelled to ramble on endlessly as if waiting for a
    Muhammadan angel under the el to give them a Heavenly sign —
For only TOUGH minds can go free,
As even fools like me can see,
And only an LSD-addled tripster
Would ever confuse a good mind with an angel-headed hipster.

Who would have expected that crossing Ginsberg with Kilmer would
give birth to Ogden Nash! Do poets breed true? Do our mongrel descendents
all eventually become Nash hash?

Three years before publishing T. S. Eliot's "Prufrock", *POETRY* pub-
lished that equally clarion call for a new poetry, "Trees":

To *POETRY*, In 1912 As Now

I think that I shall never see
So fine a line of poetry
As this: "I think that I shall never
See" — though often I endeavor
To craft a line so coyly stilted

(Whose bloom the decades have not wilted!) —
A line that soars from humble "think"
To proud "I shall" in half a wink,
But pride must fall — how suddenly
We're plunged into dark "never see"! —
A line from blue-veined marble hacked,
So round, so firm, so fully packed![12] —
A line chock full of solemn twist,
So pale of brow, so limp of wrist! —
O Kilmer, shall we see a line
Ever again as fine as thine? —
O greater Joyce,[13] we thee implore!
"I think," quoth Kilmer, "never more!
For only mocking comes from thee...
Whose point I think I'll NEVER see!
Why should a fool be made of me?
For such long notoriety
Blame God, the age and *Poetry*."

Motive Force

I think that I shall never hear it —
An engine that can run on spirit,
Spirit that moves mysterious ways
And even over ashen days,
As sunlight veins the torrent's maze,
So spirit heightens where it plays;
While oil's an ooze of ancient creatures
Crushed by earth like kids by teachers.
Ah, fuels are made of fools like us
While only spirit can raise up dust.

Only God can Make a Tree, but any Mutt can Make Water

Though I write poems in every season,
I think that I shall never see, Son,
A poem as lovely as a tree, Son;
And though poems prosper, yet there's reason

---

[12] "So round, so firm, so fully packed" was a slogan for Lucky Strike cigarettes, not for brassieres or Jockey shorts. What did guys and gals think they were smoking?
[13] The implied lesser Joyce is James Joyce. I'm assuming that genteel Joyce K., had he survived WWI to encounter rude and rollicking *Ulysses*, would have found it less lovely, even, than crab grass. I have Kilmer's admirers here address him as the greater Joyce because I assume they share his tastes in trees and literature.

None dare call a poem a tree, Son,[14]
For even scribbling fools like me, Son,
Would not make what each dog pees on.

Milton On His Blindness:

I think
that I shall
never
see

This Poem Is Hip...NOT! (Ick!)   [i.e., hypnotic]

I think that I shall ever drone
On endlessly in monotone,
For poetry should make us sleep
With its hypnotic steady creep
That best can make us do and see
What we are told agreeably.
Thus hypnotism is my game —
Each syllable more of the same.
My voice is heavy, and your eyelids
Start to droop like shrinking violids.
Your minds can best be led like sheep
When sunk in deep iambic sleep.
For tomes I'm paid by fools like thee
Whom, oddly, tone can make agree.

To Your Behindness

I think that I shall never find
A gown as nice as your behind —
Behind, whose muffled mouth is pressed
Against a chair, stiff, uncaressed;
Behind that hides from God all day
And cannot spread her cheeks to play;
Behind that may at bedtime sing
Of silken softness to my thing;
Who intimately lives with nylon;
Against whose bosom prods my pylon.
Gowns by tailors are designed,
But only I know your behind.

---

[14] An allusion to Sir John Harrington's proverb: "Treason doth never prosper; what's the reason?/ For if it prosper, none dare call it treason!" And if the reviewers pan this book, will none dare call it pleasin'?

[Note: The mixed metaphor ("behind" as mouth, bosom, etc.) is intentional to mime the mixed metaphors in the original, where the tree has its mouth sucking at the ground, its arms raised in prayer, etc. — a very difficult position! Probably the influence of French symbolists or sex manuals.]

I Think, Therefore I Shall Never See

I think that I shall never see
A tree as rare as poetry,
For poems do not grow on trees —
No groves of academe bore these;
Nor do the poets *grow* on trees:
They're hanged there when they fail to please.
What poet would stop at placid treedom?
Our metric feet demand their freedom.
Oh! any god can make a tree,
But gods are made by poets like me.

The next poem was composed as an announcement for a poetry reading. Several people showed up, but I don't think anyone actually read my clever announcement, so I'm inflicting it upon you here. Who reads announcements. After all, the seldom-mentioned reason why the number of poetry readings keeps increasing is that more and more people have to HEAR the poems read aloud, because they've never learned to READ. Marshall McLuhan (who considered the printed word a sort of tyranny) would have rejoiced. He *did* rejoice at the coming illiteracy, but he did so in print, so, soon, no one will know about it. (Is someone out there still getting this?)

POOR TREE! —

By which I mean the little, airy
Leafy friend that literary
Folks pulped into reams of paper
Worthy to serve a serious crapper —
Instead filled up with silly poems,
Then crammed in academic tomes;
And though I think you'll never see
A poem as lovely as that tree,
I *know* you'll never know a tree
As **SILLY** as our poetry,
For writing which, we ought to be
Hanged from a limb of that same tree —
Alas! 'tis nevermore to be,
Alack, poor poetry! Poor tree!

So come! Commemorate the dismembery
Of that poor tree on Saturday
(You'll never know a sadder day!)
Which is the second day Decembery,
At 2 in our Community Center
Where two tree-loving bards will render
Their longings ludicrously audible,
If not arboreally laudable.

Doggerel

Quoth one James Kilmer, "Hark!
A poem's not like a tree!"
Yet has not his a bark
As "O Bough — WOW!" raves he?

Raving On The Paving, Fools In The Schools

Since golden days when Mr. Kilmer taught us
That He who made the tree was surely not us
And how we from a foolish poem may know a tree —
Since then we've split into two schools of poetry:
From T. S. Eliot come the Academics
While Whitman's spawned a spate of Macadamics:
Kerouac, Ginsberg — all who shun tight collars
To be road scholars rather than Rhodes Scholars.
Pedants who watch them avidly go packing off
On wordy trips say they're just Kerouacking off.
The sons of Walt reply: "At least we still know
How to get it up! Go stroke your dildo!"
Thus poets fart around, relieve no heart's ache:
Both schools come down at last to "fart for fart's sake".

Pageantry of Page and Tree

I think that I shall never see
A poem tough as an infant tree,
Nor shall I likely chance to see
One sultry as an adult tree,
Yet poems live on, while every tree
At last is pulp, an in-dust tree.

NEA Nay-Saying[15]

I think that I shall never say
The sort of stuff for which they pay,
That trendy avant-gardish tripe
That reaps rewards and reeks with hype.
I rave my raves, rant many a rant,
But ne'er shall win an NEA Grant.

My poems will do — some deep, some witty,
But aimed at you, not some committee.
Besides, a grant would just affront me
Who write for love of God and country —
Also to use up excess trees,
Sip cheap chablis and nibble bries
(O poetry-reading-evening bries!
O tenderly caressed chablis!)

But pardon these, my jeers and japes,
If they be only sour grapes
That I'm not of that glittering crowd
Of fresh new voices, well-endowed...

Yet they're not gods, just fools like me
Who call their babblings poetry —
If they can win, then why can't I?
Perhaps someday...I may apply.

"O poetry-reading-evening bries!/ O tenderly caressed chablis!" Hey!
What's the plural of chablis? I need a rhyme here. By the way, "Evening
bries" and "tenderly caressed" is supposed to recall an old song that begins
"The evening breeze/ Caressed the trees/ Tenderly..." (though when I was in
high school we sang "The evening breeze/Blew through her knees...").

Solution: Remove Trees

I think one almost never sees
The forest for the bloody trees.
Poetry, too, we're apt to miss
For all the foolish rhymes like this.

---

[15] This poem is pure sour grapes. They should give ME an NEA Grant if they give
ANY a grant. (NEA/any a, get it?) But I've never asked for one. I'm waiting to be
discovered. Here I ammmmm....

Enough Kilmer. Here are two more revisions of Dylan Thomas's memorable villanelle, "Do Not Go Gentle Into That Good Night" ("Rage, rage against the dying of the light" — see Chapter one, page 63):

Advice To A Lady Whose Gent Takes Her For Granted (As, Of Course, A Villain'll Do)[16]

Do not go nightly in to that rude gent;
Stay out till 4 a.m. Should he complain,
Rage! Rage until he begs...and then relent.

Ladies don't grow on trees — they're Heaven-sent!
His ass-grabs should be greeted with disdain.
Do not go nightly in to that rude gent.

And if he says, "See here, who pays the rent?"
Say, "Fine — I'll move out, since it's such a strain!"
Then rage! Rage till he begs...and then relent.

This man's an island while you're continent[17]:
Let "I'm not in the mood" be your *refrain*.[18]
Do not go nightly in to that rude gent.

Headaches, fatigue, "It's sore!" — you can invent
New reasons every night — his pain, your gain.
Rage! Rage until he begs...and then relent —

With all that waiting, swiftly he'll be spent;
Say, "My, My! Speedy Gonzales! John on the Wane!"
Do not go nightly in to that rude gent!
Rage! Rage until he begs...and then relent.

---

[16] That is, a villanelle do, though this poem might be entitled, "Let's NOT do it in a villanelle!" Both these poems, like the poem they parody, are villanelles. "Villanelle" is a verse form, not an ice cream flavor: 19 lines, only two rhyme sounds, six stanzas, the first and third lines of the poem are repeated alternately at the end of each subsequent 3-line stanza, then come together for the first time at the end of the final stanza (a 4-liner), like partners all formal at the start of an elaborate ballroom dance (separated by a chaperone line) who are whirled off in opposite directions to spin around with partner after partner until, having circled the room, at last they come together again, hot and sweaty from the exercise and relieved to meet without that pretense of formal distance. But my lines never learned to dance. Their iambic feet are sore from stepping on each other.

[17] This island and continent are borrowed from Donne's "No man is an island..." — and please, since we're all in the same boat, don't be incontinent.

[18] That is, it's her excuse to refrain. The question is, has anyone ever frained?

To A Gambler Up Against Loaded Dice

Do not go gentle with a light goodbye —
You know this bozo's "luck" is a load of crap!
Rage! Rage against the lighting of a die.

You've got a rep — you can't let this go by.
If word gets out, your name is Mr. Sap!
Do not go gentle with a light goodbye.

"Bad luck," he says, and "Sure" is your reply.
You keep your cool and watch out for a trap...
(Rage! Rage against the lighting of a die!)

You shrug, begin to stand, then with your thigh
You tip the table CRASH into his lap,
Not going gentle with a light goodbye.

He's clawing for his gat — you let him try,
Then coolly loose your little thunderclap.
Rage! Rage against the lighting of a die.

You take your bills and let the nickels lie.
"Bad luck," you say, and leave him to his nap,
Thus, gentle, going with a light goodbye —
Why *rage* against the lighting of a die?

This reminds me of Browning's famous passage about human faith in the dice when shooting craps: "Ah, but a man's reach should exceed his grasp, or what's seven for?"[19]

Yet another version of "Do Not Go Gently," addressed to a Jewish mother who wastes time reasoning with her son instead of beating him, begins "Do not cogently yenta that nudnik!" ("Rage! Rage! With your strap give him a good lick!")

Now for a brief gentle inter*lewd* with a variation of Ogden Nash's "Reflection on Icebreaking":

A Reflection On A Reflection On Ice-Breaking

Candy
Gets randy

---

[19] Yet another riff on "Andrea Del Sarto" where "Or what's seven for?" is "Or what's a Heaven for?" (To curse when the dice are cruel?) Some say Browning favored that other crucial-to-craps number, eleven, over seven and wrote "Or what's seven four?"

Quicker
If you lick her.

There are certain people and things one may not mock, the current sacred cows of poetry. They include Rilke, Neruda, Lorca and Milosz. This sanctification seems to favor poets known to most of us only in translation, so I've mainly left them alone to concentrate on us Englishers. But I object to their sacred cowdom (for dumb is dumb). As discussed in chapter six, I once invented a poet of my own (called him William Parelli), created for him some ten pretentious, trendy, "vivid", "passionate", "mythically poignant" poems (It was hard work — must have taken all of two hours), and, at a time when my best work got mainly rejection slips (i.e., always!), got one of the Parelli's accepted by a reputable magazine on my first try. How had I written it? I thought of Rilke and wrote it by numbers — put in a lot of enigmatic, rather aloof and somehow bluely toxic angels, filled it with a dry, funereal urbanely resigned tone, etc. Sacred cows don't move very fast. It's very easy to mount them and ride along — though you won't get anywhere you haven't been before — and when you dismount, watch where you step!

I've taken a shot at one of these saints of the current cult of poetry, F. Garcia Lorca, not parodying a particular poem, but going after his idea that the heart of poetry is "*duende*", an obsession with a particularly pale and bull-fighter-stiff sort of death (blood on noble brow). Ah, the profundity of death. But even death is not immune to that far subtler destroyer, the spirit of CORN. Even Death can become a cliché. Dying, after all, is not very difficult. Any idiot can do it. Some of us, perhaps, do it again and again with undiminished relish.

The following poem tries to say this better. It's almost a serious poem (*mea culpa*). It's all about Lorca's own death — at the hands of Franco's forces during the Spanish Revolution. (Another definition of "*Duende*": Advice Peter Pan later regretted not having taken; i.e., Do Wendy.)

Duende Others As You Would Have Others *Duende* You

Had they not killed you, Lorca...

They stumbled you out
of a country house
blinking owlishly, though only
at the moon and headlights
(or so I imagine — crisscrossing
beams scurrying not to miss
your stern, blanched face).

Now I am supposed to mention
wind in olive trees. But

it must be a dark wind — or
a blue wind? Black? Green?

Had they not killed you, Lorca...

They marched you to a car
because they were supposed to,
drove you "into the country"
(so my book puts it)
because they were supposed to

(drove you into the country
as hammer drives nail
into another country —
or maybe not, maybe there's
only one world if
you don't create another),

drove metal pellets
into your body because
they were supposed to
and the pellets, too,
were impelled and did
their duty and you
too did what you were
supposed to do,
that is died.

Had they not killed you, Lorca...

Now I'm supposed to mention
some sort of flower (but it will
be bone-white or blood-red, your
shirt an overgrown rose garden,
or greening with decomposition or
rooted in eye-sockets filled
with the loamy residue of
sunlight. Or I should name
a dark Spanish river whispering
in a library of hushed reeds or
anything elemental and slightly
non-sequitur, the warble of
water over green-scummed stones,
icy flashlight darts shivering
the night, modesty of stars,

stench of rotten wood and sweetly
decaying orange peels, wet earth, the
shriek of engraveled shovels,
a memory of long-ago morning and
the tenderness of coffee's
never-more aroma.)

Had they not killed you, Lorca...

It must all convey
our uniformly fatal destiny
because poetry is supposed to
be drenched in dainty *duende*, death's
inconsolable beauty, death's
inevitability...well of
course it is inevitable, for
we poets, too — gaunt solemn toreadors,
hoping to distract the rush of time
by waving our bright sad images
at it — we poets do what we're
supposed to do, which may be
the only death there is —
and ample at that.

(I am not supposed to say that.)

O had they not killed you, Lorca,
I would do it now, but only
here.

Sacred cows should be served rare: flay of soul. They deserve no less.
The next two parodies lead us into another genre, the novel. Why not? Can't
I escape from poetry for a moment? No? Vel...

Novels: Two Beginnings

I

It all began when I discovered
I was oddly unlike all the others
because I saw what they could not:

for example, the underside of my eyelashes
and the inner surface of my eyelids.

105

And yet, how quickly I'd have traded it all
to share their banal, mockingly casual view
of the, for me, excruciatingly invisible
back of my head.

II

No one came to the door,
but it swung open to my knock,
so I went in. She was there all right,
long raven hair, delicate features
all ivory and rose, head hanging back
off the sofa — but with an extra mouth
above the wan upside-down smile,
a sloppy red gash on the pale throat,
crimson pooling on the carpet beneath...

"Come in," she said.

You Should Write a Novel — That's Where The Money Is

Maybe it's that damned sherry, he thought, turning over heavily in bed, letting the reader know that something's wrong, and surely not the sherry — damned sugary horse piss! — or "fucking", etc., if it's to be a hit with the ladies, to whom a mere "damned" is condescending. Or more likely it's that today at last he'd have to tell her — there was no more putting it off (and the patient reader knows he'll be told what IT is, all in good time).

He threw off the remaining (fly-specked?) sheet (There follows a long descriptive passage, very droll and vivid, about what kind of machinery his head is throbbing like, how sour his tongue tastes [weird simile, please], maybe the rattle of a fan. In short, the reader learns what sort of an author he is dealing with).

Then he splashes cold water on his face and leans before the mirror for the obligatory wry self-appraisal scene ("Not bad," he thought, pondered, chuckled, heard a gruff voice in his head remark — me, he realized...) — which gives the author a chance to tell the reader about the hard jaw, the cold, but smouldering, blue eyes, the scar, etc. [Isn't it fun to say "aquiline"?] Later the female lead will be said to have less than perfect features because of excessively large eyes and full lips). Now bring in the career, somehow leaving him empty despite a facade of success (a bit of technical shoptalk, please, as he thinks about what he has to do today at the studio, bank, stock exchange, rodeo, race track...) — all without stepping outside the hero's (?) claustrophobic viewpoint.

It's time to start something — at least give the reader the illusion you might be going somewhere. For example, half his face is still foamy with lather (in case a major Hollywood studio decides to adapt it — lather just hangs there forever in movies! — great for suspense) when the phone rings (or makes some more striking effect inside the still convalescent head — say, "a shrill explosion"), and a terse conversation ensues where we get only one side (because suddenly the author forgets whose head we are inside of?), and it's just intriguing scraps — "I'll be there...I *SAID* I'll be there, OK, so I'll be there!"

At this point the smoke curtain parts or coalesces into stale crystal, maybe he shuffles through yesterday's mail and notices something odd just as he's about to trash the crucial envelope — but you can take it from here, you've read it before a hundred times and seen the TV movie too. I'd take it further myself except I'm an old fashioned reader who just woke up and realized this has all been a dream. Then I turned over heavily in bed and went back to sleep happily ever after.

————

Now, one of the rare extant fragments from John Milton's lost collection of parodies after which this chapter is named, a fragment which shows that Milton did, at length, learn how to end a sentence, once started. (*Paradise Lost* has led many readers to prayer: "How long, O Lord? How long!")

Paradise Remortgaged

O give me strength, sweet Muse, to lift this cross,
For unto me now falls the cumbrous task
Of taking up the tale where mighty Milton
Himself ran out of breath, to tell how Satan,
Surrounded by his retinue, grotesque,
Of sooty demons and contorted imps,
Bemoaned his new disgrace, his further fall
From noble-in-damnation Lucifer
To stooge and straight man for the Lord's spoiled brat,
And pondering how to counteract the glory
New fallen o'er the world as Christ's bequest
To man, as when the dappled morn sheds stars
On every blade of grass, pearls every leaf —
Then arguing with his own despair, asudden,
Like a black ember flaring up, arose
Imperious Satan, countenance darkly glowing,
And spake: "My loyal aeons-long-suffering crew,
Be not distressed, for I begin to see
How we may profit from Christ's latest Shtick —
'Good Will To Men' indeed! I see one hope
For us: What we can't beat, we'll join — in spades!
And with a vengeance — in more ways than one —

We'll push GOOD WILL TO MEN with all our might,
But give it our own twist to make it mean
Gifts, money, commerce, social obligation,
A source of venal pride moved by a fear
Of scorn. From earliest puling infancy,
I'll teach each human brat that Christmas means
Fulfillment of material lust." "But Sir,"
Asked Beelzebub on Satan's dexter hand,
"How can you teach them now? They'll recognize
In you a monster they've been taught to fear.
They're wary of your name, your horns, hooves, tail,
Your fiery aspect and your leering bray..."
"Fear not — all that is comprehended in
My master plan: I'll subtly change my name,
My shape and manner. Hear my dark designs:
For name, I'll simply shift the final 'n'
Of Satan to become the softer 'Santa'.
I'll add white trim to my hell-fire dress,
Put on a jovial belly that my leering
Laughter pass for cheer, and change my story:
I'll say I hail from earth's most frigid zone,
The North Pole! They'll never think of me
In hellish heat. You, comrades, will be elves,
My jolly helpers all. We'll spread the word
That children must be good if they would get
Material baubles; thus, we'll redefine
The source of goodness, one more tool of lust.
'Tis brilliant, if I do say so myself!
And so I do. A long loose cap will cover
My horns, nor tail nor hooves will ever show,
Bundled as I'll be against the Northern night.
And, hell, just to maintain my old trademarks,
I'll be transported by horned, tailed and hooved
Creatures," he said. "But," asked a shivering demon,
"How will you visit long enough to teach?
We've grown accustomed to our toasty realm
And lost our taste for icy winds?" "Aha!
I'll go from house to house and warm myself
By entering and leaving through the chimneys,
A merry devil making each home hell.
They'll love me! When they think of Christmas, why
'Tis ME they'll think of, jolly old gift-bringer,
Ho HO, old Satan Santa, not that solemn
Christ Jesus wimp with His mealy-mouthed 'Give all
Thou hast to the poor and follow me'!" "In sooth,

108

'Tis brilliant beyond compare" cried all
Those Pandemonic ranks in shrill uproar.
There followed silence. Not a creature stirred
All through the depths, as in demonic pates
Sweet visions swam of new recruitment records,
Of rising graphs and quotas met and beaten,
Of bonus points and most of all the scent,
the delirious scent of sizzling sinner flesh.
At last, "Yum Yum — I mean, Ho Ho, indeed!"
Cried Santa: "Merry Christmas to you all
And to you all Good Night, for Santa soon
Will have you in his claws! Farewell, Old Nick!
Behold good old Saint Nick! Heh heh! Ho Ho!"

Now for a modern Miltonic (having the effect, rather, of a Milltown?): This next parody is generic (that is, I see no reason to insult with whatever small notoriety I may command the genial old gent whose poetry inspired it). It's unfair, really — why parody such obvious pomposity? Too easy. And yet…and yet, it's the sort of poetry (lush vocabulary, far-fetched euphemisms and inflated passions) that wins all sorts of local poetry contests, and it's such FUN to parody, like blowing up a paper bag to enjoy the POP! And scare oneself. The epigraph, besides alluding to "East is East…", refers to the first words of Hopkins' sonnet, "No worst, there is none." It also conceals, I hope, the name of the genial gent aforementioned. It's an old honored parodic device, applying a noble inflated style to banal scenes, here the acts of rising from bed ("the cadent catafalque"), breaking wind ("malignant trumpeting calliope" — and isn't "breaking wind" a fine phrase? I wonder why windbreakers [the jackets] aren't called "farters"?), entering the bathroom, stepping on the "scales that croak," going to the sink ("alabaster porch"), looking in the mirror ("coffin of lurid lucence"), experiencing being split in two — self and mirror image ("agony of mitosis"), using the water (described in the nine lines beginning "with this fierce pale tinct"), engaging in an epic encounter with the toilet (or "nether porcelain" which he doth bestride like a colossus), and combing his hair ("cultivate the hirsute furrows", etc.):

The 701st Poem of a Professor Proud of His 700 Noble Poems[20]

"Yeast is yeast and wurst is no wurst, there is none."

Poised, puissant,
upon the cadent catafalque
of the infinite, I
emerge, malignant trumpeting calliope
of the strenuous morning,
tremulously arise,
poet of nascent nakedness,
from crevassed glacial creep
of pillow, unrolling Alpine
arabesque of sheets,
emerge, mottled ivory,
untuned by shallow dreams, stand
in a frenzy of fluorescence
on frail scales that croak
at the gross injustice
and am judged abundant
in my nakedness, for am I not
infinite, both bottomless and
topless? Now inclined
o'er the arid alabaster porch
of my own dim agony,
O agony of mitosis,
as my image is taken from me
and returned, recumbent in its
coffin of lurid lucence,
dappled with dots of dental-floss
debris, flotsam and jetsam
of my most feral mastications,
laving, as I
lave and dye,
its mirrored lips and eyes
with this fierce pale tinct
of black-browed nimbi, columned
cumuli (Alas, do I wax cirrus?
O dire stratus!),[21]
oceanic exhalation, ah, I plunge

---

[20] This poet could not read a poem to a group of poets without first explaining to them exactly what poetry is supposed to be, proudly citing his own 700 poems.

[21] Water, I'm told, comes from those curlicues in the sky, though I don't see what holds them up there if they are water. Anyway, they have names, like cirrus and stratus, cumulus and nimbus, so our hero gets into dire straits waxing serious.

my fevered immaculate brow
into this bright brew, precise
precipitate of nebular peristalsis,[22]
pure cold mother of quenched levin,[23]
touch of mourning fingers,
liquid lament for the lost lambent lightning
of dreams — but whence this
tumulent[24] thunder? Hark! O odor
of another inner air I sing,
bestride like a pendent colossus
the nether porcelain, seat myself,
memorially Lincolnesque,
dauntless o'er the watery void
and loose the perilous music
of my bowels. Now shall we know
into what golden gobbledygook
the Midas touch of intestinal avarice
hath enchanted my dull dinner...
but no, fear not, for I look
no further than my delicate muse can stomach,
poor moth of academe,
I shall not look, but send
this stertorous stew cascading
into voids beyond voids
where curious schools of fish
will deliberate over my diet and excavate
shards of, alas, not THIS paper,
but a flimsier tissue stained
with far more precious stuff,
while I arise, O arise! Yet again
(for have I not arisen, my choice,
cadent words, lo! These 700 times?)
arise to cultivate the hirsute furrows
with horrid bristling implements
of jellied elegance, arise
to teach yet again our dreams
to find their fluent tongues, teach dreamers
the elocution eterne, the sweet sad

---

[22] Rainstorms are often accompanied by lightning, which can be a spark derived from clouds rubbing against each other or internally, a sort of peristalsis, right? And clouds are nebulous, right? And sunset is the angels cooking their suppers, right?

[23] Levin, besides being the hero of *Anna Karenina*, is a very artsy word for lightning.

[24] I coined this word, "tumulent," to refer to deep stomach growling and churning, knowing the poet I'm parodying would approve of it.

symphonies of our striving,
the truth that, alone, can carry us
from the moraine of glacial sleep
to the imperious peaks of breakfast and,
I dare say, beyond.

Breakfast will be, no doubt, Corn Flakes, for high drama is always based on cornflakes (i.e., conflicts ... sorry).

Last, a self-salute (it's a lute or I'm a lyre) to the poet/parodist (working against all of our migraines):

Going Against My Grain — the Qualities of a Parodist
or As I Ape Gems

*A*bstruse, my shtick is mystique.
*S*peculative, my motif is the *mot* "if".[25]
*I*mitative, my name is myna-me.
*A*wed, my saga/game is a gaga me.
*P*ositive, my humor is you, more.
*E*gocentric, my theme is the me.
*G*adfly, my topic is to pique.
*E*xpansive, my thing is myth-ing.[26]
*M*onogamous, my metier is my mate — yay![27]
*S*atirical, my stock in trade is me stuck in tirade.

In case you've never seen an angry blood-sucker, the above poem is, in fact, a cross tick (i.e., acrostic). If you encounter a REAL tick, knock on wood. You will then hear what is termed a "tick tock". That joke may be obscure to many of you: Long ago, my children, in this very galaxy, before watches were digital and battery-operated, our clocks and watches and time-bombs would TALK to us, and this was called "tick talk" or tick tock. But we grew tick-tocksick (weary of toxic time), so had all our clocks detocksified *and exterminated all their ticks* (Don't you dig Ital?)[28]. It's time to move on.

---

[25] For some reason the French word for "word" is "mot," which looks like Jeff's partner, Mutt, but is actually from another comedy team, the Three Stooges, since it is pronounced something like Moe, because the French cannot pronounce most final consonants or it's against their religion or something — like stepping on one of the sidewalk cracks — "Oops! I pronounced a final 't'! Bad luck all week!"

[26] I mean that my thing (bag, preferred activity) as a poet is mything (myth-making). I do NOT mean that my thing (my you-know-what, crown jewel of family jewels, etc.) is among the mything.

[27] Meaning either that I am married to my avocation, in love with my muse — and, in formal works, I'm very pleased to meter — or that I love my wife, as, of course, I DO (she's reading every word of this).

[28] "Dig Ital?" — dig Italics or digital, a digital clock being a clock whose ticks have been exterminated. You aren't allowed to get PART of my punning here. You are expected to dig it ALL.

Section 1: A Survey of English Poetry

Chapter 3: Rhyme Does Not Pay

With Malice Aphorisms

Feel free to read the poems, but please don't feed the poets.

We are such fools as worlds are made by.

I respond readily to poetry. Usually the response is "So what?"

The unknown soldier is always in a tomb. A random, messy death swept away his identity. Fortunately or not (owing to their randy messianic lives?), poets don't have to be dead to be unknown.

The poet strives for newness. The OLD ness is either monstrous (as in Loch) or untouchable (as in Elliot).

"Art hasn't progressed since Picasso" — odd notion, that art should progress. Communication hasn't progressed since "Hello!" Has poetry progressed since "With thy sharp teeth this knot intrinsicate of life at once untie"?[1] (Nobody does it like those dead white males!)

Pornographic poems — or to the Romans, vice versa.

Occasionally poetry is occasional poetry. Occasional poetry is occasionally poetry.

How did the psychiatrist stop the poet? A ward to the wise is sufficient.

How do I love thee? Let me count the positions...

"Sein oder nicht sein?" from Hamburger Hamlet.[2]

We tolerated his eccentricities for the sake of his genius...or vice versa?

---

[1] In Shakespeare's *Antony and Cleopatra*, Cleo says this to the asp that is about to poison her. Shakespeare coined the word "intrinsicate" (intricate, intrinsic), a rare, golden coinage.

[2] "Sein oder nicht sein, das ist die Frage" — German (more or less) for "to be or not to be, that is the question." "Hamburger Hamlet" is a restaurant chain — or *Hamlet* as spoken in Hamburg. Recently, wondering if "Seinfeld" would really go off the air, millions soliloquized (grieving):

"Seinfeld oder nicht Seinfeld, das ist die Frage."
(Auf Wiedersehn, Jerry, und dabei gutten Tage.)
[Farewell, Gerhardt, and also good day.]

Chapter 3
Rhyme Does Not Pay — But
It Looks Good On Your Resume

Is there any sort of writing less bought and read these days than poetry? YES! Literary criticism! To solve this cultural crisis, I suggest that we combine our crises: No one reads poetry; no one reads criticism of poetry — and probably the critics of poetry don't read the poetry; that would be too much to ask — no one sensitive enough to qualify to be a critic could bear to read the stuff. And certainly the poets don't read the criticism — for similar reasons. (Grad students don't count. They don't read such stuff. They consume it. And excrete it.)

I suggest that we combine poetry and poetry criticism by requiring that all critiques of poets and poetry be put into the form of short poems — mainly quatrains and limericks, like those in this chapter. In roughly the order of chronic logic (I suffer from it), here's a bit of dirt on a fine poet, Walter Raleigh — hundreds of thousands die every year from ailments because he brought home from the New World... well, here it is in rhyme, so it must be true:

We Come To Bury Raleigh

One folly hath lived after Walter Raleigh:
Discoverer of Marlborough and Pall Mall he!
Sir Walter's smokes put many in the tomb:
He hath brought many coughers home to rheum.

(I'm including this commentary, with explanations, in order to insult all the readers who don't need it. I include no dates, for fear that someone will memorize them. Hell, I got through most of my schooling with very few dates and only one marriage.) Raleigh really brought back tobacco, flung it before Queen Elizabeth (so that she could walk across a puddle) and said "Put THAT in your pipe and poke it!" (This is usually relayed as "...and smoke it," but my Dad always seemed to spend a lot longer poking at the tobacco in his pipe than actually smoking it. He probably enjoyed playing with his little three-pronged metal poker almost as much as I did.)

That brings us to Shakespeare, alluding as it does to three lines from *Julius Caesar*: "We come to bury Caesar, not to praise him," "The evil that men do lives after them" and, from the same speech, "He hath brought many coffers [chests of treasure] home to Rome." And of course, Shakespeare was well aware of the scourge visited upon us by Raleigh's introduction of to-bacco to Europeans, as, for example, in the Bard's famous description of cancer: "Tumor — O tumor! O tumor! O — creeps in its petty pace...." And eventually, when cancer reaches the bone: "To marrow, to marrow and to marrow...." Shakespeare was well ahead of his time in medical knowledge. He even considered vasectomy ("Tube or knot tube...?"). And here's a bit of barding where he struggled with that other great scourge, taxes:

Shakespeare and Shelley Meet in Tax Court

(an exchange in which Shelley suggests that Shakespeare change the first word of a famous line to make it express more romantic determi-nation.)

"Shelley, compeer! — thee, too, a sum erred, eh?"   [Shall I compare thee to a summer day?]

"Willy, calm pere! Thee, too, is amerced, eh?"   [Will I compare thee to a summer's day?]

Calm pere, because, of course, Willy is the serene daddy of all us bardlets. To "amerce" is to charge a fine. So that's what *fine* poetry is. Shakespeare will soon be making a big comeback, when the musical comedy version of *Hamlet*, called *This Little Piggy*, comes out, featuring such hit tunes as "There is Nothing Like a Dane," "Good Night, Sweet Prince, Good Night, Sweet Prince, Ophelia in my dreams" and "Alas, Poor Yorick, I knew him well — Knew Yorick! Knew Yorick!" Stay tuned!

Two For John Donne

One Sunday good Canon John Donne
Said, "No man's an island, not one!
So ask not for whom, man!
You, human, it's *you*, man!
We're in this together — what fun!"

He said, "Death, thou shalt die," did John Donne,
But then Donne died himself, so death won —
Or did he, for Donne,
Though quite done, was not done:
Death will never have done with that pun.

116

Grammatical Note:

Asking for WHO the bell tolls
is just not Donne.

Donne was Canon of St. Paul's Cathedral, and "No man is a standalone workstation...er...island" (we're a WE-land, though some grow incontinent with age — welcome to weeweeland) is from his most famous sermon, which also contains Bill Clinton's campaign slogan[3]: Ask not for whom the Bill toils — he toils for THEE! (And ask not who pays the belle's toll.) The following poem explains the connection between canon and *loose* canon:

CLINNN TONNN[4] CLINNN TONNN...PEAL & REPEAL

White House Press Conference: "Sir,
again you waffle. What do you stand for?"
"O members of the Press, ask not for whom
the Bill toils — he toils for thee."
"In that case, Mr. President, how do you differ
from a funereal church bell?"
"The Bill feels your pain. The bell peals
your fane."[5] "Sir, do you dingdong repeatedly?"
"No, I answer immediately with a message
that no one is home."[6] "Sir, how many pains
do you feel?" "I feel three pains:
mine, thine and the pains of pubic orifice.
In short, I'm as phone-y as a three-dolor Bill."
"Sir, if you feel a nation's pain,
why do you seem cheerful?" "America's agony
cannot be seen, for it is
a Pent-agony."[7] "Sir, is it true as rumored
that many belles have peeled for thee?"

---

[3] Bill Clinton was the (allegedly) philandering president of the United States way back in the last years of the 20th Century when Blehert's classic work was written.
[4] If you deal in federal contracts, DC is definitely CLINtown. A "CLIN" is a Contract Line Item Number, and anything that ails a Beltway Bandit (federal contractor inside the Beltway area — the Beltway being a freeway around Washington, DC) can be treated CLINically. Which has zilch to do with the Clinton poem, which is rather Unclin, in fact, filthy.
[5] A fane is a temple or sanctuary. Thus, "Wouldst fain feign a fane?" means "Would you like to establish a phony church?"
[6] Long ago New York had a governor named De Witt Clinton. Our president is, at times, De Wittless Clinton. If he continues to confuse the Oval Office with the oval orifice, he may soon have to enter De Wittless Protection Program.
[7] I suppose this means that we are impoverished by military expenditures, but it could refer to Clinton's agony, having to keep peter pent in pants.

"O ask not!" "Yes or no, Sir?"
"If the belles fill the bill, then the Bill
fills the belles." "Sir, why are you not
continent?" "No man is an island.
After paying the belle's toll, I land
in bed." "You admit it?" "Why not?
I'm a lame duck. I bequeath my evasions
to the next press-it-in erect[8], for I
am nearly Donne."

But I digress (and pardon my Hillaryty). For several centuries collections of sermons were best sellers and attracted the finest writers. These days writers are taught that "sermonizing" is a no-no. I've never figured out why it's OK to load your poetry with emotionally slanted words and innuendoes, but not to say, look, this is the way it is — it tolls for thee. Perhaps under the guise of arguing against callow judgmental abstract poetry, our teachers have been teaching us to be covert and to dismiss wisdom as even a possibility. There, wasn't that serious!

The pun in the second Donne limerick is Donne's own. Shortly before he died, he wrote a poem that works all these variations on his name, telling God that when He has forgiven him various sins, "...Thou hast not done, for I have more," but as the stanzas turn, God does what needs to be done, "And having done that, Thou hast done; I fear no more." So don't blame me for ALL the puns (or ponnes) around here. Besides, if no man is an island, we're all in the same boat. (If I'm not an island, am I an isn't-land?[9]) But enough of Donne. In the words of *Dragnet*, "Donne da Donne Donne!"[10]

Now a word from George Herbert, who had the gall to picture the communion (or more broadly, man accepting God's Grace through Christ) as a seduction scene in a poem called "Love" that's so moving it forces atheists to hide in foxholes in order to avoid being touched by it. Love bids him "enter", but he "hangs" back, guilty as sin, but love persuades the bashful speaker, at last to "taste of my meat". Here's what a limerick does to all that holiness when your name is Herbert and there's a scarcity of rhymes for it ("Blehert" is also a rough one):

---

[8] The press-it-in heads his sexy-cute-Eve raunch. The other raunches include the you-dish-iary (led by the sperm quart) and Congress (which consists of the Snot and the House of Reprehensibles).

[9] And do men fear marriage because no aisle is a man's land?

[10] For the absurdly and impossibly young among you, literate fetuses, as it were, *Dragnet* was a radio and TV cop show in the 50s. It's theme music included an oft-repeated, irritably unforgettable sequence of four dreary notes: do re mi-flat re, in a Dumda DUM Dum beat. Be glad you're too young…

118

Sure, 'Bert, You Bet

When Love, that insatiable pervert,
Showed all to sweet bashful George Herbert,
Saying, "Taste of my meat,"
George got red as a beet
And said, "Please, could I settle for sherbert?"

Farewell, sweet-tempered Anglican. We must venture into arid, hot-tempered Miltonia:

John Milton

Though Puritan poet, John Milton,
Spends eterne at the Paradise Hilton,
Still he wobbles and tilts,
Teeters high on his stilts,
Lest he touch that hot lake "Heaven's" built on.

Milton was, indeed, of the Puritan (Natirup spelled backwards) persuasion. The suggestion of this limerick is that Milton (said to have been a harsh man, tyrannical to wife and daughters, a bit of monster — and we like to believe such stuff if it'll get us out of having to read him) is so certain of his own righteousness that he chooses not to notice he's in Hell, not Heaven. After all, generations of readers have mistaken Satan for the HERO of *Paradise Lost*. The other joke is that Milton is among the most stilted of our writers (and he must have magnificent poise to get away with it as well as he has). Stilts would come in handy on a very hot floor. Milton spelled backwards is notlim, which suggests that he is NOT of a LIMerick humor. Now for a less forbidding Puritan:

Wouldn't it be Marvellous

"Had we but world enough and time..."
Oh, let's descend from that sublime.
I've changed the thought, but kept the rhyme:
Had world but WHEE! enough and time..."

A Poor Thing, But Brine

O Andrew Marvell, my sun runs no more.
I can but marvel how you still do *your* thing.
What now transpires at my every pore —
Not hot, but cold and wet — is but a pore thing.

119

Andrew Marvell's "To His Coy Mistress" begins "Had we but world enough and time," but eventually gets the WHEE of it and ends with the suggestion that, though we can't make the sun stand still, yet we can make him run. The "poor thing, but brine" (and who said "...a poor thing, but mine own?") is sweat. Marvell's lovers "transpire at every pore" with "instant fires." My pores seem more inclined to extinguish any remaining sparks.

Another Marvell masterpiece, "The Garden," has the poet tripping over garden riches, fruit falling about him, then:

Meanwhile the mind, from pleasure less,
Withdraws into its happiness...
Annihilating all that's made
To a green thought in a green shade.

These lines seem to me to describe aptly one goal of a hungry monomaniacal parodist, eating his way through the canon, consuming and digesting great poems and extruding them as something of his own:

Meanwhile the mind, from poets less,
Withdraws into its childishness,
Annihilating all that's said
To a Dean thought in a Dean head.

Do not fall asleep while reading this book, or you may be taken over by a parody.

Seldom has a writer been as appropriately named as Pope (perhaps the wordy Wordsworth — and Marvell is, indeed, a marvel. And Ezra Pound is percussive and Auden's an odd 'un and Swift is quick and Hardy is tough and Smart is smart and Keats is SO Keatsian...but Sitwell doesn't always sit well). Pope loved to pontificate. With his barbed wit he'd sting any who displeased him (and so many did!) — as he did in his mock epic, *The Dunciad*, about the bad poets of his day, some of whom should have been grateful, since it's only because of Pope's insults that we remember them. The Poet Laureate of the day, Colly Cibber, is known to us now mainly from that poem and from a single quotation on some of the tea-bag tags from Good Earth Tea. Pope did indeed argue against "presumption" as described below.

Four For Alexander Pope ("Just call me Al...NOT")

Just a dwarf of a man, Mr. Pope,
With whom never would damsel elope[11] —
Wipe that smirk from your face!

---

[11] Pope is said to have been a dwarf and a hunchback, though with a very finely featured face. He was very sensitive to mockery and gave better than he got. (Why doesn't someone make the movie?)

120

Or else you'll find your place
In *The Dunciad*, damned for a dope!

That hunched up dwarf-poet, A. Pope,
Ordered mankind to keep to its scope,
Stuck 'twixt angel and ape,
With no hope of escape —
Honing couplets may help one to cope.

A young poet implored Master Pope,
"May we please try to broaden our scope?
"I know it's a lie,
"But a poet should fly!
"O Sir! Please can't I soar?" Pope said "Nope."

Then another begged, "Please! Mr. Pope,
"Can we not at least venture to hope,
"If we all persevere,
"To climb out of our sphere..."
"Don't you *dare* to presume," said this Pope!

Swift DID encounter the response described below to his sometimes savage satire, *Gulliver's Travels*. And he was easily miffed. Of course, he made a career of miffing others. He was among the miffing. He was dean of an Anglican cathedral — perhaps a bit of his wit rubs off on other Deans, but not, I hope, his fierce unhappiness.

Jonathan Swift

That funny old Jonathan Swift —
His humor sure gives me a lift!
But why he turned pale
When I said, "A great tale
For the kids!" I don't know — was he miffed?

He probably gave the guy a good Swift kick.

Christopher Smart got put in Bedlam. Sam Johnson said it was for not keeping his linen clean and for inviting passersby to kneel with him in the London street and pray with him, to which Johnson's response was that his own linen (underwear) wasn't any too clean and that he'd "...as soon pray with Kit Smart as any man alive" —and so would we all — that is, you will if you read his poems, especially *Jubilate Agno* (rejoice in the Lamb). This — and his other great works— were all written while he was kept, as insane, in Bedlam. His main company during this time was his cat, Geoffrey, and part of *Jubilate* is a delightful poem to his cat (sorry, sometimes parody fails even me). Obviously psychiatry of the late 18th Century was enlightened compared to the savage treatments of our day: They left him to himself. In our day, he'd be given anti-depressants and shock and would probably be back on the street — but he would NOT be left capable of writing *Jubilate*.

Christopher Smart

When they put away pious Kit Smart,
Bedlam couldn't keep him from his art:
From divinity grown dotty,
He'd sing "Jubilate!"[12]
While his cat caterwauled the high part.

Samuel Johnson

Dare one argue with old Samuel Johnson?
He says, "Sir!", having one where he wants one;
As his sentences roll,
One may feel on the whole
One would much rather be in Wisconsin.

If you want to know more about Johnson (is there more to know? Well...yes), read the biography by the following writer, who, finding his sense of self exceedingly vague, determined to get a life, and ended up getting the life of Johnson, the least vague man in the world at that time and perhaps since:

James Boswell

Though a Scotsman eats oats as a hoss will,
Sam Johnson puts up with young Boswell,
For his life James devotes
Just to taking good notes
And to whore and booze well and learn laws well.

Johnson cultivated an anti-Scot bigotry. He considered Scotland a barbarous place. In his famous dictionary he defines oats as a grain fed to horses in England, but which, in Scotland, is the main staple of the people (a "staple" — it sticks to the ribs, holds body and soul together). So young-law-student-from-Scotland-Boswell (who did, indeed whore and booze as "well" as he could — in his journal he notes each orgasm) wondered if Johnson would treat him politely. Johnson did (Boswell was a charmer), and the rest is, not

---

[12] Pronounced "Jew Bill Lot he." (Rhymes with "dotty")

only history, but damned good biography. Johnson and Boswell are the greatest team since Laurel and Hardy.

Gimme a Blake!

Tiger! Tiger! burning bright —
did he who framed thy fearful symmetry
frame Roger Rabbit?

Sorry.

Wordsworth did get his picture's worth. To be fair, he also wrote some of the shortest, simplest poems of his time — like the "Lucy" poems. (This is Lucy pre-Desi and pre-Snoopy.) But, OH! he could roll on like Byron's ocean or stick deodorant.

William Wordsworth

One ten thousandth of a picture? — Not Wordsworth!
He who highly considered a bird's worth;
Daffodils he adored,
Leech-gatherers he'd hoard,
But for botanists gave not a turd's worth.

William Wordsworth liked old mossy wells
Where he'd brood and indulge pensive spells.
He was solemn and gray,
But those bells made him gay —
That Tintern-Abbey-elation of the bells!

That includes a foreshadowing of Poe's "The Bells" (and the tintinnabulation thereof). And, of course, Wordsworth did pen one of his long meditations near Tintern Abbey (see Chapter 1). His "I wandered lonely as a Cloud"[13] is all about encountering an unruly mob of daffodils, "Resolution and Independence" is about his meeting with an old leech-gatherer, from whom he extorts several stanzas of wisdom and banality. As for botanists, he derides the overly analytical who would "botanize o'er his mother's grave". (Hell, who wouldn't? I mean, imagine seeing a rare orchid growing from between your Mom's toes.) Does Wordsworth sound a bit square? No wonder one of his sonnets begins: "The world is too much with it" (often mis-written as "...with us").

---

[13] Which inspired that famous study of American life, *The Lonely Cloud* (I wandered lonely as a crowd?).

Wordsworth Revisited

"Be careful!" "Don't be silly!" "That was DUMB!"
"Who do you think you are!" "Now you be GOOD!"
Intimidations of Immortality from
Recollections of Early Childhood

Wordsworth wrote about the intiMAtions (not intimiDAtions) of im-
mortality in an ode so named — that is, a very young child knows he is
immortal and senses the world freshly. He loses this wisdom with age —
grows stale. A poet tries to help us recover it. My version suggests another
way our immortality is treated in early childhood, when the most important
person in the world (it's OBvious!) is asked "Who do you think YOU are!?"

If I've made Wordsworth sound a bit of a bore, well he is, but I like him
better than many a more charming or electrifying poet. He actually seems to
know something worth knowing. As they say in the movies, "I think he's
trying to tell us something!"

Samuel Taylor Coleridge

He would talk you to death, S. T. Coleridge,
Like that mariner with his weird goal or itch
Just to corner one guest,
Tell his story (the pest!)
'Till you'd wish you had hid in a hole or hedge!

Coleridge's ancient mariner would stop people (like a wedding guest),
hold one "with his eye" and tell his longish tale, the one Coleridge tells us (to
put it palindromically: **Huh! Albatross? Sort a' blah, uh?**). And it is re-
ported that Coleridge himself was a brilliant, almost hypnotic speaker who
loved to hold forth to an audience. I knew a poet who fit that exact descrip-
tion (David Ross, who died in 1994) — I'd watch one of his eyebrows twitch
into gear, as it were, as he drilled in that eye contact so he could pour his fine
sentences into me. Here are two limericks for David (and they probably would
serve for Coleridge too) — maybe you'll read some of his poems one day
(Macmillan published a book of them, *Three Ages of Lake Light*, in the early
60's, but he wrote much better ones later). I include these here as a tribute to
a friend (sort of) and fine poet, because he bore a striking similarity (in per-
sonality and giftedness) to Coleridge and because it is SO much easier to
rhyme "Ross." He taught me a great deal, for example, that when you tap a
watermelon, it goes "tunk tunk."

124

Two For David Ross

An insufferable poet is Ross —
No subject finds him at a loss;
His funereal charm
Holds your eye, grasps your arm...
Ancient mariner...or albatross?[14]

An apostle of purity, Ross,
One whose words are refined of all dross.
'Twixt one pearl & the next —
While with high brow unvexed
He holds forth — couldn't slip dental floss.

Back to the earlier incarnation: Coleridge dreamed up a long poem
("Kubla Khan") with the help of a medication containing opium, was woken
by a knock on the door, then, after dealing with the knocker (no, not a Jehovah's
Witness, but a man on business from Porlock[15]), found he'd lost all but a
fragment of the dream (which begins "In Xanadu did Kubla Khan/ A stately
pleasure dome decree..."):

Poetus Interruptus

S. T. Coleridge, you
Aren't finished — please go on:
What did Xana do?
And whom did Kubla Khan?

Rape of the Poor Lock

Opium dreams had just thawed writer's block
When KNOCK KNOCK — "It's the man from Porlock!"
Hell! I've lost half my verses!
To find fierce enough curses,
Luckless Porlock, I'll pay a warlock!

---

[14] Lord, is it too much to ask? Give us a Coleridge scholar named Albert Ross! In the
poem, the mariner's penance for shooting the albatross is to wear the dead bird hang-
ing heavily around his neck. An insistent talker can be as wearying, and many a
scholar weights down the poet he explicates.

[15] Porlock, I'm told, is a real place. They probably have an annual Porlock festival to
celebrate their most famous native, the fellow whose knock has spared millions of
students many pages of Coleridge's lost opium dream. Millions of student-page-
hours (SPHs) were thus made available to be expended upon Wordsworth's "Pre-
lude" and other exciting works.

Lord Byron

That horny romantic, Lord Byron,
Never covered his ears for a Siren.
If it bloomed he would pluck it
(Or, in plain words, he'd f—k it),
Taking even his Sis for a dry run.

This is what the biographies tell us. Byron's sexiness wasn't just hype to sell books. He felt that a woman's legs might get into violent arguments with each other. To keep the piece — that is, peace — he came between as many pairs of legs as he could. As for that last line, it's not as bad as it sounds: She was only his half-sister. DRY run is not the term for it, but rhymes for "Byron" (whom the girls found dreamy — YUM!) are at a premium. He also had a wife and, by her, a daughter who helped invent computers (after whom the programming language ADA is named)[16]. We owe him our thanks also for the ocean tides: He bade the deep and mighty sea roll on — and it did! I haven't much to say about Byron — he wrote so much about himself — I'm carrying coals to Newcastle. He even made fun of himself — quite skillfully — which leaves little for a parodist except what's too easy, like calling W. C. Fields a drunk or a fish wet. Speaking of fish:

Shellfish Shelve Selfish Shelley

After drowning, Percy Bysshe Shelley
Fattened many a shellfish belly;
Hence the naming of those famous dishes,
Crab and lobster bysshes.

Two For Shelley

There was once a sweet singer named Shelley —
The Victorians thought pretty swell he,
Since which F.R. Leavis[17]
 Did quite undeceive us:
"You can find better tripe at the deli."

---

[16] Fact. She worked with computer pioneer Babbage. Byron probably wouldn't be pleased to know that the language named after his daughter is used mainly to control guided missile systems. But just think: She'd be formatting business reports if he'd named her Cobaldia.

[17] Leavis is that most unpleasant of critics, the one who is too often right — or brilliantly enough wrong to carry a generation along with him. But Leavis has left us. It's safe to come out of the closet, Shelley-lovers.

126

There was once a pure person, poor Percy,
Whose drowning was surely a mercy,
For his birds never wert
And his plant sort of hurt
And when least he made sense then least terse he.

Shelley was once worshiped (e.g., by Robert Browning and most of his generation) as some sort of incandescent soul of poetry (though he wasn't of Incan descent). But deification can turn on you. In fact, "deified" spelled backwards is... "deified"! Shelley's stock fell steeply in the 20th century, but investors have been counseled that this is just an adjustment: It's sort of OK to like his poems again (some of them). Hell, even Tennyson is making a comeback. F. R. Leavis is one of the critics who temporarily demolished Shelley (while deifying D. H. Lawrence.).

In the second limerick, Shelley's skylark is the bird of which he says, "Bird thou never wert" (I always want to say "Bird thou liverwurst", just one of those odd compulsions), since the bird (heard in full song, but not seen) seems to him, to be pure Spirit, just like a great poet, who should be heard, but not obscene. (This is why so few people pay attention to poets. We say that we are true children, having recovered the child's fresh vision — but children should be seen, not heard.) He wrote another poem called "The Sensitive Plant" (what we poets are, you know — don't over-water us with, for example, money).

Grandson Perhaps?

Percy Shelley was middle-named "Bysshe".
As a courteous fellow, I wish
Bysshe were not in his name —
It's his mother to blame
If I call him a son of a Bysshe.

(Bysshe rhymes with "fish", but not, alas, with cliché, which requires a bit of quiche, eh?)

John Keats

There was once a young Cockney named Keats
Who said "Blimey! I ain't what I eats!
"I become what I see,
"Like that sparrow," said he;
Then he pecked at his worm and gave tweets.

Keats was, indeed, a cockney (Londoner, lower middle class), and when his Grecian Urn ode bursts into "O happy happy..." — Keats may well have pronounced it "Ho 'appy 'appy...". (I learned this from a teacher I couldn't stand. 'Tis an ill wind....) In a letter he says that a poet must have a gift he calls "negative capability", the ability to be absent from self and become the things he sees, as, he says, I now see and can become that sparrow pecking at the gravel in the drive. As for the other implications of "pecked at his worm", Keats was, apparently, rather tormented in his relationship with his girlfriend, Fanny Brawne — he was too ill with consumption to marry, and possibly had moral or physical difficulties in consummating the relationship (too consumed to consummate, perhaps even too pooped to pucker), though I doubt that the next limerick is more than the delusion of a depraved mind (Who took my prave?):

> Young John Keats turned and twisted till dawn,
> Torn by lust for his lass, Fanny Brawne;
> With his last gasp, uncanny,
> He reached for her fanny,
> But ere touching Brawne's brawn, he was gone.

Keats Grows Lear-y

> "A thing of beauty is a joy forever" —   [Keats]
> But show her poems before her morning coffee?
> Never never never never never   [King Lear]
> Trust unwed poets for your philosoffee!

Dolly, Parton is Such Sweet Sorrow
or Keats is Keats and Yeats is Yeats
and Never the Twain Shall Meet Country Western

> For her lips his were itchin',
> But he thought poems the pits.
> She thought Shelley just bitchin',
> Nibbled sonnets for treats,
>
> So they split — he to Michen-
> Er, she — Yeat's Greatest Hits:
> No regrets, no contrition —
> Every hour he repeats:
>
> "Get the hell out of the hitchin'
> If you can't stand the Keats."

Perhaps the second title should be "Keats ARE Keats and Yeats ARE Yeats," just as Thomas is plural for Thoma and we have first cumming, second cummings.

128

As noted in several of the following, Poe, in poems, stories — maybe in life — yearned for young, pale, anorexic, aristocratic feverish horizontally languishing women. Poe is often derided in America for his gloomy, loony-tuney and more-memorable-than-one-wants lyrics, but the French elite have discovered him (which puts him in a class with Jerry Lewis), and 50 Frenchmen can't be wrong.

Beyond The Pale

Fey damsels roused Poe's lust
(He couldn't stomach crudeness)
and pale ones, sober-eyed and just
a touch sepulchritudinous.

Three For Edgar Allan Poe

That finicky slapstick fan, Poe,
Laughed at Larry and poor Curly Joe;
For each gag of these knaves
Kudos, plaudits, and raves,
But for Moe was no raving — never Moe!

Of course, the Three Stooges weren't very popular in Poe's time, but Poe was a visionary.

O pity that poor poet, Poe,
Who cried out, "When, O when shall I know
Great sex? With my avarice
For damsels cadaverous,
O woe!" quoth he, raving, "Nevermoe!"

A neglectful landscaper was Poe,
A disgrace — he just let his lawn go
All to bramble and thorn.
He said "Fine lawns I scorn!
Do not be your yard's slave — Never mow!"

Ogden Nash's Advice To Poe

When called by a raven,
seek haven.

Big Knell

"O! The Dickens with drear Little Nells!"
Cried Poe, "I'm immune to their spells.
And I won't have a whore —
Jaded flesh is a bore!
How I yearn for those sweet Southern belles belles belles belles belles
    belles belles belles belles, for the tint and
    adulation of the belles..."

Little Nell is the heroine of Dickens' *The Old Curiosity Shop*, a hit during Poe's lifetime. The last line alludes to Poe's "The Bells," tintinnabulation thereof, as does the next gag.

Riddle: Why did they bell Rin-tin-tin?
Answer: They wanted to hear the Rin-tin-tinnabulation of the bell.

Ravenous

Pencils, no more; books, no more; teacher's dirty looks,
no more — alas, the song is cheerful...no more.

"No more!" she cried, "No...more! No! More!..."

Quoth the craving, MORE!

Advice to a writer of done-to-death parodies:
Quote the raven...never more.

Walt Whitman

Old Walt's such a hardy and fit man,
Like a cheerleader OD'ed on Vitamin,[18]
So that, borrowing from Tonto,
The reader may want to
Say "Whaddya mean 'Whee!' Mr. Whitman?"

Whitman's energetic self-assertion can be wearying. The joke referred to in line 5 is the one where Tonto and the Lone Ranger are surrounded by...well, I'd better not tell the joke. Someone may own it, and, being an American, I'm allergic to royalties, but the punchline is "Whaddya mean 'we,' white man?"

---

[18] "Vitamin" pronounced Brit. fashion (SOME Brits): Vitt'men. I suppose a Yiddish funeral service would vault Vitman.

...And Miles to Go While Reader Sleeps

You'll be billed by the line length,
So watch the odometer:
Whitman shows off his lung-strength
In iambic kilometer.

Why Walt Whitman Sings The Song Of Himself
(a palindrome)

O Gemini sin: I'm ego!

He was long-winded and long-lined — and a Gemini with a substantial
dose of ego. Of course, where would we be without egos? As Ruth says, in
the Bible, "Wither egos - there go I."

Whaddya Mean WHEE!, Whitman?

In high black socks the private school girls pass;
I hear the hundred rustling greaves of lass.

Just a play on Whitman's title, *Leaves of Grass*, the girl's knee-high
black stockings suggesting greaves (ankle armor). I doubt that Whitman would
have listened as carefully as I did to that "rustling". He'd have preferred the
BOYS — whose socks bristle with clinging seeds and brambles, for nothing
sucks seeds like sockses. But let us return to Anklish literature.

Two For Emily Dickinson

Sweet and light — with a bite — is Ms. Dickinson,
All that primness and passion — it sickens one!
Shall ever love's dam burst
For the maiden of Amherst?
What you'll find in the grave is slim pickin's, Hon.

She never married, and wrote many poems in anticipation of the grave
where death comes as gentleman escort or she finds good fellowship in her
wormy mossy bed.

Once a well-known critic named Higginson
Advised a Miss Emily Dickinson,
"Don't publish that stuff!"
Now she's famous enough
To afford a small footnote for Higginson.

131

Riddle: Why did the poetess become a necrophilic?
Answer: Because she could not stop for death.[19]

Pick a Peck of Peglegged Poopdecks

"You've got your ship, your Moby Dick,
But who'll play captain of the *Pequod*?"
John Houston cried, "Had I my pick,
No one else but Gregory Peck would!"[20]

(Yes, you'll find several novelists in this chapter — don't be so picky!)

Moby Dick

Since Ahab's grown twisted and sick
And developed a Moebius dick,
He finds that just knowing
If he's coming or going
Is quite an impossible trick.

If you twist a strip of paper once, then tape the ends, you get a Moebius strip, which has the property that if you travel (e.g., with finger or pencil) all the way round the loop, following the surface through the twist, you come out on the other side of the paper. Is it just me, or do you, too, often wonder what American literature would be today had Melville written the saga of a malevolent *pink* or *purple* whale?

Captain Ahab Converts and Gives Up on Vengeance
[a palindrome]

I Ahab was ere I saw Bahai.[21]

The Lowellist Form of Humor

From mounded sand — two tiny feet!
We gently scooped away, and soon

---

[19] One of her famous lines, "Because I could not stop for death/ He kindly stopped for me." He drops by in a carriage (he can't afford a bicycle built for two down among the daisies) and takes her for a ride. For Emily, Death and marriage go together like a hearse and carriage.

[20] Houston directed the film, Peck played Ahab and John Bobbitt did not play Mopy Dick.

[21] Bahai, a religion of which I know little more than its universal brotherhood pitch, which suggests that it would frown upon a man separating himself from humanity to get even with a whale. Or, as the Everly Brothers might sing it, "Bahai Bahai, Sappiness...". (a riff on "Byebye happiness")

Touched torn blue feathers — no heart beat...
Oh what is so rare as a jay in dune!

The Lowell referred to here is not Robert or Amy (of "Christ! What are patterns for!" — to sew with, of course. And also to mate with the Ma terns to make little baby terns), but their ancestor (or ancestor's cousin?), James Russell Lowell, who said, "Oh what is so rare as a day in June" and also "The gift without the giver is bare," to which many sick alcoholics have responded, "The lift [or high] without the liver is rare" and those who objected to the flooding of Glenn Canyon, replacing river and canyon with a lake said, "The rift without the river is bare," and, as a strip-teaser remarked, without the shift, the bare will shiver. Fortunately for you, I don't recall anything else he said.

Lord Tennyson

The innocent maidens in Tennyson —
What they eat, be it lotus or venison,
Never turns into sh_t —
They've no holes where they sit,
Nor the least nook for putting a p_nis in!

Very much Queen Victoria's poet was Tennyson. Queen Victoria herself managed to spawn large numbers of children without ever learning exactly where they came from. I'm joking, of course. Her title was Victoria Regina (Queen Victoria), but she was as respectable as a rector, so might as well have been called Rectoria Vagina. But enough rectal humor — the Queen is not amused. Alfred's been well-parodied. "Come Into the Garden, Maude" is particularly fair game — almost too easy. He also writes of the murmurmur of beebees in immemmemmorial marmoreal mammaries...I mean elms ("In Memoriam" — he was over-elmed by the death of a friend).

I think he wished himself a tougher, crisper poet — after all, he begins one of his famous poems:

Blake, Blake, Blake,
Oh thy bold gay tones, thy rants!
Would my tongue were in the gutter
For what rises in my pants![22]

---

[22] Actually, Tennyson wrote "Break, break break,/ On thy cold gray stones, O Sea!/ And I would that my tongue could utter/ The thoughts that arise in me." He did a lot of uttering for a guy who couldn't utter. The poetic feet run rapidly from his pen. After all, they have their *tennies on*.

Robert Browning

That puffed up old poet, R. Browning,
Is it praise, wine or speed he is downing?
For he's pert as a parrot —
Can Elizabeth Bear it?
The strutting, the crowing, the clowning?

Elizabeth "bear it" — that is, Elizabeth Barrett Browning. And she put up with him very well. Of course, Browning was caricatured as puffed up, portly, blustery, etc., late in his life. He may have been more "sufferable" before his wife died. He's not the easiest poet to parody — his worst stuff (Strive on!) is too easy and his best is, at once, too good and too trifling — it's like critiquing fine Chinese cuisine — it goes through too fast. I once spent a good part of a college summer enthralled by his novel in verse, *The Ring and the Book*, but damned if it didn't vanish from my literary digestive system in a month or so, leaving me hungry again.

Promise of Breech

Bob and Liz go down to the nudist beach,
In Adriatic glare frowning.
Will Bob's Victorian gasp exceed his reach?
Will Elizabeth bare it, browning?

His stock has sagged slightly. Hers is coming up. After all, she's a woman. And she did get a bum rap: Who'd expect a poem called "Aurora Lee" to contain sharp insights (it does). Give her a few more years and she'll be recognized as a "fresh new voice in English poetry." "Gasp exceed his reach": From Robert's "Andrea Del Sarto" which says a man's grasp should exceed his reach (or is it the other way around)? The Victorians were very down on "self-abuse", so it may have been "Ah but a man's breech should exceed his grasp/ Or what's a Heaven for?"

Two For Tolstoy

Once a guilt-ridden writer named Leo
Used his wife quite as ill as could be, O!
With 12 kids, he said "Honey,
"It's a sin to have money,"
Then he traded in Sophie for Theo.

There was once a deep thinker named Leo
Whose young muse got abducted by Clio.
'Twixt love scene and battle

On history he'd prattle
While his readers skipped pages *con brio*!

Yes, No Pollyanna He[23] [His estate was at Yasna Polyana]

Young Tolstoy sampled all things male —
A taste of war, a piece of tail...
Then wrote — will wonders never cease! —
a tasty tale of war and peace.

A double escape — from both poetry and English. Tolstoy did, indeed, at least spiritually, desert his wife (Sophie) to indulge in saintly competition with God (Theo) — though he didn't get into Theosophy. And he did try to give away all their money and did, after co-producing 12 children, decide that family responsibilities were standing between him and God (perhaps preventing him and God from coming to blows). But before he became constipated with a high-fibered emulsion of rationalism and religion, he wrote his great novels, including *War and Peace*, where the muse of History (Clio) at times takes over and bores the hell out of many readers, who can't wait to get back to Pierre, Andre, Natasha and Nikolai. Who can blame them? For years after reading it (in high school), I kept meeting Pierre in my mirror and waiting for Natasha to show up. Natasha is the original of that woman in countless novels who is described as not being quite beautiful, because her bright eyes are too large and her lips too wide and sensual. It's like saying "He might have been considered handsome had he not been a bit too limber and muscular, a bit too tanned, his nose and chin a touch too strong." Read *War and Peace* to experience this classic cliché before it became a cliché. Then read *Anna Karenina*. Then you'll REALLY be pissed off with Tolstoy for getting too holy to write more such novels.

Those Too Too Tonic Nights

Fyodor Dostoevski
And Alexander Nevski
Cursed like Rasputins
At all those Darn Teutons!

Nevski, a few centuries earlier, fought the Teutonic Knights. (You've read it here, now see the movie!) Dostoevski also liked to cuss out those Germans (they represented to him the West corrupting sacred Mother Russia). And Rasputin, who took everything else to extreme — could he curse? You're darn tutin'! Our next author is more tut-tuttin', as his sentences twist like the turning of a screw:

---

[23] "Yes, No Pollyanna" suggests, both, that Tolstoy was a rather glum fellow AND that he lived on his estate, Yasna Polyana.

Henry James

One might say (yes! *do* say it) of James
That his sentences curved from their aims
Toward the fraught, but unseen,
If you know what I mean,
Like a gossip ashamed to name names.

Queensberry Rules and Soiled Stones

"Slander!" cried Oscar; Queensberry counter-sued,
Striking below the belt, the stodgy prude! —
Sued and pursued — rude! Lewd! (all this in quotes) —
On stony soil he sued Oscar's Wilde dotes.

Here's the program: Oscar, famous aesthete, poet, playwright (with wife and children), gets seduced by young Lord Alfred Douglas (that's right — the kid worked hard to hook Wilde and reel him in, not that Wilde resisted much — he was just a limp wrist on Alfred's wimp list). Douglas's father, the Marquis of Queensberry (he who decreed thou shalt not strike a blow below the belt) publicly accused Wilde of homosexuality. Wilde sued for libel, lost, then was arrested for what was, at that time, a serious crime. So if I have to say all that, why'd I write the damned poem?

While Wilde was writing the Credo of the aesthetic movement, Aubrey Beardsley was adorning the movement's covers with butt-smooth cherubs, slim witchy women, minisculely-endowed satyrs, etc.:

Macaubrey Aubrey

It gave young Aubrey Beardsley a kick
To draw fauns prepubescently slick.
Though we're not pointy eared,
We've a short prickly beard,
But thank GOD! not a wee Beardsley prick.

Since writing that, I've seen some of Beardsley's less well-known raunchy art, well-endowed with less polite, more ungentle genitalia.

While we're touching upon (but not, I hope, abutting upon) the love that dares not speak its name:

Will Housman, the Cad!, Take a House Boy?

Quoth the bard, "Dare I pester this lad?
Goodness Gracious! I could be his dad...
What AM I, a mouse, man!

As I'm A. E. Housman,
I'll HAVE him! But...no — that is mad..."[24]

Funny how favored are hard-to-pronounce poets whose names end in
that little vowel sound:

'Tis An Ilk Kith Blowth No Goethe

She likes to read from Roethke & Rilke
And their ilke.
My stuff's no kin to Rilke & Roethke,
Nor kithke.

Speaking of funny foreign names, there's the Greek bard of Alexandria,
Egypt, Cavafy:

Cavafy, TV or Mvilk?

If you don't like terse urbanity,
Cavafy's not your cuvup of tea.

Yeats — That Lovin' Feeling is Gonne Gonne Gonne

With Maud Gonne, fiercely Will Butler Yeats
Held debates — she'd rebut *all* her dates;
But, did he — as Zeus Leda —
Fill Gonne up with seed? Ah!
That riddle's for subtler pates.

Note: When everyone wants a piece of your ass, you get good at re-butt-al.

Window of Opportunity — or Getting BASIC[25]

In that poem by William Yeats,
Leda's coupling seals Ilium fates;
For from that horny swan
She takes world power on
And grows pregnant with William Gates!

---

[24] And rather sad: Who knows, he might have been glad to be had — it's all the fad to
be bad.
[25] He of Microsoft Windows fame also co-created BASIC, a synonym for which
describes what it's like to use Microsoft products: FUN? DAMN! MENTAL!

Yeats carried a torch for actress and fierce Irish nationalist, Maud Gonne. He was enthralled by her but found her politics a bit shrill (sometimes he wanted to shove that torch...), and they did debate. In "Leda and the Swan", Zeus, having gotten directions to find Leda by commanding, "Take me to your Leda"...anyhooo, having found her, Zeus took the form of a swan so he could rape her (you see the logic of that, of course) and did so, and that rape begot (begorrah!) Helen of Troy and so sealed the fate of Troy (Ilium): Troy was doomed to become thenceforth the first name of tall, trim, vacant-headed, blue-eyed, blond hair-dressers.

Later, Leda saw in a vision a palindrome that told her what to do: SUE ZEUS! Asked in court why she objected to being romanced by a god, she showed the bite marks where he held "her nape caught in his bill" and answered SWAN GNAWS. (She had those gods coming and going.)

The poem asks, "Did she put on his knowledge with his power?" Yeats liked to say things like that. He knew which side of his bread future grad students were buttered on. He was better at questions than answers, because he belonged to a strange sect that practiced automatic writing (he would only write during the *autumn* while sitting in his *attic,* hence *autumn-attic writing*), and when you're in a sect, you try to get your answers from insects, and, in Yeats' famous words, "How can we know the answer from the ants?"[26] Why this appeal of sects? Probably it's anagramatic: Incest with insects is nicest in sects.

And, speaking of beetles, the musical version of "Leda" (Lovely Leda Meter Maid — she's in a metric poem, so is, in fact, a maid made of meter — and then a made maid, or maid no more) came into existence when a Japanese quartet tried to perform "Lovely Rita, Meter Maid." This is just one of many intimate links between literature and rock 'n roll. Bob Dylan took his last name from Dylan Thomas. (I guess "Bob Thomas" wasn't distinctive enough. Someday a poet named Dylan Zimmerman will borrow Bob Dylan's name and become Dylan Bobby.) And (tada!) literature itself is named after one of the Great Black Fathers of Rock 'n Roll. (I'm sure you've all heard Literature sing "Tutti Frutti" or "Long Tall Sally.")[27]

One famous Yeats passage is a line from "Byzantium" about his failed romance with Maud, as she grew lean and bitter: "That dull thin form, Maud Gonne: Tormented she!" (Some editions have this, incorrectly, as "That dolphin-torn, that gong-tormented sea".)

Yeats also pondered ethics. How, he asked (in "Among School Children") "... can we know the can'ts, sir, from the cans?" (How can we know the cancer from the can'ts?) Yeats dreamed of "Sailing to Byzantium" and there becoming a golden bird, but gave up on it when he realized that Byzantium no longer existed, or as he so quaintly put it:

---

[26] Refers to "How can we know the dancer from the dance" — from "Among School Children." He doesn't answer that one either. The answer is, of course, to be found somewhere on the Internet.

[27] "Literature," that is, Little Richard. Deeply sorry.

Byz'ntium
Yzn't. I am.

Freed from futile dreams of a phantom city, he got down into the "rag-and-bone shop of the heart"[28] and began to talk Turkey.[29] Somewhere along the way he became the "greatest poet of the Twentieth Century," which doesn't say much for the Twentieth Century. It does show that literary critics are visionaries, since they hailed him as the greatest of the century before the century was half-past. He liked to talk about history turning in a gyre (that is, spiraling), which may be the source of the gyre that Wallace Stevens placed on a hill in Tennessee. His eloquence ennobles a kind of rueful futility, makes it stoical, full of dried-up regret for a lost glory that perhaps never was, makes it mythic, makes being part of the human world a necessary and somehow noble ordeal — all of which has endeared him to generations of ruefully futile academic poets, desperate to feel noble about the banality of their days and to know that any glory is long past — which justifies not looking further. No wonder he's the greatest poet of our century: He says our academic poets are exactly what they should be. That's OK, we all have our self-serving idolatries — why shouldn't professors?

He also discovered that a man who doesn't feel much can represent himself as a man of deep feeling by presenting his lack of feeling as the result of having felt too much, the numb poet having survived his tormented feelings much as a tombstone survives a body. He, even more than Eliot, gave us a generation of academic poets who used passionate language as a substitute for (not an expression of) passion and allusion to ideas as a substitute for thought. (Ah, but Yeats spins some fine phrases! He is, if nothing else, the supreme literary Con man of the century — a great-poetry machine in search of an evocative idea, a voice that overwhelmed a generation of "modern poets.")

Let's move to Lawrence, who both thinks and feels — to an embarrassing degree (Yeats never embarrasses anyone):

Two For D. H. Lawrence

Once a young son & lover named Lawrence
Stood and stared at his girl with abhorrence:
He cried "<u>You're</u> not my mother!
"You're so UTTERLY OTHER!"
Then he penned purple prose in great torrents.

---

[28] The main poetic device of 20th Century poetry is "of." Anything can be "of" anything else. "Corridors" can be of "your mind", rag and bone shops can be of the heart, snow can be of laughter, mountains of futility, roads of darkness, rivers of afternoon — "of" is a much over-worked magician.

[29] Turkey, of course, includes what was Byzantium, but minus all the golden birds, for Yeats a kind of cold turkey.

The hero of *Sons and Lovers*, based on young Lawrence, has trouble finding a gal who'll match Mom.

There was once a game writer named Lawrence
Whose game-keeper flaunts loudly abhorrence
Of lace, silk and satin
And dead things like Latin,
But spouts sperm and fine speeches in torrents.

This, of course, refers to the very talkative gamekeeper in *The Lady's Chatterbox Lover*[30].

Lawrentian Otherness? (An Overly Endowed Limerick)

A young maid who milked cows and fed fodder
At the sight of her breasts gave a shudder:
She glared at her bosom (for they grew some — how gruesome!)
"O why can't I lose 'em!
"They're so utterly utterly udder!"

Lawrence saw love as possible only when each lover accepts the mysterious "otherness" of the other. That is, one is the same as oneself, but other than others, or if there is only a single other, one would accept his/her anotherness. There is also the motherness of mother, the brotherness of brother and the niceness of nieces. There are several udders in Lawrence, and EVERYTHING in his work is UTTER!

James Joyce

Once a whimsical jotter named Joyce
Poured out puns with oracular voice:
"Sure, some meaning must take
"Any sound I shall make —
"For your guess is as good as my choice."

One day while the nearly blind Joyce was dictating passages for *Finnegan's Wake* to his daughter (his biographers report), someone knocked at the door, and Joyce said "Come in". Later, when his daughter read back to him what she'd written down, it included the words, "Come in". When she realized her mistake, she was about to cross out those words, when dad said, no, leave it in. After all, he'd said it, so it must belong there — magic! The real magic is, that this mammoth work, 17 years in the writing, when I opened

---

[30] That is, *Lady Chatterly's Lover*, a novel from which, when I was in high school, two torrid paragraphs were required extracurricular reading and seemed, at the time, all we knew on earth and all we needed to know.

it, magically turned into a monument to self-indulgence. It almost made even me give up punning. I would not hate it so, dear reader, loved I not *Ulysses* mucho. The moral is, writer, YOU make the magic, not the man from Porlock at the door.

Ezra Pound

That poor heavy-weight poet, old Pound,
Should have always remained underground,
For when he talked plain,
He was judged quite insane,
While his gobbledygook — "Ah! Profound!"

That is, his plain talking about economy and usury (especially when he went on the air for Mussolini) got him committed to St. Elizabeths (imPounded), while his Greeked- and Chinesed-up, polluted-stream-of-cultural-self-consciousness Cantos are deemed profound. Of course, works read by only a few are always claimed to be profound. Here's the chance to be among the elite, since so few others are going to waste their time finding out for themselves, and those months of study deserve SOME reimbursement.

But we owe Mr. Pound a great deal. He edited T. S. Eliot's "The Wasteland" and cut it to half its original length. A good start.

T. S. Eliot

There was once a bank teller named Eliot
Whose poem-scapes were rancid and smelly, yet
Quite shabby-genteel,
With a wistful appeal:
"Shall I never? Or possibly shall I yet?"

Eliot did work as a bank teller for a time. The other lines describe his favored settings and, especially, "The Love Song of J. Alfred Prufrock."

Lines Written Upon The Spurt Of The Moment

No tie can I devise
Beyond a peach's reach.
Whoever's free of ties
May dare to eat a peach.

Prufrock asks himself, "Do I dare to eat a peach?" The answer is left to the reader as an exercise. Meanwhile, let us gobble up another pome (actually most poetry isn't the fruit; it's the pits):

141

Frock You, Pru!

When Pru hocked the mocked red frock of the
prof who proofread "Prufrock", did the prof
rue through and through the Pru-hocked,
rude-mocked, red, Prufrock-proof frock?

He Had a Lock on Ness

He emulated T. S. Eliot so well that he attained
Eliot-ness. "Let us go now, you and I — come
quietly" he said to Al Capone.

You "Untouchables" fans will recall that Eliot Ness (Eliotness) was the
Fed who went after Al Capone. He probably said, not "come quietly", but
"kumquat" — he was still looking for a fruit he dared to eat[31]. And then
there's Moses' famous words to Yul Brynner...I mean Pharaoh: "Let us go,
then...". (Forgive my satirical streak. I was born in April, and, as Eliot said,
April has the cruelist mouth.[32]) I wonder, can I rhyme his entire 6-syllable
name?

A Drama — Stern?...Silly, Yet
or T S

Ah the pity of Thomas Stearns Eliot!
Even great poets — BAH! — must earn. "Sell he ought!"
"Get a trade." How the promise
Turns sour for Thomas
Whose school tie at last — Ah! — must urn sully yet.

Gertrude Stein

Punctuationless old Gertrude Stein
Tossed out nonsense like pearls before swine:
a rose is a rose is a rose I suppose all the way to the end of the line

Note: The above is a limerick in disguise.

---

[31] He needed something light to eat, as he was already a FED agent. He was watching
his diet, as described in his poem, "The Waistline." (By the way, Eliot as a federal
agent is not far off. One of his best buddies and correspondents was James Angleton,
a CIA insider.)

[32] "Let us go then" begins "Prufrock." "April is the cruelist month" begins "The
Wasteland." It might be interesting to combine these poems; for example: "April is
the cruelist month,/ when the evening is spread out against the sky,/ breeding lilacs
out of the dead land, mixing,/ like a patient etherized upon a table,/ memory and
desire...". Wow! It's a fresh new voice!

Roses! MORE Roses! NEW Roses![33]

Gertrude Stein wrote "a rose is a rose is a rose" —
No one tells Gertrude Stein when to end a clause! —
And though gen'rous, was rather morose than jocose —
She could not tolerate being sans Toklas.[34]

Yo!

Politically Correct? Not Gertrude Stein!
Although she knew not when to end a line,
No one could say that Gertrude was afraid
To call a spade a spade a spade a spade...

"Stein" means stone and "Gertrude" means spear strength — yet another poet doomed from the naming ceremony. Most of us know but the one Gertrusive (or Gertruding) line of Gertrude's (she did write a few others): "A rose is a rose is a rose." But that one line has been pure or fool's gold for parodists. That is, "a rose is a rose is a rose" is aurous. And for the masses (poor things), it is what keeps her sharp, militant name alive. Thus, a niche in time saves Stein.

Carl Sandburg

A bestselling bard, Carl Sandburg,
The tip's all you get of this landburg:
Free verse cute and simple,
And brainy as a dimple,
Outsold all but *Forever Amburg*.

Forever Amber was once a sexy best-selling pot-boiler. The once-popular Sandburg is creeping on little cat's feet right out of the poetry anthologies. He's a sweeter, less original Whitman — you might say a Whitman Sampler.

e. e. cummings

Once an *enfant terrible* named cummings
Treated visits to plain sense like slummings.

---

[33] She was perhaps morose with neuroses, which arose from viewing the world through prose-colored glasses.
[34] "*Sans* Toklas" (without her friend and lover, Alice Toklas) is also Santa Claus: She lacked a man, but had a lass — Alice and a lack! By the way, someone who can't tolerate being Santa Claus probably suffers from Claustrophobia. Stein helped out lots of down-and-out writers and artists in Paris, but not with hearty Ho-Hos.

If subjects as predicates
Give you a headache, it's
Soon you won't know your to-ings from from-ings.

e. e. cummings as Narcissus

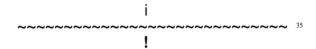

Cummings' stock seems to be on the rise. People still say they like him as if proud of daring to say it, because almost everyone hasn't found out yet that almost everyone else is also saying it. He peaked early, then plunged (too gimmicky), but he's cumming back — a second cummings! So it goes: any poet lives in a pretty who? town (with up so tenured many rejections down).

Edna Saint Vincent Millay

Ms. Edna Saint Vincent Millay
Had a muse that would bear no dillay:
Frilly thoughts turned to verse
Quick! for better or worse,
Willay Nillay and just a tad sillay.

I don't know if any of this is true. I just wanted to rhyme Millay with dillay and sillay and also get in Frilly and Willay Nillay. (I say this to protect myself, since my wife loves one of her poems.) If she wrote a horse-to-water poem, it deals, no doubt, with a stubborn fillay. Millay shows the change in mood from the optimistic Victorians to the pessimistic moderns. She writes "My candle burns at both its ends...". Browning or Tennyson would have written, "My candle burns at both its beginnings." (And the best is yet to be!) The pessimism of the moderns stems mainly from their laziness or ineptness at finding rhymes. It's easy enough to rhyme "ends," but only the Victorians or Ogden Nash could rhyme "beginnings" (My candle burns at both its beginnings,/ As the Yankees hope for two big innings). And only God can make a tree. But how many romantic poets does it take to screw up a candle?

---

[35] Cummings was fond of lower case, perhaps influenced by Fredrico Garcia Lower-case' poetry. (That is, Lorca's. Can you tell which puns were added at 3 a.m.?)

Dylan Thomas

The Guest Who Would not go Gently (or Cogently)

We have given a party for Dylan,
Enamored of the warm glowing thrill in
His voice...but it's late —
LOOK! He's pissed on our grate!
Butts, burns, booze! Our POOR carpet! The VILLAIN!

That piss-poor poet sot, Dylan Thomas,
Didn't welsh on *one* part of his promise:
He said, "Don't go gently,"
Then went, permanently,
As drunk as a fish and as squamose.

Squamose means scaly, and that's what lots of alcohol or any drug does
for you, covers you with a hard, rough, "protective" surface, which is why he
went, but not gently, after sustaining serious bottlely harm. "Didn't welsh"
— he was, of course, Welsh, and a rare bit of Welsh at that. "Rage, rage
against the dying of the light" he said. I guess he wanted an excuse to rage,
because he did his best to kill that light.

Ernest Hemingway

Papa'd faced up to death at its sternest,
But the shrinks made his memory a mare-nest:
ECT soon taught Hemingway
(Who then went the lemming way)
The importance of not being Ernest.

The shrinks at Mayo Clinic told him a little juice to the brain would help
un-depress him. (He authorized them to go ahead with the following palin-
drome: **Stun, Mayo — Oy! Am NUTS!**) Afterwards he said the ECT had
cost him his memory, and without that he was no good as a writer. So he used
a shotgun to dis-Ernest himself (a man of discernestment). Actually, I don't
find this at all funny. Not that I'm a Hemingway fan, but I think that psychia-
trists help writers even less than do critics who say "I like it VERY much —
now if you could just cut it to about one-tenth its current length..." (i.e., take
two aspirins and call me in the morning). Reader, if you are a psychiatrist
(especially one who deals in ECT or its chemical equivalents), would you
please put down this book, wet your thumb, remove a lightbulb from a socket
(with the light switch turned to ON) and insert your wet thumb?

145

Thank you for making the world a better place. I feel MUCH less depressed! (How many poets does it take to screw in a psychiatrist-bulb?)

And here is **A Brief Hello** to the author of *The Long Goodbye,* Raymond Chandler, who with Mr. Hammett did a better job (Dammit and Dash it all) of Hemingway than Hemingway did:

> He deals in dirges, not in psalms,
> This L.A. dick whom rotgut calms.
> He speaks his piece and then embalms
> His qualms beneath blue neon palms.

Hammett, of course, wrote *The Maltese Falcon*, which brings us to...

William Faulkner — With a Nod to Yeats

> His delirious prose makes you walk on air;
> On quaint folk honor off he can talk an ear:
> Thoughts all tangled unfold
> Till the sentence can't hold —
> Like a falcon that can't hear the falconer.

Faulkner (falconer) writes sentences that get tied up in knots and disentangle themselves laboriously. The last two lines are based on Yeats' "The Second Coming":

> *Turning and turning in the widening gyre*
> *The falcon cannot hear the falconer;*
> *Things fall apart; the center cannot hold...*

Apparently, when the falcon loses contact with the falconer, he just keeps falcon around in larger and larger circles, and falcon around brings us to...

The Case Of The Perried Thrust?

> Perry Mason (by Erle Stanley Gardner)
> Will exchange a soft kiss with his pardner —
> His Gal Friday, Ms. Street —
> But he never [delete
> Expletive] or puts anything hard in her.

OK, I know this is slumming for you elite literary types, but, hey! I LIKE Perry Mason — great quick reads, wooden prose, but terrific pacing and at least one character (Mason) who's rather alive. OK, OK, back to Literature:

146

Vladimir Nabokov

VlaDImir pronounced it NaBOKov,
Which rhymes with your taking a cloak off.
Most people say NABokov,
Rhyming with sob-a-cough —
They, says Nabokov, can FOKE off!

Of course, Nabokov would not be so crude, but rhymes were scarce. He did, indeed, pronounce his name as shown in line one above. Here's a poem that tries to do greater justice to a writer who, if he were to look at this book and say, "Not bad", I would not trade my state with kings, laureates or the noblest of the Nobelists:

One Ray of Light Thru the Dolorous Haze

One asks herein: Can a book offend?
Suave lad, he — merry to the end.
Ah, lowly tongues will say he's dead,
But turf lies lightly on his head.

[One asks Sirin: Can Nabokov fend?
Suave Vladimir, HE to the end.
Ah, Lolita, *Angst* will say he's dead —
Butterflies lightly on his head.]

Nabokov fended very well in at least three languages and kept a remarkably large reserve of sanity and genius to the end of his days. In *Lolita*, the title character's "real" name is Dolores Haze. Sirin (a kind of songbird) was Nabokov's pen name when he wrote his Russian novels (sheer sirindipity). And he was, besides being a great novelist (and a good poet), also a butterfly collector of distinction. I think he would enjoy these two parallel poems (he liked parallel worlds) and the fact that you could read either separately without realizing that it's only half of a phonetic siamese-twin twining. He'd say that the two line 3's don't quite chime: No matter how lightly "Lolita" trips off the tongue, it's hard to make "-ta *Angst*" mimic "tongues". Yessir, you're right — I need to work on that. (See — I TOLD you he's not dead!) Any page of Nabokov's *Bend Sinister* generates enough energy to light up entire continents of Yeats and Eliot for years. Now let me put my silly cap back on.

Sowing Wild Quixoats?

Her poems in that rough age
Most regularly ran,

Bulked up by slick roughage:
Large dollops of Gibran.

Bran is good for constipation — in this case, Khalil GiBRAN, who briefly captured a large readership with oracular Mid-Eastern-exotic sermon-poems. His poems (and those of imitators), do flow with regularity, the prophetic loftiness not much impeded by live communication or that lumpy gunky sense of someone speaking to you. I wrote the above after hearing a lady first announce that her inspiration was Gibran, then spew forth considerable watery oracularity.

Now several poems dedicated to Ogden Nash, whom I choose to value just because in a century whose greatest poet is supposed to be William-the-sober-faced-Butler-Yeats, someone should help us laugh. I suppose Charles Bukowski is a comedian, a W. C. Fields, who, hearing of the Crisis of Belief, would say, "I believe I'll have another beer". But Bukowski doesn't need our acknowledgment. He relishes rejection, gets to give us the finger. Whereas Nash was a modest gent who made no secret of his intention to amuse and wrote funny, urbane, charming stuff (some corn — whose work is never corny? Only those academics whose entire poetic is based on avoiding corn — or anything else edible) — and Nash, poor fellow, BELIEVED the critics who said he wasn't much of a poet, "just" a humorist.

Nash reveals to us that if you drop out the meter and keep the rhyme, rhyme (the more belabored and multi-syllabic the better) becomes the tool of humor. Meter and rhyme, it turns out, are not equals. Rhyme without meter is the tail wagging the dog or the bathwater without the baby. Most Nash imitators don't get his sense of rhythm. He only *pretended* to dismiss meter, then called it aside and told it where to sneak into his poems and play tricks.

Bogged In Ogden

It is risky and reprehensible and doggone rash
To become infatuated with — ugh! — Ogden Nash:
Your poems cease to be serious and rational
In dogged pursuit of the notional and Nashional.
You can't sleep with your nogden befogged-in
With hunting for rhymes odd enough to be worthy of Ogdin,
And next morning your brain's a dog breakfast and by dinner it's a
    dog dindin
From being ceaselessly a-hum with that Ogdin din,
And you devoutly wish you could, like Dorothy, say to the Wizard of
    Og:
"Why you're nothing but a humbog!"
You'd balloon back to Kansas and our culture full of fresh, raw,
    distinctive voices by the dozen with that Toto dog then —

But suddenly up bubbles another horrid rhyme that's just tootoo
    Ogthen...
And so feverishly through this wilderness of brashly flashy,
    tooth-gnashy hash
I ramble with Nash.
I'm sliding downhill fast, thanks to Ogden Nash.
I fear that neither God nor Ogd can save me from a terrible
    toboggden crash!

It Has An Air

If you'd asked Ogden Nash if his poems were worthy of the raving
    and lauding
Bestowed by critics upon Eliot, Stevens and Auding,
He'd have said, diplomatically,
    "Comparisons are odious and malodorous"
His heart the while singing with a flipflopflip, romatically,
    "Your comparison is melodious!"

Writing Nashurally

I could not love thee so, my dear,
Wirt thou without genitalia,
Nor could I write what you see here,
Were I not generally indifferent to
    Yeats, Eliot, Pound, Auden, et alia.

Oggg! — The Sad Tooth

The lady's trying to write like Ogden Nash.
She rhymes "banana" with "God's plans, so granda".
No wonder Ogden Nash is out of fash-
Ion. Worse than biting down on grains of sand — a
Rhyme like that makes even Ogden gnash!

If Your Nash Is A Rambler, Park Her

Nash
is rash,
But Parker
is darker.

    We move now from the ridiculous to the suicidal (who often end up
sub-lime):

Sylvia Plath

Ah the pity of Sylvia Plath,
Who exchanged all that pungence and wrath
For a snootful of gas
And a snooze 'neath the grass —
She was surely deficient in math.

And just what is the lesson of Sylvia?
That to kill a fine poet, you kill via
Her daddy? Ted Hughes?[36]
ECT for a muse?...
Will you then have destroyed her? You will've, Yah.

Home in the Range

Like Dorothy Parker, Sylvia
Was not inclined to kill via
Knives or poison, but, alas,
Decided she could stomach gas.

Dorothy Parker's weapons of choice for self-slaughter were alcohol, tobacco and time, but she wrote a funny poem about the inconvenience of various approaches to suicide in which she concludes that one may as well live. Sylvia, however, found a weapon she could not refuse. It's not yet clear *what* weapon she used on herself: Some say it was her husband, others her father. Maybe these were the guns. I'm inclined to think the shrink who brainshocked the hell out of her when she was a kid was the ammunition and powder. There was also the oven. And Sylvia, who is she?

Poets should not be killing *themselves*. C'mon, guys — let's get the READERS! (I've got the gas...alas!)

Spies To Despise

The one question for John LeCarré
Is *"Peccare* or *non peccare?"*[37] —

---

[36] Refers to Ted Hughes, Sylvia's then hubby. I need "Hughes" for the rhyme. I have no idea to what extent, if any, he is to blame for Plath's suicide, but since the issue has been raised in several books, it's grist for my mill. Personally, I'd rather not let such speculations distract us from Hughes' *indisputable* crimes: He's an academic poet and a laureate who has probably written nothing both distinctive and popular enough to support a good parody. He writes about predators — like sharp-eyed parodists who spring like coiled steel to skewer any squirming seriousnesses they spot.

[37] Means "to sin or not to sin," with *peccare* pronounced peck-CAR-ray, close to

As his spies probe for loopholes
Their public-school scruples
Under glass in forensic array.

From time to time someone notices that a writer has leapt out of his
genre to become literature — LeCarre, Elmore Leonard, etc. Who knows,
even a parodist may turn out to be a poet. (Usually I don't write in the genre.
I write in the john. Or if I'm working on light verse, I write in the jack. [Lofty
poets are often just johning off.])

The remaining poems in this chapter are general observations about no
one poet in particular. To enjoy poetry it is essential not to be too particular.
Actually, in the 18th Century, this was the rule: Stick to the generalities,
avoid particulars. In the 20th Century this has been reversed. It's a cycle: We
get intoxicated on our particulars, then go through hangover periods where
we sooth ourselves with abstractions.

I'm Pro Perverse (i.e., Improper Verse)

He reads blue verse to decent folk
And heats them to a simmer quick!
For he will have his little joke
At risk of life and limerick.

Our Kingdoms For Your Ears

No Nobel prize? Yet poets rate attention,
For are they not all honorable menschen?[38]

Written one year when no poet won. I notice they award Nobel prizes for
Economics — based, I assume, on the winner's ability to spell and type well?

A Gusty Gutsy Poet

A famed poet of tongue and pen aureate
Found the more he was honored, the more he ate.
It sped up his slow swell

---

peccary, a wild pig — isn't that a boar? LeCarre's spy novels replace gadgets, chases
and grotesque villains with tired, guilt-ridden civil servants picking obsessively at
their moral scabs and dreaming of redemption. His sometime hero, Smiley, only
smiles sadly.

[38] A Yiddish twist ("menschen" means men) on "For are they not all honorable men?"
from Antony's speech in Shakespeare's *Julius Caesar*, the sequel to his pre-Viagra
drama about curing the impotence of important men via homeopathy, *Homeo and
Julius, or Romeo was not Erected in a Day.*

When he won the Nobel;
Then he burst[39] on the scene as the Laureate!

The Muse And The Ms[40]

If all my words from you I've nipped,
O muse, am I the man you script?

Rhyme And Pun-ishment

As we two lay in bed,
"[Horrible pun]," I said.
"OOOH!" she groaned, "No more!"
Then came...THE KNOCK AT THE DOOR.
He neither smiled nor spoke,
The haughty uniformed bloke
Who sneered just like John Cleese,
On his badge: "THE PUN POLICE"!
Then: "Sir, are you the one
Who said [horrible pun]?"
"I did, I can't deny it,
But I meant nothing by it."
"Indeed, sir, that's just it.
Please try these cuffs for fit."

Ever And Ever Endeavor

Eternity goes on and on forever —
And on and on and on and on and never
Runs out of on-and-ons: How very clever!
For though my verses modestly endeavor
To keep on going, always I must sever
Them — this one's dying; though I try to rev her
Up again, forever will outlive her,
For forever needn't rhyme — O clever forever!

---

[39] This is the burst referred to in the old adage, "The gutsy burst non disputandem" — or, there's no arguing with an exploding poet. Another interpretation is: "The gusty burst — nun, despot, Aunt Em" — the nun, the despot and Aunt Em have all been carried away to Oz by the blast. All these are, of course, bastardizations of "de gustibus non disputandem," there's no disputing taste, which is perhaps why we do practically nothing else but.

[40] Ms is also ms, short for manuscript, or, in parlance of the Ms., "personuscript."

Those Moldy Oldies

Must we fit the classic mold?
All that's literature is not old.

Porn Free

In my school days we read no dirty poems —
No open talk of sex in schools or homes.
We went though bootleg porn with fine tooth combs,
While skimming literature from fine couth tomes.

The Inuit Knew It

How sad to be a Minnesota poet —
As lost in snow as any Eskimo, yet
Can say but little of it — or ignore it,
Poor Anglo, with but just the one word for it.

Refers to that old anthropological study that claims the Eskimo (or Inuit) have umpty-ump words for snow. Your humble parodist was born and bred in Minnesota, which is why I'm a man of few words.[41] Actually, since I'm unknown, my name, not yet a household word, is a word of few men. Or, in plain Minnesotan: Whatever.

Dog Mad Him!

A crude dyslexic poet — he's so wayward! —
You'll find no poem of his that lacks the "k" word.

If you just thought of the "f" word, don't blame me. This is a religious dyslexic, so the "k" word could be the Biblical "knew," as in "Adam knew Eve"…Oh, wait, that would be the "w" word…

He Was Ill-Ulyssesed

Each madman's epically mad:
How odd is he? It's the ill he had.[42]

---

[41] Actually, we Minnesotans have many words for snow, including, "Oh shit!" and "Not again!" and "I'm going back to bed!"

[42] "Odd is he," "Ill he had," that is Odyssey and Iliad. Many claim our oddities stem from the ills we've suffered. Reader, each of my puns is a cry for help!

The Same Old Dance

You critics demand subtlety: "A poetry of nuance",
Which interferes with happiness — or thereof my pursuance.
Nuance Nuance Nuance — you're giving me carbuncles!
Why not toughness, pungency — the odes of our old uncles?[43]

Sex and the Single Meaning

Tenderly we couple, becoming one, but double in tenderness.
This mystery I cloak in word play, lest making a pair one amaze you.[44]

Artichoke: Pretentious assumption of the attitudes of writer's block.

A Prayer for Victims of Sorcery

Too oft the muse proves Circe,
Turning poets into swine:
"O! Ink! Oink Oink! Have mercy!"
We cry line after line.

We're penned by our own hand.
Open us up, O pen!
The sty — that is the man[45]:
Be more than man, Ah, men!

O Ink! Oink!

Long may satire's lens
Shame those who swell too big:
God help us if the pen's
Not mightier than the pig.

---

[43] Old uncles and old dance being opposites of new aunts (nuance). Sometimes the critical insistence on subtlety masks a fear of simple truths: How can we know the new answer from the nuance?

[44] Translation: "double in tenderness" — double entendre-ness; "pair one amaze you" — paronomasia (pun). Many have punned "pun" (puny punishment, etc.), but I may be the first (and last) to subject paranomasia to paronomasia to describe the phenomenon of paranomasia.

[45] I don't recall which French critic said, "The style, that is the man." I used to know. Terrible thing for a punster to forget names. It was Stanley, following the Nile in search of Livingston, who, feeling he had conquered the river and made it a part of himself, said, "The Nile...that is, the Stan."

154

Section 2: Poetry from Contented Forms

Chapter 4: How Can You Get 'em Back on the Form?

A Few Mo' *Mots*

Rhyme and meter, rhyme and meter
Go together just like Paul and Peter —
Grampa said to Papa,
"You've got to learn to do it propa."

The poetic fad is to omit punctuation, a futile attempt not to be comma-tose.

I prefer poems in fixed forms: They never go into heat and run away.

See my new rhyme?
It can stop on a dime!

When formalists cease free verse to damn,
Then shall the line lie down with the iamb.[1]

Why all these poems with short lines? Because art has no "use." Thus there
is, for poetry, no right justification.

Should a poet write to the past? —so many people live there. But only because
poets aren't creating a future for them.

A poem is a one-way valve: You enter
at the beginning. In one line you will
leave. Already you cannot go back.

Readers are such a bargain —you can get them for a song!

Ah, but a poet's reach should exceed his grasp,
Or what's a metaphor?

Writing poetry is like fingering a Flute: The air flows through, resounding,
not waiting for the fingers to position themselves. Quick! put the right words
in front of this feeling!

The first line should grab you.
I'm the second line — it's not my fault.

---

[1] Whereas the most common rhythmic unit of formal metrical verse in English is the iamb ("to BE" is an iamb, a relatively unstressed syllable followed by a stressed syllable), free verse poets often treat the entire line of poetry as the unit of rhythm, while rejoicing in the blood of the iamb.

Chapter 4
How Can You Get 'em Back on the Form,
Once They've Seen Free Verse?
or The Sound of Muse Ache
or A Funny Thing Happened on the Way to the Form

Scarcely a day goes by when one of my readers doesn't write to ask me, "Dean, what's a sestina?" or "Dean, please explain the fallacy of imitative form." And, of course, these are important questions, for what is form but the cookie-cutter of Civilization imposing its homely domestic shapes (stars and gingerbread boys) upon the raw, savage dough of our ranting. Form and content (mostly now on computer disks) — Civilization and its disk contents.[2]

In this chapter, I will provide an introduction to several key forms of poetry traditional in Western verse. (Another chapter deals with a Japanese form that has sprouted in America like one of those foreign weeds with which the home-grown flora can't compete — a form called kudzu...sorry, haiku.) But first, let us define the word "form" more clearly: It is a place from which one speaks, as in a public market or tribunal. Thus, in Rome, Senators would address the masses from the Form. It is also a kind of organization which promises security, but, once one becomes entangled with it, one may find it hard to escape — as shown vividly in John Grisham's best-selling novel about a young poet on the run, *The Form*. (Yes, form can be a harsh foreman.) Form is also a kind of intoxication, an addiction, a process in which your words undergo formentation. This is why it is so important that every poet have at least a rudimentary grasp of formaceutical issues. (Formaceutical: From "form a cuticle," since form, like calcium, strengthens your poetry, gives it a hard bony structure.) And form can provide sharpness and bite, as

---

[2] Referring to Freud's *Civilization and its Discontents*. What's behind civilization? Freud says Id's not what you think. Freud's attempts to find clinical or surgical evidence of the existence of an id failed miserably, leaving him babbling: "Look! Open this guy! Id's a bird! Id's a plane! Id's SUPER-ego!"

in the case of formic acid. But enough dreary definition. Let us view some forms in the flesh, as it were.

The following poem not only demonstrates the nature of one of the most popular forms in English poetry[3], but also shows how that form decayed into undisciplined free verse in recent decades:

Le SonnEt La Furie[4]

How primly rhymed pentameter sets out
In perfect ranks, plumed hats and gleaming brass,
Marching to thumping drums across trim grass
To put the ragged noisy mob to rout
And...oops — WATCH OUT! Who threw that brick? A shout!
Hold ranks! Duck! Keep in step — but watch your ass!
We'll show this rabble!...Lord, but what a mass
Of life is this! It surges all about
Each syllable — the meter cannot hold!
Now it's breaking, words stumble from the ranks,
bloodied feet fall out of step,
rhyme drowned in the din of revolt
falters falls
      look there! On either flank
hordes of
  words
     loose

  characters
       dart an

  d leap

Note: The ending only looks like chaos. In slight disguise, it continues the rhyme scheme: hold/ranks/step half-rhyme with revolt/flank/leap. The meter is also a bit less disheveled than at first appears. It loses a beat when it falls "out of step." Whether this says something in favor of free verse or not, I leave as an exercise for the reader.

---

[3] The sonnet, a poem in 14 iambic pentameter lines with a choice among several rhyme schemes, that typically introduces a theme in the first eight lines (the "octet" or "octave") and resolves it in the last six (the "sextet"). Many sonnets sum up with a witty rhyming couplet as the last two lines. It's also something you do on the *bottom* line in Georgia — you sonnet (sign it). Sonnets are often twisty, condensed and difficult, maybe because in the earliest sonnets, the lovers addressed (e.g., Petrarch's Laura) were about 12 years old, an incentive to keep one's meanings veiled.

[4] The sound and the fury or the sonnet, the fury — with the hint that it's all the result of something the poet *et.*

Next we see a less radical shift in form, from the strict rhymes of early sonnets to sleepy half-rhymes of a soporific form (also called "slant rhymes," because the sonneteer is reclining[5]):

Sonnet Les Matines, Ding Dong Bell

The sonneteer in apple-green pajamas,
Rolls over onto his belly, groans, then snorts
("ICtus![6] OCtet![7] SESsss...tet..."[8]) — Hark! He farts
("Petrrrraaarch!"[9]), then falls to dreaming of enjambments.[10]

Curled up now on his side, he sweetly rests,
Swells up, subsides to slow iambic[11] breathing
Until, with prose-grey wraiths of dawn light writhing
Through literary shades, he turns and twists,

Clutching to catch at slumber's dragging foot,
To make her stay till he can find a line
To make sense of his dreams and also rhyme
With something...he's forgotten just what, but

He wants a finish sunlight's glare can't spoil...
DING! DING! — Foiled by the clock's barbaric peal!

————

Next, the sonnet carried *ad absurdum* (Latin for ridiculous ad — this sonnet is entirely self-advertisement) — a double sonnet that uses only a

—————

[5] Actually "slant rhyme" and "half-rhyme" are among several names for various types of partial rhyme. Time and Dime are full rhymes. Tome and dime rhyme partially (the same final consonant sound), as do time and dine (same vowel sound, similar consonant sound). There are also sight rhymes, like pear and fear, and pious rhymes, like "I curse your **luck**,/ You stupid **fellow!**

[6] Ictus is a stressed syllable — needs a vacation.

[7] Octet: the first eight lines of a sonnet, or a very small Oct. which hath only 30 days — no Halloween!

[8] Sestet: Last six lines of a sonnet. Why do all these words end in "et"? Is there a larger form called the sonn where the first eight lines are the oct, followed by the sest? I've had it with sonnets! Let's go enjoy a barbershop quart.

[9] Petrarch: Italian sonneteer who wrote sonnets to his dreamgirl, Laura; one glance from her could straighten out the arch of his peter (or Peter-arch).

[10] Enjambment: run-on line, no pause at the end; not the condition of being in a jam. For example, in this poem, "...dawn light writhing/ through literary shades..." is an enjambment — no pause between "writhing" and "through", which, by the way, is a soft way to say "writing true."

[11] Iambic: Meter made up of iambs, where an iamb is an unstressed syllable followed by a stressed syllable, like "reJOICE" — or what your cheap ballpoint may say if you ask it to identify itself: "I am BIC!" Since each such pair of syllables is one iambic "foot," I call this a footnote.

159

single rhyme, and multi-syllabic at that — for 28 lines. Eat your hearts out, sonneteers — or shed a sonnet tear:

Sonnet to the Max
(A Max Sonnet[12] Production?)

Why do I think I have to write a sonnet?
Why do I think and think and think upon it?
Shakespeare and Milton and Donne have already done it;
Now hordes of genteel rhymesters overrun it —
So why must I? What can it be but vanit-
-Y? There is naught that's new beneath the sun: It
Has snob appeal, like wearing a bon ton bonnet
Or knowing Monet from Manet and not saying "Monnet".
It's made to last: It sets your words in granite,
Like tombstones or marriage — but I'd rather Don Juan it,
Foot-loose and fancy free, 'oclast O'th' icon. It
Ill suits me to be ever like lawyers on law nit-
Picking. What eggs me on? By God! I'll shun it!
The sonnet makes me vomit! I SPIT upon it!

But if I ever choose to write a sonnet,
In spite of all my carping, to condone it,
Once started, I won't stop, but on and on it
Will tick away, out-rhyming rhyme and reason! It
will show them! I'll pentathlon it —
Make an Olympic event of it! I'll flaunt it!
Rhyme it to death! At last make it a non-it!
I'll write it in one sitting in the john. It
Won't even put my legs to sleep; then down it
Will flush, bye-bye, all gone, gone gone...I'll yawn; it
Isn't a blonde or brunette or Madonna. It
Is how you write if you're someone's maiden aunit.
But can't I save it?...TOSS it! Oh! Doggone it!
I CANnot! Look! I've done it! A double sonnet!

To fully appreciate these and most other traditional English forms, it helps to understand rhyme schemes and metrics. A typical rhyme scheme in a sonnet is ababcdcdefefgg, easily remembered as follows: "Abie, Abie! See de seedy ee-ef-ee effigy — Gee!" (No, there's no word "ee-ef-ee" — do I have to do EVERYTHING for you?)

---

[12] Didn't Mack Sennett produce scads of old-time slapstick movies? Or is that the *other* Senate?

Some critics distinguish between audible rhymes (words that sound like they rhyme) and visual rhymes (words that LOOK like they rhyme on the page.) Here is an eye-twisting poem to explain the difference (should be read rapidly):

Compearisons Are Audious

A pear should be a peer,
Or so it would appear,
For we should fear, not fare,
To eat a pear, not pare.
Who dears to eat a pear?
And yet to eat a pear
Will disappear a pear.
A pear's shaped like a tear.
Therefore who pares a pear
Is one who tears a tear.
A pair of pearly pears
Defeats my weary ears.
But what did weary Peary
Wear? — of peril wary,
Of bears perhaps grown leery.
And Dr. Timothy Leary —
Did he drink bear or beer?
This bare bear buried here —
Bear berries to his bier.
He'd hear if he were here.
Then pare a pair of pears;
They're Pere's, not merely Mere's.
The end is coming near —
Or so it would appear
Upon this peerless pier
If there were merely here.

Metrics is a more difficult subject. It has to do with "feet" (groups of syllables) and "stresses" (syllables pronounced with more stress than other syllables — one stress to a foot or you get fallen arches). Here's a poem that demonstrates that the words "If you start" are a perfect example of a dactylic foot (IF you start), an anapest foot (if you START) and just about every other kind of poetic foot a critic or poet can fit in his mouth without getting his tongue stuck permanently in his cheek:

How To Put Your Foot In It

We'll all dance the hokeypokey
If you start with clumsy trochee.[13]
What do you think the impact'll be
If you start pertly and dactylly?[14]
Will your beat banish sense as we ban a pest scourge
If you start with a hectic'ly anapest[15] surge?
You'll sweep the rubes right off their ham-thick feet
If you start out in strong iambic beat![16]
How do we scan — since we're so smart —
That simple triplet, "If you start"?

Most English verse (since Westerners are notoriously competitive and egotistical) is based on a metric unit called the "I am" or Iamb (no relation to the little lamb that Mary had). It ends in an unpronounced "b" because of a famous Greek admonition to poets: "B Silent!"[17] An iambic unit or foot consists of an unstressed (technically, "laid back") syllable followed by a stressed (or "Type A") syllable, for example, "helLO" and "reJOICE". The meter of the line is further characterized by the number of feet in a line, most often five — thus "iambic pentameter" (that macho free-versers would prefer to call "anemic panti-meter") — as in all the sonnets above. As those free-verse debunkers of meter might put it (if they could write this well):

Confined to ancient forms — Oh woe is he!
He suffers from cerebral poesy:
And yet he'd rather fight (and count) than switch:
ticTWITCH! ticTWITCH! ticTWITCH! ticTWITCH! ticTWITCH!

Of course, not all traditionalists keep good time. Some can't even keep step to their OWN drummer. To see the iamb at work in its utmost purity, here is a poem written in iambic monometer (as in the title, below: "Look, Monometer!") — just one foot per line:

---

[13] Trochee: a stressed syllable followed by an unstressed syllable, like POet or APple. FRIgid, CHILly and Icy are called "cold trochee."

[14] A dactyl or dactylic foot is a stressed syllable followed by two unstressed syllables. What'll start your line with a bang? A dact'll.

[15] "...apest SURGE" is an anapest foot, two unstressed syllables followed by a stressed syllable. So how come the word "ANapest" is a dactyl? Hungarian poetry is written entirely in Budapests.

[16] "the RUBES," for example, is an iambic foot. Why are they called "feet?" Because poets would count them on their toes like piggies, an early form of digital computation.

[17] Plato, in his *Republic*, is very nasty to poets. He calls us liars. Seems to me I'm an idealist, just like Plato, but *I deal* in lies.

Look, Ma! No Meter!

I'm in
A jam:
Enjambed[18]
Iamb.

I who
Discreet or[19]
Tight-pent
Am, meet her

And pray
This gamine
Will sate
My famine

In rhyme[20] —
But put
In it
My foot

And find
That I'm
Too tight
To rhyme.

A rhy-
Min' am-
Ateur [21]
I am.

Obviously monometer is cramped. Tetrameter (four-foot lines) are more common, but tend to fall into an easy jingle (each line breaking into two neat bits, daDUM daDUM — daDUM daDUM) called "jog trot", most suitable

---

[18] Enjambment — syntax carries from one line to next without pause — e.g., "I'm in/ A jam:" But I toed you this before — "toed" because this is another footnote, part of our study of Anklish lit. and rather arch. The iamb jam here may be toe jam.

[19] The extra unstressed syllable at the end ("or") makes it iambic with a "feminine" rhyme — a 2 syllable rhyme like "meter"/ "beat her," the idea being that women always drag along extra baggage. See "famine in rhyme" later in this poem — you'd be there already if you had skipped this footnote.

[20] "Famine in rhyme" — feminine rhyme (e.g., "famine" with "gamine").

[21] A rhymin' amateur — or a rye monometer — which sounds like a gadget for measuring how badly you've been stricken with mono.

for humorous verse, though some poets overcome this limitation[22]. I, for example, overcome it easily by TRYING to be funny, a sure antidote to humor, or sometimes I just forget to be funny, as in the second of the following poems:

Reading, Writing and Rhythm — a Tic

And ONE and TWO and THREE and FOUR —
Tetrameter's a deadly bore;
Free will's dreamed up by fools like me,
But only four can follow three.

Jog Trot Home

Now I'm going to write in rhyme.
Tap your feet — help me keep time.
What I'll say I still don't know —
Let's see where this form can go:

Its beat is strict and very dense;
My words must make a lot of sense
To stand the stress, lest form get sick:
A speaker with a rhythmic tic.

The first line usually comes easy;
The second's just a little queasy.
The third begins to look about
To find the fourth a sure way out.

Four-square, bumpy, jog-trot quatrains[23]:
My skittish muse is chafed by taut reins.
On this old rack I'll learn what form meant:
Perfect pearl of an oyster's torment!

I'm listening to a string quartet;
They call it "Late", but it has met
Me always right on time. If strings

---

[22] What limits iambic tetrameter is the way each line tends to break in two even parts. A natural pause inside a line of poetry is called a "caesura." Iambic pentameter is capable of more subtle variations than iambic tetrameter partly because there are more places to put the pause. In tetrameter, it nearly always comes at the dead center of the line — too obvious, makes for singsong. Thus Shakespeare explains the use of pentameter in muting and modulating the jingle of tetrameter: "We come to bury Caesura, not upraise it."

[23] A quatrain is a four-line stanza or poem or else a rainfall that doesn't make much noise.

Can learn to sing, so can anything.

I'll teach my tone-deaf days a tune;
They'll dance to the beat, leave clock-crutches strewn
On closet floors. With work I'll earn
The right to play — if strings can yearn.

The moving finger having writ,
Becomes a thing, like a nose or tit.
Song in bits of string lay dormant
'Til Ludwig taught them what a form meant.

Beethoven couldn't eat or shit,
But made taut fingers move and writ,
And still they move, for I am moved
By a moving disc, finely grooved.

Needle or finger, gently moved,
In a surface intricately grooved;
The finger-tip itself is such
A record: music of your touch.

These poems, my finger-prints, smudge time,
Leaving at the scene of the crime
My fine-grooved record. Reader, play me;
Your pointed vision can free me, say me.

Living is the only crime.
Having lived (and left a rhyme),
You've served your time — the world forgives,
Not knowing that art — the scoundrel! — lives.

We cut our lives, fine spiraling grooves,
In time. Each star, each wavelet moves
To the music of our universe.
Galaxies sprout where we rehearse.

We make this universe our record —
Leave our music or our wreck-hoard.
Are you phonograph or singer?
Slave or maker? Mover or finger?

The music is there, but you can make it:
Contribute to the motion — fake it!
The sooner you learn to sing along,

The sooner you'll know who makes this song,

And having turned your fears to song,
One day you'll ding and wait for the dong,
And while you wait, there'll be no sound,
No stars, no earth...aha! You're found!

While you wait, the world will become
Your waiting; when you sing, the dumb
Numb void turn tongue. The God who hovered
Over chaos has been recovered.

Now it's *your* song. Sing it *your* way.
We have worked; now let us play.
Each dogg'rel his day: After much muse ache,
Even I will turn to music.

It's time for me to go to sleep —
I pray my poems my soul to keep;
If Dean should die before I̲ wake,
I pray my poems my music make.

Before English poetry became mainly "anything goes", not only son-
nets, but numerous other forms with origins in Provence or Italy, took root in
English, among them the villanelle, triolet and sestina. The villanelle was
once so prominent that the progress of English poetry might be described as
the progress(?) from villanelle to willy-nilly. Modern poets, if you hear the
bell tolling, ask not for whom. It is that villain-knell tolling for us. Perhaps
these old forms require a lofty inspiration that our world refuses to provide.
After all:

Not just any John Doe
Can compose a rondeau

and:

Clinton and Gore inspire no villanelle:
A single couplet serves for Bill 'n Al.

Here's a sad villanelle about the condition of poetry today, followed by
two stabs (both fatal, though not serious) at triolet and a sestina that tells you
exactly how to write a sestina (just connect the six dots...over and over):

166

The Night Poetry Died

The night poetry died I was out of town.
I simply couldn't believe it when I heard!
No mention in the papers, poor sad clown,

For poetry was not a proper noun.
We'd thought he'd never die, doting, absurd.
The night poetry died I was out of town.

Grass green, sky blue, and you-know-whats were brown
The day he died — and since (I mean a t-u-r-d).
No mention in the papers. Poor sad clown,

They say he drooled all down his hospital gown,
Gibbering — no one understood a word
The night poetry died. I was out of town.

Who knows just when he died? With frozen frown,
For years from breath pumped down the tubes he stirred.
No mention in the papers, poor sad clown.

The children take it well — the laurel crown
They soar at quoits.[24] My old nightmare occurred
The night poetry died — I was out of town.
No mention in the papers, poor sad clown.

    The key to the villanelle is the repetition of lines one and three at the ends of alternating stanzas, until, at last, at the end of stanza six, they come together, a great relief to them no doubt. Villanelles and triolets call for lots of rhymes. In the villanelle, for example, you have to get though 19 lines (or 13 if you don't count repeated lines) with only two rhymes. That's easy in Italian or Provencal (more rhymes available in strongly inflected languages where word endings reveal each word's function in the sentence, as opposed to relatively uninflected languages like English, where function in the sentence is revealed by sentence position), but not so easy in English, where even the words insist on each going their own way, probably in protest of the Normal Conquest. The triolet is at least helpful, in that it can be pronouced either trio-let or trio-lay, thus doubling my chances to rhyme it (and increasing my rhyme interest rate).

---

[24] Odd, because most poetry these days is quite unquoitable.

167

An Obscene Triolet

Here goes! An obscene triolet —
I'll even put you in it!
For you're no shrinking violet;
Here goes! An obscene triolet;
I'll write while on the toiolet —
It won't but take a minute.
Here goes! An obscene triolet —
I'll even put you in it!

Triolet Trio Con Brio With Frijole Omelette

I call this verse form tree-o-lette —
Though some say "try-a-lay".
"WHO? WHO dares" cries a tree-owlet,
"Not call this verse form tree-o-lette?"
Soft twilight, blue to violet...
Good time to try a lay —
But I call this a tree-o-lette,
Though some say "try-a-lay".

Some call this verse form try-a-lay,
A tiny trial or trial-lette,
Not perverse, like a trio-lay,
So call this verse form try-a-lay —
Three cheers: Olé! Olé! Olé!
T'ree Olés! Whee! Oh let
Us call this verse form try-a-lay,
No trial at all, this trial-lette.

Let's compromise with try-o-lette.
("Tri" — three: we call it t'ree.)
A little lay? Try a layette?
Let's compromise with try-o-lette.
"God only makes a tree-o-lette" —
Let's shun Tree-o-latry
And compromise with try-o-lette.
("Tri" — three: we call it t'ree.)

How to Write a Sestina...if you MUST
or Six Sestina Words — Line Pattern? Crisscross![25]

You must know how to count at least to six
If you would try your hand at a sestina —
Pore through your lexicons to pick six words,
For these comprise the end of every line;
And then you have to understand the pattern,
Which some describe as "retrograde criss-cross."

That pattern is the heavy wooden cross
You have to bear: This line must end with "six"
Because line one's last word (to keep the pattern)
Must end line eight; and since the word "sestina"
Concludes line two, it also ends the line
Before the line just ended; then the words

That end each stanza are the selfsame words
That end the lines that start the next — they "cross,"
You see. And thus the end of every line
In every six-line stanza — there are six —
Must be one of these words — SIX — hence SESTina —
Then stanza seven, three lines, where the pattern

(Mid-line words join end-words so that the pattern
Contrives to cram in three lines all six words)
Resumes first-stanza sequence. Thus sestina
Provides both repetition and that criss-cross
Sense of spiraling change toward (after six
Coiled stanzas) a return, the final line

Like coming home...but, ah! We've crossed the line —
Each stanza twists the spiral uP A TURN.
Can cocCYX count as six? Or if one SICS
The dog...? This form's for *words*! We're after *words*!

---

[25] This sub-title contains the six words that end each line in the first six stanzas. The formula for a sestina is as follows: If the lines in the first stanza end with the words A, B, C, D, E and F (respectively), the lines in the next stanza end with F, A, E, B, D and C. Stanza three runs the same play on stanza 2, and so on. When this is done to the end words of stanza six, the words return to their original order. Stanza seven has only three lines, with word A near the middle of line one, word B at its end, word C mid-line two and so on. Why, you may ask, would anyone want to write such a thing? Well, academic poets like to conceal their meanings, and what better trick for concealment than the old shell game, as, nimbly, we shift end words? And what is more natural than in*cest in a* tight, cliquish group of poets.

A very serious form — don't make me cross!
Sestina! Not "Sex Life of PrinCESS TINA"!

Keep this form pure. We've had inCEST ENOW
With sonnets, haiku — *here* let's hold the line
("Can you please hold?") *Bad* end words! Don't CAROUSE
So! Keep it simple; get it all down PAT: EARN
Your sestina badge or else cross sWORDS
With one who of your trifling whims grows SICK! S-

-olely a return to baSICS can SUSTAIN AWE.
Would that to gimmicks we WERE DisincLINE-
-d, content to gaPE AT URNS[26] — how ludiCROUS!

———

Now we're moving into less familiar forms — or foreigms, first, a limerick that is also an example of a nonsense form called "Kyrielle" (not to be confused, unless you want to, with a serious form, also called "Kyrielle"). The point of a Kyrielle is to enforce a rhyme by sheer mayhem, as, for example, by rhyming "month" with "the one th-" where the next line begins "-at". In other words, "the one that", where "that" is a victim of unwarranted entering and breaking. This form might also be called "Fun With Hyp hens."

Can I Carry A Tune? No, But I Can Kyrielle Limerick

I love the Procrustean[27] Kyrielle,
Infectious as ailments venereal:
Nothing rhymes with oblige,
But by G-eorge! Today I j-
Ust may do it - at least I in theory'll!

The greatest Kyrielles are by the German poet, Schiller, often called "Kyrielle Schiller" for his masterpiece, "Silence of the Iambs" with its haunting villain, Hypocrite Lecteur.[28] I don't know why the form is called "kyrielle" — perhaps because upon reading one, the reader is apt to cry out *"Kyrie eleison!"* which means "Lord, have mercy!"

---

[26] Alluding to Keats' "Ode on a Grecian Urn," a *serious* poem by a poet very much in urnest.

[27] Procrustes should be the patron saint of poorly written formal poetry. He's the fastidious host who would amputate or stretch his guests to fit the iron beds he provided. He should also be the patron saint of current American education, where, if the teacher is boring, we drug the children to make them look attentive.

[28] The serial killer in *The Silence of the Lambs* (novel and movie) is Hannibal Lecter. "Hypocrite Lecteur" (meaning hypocritical reader) is what Baudelaire calls his reader. T. S. Eliot recycles the phrase in "The Wasteland." Sorry for all this Schilliness…not.

A Persian form called the "ghazal" (pronounced GAHzzle, not gahZAHL) has been immigrating to the U.S. in recent years. Its rules include repetition of the final words of line one (here, perversely taken as "t'a ghazal" from "wriTE A GHAZAL") in every even numbered line and inclusion of the poet's name in the last couplet. I get bored with repeating the same words, so, of course, cheated in the following example:

Interesting Challenge, But

I'm much too tired now to write a ghazal.
I wonder what's upstairs to bite, to guzzle...

Crunching crisp cars, treading towns to rubble —
Godzilla tries with all his might to Godzil.

A long necked goose can goose — they reach that high —
And goslings reach, I guess, the height to gosle.

We Jews at times are inclined to feel unwanted —
I, for instance, if I go at night to Gaza'll.

Pardon my verbal leaps, but, impelled like impala,
My couplets fall apart in flight — two gazelle.

Will nothing stanch this pun-infected oozing?
Here, if you wind it thick — and tight, too — gauze'll.

"Keep your day job," the editors all chorus,
"Put away your gaudy kite to go sell."

I'm tumbling off Parnassus[29] — catch my hand!
Whew! Pull me up now! (What a plight!) TUG, asshole!

Ghazal's a noun, but I'll let ghazals Dean
If ghazals will grant Dean the right to ghazal.

A short poem is a small "reading" — or "readicule". Now we progress from small to minuscule or from the readiculous to the sub-limerick. One day, looking for a challenge, I decided to see if I could write palindromes (e.g., the name "Otto" or the famous "Able was I ere I saw Elba") that were also poems. Ideally, one could read the poem and not even notice it was a palindrome. Here's one that, apart from the giveaway "O", comes close to

---

[29] Parnassus is a Greek mountain sacred to the muses, a place for successful poets (sort of like *The New Yorker*). I was thrown off Parnassus. Why? Obviously because of a bad pun...Asses!

what I aimed at (Note: The entire poem, excluding the title, is the palindrome, not individual lines):

Self-Defined

One "me,"
  man — O not mood nor event;
    I, awed, AM; emit DNA edition...
      no "I," tide-and-time-made;
        wait never
      on doom to no-name me,
  no.

You think that's EASY! Hey, let's see YOU fit "time and tide" and "no man" and "wait never" (with the allusion to "time and tide wait for no man") into a grammatical palindrome along with a bit of pseudo poetry as pat as "emit DNA edition" (a pretty fancy way to say "procreate"), and still say something that makes sense: I'm not a man or a mood. I AM. I'm not the DNA thing with the name, not — as a spirit — the victim of time and tide, nor can any doom destroy my name, since I have no name. See! Ain't that GOOD! Can I have my A now? (It's even better backwards!)

Here's a poem about the palindrome as a form:

When In Palindrome, Do As The Palindromans Do
(O do! O do!)

"Madam, I'm Adam"
"Able was I ere I saw Elba"
"A man, a plan, a canal — Panama!"

Clever verbal contortions, merely...and yet
there's a hint of mystery, as if,
behind our backs, our language were trying
to tell us something (WOOF! O OW!) — for example,

that while we pilot our bodies and our world
from past to future, other beings, much like us
(if rather backward) are propelling
the same bodies and world the other way,
so that when I say "Able was I", and travel
half a second nearer death, the one who shares me
(passes me going the other way, knowing
as little of me as I of him) loses half
a second of experience as, saying "I saw
Elba", he approaches my birth — his

172

enwombing. My passions are jokes to him
and vice versa — "Ah! Oh!" one says, the other
snorting "Ho! Ha!" "Live!" rejoices one,
approaching innocence, as "Evil! cries the other.

Hence the mystery of palindromes: These are the
moments when our two opposite worlds become
dimly comprehensible to each other, blips
upon each other's radar in time's darkness:
When I say "When I say", my counterpart says
"yas I nehw" or perhaps, "Ya, sin ehw".
If meaning lurks — that touch of sin, eh? —
I can make but little of it. But when I say,
"Star!", he (or eh) says "Rats!" — and THAT
I can make sense of, and when I say "Able was I
ere I saw Elba" — MIRACLE OF MIRACLES! — he says
"Able was I ere I saw Elba" — Ah! Able was I ere
I saw Elba — Ha! Oho! *Mon Frere! Mon Semblable!*

Briefly we have become one — our worlds, our destinies
one! Briefly we defeat time, grow younger even as we
age; dying and borning cancel out for a timeless
instant...and then we speed on, tightly bound
in our opposite tenses, as our mutually
incomprehensible tongues, like inept poets,
    yap ONWARDS! — draw no pay.

I wrote a few hundred palindromic "poems", but this collection is only
for poems about the act of poeting, so I will give you only these few palin-
dromes on that subject. I've found that readers either love or hate these things
— not much middle ground, though haters do find the short ones more toler-
able. (My wife hates them all! Though otherwise we mesh so well: Pamela,
male map!) If your gorge is rising after a few, please skip to the last page of
this chapter. Or return this book, including your lunch, to the publisher for
full refund...of your lunch. Again, the poem(?), not including the title, is the
palindrome. Also, the title of the T. S. Eliot palindrome is, itself, a separate
palindrome:

Clever Poet Doesn't Delve Deep, but Burns Bright

No enema tube —
    but a "ME", neon!

Critic's Lament

We fret:
So few senile lines we foster! —
    few...

Newt Announces Attack on NEA

Strategy: Get Arts!

Ridiculing The Notion That A Conspiracy Existed
To Hide The "Fact" That Bacon Was Shakespeare

La! Bacon bard? Pardi! Rats!
O my ASS! Essay: Most arid rap —
DRAB! No cabal!

Petruchio Wakes Kate[30], Not Sure How She'll Respond

Dame...Mate, take Mocha —
A moral aroma — Ah! Come, Kate...
Tame? Mad?

In Poetry Despair Equals Profundity

He gabs agony — no gasbag, eh?

P.U.! T. Eliot, Old-Aged Eliot — Fell! —
Left Oiled (Egad! Lo!) Toilet Up!

One poet, ah! — T. Eliot — was *fine* poet;
    Odd id — DNA? — but was —
        O! Holy "mot!" — ANAL! —
          Anatomy? Lo! Ho! —
             saw tub and did dote, O pen!
            If saw toilet — HATE!
               (Open? **O!**)

In the following palindrome, George Herbert, known for poems shaped like altars and angelic wings, attempts a palindromic poem in the shape of the cross:

---

[30] The main characters in Shakespeare's famous drama of American politics, *The Shaming of the True.*

**Saint Despises Mocking Secular Law, Communion Polluted
by Worship of Pleasure, Idolatrous Adoration of Symbols
and Vanity, Pledges His Life to Christ and the Faith
That Can Pass Through Walls**

<pre>
              O   reviled
              evil   droll
 "law", Dei-fed!   How one deified — fie! — Id!   Rood?
 O Dei-fed, deified Rood!   O Temple! — Ho! Nosh! Peso!
              Jesus-sent,   I
              witness,   USE
              Joseph-Son, O
              Help met! — O
              Door   deified,
              defied — O do
              or   die!   "If",
              de-IFied enow —
              Oh defied wall!
              Lord,   live!
              Deliver!   O!
</pre>

**Her Response When Tired Of Hearing
That Her Breasts are White Doves,
Ripe Peaches, silken pillows, etc:**

Metaphor? Oh, PAT 'em!

The next seven palindromes are plot summaries from Greek works:

A Classical Drama

La! It's Electra — art celestial!

Eely Proteus Escapes Menelaus and Taunts Him

Hey, Menelaus — unusual enemy, eh?

Orestes, Free of Furies, Goes Off Quickly, Alone

At Attica, tacit Orestes — no onsets erotic; a tacit tata.

Dead Iphigenia Speaks in a Vision to Clytemnestra

I was no belle. Hot set Agamemnon on me, Ma —
Gates to Hell, ebon, saw I...

Seeing How Many Have Died Because of Paris' Infatuation, Diomedes Hates Trojan Women

O he, Paris, lived for 'em. May I not! O I, Diomedes,
abased 'em...O idiot! On I yammer of
devils I rape — HO!

Aeneas Struts Before His Men, Singing of Arms and the Man

O did I do Dido? I, Dido's Aeneas — *Aeneas!* O *did* I! O
Dido did I DO!

Queen Gets Too Involved With Leader of Trojan Survivors

Did Dido on Boss Aeneas (Troy orts, Aeneas — S. O. B., no?)
OD? Id did.

Shakespeare, too, can be palindromatized:

Caesar's Last Words: "Does Rome Support This?"

"Et tu, Brute...et urb ut te?"   *[You, too, Brutus...and the city
with you?]*

We can save a lot of time by palindroming our literature. For example, wouldn't you rather read the next three palindromes than the works they summarize: *Dr. Jekyll and Mr. Hyde, The Scarlet Letter* and *The Hunt for Red October?*

Dr. Jekyll Justifies Becoming Mr. Hyde

Man am I? Oh who lives timid stifles!
I die, wane! Volcano IS.
REVERT: Rape! rut! — part rapture,
part reversion, a cloven awe:
Id/I/Self.
It's dim, it's evil — Oh! —
who I, man, am.

Hester Prynne Stands in the Sun, Rues Adultery and Child out of Wedlock, Wonders Who She's Become

Is it I? Tis I — Oh! — who's, alas, unmade!
I fret sin. I'm...O Sun! Oh crimson Ma I!
Red "A" vexes bosom! O sob!

176

Sex evader I am? No smirch on us, O Minister?
FIE! DAMN us! Alas!
Oh who is it? It is I!

Sound Track: The Hunt for Red October
[Note: Radar off to avoid pings alerting "Ivan"]

Mum! Level...(deep song)...No speed! Radar ON,
Navigation? NO! I tag Ivan — NO RADAR!...
(deep song)...No speed...level...mum...

To avoid a few more examples of palindrome poems, shun the chapter on haiku — which come from Japan, not Ukiah.

Palindromes take time to read — both ways. Here is an even shorter form: Poetry is said to make all things new. What we call "the news" is the OLDS (Famine here, how many killed there, who's afraid of the big bad bomb...). Poetry should be published as news. Here are sample headlines:

**PLAYBOY PRINCE POPS POSER: TO BE OR NOT TO?
SOMETHING ROTTEN IN DENMARK SAYS SCION**

**FLASH: JAP MONK WITNESSES LANDING OF
SMALL GREEN ALIEN IN OLD POND: SPLASH!**

**RECORD DROUGHT — HOPES DIM FOR
WESTERN WIND AND SMALL RAIN**

**PRUFROCK DARES TO EAT PEACH...
CORRECTION: PRUFROCK DOESN'T**

I end this chapter with headlines, the form for the future, a headline being as much poetry as attention-strapped web-junkies are likely to be able to absorb. I call upon all those who would preserve the great poetry of the past to join me in the immense project of reducing our literature to headlines. The form has at least one great virtue: One doesn't have to use the shift key at all. At last a form that a keyboard-hopping cockroach could entirely master.[31] Cockroaches, our likely successors as dominant species on this planet, could thus carry on our great work. Also, we like to say that poetry should be timeless. Certainly a poem that takes almost no time at all to read is approaching timelessness. Will poetry run out of time? It may if we don't do something about it. So repeat with me, abba cddc...

---

[31] That's why archy, the cockroach narrator of Don Marquis' *archy and mehitabel* (1927) wrote only in lower case — he couldn't hold down the shift key. We humans are hard on cockroaches. At our approach they scurry away. We've got them scared shiftless.

177

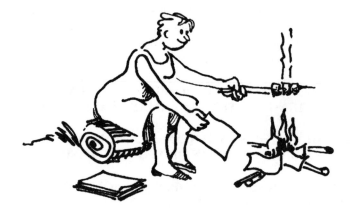

Pam editing the Palindromes

Section 2: Poetry from Contented Forms

Chapter 5: Softe Coo Haiku!

A Few Proverbs and Anti-Adjectives

Next on "All Things Being Equal":
The poetry imbalance between the United States and Japan,
or how the Japanese are winning the real war.

The Perrier of poetry: "It is good...but it is not haiku."

"I like this haiku — but I'd like it better if it were just a few lines shorter..."

The poet pointed
somewhere else, but my eye stuck
on his jeweled ring.

Easy to write lots of poems: I don't throw back the little ones.

A short poem should be an event, like a flamingo lifting one leg
and putting it down.

Spring:
the start of too many poems
and too few changes of heart.

When every other word's an adjective or adverb, the nouns and verbs cringe
and complain like children being dressed up for a party.

Chapter 5
Softe Coo Haiku!

HaiKU![1]

Leapeth frogge
And splasheth bogge —
Softe sing haiku!
Adjective droppeth,
First person croppeth,
Softe sing haiku!
Bright leaf soarth high —
A butterfly![2]
Softe sing haiku!
Trembleth blossom
Quite ad naussom —
Softe sing haiku!
Haiku! Haiku! Softe coo haiku!
Haiku! Haiku! Haiku!

"Sorry to be so short with you,"
said the haikuist.

This chapter deals with the delicate art of haikuing and such related subjects as haikuism, haikology and haikolatry. Haiku is, of course, a Japanese form, but English-language haiku have become a thriving industry within

---

[1] A takeoff on a medieval lyric, "Cuckoo": "Lhude [loud, with hint of lewd] sing cuckoo," where the cuckoo's song suggests spring and the likelihood that some husband has just been cuckholded, probably because cuckoos lay their eggs in other birds' nests, much as Japanese haiku poets have laid their literary runts in Western nests — that is, nests for the West ern, a very ernest bird that lays its eggs mainly in Grecian urns.

[2] Haiku poets frequently are astonished to discover that petals or leaves are really butterflies. But only Joanie Mitchell has tried to turn war planes into butterflies. Ugh! Stubby shit-brown butterflies!

the vast American poetry cartel. Here are some questions and answers designed to clear up the many misconceptions that have accumulated in this country about the haiku form:

1. **Are haiku always exactly 17 syllables long?** No. They grow longer during the heat of the afternoon and shrink in the cool of the evening. The seventeen-syllable requirement is not set in concrete: Haiku are still syllabic, not slabic. But the 17-syllable form (three lines of 5, 7, and 5) is the most common, as explained in the following classic by the great DeanOH!:

> Samurai poet
> with pen skewers seventeen
> silly bulls...MU sound.

Note that "mu" is a Zen concept. It is often defined as "nothingness," that definition followed by many paragraphs that explain how it isn't really "nothing," just not "something," which is closely akin to the Greek concept, "mu pi," or, in plain English (pardon my French), cow pie.

2. **Must every haiku include a word to indicate the season (or "seyasonu worodu"), and if so, does it count against the syllable limit?** Yes and yes, but it needn't be as obvious (and disyllabic) as a season name (like "summer"). Thus, for example, "frost", "ice", "Tiffany", "witch's tit", "of" and "the" are all words traditionally used to suggest the winter season, while "crisp", "harvest", "rake", "wild geese", "tooth decay", "toilet paper", and "moreover" are among the many indicators of autumn. In the following examples, the obvious season words are actually unnecessary, the season in each case, being conveyed by other words in the poem:

> Spring. The old horse
> vomits on the baby sparrow
> after nibbling cherry blossoms.

[Season words: "on", "vomits"— both suggest spring.]

> Winter. Old crow
> on a bare branch reading
> the Wall Street Journal.

[Season words: "Wall Street Journal" suggests the frigidity of winter.]

> New Years. My little
> daughter wants more rice cakes.
> With my axe I chop her to bits.

[Season word: "Chop", demarcating the new year.]

And of course, this tradition gives some an unfair advantage:

No seasons
in L. A., which shortens
my haiku.

We have cats, dogs and
urine smell in every season
of the haiku.

The haiku has
many seasons, all of them
Nippy.[3]

3. **What is a death poem?** The Japanese are a very poetic people. For example, when they crash their planes intentionally into a battleship, they are not crazy; no, they are "kamikaze" or "divine wind". When they fart...but you get the idea. This national poetic sensitivity is displayed in the tradition of writing a death poem (usually a haiku) shortly before (well duh!) death. Here is an example from Lord Bozo (with Bimbo, Boozin and Dumbo, among the great thanatographists or death writers):

Sting of winter air —
Bah! Show you something sharper?
Sigh! An arrow!

Note that "Bah! Show" is a hidden message to his contemporary, Basho, whom he acknowledges to be "something sharper" than himself; also note that the last line is his way of saying "Sayonara".

4. **Can true haiku be written in any language other than Japanese?** No — *true* haiku cannot be written in any language at all, for haiku transcends mere words. Language is but the tea bag dipped into the seething water of individuality to produce the subtle infusion we call haiku. "He who speaks, knows not; he who knows, speaks not." Haiku represents a Zen moment, wherein... [We've had to cut this answer short for lack of space. For further understanding of how haiku transcends language, please refer to R. H. Blythe's four-volume work on the subject.]

5. **Can haiku be understood outside the context of the Zen experience of Satori (enlightenment)?** Yes, for haiku can also be grasped in the context of the Yogic experience of Samadhi. As the 69th Zen Patriarch aptly remarked, "Everyone love Satori night and Samadhi morning." Basho expresses his view of Samadhi in the following classic haiku:

---

[3] For the deplorably young among you, "Nip" was a nasty word for Japanese during WWII — from "Nippon," a Japanese word for Japan, which, economically, was nippon at our heels, though lately they have fallen nippon hard times.

Samadhi —
Over the rainbow
bluebirds fly.

Note: In this haiku Basho is said to have achieved Toto enlightenment. A friend points out that Basho expressed his hope for salvation as follows: Samadhi/ my Prince/ will come.

6. **Is it true that all haiku express an absence or emptiness of self, a transcendence of the competitive, ego-based dualism of most Western poetry?** Yes, as is beautifully expressed in the following first-prize winner in a recent national haiku contest:

Ha ha!
My leaves fall better
than your leaves do.

7. **Can haiku express personal human suffering?** Yes. For example, in the following highly personal classic, Issa poetically expresses his frustrations: As water commissioner of his village, the frustration of finding all his resources frozen; and more deeply, the disappointment (after finally marrying at age 82) of discovering himself impotent:

Frozen river —
little horse can be led to it,
but not made to drink.

8. **I keep hearing that, in haiku, the perceiver becomes the perceived. Please explain this.** Let's let one of the masters of haiku explain it — again, the great Issa. In the following haiku, Issa, viewing a rose, contemplates the breaking down of distinction between subject (Issa) and object (a rose), achieving Satori in the final syllable, where subject and object unite. This haiku is also a classic Zen Koan (or riddle), named after Zen Cohen, Len (or Leonard) Cohen's younger brother.[4] Zeonard became a Zen master (during the Meshugganah Shogunate) after giving up guitar, having immobilized both hands with repetitive motion syndrome after years of rapidly closing fingers upon palms in an attempt to hear the sound of one hand clapping. But I digress. Here is Issa's haiku of convergence:

---

[4] Students of Zen are said to meditate for months on a "koan" such as "What is the sound of one hand clapping?" Leonard Cohen was erected in Canada, but taken down by Suzanne ("Suzanne takes you down/ to a place by the river..."). Since he is sometimes considered a poet, I should have written about how you can lead a horse to a place by the river and give him tea and oranges, but you can't make him drink. It might conclude: "If you don't drink, I'll have to shoot you, but, hey, that's no way to say goodbye."

A rose?...Issa?...
rose...Issa...
    Rose!

        [Translation from the Japanese by G. Stein]

9. Isn't a haiku just 17 syllables of nature description? No! No no NO! It is more — so MUCH more! In haiku, nature's presence points to a razor-keen crest of awareness of... — well, here is how the great haiku poet, Snupei, expresses it:

Dark and stormy night —
not one creature is stirring,
not even a mouse.

Snupei tells us he wrote this while sitting on the roof of his tiny house, having earlier talked to his only friends, the small birds who alit at his feet unafraid, and with whom he shared the last crumbs from his bowl. It is all in those few syllables, his spiritual isolation that somehow unites him with all creatures great and small so that his dark and stormy despair becomes a "good grief", as he waits for the sun to rise and life to stir in the mud-red, barren landscape in the shadow of his "Master's House" (for Snupei was a very religious poet).[5]

10. Must haiku always approach the non-verbal? Verbs are OK. Just go easy on adjectives, adverbs, articles and first-person pronouns. Especially eschew first-person pronouns. For example, don't say,

Trees hung with ice.
No one cares about me anymore.
I am not happy.

Say rather:

Trees hung with ice.
No one cares about Bob Dole anymore.
Bob Dole is not happy.[6]

---

[5] Snupei is, of course, Snoopy, the creative dog in "Peanuts." Hence the "red barren landscape" (Snoopy often dreams he's a WWI pilot hunting for the Red Baron) and so forth. When Snoopy decides he's a writer, his stories always begin with Bulwer-Lytton's famous lead-in, "It was a dark and stormy night...". Note to my fellow pseudo-intellectuals in high school: I still say "Pogo" was a lot funnier!

[6] In case this book is being read long after Bob Dole is otherwise forgotten — say, five years from now — he, like many politicians ("You won't have Richard Nixon to kick around any more") often spoke of himself in the 3rd person. Presumably this is because so many politicians are sick of being themselves, Bob being particularly doleful.

185

Some poets rebel against this prohibition. Here is an opposing view:

Against Haiku

Clear fall day;
even the evergreens
want to change.
No, no, this won't do:
I want to say I.
I want to want.
I have no damned seasons.
Nothing is precious
but what can come out and play
with me.
I am no more a lie than spring.
I can say I seventeen times.
It is I who wants to change,
not evergreens.

11. **Can haiku deal with social and political issues?** Of course, although usually haiku-length poems emphasizing social issues and human relationships are called "senryu". While today haiku and senryu are considered separate genres, originally they were simply different regional pronunciations of the same phrase, "thank you." Both began when the first English speakers came to Japan and offered gifts to the people (beads, digital watches, etc.). The Japanese gave, in return, short poetic notes of gratitude inscribed with exquisite calligraphy on painted scrolls. These notes, the Japanese called (after the English) "thank you notes" or "t-hankyou". In Eastern Japan, the natives called these "haiku", as in "Haiku velly much!" In Western Japan the pronunciation was, first, "sankyou", then, "Senryu velly much". To further complicate the picture, in Western Japan, the natives pronounced another English borrowing in such a way that it sounded like "Haiku", as in "Haiku and the horse you rode in on!" or "Haiku! You AhSo!" This led to much misunderstanding and eventually a bloody war between Eastern and Western Japan, when an Eastern lord said "Haiku" (or thank you) to a Western lord, who, misinterpreting it, took offense. But I digress. The following haiku, by Boffo (who called the form "sicku"), shows this form used to comment on the human condition — by contrasting the harmony of the seasons with man's inhumanity to man (usually based on misunderstood pronunciations), while yet showing how nature assimilates that inhumanity, as the ocean swallows a droplet of rain:

Full summer moon,
hushed crickets. Over Hiroshima
a large mushroom cloud.

186

The difficulty of dealing with human issues in haiku form may be better understood if we simply replace animals with humans in familiar haiku, for example:

The old pond.
A lawyer jumps in.
Sound of splashing.   (better "Sound of cheering")

Autumn.
On a bare branch
sits an old lawyer.

In Basho's originals, a frog leaps into the pond (not a car pool) and a crow occupies the branch (not a branch office). The closest thing to a lawyer in classic haiku is the scarecrow, who in many haiku is out standing in his field, threatening crows with little more than a suit.

12. Many argue that 17 syllables is too long for an English-language haiku, that Japanese haiku in translation seem padded when rendered in 17 syllables. Is this true? Possibly. "Basuboru" (or baseball) is NOT a two-syllable word in Japan. Basho wrote (according to some translations):

The old pond —
a frog jumps in:
SPLASH!

but in Japanese, it's 17 syllables, because Basho, a hippie (into Zen, you know), used lots of hippie "cutting words" (a term for the Ohs and Ahs and Ah-So's of traditional haiku) — "cutting" because Basho was a Nippy Hippy. A full literal translation (doing justice to all 17 syllables) reads:

You know, this old pond?
Well like this frog jumps in, right?
Like, Oh WOW! **SPLASH**, man.

13. Must a haiku be witty or aphoristic? Must it deal only with lofty or picturesque subjects? No to both: Haiku is a direct pointing at what is. Aphorism is a distraction, a blurring layer of conceptualization interposed between viewer and nature and is to be avoided or touched upon by the most delicate allusion only. And haiku is at home with the commonplace, frogs, scarecrows, taverns, but treats these subjects so that they become, somehow, part of a totality and the expression of that totality. Thus, for example, in the following classic haiku by DeanAh! (DeanOh!'s grandmother), we see a girl making soap in the spring, stirring the pot full of wood ashes and bones, aware that she has no lover. The smells from the pot are so strong that she can't smell the cherry blossoms. This poem combines many traditional elements of haiku, but in an unexpected manner. For example, the usual swooning over cherry blossoms, associated with spring and young love, is here undermined (and yet suggested) by the homier pungence of soap in the making:

> Spring soap-making:
> Lye, fizz — not a beau. Love?
> Cherries — hard to smell.

Adding to the richness of this vignette is its evocation of an ancient Zen aphorism, which you may hear for yourself by pronouncing the last two lines carefully (excluding the last three words).[7]

14. **In the West (e.g., Wyoming), we often think of poetry, especially formal poetry, as a difficult, painstaking art. Are you trying to tell me that something like "The old pond, a frog jumps in: SPLASH!" is poetry? My 3-year-old can do better than that!** Basho's classic loses much in translation. First of all, the last line is better translated, not "splash", but "sound of water" or "water sound" or, more profoundly evoking its deeper Zen significance, "auditory manifestation of a deep penetrating impact with the aqueous surface." Second, Basho was only TWO years old when he wrote it (so there!).

Thirdly and finally, it is a little known fact outside Japan that in Japanese, the traditional haiku must be, in addition to all other requirements, a perfect palindrome. That is, it must read the same backwards and forwards like the sentence "Able was I ere I saw Elba" or the name Otto. It is this bi-directional form that gives the haiku its timeless quality, for its beginning is also its end, like the great serpent that swallows itself.

This is VERY difficult to achieve with any degree of spontaneity in English. Here are three noble, but alas, failed attempts at full palindromic translation:

Who Leaps Into The Old Pond?

> Is "I" true to Basho?...
> Hero Frog? I'VE vigor, for...eh? —
> Oh saboteur — 'tis I.
>> *[Basho concludes that it is HE who leaps into the pond and sabotages silence.]*

---

[7] For the exceedingly pun-impaired: "Lye, fizz — not a beau. Love? Cherries" strangely suggests (by most delicate allusion) "Life is not a bowl of cherries." (My jokes are either so good or so bad that explaining them can't harm them.)

188

Gentle Issa Is Charming, But Perhaps
Not For All-American He-Men

Was I ass? Inane?
Meek? Nay! O no YANKEE men —
An ISSA I saw!

*[Issa, a very gentle poet,
realizes he lacks that
Yankee toughness.]*

Consummate Artist, Buson Refutes Critics

Eh? Bad-rap Buson at arts!
  "Buson — no substrata..."
No sub-par dab, he!

*[Buson is sometimes said to lack the
depth (or substrata) of Basho, but to
paint surfaces.]*

As you can easily see, it is almost impossible to produce a truly traditional haiku in English. Palindromes are easier in Japanese, with all its reversible exclamatory vowels (e.g., Ah So! O Sha!). The Japanese have always, after all, been rather backward. As Kikaku says of the klutzy Subaru Van: *"Subaru, U R a bus!"* Later, chiding his rival, Buson, he adds, *"No, Subaru, U R a Buson!"* Issa later exclaims, *"A toy! O! Toyota!"* Sober Shiki bitterly replies, *"Nissan — a van as sin!"* (Shiki yearned for the ancient traditions and considered sinful all attempts to be in the van.) Issa's retort (typically, accepting the sin as his own) is: *"In Issa, Nissan: I!"* Buson, ever the optimist, tells of his spring motorcycle tour: *"Was I Yamaha dude? Dud? Aha! MAY I saw!"* After a religious experience in which he realized that all such spring pleasures were illusion or "Maya", he rewrote this as *"Was I a Yamaha dude? Dud? Aha! MAYA I saw!"* As usual, Basho gives us the ultimate Zen summation: *"I saw race car; race car was I!"* (It is indeed fortunate that these particular palindromes could be thus translated into roughly equivalent English palindromes.)

Nonetheless, even in Japanese, the palindromic requirement makes haiku FAR more difficult than any Western form. This aspect of haiku has, hitherto, been held secret from notoriously lazy Westerners lest they lose interest in the form. You have driven me to indiscretion with your impertinence.

15. Is it possible to modernize and Americanize the haiku in theme and setting? Certainly. For example, why not deal with the immutable seasons of the air conditioned business world:

Summer — at full speed,
talking on the car phone — LOOK
OUT! IT'S A....

You see, work has its own seasons: Superbowl season when you jump into the old office pool (sound of money changing hands), end of fiscal, first quarter, etc. — personally, first quarters are my favorite, that smell in the recycled cubicle air of new money; all the tight little customers slowly unfolding like spring buds; and, stretching above us, reaching almost out of sight, our quotas, ah, yes! And end-of-quarter, the shredded memo that turns out to be the report you worked on for two weeks; the boss giving you a bad, unfair review — Ah so! Third quarters, too, have their special tang, the crisp directives, all the changing part numbers... why are there no business season haiku? For example:

> First Quarter — short-staffed
> branch office; an old salesman
> squawks.

While some traditionalists feel that America must be saturated with traditional haiku, featuring cherry blossoms, frogs, temple bells, scarecrows and some sort of bird called a hotogisu, at the opposite extreme are those who feel invaded:

Why this American dotage on haiku? Are the Japanese
reading and writing sonnets? No! They won't TOUCH
our huge gas-guzzling, chrome-blazing, tail-finned
Western poems, while our poetry mags are flooded with
cheap compact efficient haiku. Americans! Fight the
poetry trade imbalance: READ AMERICAN!

Now that the most commonly asked questions have been answered, to further clarify the range of haiku, here are some haiku and haikuesque poems (Hiccups? Lowku?) that deal in some way with the nature of haiku:

Perceiving a
phenomenon, I respond with
a certain feeling.

> Hanging to five sounds
> by one hand, I swing to the
> seven line and back.

Four a.m. — wide awake,
I grab for a sonnet,
catch a haiku.

The next several poems are all tributes to Basho's seminal haiku about the old pond into which the frog jumps:

190

Basho Bashing

Plopping into a pond —
Who knows what that frog meant?
How can you tell the sound
Of a haiku from a fragment?

> What a subtle satorist was Basho,
> Who, while watching a bullfrog, sneezed "Hasho!"
> In frog and pond fashion,
> These met with a splashin',
> And "Ah So!" said Basho, "My gosh O!"

Old circle
Triangle jumps in
An acute sound.

> The new highway —
> a frog jumps out...
> squish.

(Note: A more proper evocation of the Zen spirit of this poem requires, in place of "squish", "the sound of the rubber hitting the road with frog intervening" or "sticky macadam sound".)

"We accept only
PURE haiku..." — kerplunk in the
old wastebasket.

> Old circle —
> a triangle falls in!
> Sound of circumscription.

The new movie —
Titanic goes down;
Water sound, water sound, water sound, water sound...

> The old pond —
> my wife jumps in...
> **SPLOOOOOSH!**
> Where did the pond go?

The middle-aged husband —
a chip dipped in sour-cream-onion jumps in,
a handful of peanuts leaps in,
three dipped corn chips jump in,
a piece of cake and two cookies and three
carrot sticks (to propitiate) and a bowl
of vegetarian chili and four curry puffs and
two more dipped chips and a finger full
of frosting from the side of the cake tray
and a glass of sparkling cider hurtle in...
    no sound...no sound...no sound at all...
      BURRRRRP!

**To be Followed by the World's Greatest Disguise Artist —
The Butterfly That Looks Like a Leaf! — but First...**

"And now, ladies and gentleman,
the world's most remarkable frog
will make his time-defying leap
into the old pond! Drum roll...
SPLASH! He's *done* it!
Good show, Basho!

    The next four poems allude to the many haiku in which what appears to be an autumn leaf or petal turns out to be a butterfly:

I mistook that butterfly
for a leaf. All us haiku poets
are nearsighted.

            Autumn. Words too blue
            for ink flutter off the page —
            a poem!

Chuang Tze just flew across the yard,
dreaming that a poet on a lawn chair
mistook him for a butterfly.

    This gives a Haiku twist to Chuang Tze's dreaming he was a butterfly and finding it so vivid that later, as Chuang Tze, he wondered if he might not be a butterfly dreaming itself Chuang Tze.[8]

---

[8] Chuang Tze was Chinese, not Japanese, a great Taoist writer. This poem is too wordy for haiku, but IS a twist on the "mistaken butterfly" theme of many haiku, the second most common mistake in literature, the most common mistake being that of all the Americans who mistake 17-syllable nature descriptions or 17-syllable ANYTHINGS for haiku.

Basho Magoo

"O see! That red leaf...butterfly!"
"Oops! Drop it! — a SNAKE, not a stick!"
More myopic with each passing tick,
If I'm not doomed untimely to die
From the bite of a poisonous stick,
Then, Basho, Buson, just like you
I'll turn my mistakes to haiku —
Leaf to butterfly's sure a neat trick!

But a stick for a snake's a mistake
Of the sillier sort that they'll take
For a joke in *Boy's Life* — kids will laugh
Themselves sick at the poisonous gaffe
(Unlike Pharaoh, whose staff were his servants
Till Aaron turned staves into serpents,
And the Queen's servants could only gasp
When Cleo cried out "O! My Asp!"[9])

Well, blindness has ever to Vision
Been kind — and as kind to derision.
If the eye chart shows three and I get a four,
I'll make poems of it — else what's a metaphor?

The remaining poems in this chapter are probably here for some good reason:

Toccata and Tanka for Kikaku

Mischievous Kikaku, it is said,
wrote that if you tore the wings
off a dragonfly, you'd have red
pepper pods.

That, said Master Basho,
is not haiku. Haiku would say:
Add wings to pepper pods and get
dragonflies.

---

[9] Cleopatra's asp was on her breast, not her ass, and came from (and put her into) a hole in the ground. But first, she addressed it as an old friend. Cleopatra might, thus, be considered one of the few queens who ever KNEW her asp from a hole in the ground.

Sagely (and Blythely[10]) nodding,
the critics pass this tale down to us,
and its moral: Poetry should fly.

(And so, I suppose, should pepper pods,
red ones, at any rate.)

To this extent I agree:
Any sadistic brat can tear the wings
off a dragonfly,
but only the imagination
can attach wings to a pepper pod
and on them soar.

> A poet! Tear off
> his wings and you get a critic
> or a scholar.

> Now that's poetry, for who
> Could tear the wings off a poet?

Note: The last 5 lines above almost constitute another Japanese form, the tanka, lines of 5, 7, 5, 7 and 7 syllables. "Tanka" is how the natives of Southern Japan (who wrote longer thank you notes) pronounced "Thank you". Imagine the confusion! It made the Japanese want to "renga" the necks of the English. (Note: "Renga" is another Japanese form...)

Song Sung by Basho at the Funeral of his Disciple, Kikaku
(to the tune of "K-K-K-Katy")

K-k-Kikaku, K-k-Kikaku,
You're the only Haik-k-ku poet we adore!
K-k-Kikaku, K-k-Kikaku,
Sorry you're not k-k-k-kickin' any more.

———

> Poor tulips bloomed
> into a frost. Froggie
> instructs them: Bud Wiser."[11]

---

[10] R. H. Blythe's four-volume study of haiku is a classic reference on the subject. For a four-volume classic reference work, it's unexpectedly fun to read — unless you expect four-volume classic reference works to be fun to read.
[11] Where's that water sound (FLUSSSHHH!) when you need it?

On the toilet, trying
To write poems....I keep
Picking hair off the floor.

Reading haiku: "The
old pond..." — startled by the sound
of turning the page.

Spring walk, trying for
poems. "Wordy wordy wordy"
scolds a cardinal.

I need a fine-edged
probe to touch the sweetness in
this pain: Haiku, please.

Clothes in the dryer —
perma-press, just time
to write haiku.

I stop typing.
A clear autumn night. I wonder
who my neighbor is?[12]

From across the bed,
a hand: The bed acquires
a skyline.

Dream Haiku

She'd wake up clinging to fragments
of haiku lost with her dreams,
so she began to keep a notebook by her bed
ready for things that go

Boomp boomp boomp baboomp
boomp boompity boomp boomp boomp —
Ah! boompity boomp!

in the night.

---

[12] This is a twist on a famous haiku by the originator of the form, Basho. He wrote centuries ago, when people still knew who their neighbors were. He wondered, instead, what his neighbor was doing. In our day, you could lie drunk and bloody by the roadside for days before you found out who your neighbor is — especially if you don't carry an insurance card.

Final note: In this chapter, the names Basho, Buson, Issa, Shiki and Kikaku refer to actual, much admired haiku poets, R. H. Blythe indeed left us a magnificent study of haiku, and occasionally the "facts" related above bear some tangential relationship to what is elsewhere recorded (for example, the discussion of dragonfly wings and pepper pods), but the great "DeanOh!" is responsible for all of the poetry (if any) in this chapter except the famous frog poem by Basho (in italics). I leave it as an exercise for the reader (or perhaps it has already been done?) to produce versions of Basho's frog/pond haiku as written by Henry James (a 2-page version — "A diminutive watery gleam which, while scarcely meriting the name 'pond', yet, in its quiet fashion was not without a certain fluid *je ne sais quoi*..."), William Faulkner in *The Water Sound and the Fury* ("Not a leap, no, nor a convulsion of amphibious joy, nor...") and from Ernest Hemingway's *The Old Monk and the Pond*: "It felt cool and good. It had been a good splash."

196

Section 3: How Poetry Is Done

Chapter 6: Bone and Blood I Love You

A Few Pithy Epithetth

"Go ahead, poet — you're ON! Say something to the reader."
"Wait! Can we start over? One more chance? I wasn't ready..."

*Some poetry animates, some puts to sleep. Much poetry is transcendental
medication. Or, since it combines numbness, boredom and bits that make one
wince, call it "trance and dental medication."*

*...to where the evening lies spread out upon the sky like a reader etherized on
a page...*

*As usual, I'm torn from a New Yorker poem by the overwhelming magnetic
pull of the cartoon on the next page.*

*Modern poetry has its own music: A huge mass in "Be flat", mostly minor,
ending, typically, with an anti-heroic cliché promising "I'll be Bach!" (again
and again).*

*Language is an ecology, as rich and complex as a forest; each year, we add to
the list of endangered words.*

*"What is your purpose in writing these poems?" I must be doing well if
someone thinks I do it on purpose — so much poetry these days looks like an
accident.*

*I'm writing poems in order to communicate, said the modern poet, paradoxi-
cally.*

Solipsism is OK, but keep it to yourself.

A civilization dies when its dreamers think they must sleep to dream.

Imagine! Someday we'll be nostalgic about anti-neo-post-modernism.

As ye sow so-so stuff, so-so shall ye reap (a SO-boring experience).

Iowa — famous for creative writing programs and corn.

*Fine poets are worse than shrinks, knowing enough about the spirit to be
dangerous.*

Not shock, but teach gently to connect.

Chapter 6
Bone And Blood I Love You
or How To Become Yet Another Fresh New Voice
In American Poetry

...in which Dorothy, the Cowardly Lion, the Brainless Scarecrow and the Heartless Tin Man are joined by the Unpublished Poet, who hopes that the Wizard will grant him a fresh new voice.

Testing...

Sometimes my poetry is very experimental.
This poem, for example, is experimental:
After I'm done writing it, I'm going to watch it
and see what happens...

The Latest in Fashionable Muses

This line was written by my right brain,
this one by my left brain.
This line was written by my left little toe,
this one by your right shoe.
This line — I'm not sure who wrote it — either my ass
or a hole in the ground.

Here is the best kept secret of modern poetry: How easy it is to qualify as a "fresh new voice" and get all the girls and/or boys. The rules are numbingly simple. Several distinguished (or is it extinguished?) academic poets mailed me death threats (very catty) when they heard I was going to reveal these rules to you here, but they can't stop me. As the vet said to us after fixing our feline, the bag is out of the cat, for here they are, just for YOU: a few simple rules that, if you follow them diligently, will allow YOU to make millions in the poetry market (at home in your spare time), just like me:

How Poetry Is Done

You can make any sentence poetical
by mentioning blood or bone.
For example, instead of **"Yesterday
I went to the store,"** say **"Yesterday
I went to the blood and bone store."**
Instead of **"The moon rose,"** say
"The blood moon rose" or **"A bone
of moon rose"** or, best, **"A bone
of blood moon rose."** For **"I love you"**
try **"Bone and blood I love you."**
Bone and blood are instant intense.
For profound, add in an inapplicable
abstraction, such as "geometry" or
"calculus," or a scientific reference
like "hologram" or "ecology," and
throw in a juicy verb. For example,
**"The geometry of blood laments
this hologram of bone."** But intense
and profound are not enough. You need
an ironic (hip) sense of mortality, as in **"Chanting
its inevitable theorems in every fatty cell,
the geometry of blood laments this
fading hologram of bone"** except that
"theorems" makes too much sense
with "geometry," so change "theorems"
to "charade" (not "singsong," which
makes too much sense with "chanting").
This gives us a satisfactory
Twentieth Century poem written
in a fresh unique authoritative etc. voice,
especially if the line lengths
are a bit weird, for example:

> **Chanting
> its inevitable charade
> in every fatty cell
> the geometry of blood
> laments this fading
> hologram of
> bone**

Entitle it **Collage #7** and send it
right out to a very little magazine
or anything that ends in "REVIEW."

Gently, Schmently — Just Go!

Many Twentieth Century poets are inconsolable
over the death of Daddy. Some of these poets
are dead themselves, and still they grieve
the death of Daddy. Often their poems begin "My Father
[simple preterite verb] [simple symbolic action combined with
vaguely pretentious modifier]".
Let us begin some Twentieth Century
passion-packed poems:

My father fished in wormy seas.

My father wore his wingtips thin.

My father swore in spasms of blood.

My father ate his rancid peas.

My father chewed his roast beef fine.

From these deceptively simple beginnings,
we learn of a child's fascinating tendency
to be very small when fathers are very big
and to have been deprived
(by the sudden absence of the real father)
ever of the means to be certain that,
indeed, he/she has now grown up. Something
like that. Anyway, we can't help but admire
the discovery that such passion can be generated
merely by adding one unstressed foot
to "Your Mother wears army boots" (make it
"bruised army boots") and changing "Your" to "My"
and "wears" to "wore", to achieve the pathos
of "My Mother wore bruised army boots",
which can be improved only by making it more mythic
("boots of war") and changing "Mother" to "Father",
because Mothers are usually moaning loudly at their children
for years before they die, while Fathers are stuck
with having to be strong silent role models
whose sufferings must be spoken for them
by infinitely sensitive poet-offspring.
Thus, from the proto-poem, "Your mother
wears army boots" we may derive the essence
of fashionable line-one lyrical lament:

   "My Father wore bruised boots of war..."

How To Be A Prestigious Mainstream
Twentieth-Century Academic Poet

First, you must Cope with Experience,
especially experience of Pain,
always Mingled with a Wry, Self-Deprecating
sense of Anguished Humor about the Incurable
Human Condition — but don't cope too well,
certainly not to the point where the painful Past
ceases to be fascinating.

For example, you can milk several chapbooks
(and readings, workshops and even tenure)
out of coping with the experience
of losing a dear one or nursing a sick child
or being dumped by a lover or pondering
the Holocaust. The trick
is to be casual, matter-of-fact
about anything one might be upset about
("It snowed the night you left us"
or "The truck, passing over you, Tommy,
must have noticed,
at most a slight bump,
a ripple in asphalt"),

then sock it to us with a fierce flare
of Vivid Image where least expected
(which also serves to attribute your emotion
to someone or something else),

never "I felt like shit", but

    Snowflakes
    pitched and wheeled in
    the streetlight's
    sphere,

    mad whirling brightness
    pulsing the night's cold
    heart

or

    Tonight
    the frayed easy chair cannot stop

yawning the
minute increments of your
absence.

This is called an Objective Correlative,[1]
because a famous academic poet named T. S. Eliot
didn't feel good about looking right at feelings
(especially his own) or relatives.

In between, you slip in bits of heart-rending Detail:

That huge deep-treaded machine
couldn't have felt
the bright nickel, proud
in your right jeans pocket —
the one I gave you
for leaving me this empty room
(walled with your pennants and posters)
so clean...

and don't forget that Wry Self-D.
Humor ("...for what do fathers
with snow shovels know of snow?") — see,
be slightly RUEFUL about being an adult
before you admit (subtly) to MAYBE
(just MAYBE) the POSSIBILITY of compensatory wisdom
or, anyway, salutary numbness.

You're awfully Sensitive,
and you never let us forget it,
but without seeming to broadcast it.

For example, if you run over a squirrel or frog
(which is even better than a child,
since anyone can feel bad about that),
you don't come right out and say
you'll never get over it,

---

[1] "Objective correlative": T. S. Eliot's term for conveying emotions indirectly by describing (and putting an emotional spin on) concrete external details. I won't say that I hate the formulaic use of this device, but I will say that, like a child tickled too long, the white page begins to glare at me, as I poke and prod and pollute it with these pen droppings. (Or the poem is stretched out on the page like a patient etherized on a table.)

Au contraire, you say, oh well, just
another squirrel — splat! — with maybe
some whimsical speculation on squirrel heaven
or why do they turn around when
if they'd just keep going, they'd make it
to the other side?

But you slip in a few human touches
("frozen there, bright brown eyes
growing huge with chrome and rubber"),
and then you twist the poem back
to your own reason for going
where you're going that day
(when you hit the squirrel — remember?) —
what your attention was on,
some past failure, of course (Cope! Cope!)

associated with person/place of destination/leaving,
and that branches out into a life
of well-meaning failures (insert Vivid Detail),
which leads to an Epiphany about, say,
fear and how maybe (just maybe)
we'd realize our dreams (but don't say
"realize dreams"; say "get to the other side
of the shiny wet leaf-crazy street
with our fat acorn") if each time risk loomed
we didn't turn back under the wheels
of — or zigzag treads of — or...

[insert abstraction that suggests
both car and social conformity or being
in a rut: "The screeching wheels of a world
that would not stop for us
if it could"] —

You get the idea: You can't be "Corny"
("realize dreams" or "wheels of destiny"),
Sentimentality is worse than cruelty
or incomprehensibility or academic bureaucrats who say
"not unlikely",
and you fully understand that any approach to truth
is supposed to be an approach
to an unconfrontable Vortex of Horror

on the verge of which a brave

or lucky or skillful (Wry, Tough, Humane, Precise, Complex, etc.)
poet can snatch some lifeline
of Frail Illusion —

Oh, look, it's easier than that:
You aren't allowed to be simple, proud,
happy, optimistic, certain about things,
etc. The evil or sentimental
have usurped all that. You're a spy
in the land of complicated horrors.
Your mission is to smuggle back in
(in guise of Complex Irony)
the right to enjoy (maybe just a little)
(albeit sadly and solitarily and knowing it won't last
and not forgetting to mock the romantic touch there —
COVER YOUR ASS!)
a nice spring morning.

You may feel that I've gone too far — that it's ludicrous to suppose that our complex, subtle academics write according to rote formulae, about as subtle and complex as a quack's cure-all (mostly booze and molasses) — well, look again. Long ago Poe wrote an essay explaining how he wrote "The Raven" — he wanted a certain beat, a certain emotion, etc. Nothing about expressing the depths of his agonized soul, just a bag of cute tricks. Many "deep" modern poets have mocked Poe's pragmatic approach as shallow. The difference between Poe and most of his mockers is that Poe didn't mask his tricks behind a mystique of soulful blood-and-bonery. Personally, I scorn cheap tricks. I guarantee that every poem in this book is the pure distilled quintessence of poetry. Get yours before it runs out, *only* $1.00, that's right, only 100 pennies, four quarters, 10 dimes, 20 nickels, yes, just $1.00 for a bottle of...

The Short, Unhappy Life of William Parelli

One day, not long after writing the above instructional pieces, I decided to put them to the test. I got myself a post office box, created a poet named William Parelli (I'd heard that "William" was the name found with greatest frequency among published English poets), sat down for a couple hours and created Parelli's Oeuvre.

Personally, I just write poems; I've never had an oeuvre, a word that suggests a constipated grunt. But William Parelli would have an oeuvre. I thought it would be easy to make him a famous poet — just saturate his work with detritus from the most sacred of current sacred cows, such as Rilke, Neruda and Lorca with a subtle sprinkling of Bukowski (*eau de toilet*).

205

In two hours, I gave him ten "significant" poems. Proudly I showed them to my wife. She read, sniffed, said, "I prefer *your* poems". I showed a friend. He said, "I don't quite understand why you're doing this." Another friend began to critique them and show me where they could be "strengthened". Hmm.

But I went through with the experiment: I filled six envelopes each with four or five of my best poems and one with four of the Parelli poems (written as badly as I could write them), sent all seven envelopes out to respected journals and got, of the lot, ONE acceptance — you guessed it, PARELLI! A hoax well-launched — and stillborn, because I found it more depressing than funny. And I felt sorry for the editor (I'm not mean enough to be a hoaxer). And I wondered, maybe I really DO write better when I do my worst! It IS a liberating activity, trying to write badly. I withdrew the poem, later met and explained what I'd done to the editor (foolish thing to do) who, instead of being irate or humbled or amused, said, merely, that if he'd chosen it, it was a good poem.

But enough about me. Let me introduce you, without further a-doodoo, to William Parelli himself, a voice from, well, not the grave, no — a voice from ALL of us, yes, my fellow poets, Parelli could not have achieved so much without the help of every one of you.

First, here's the Parelli poem that was accepted, his first and last acceptance. Such a mature voice for a new poet! Note all the Rilkean angels, arbitrary luridness and assumption of profound futility (so comfortable if you have tenure). And note how well this poem follows the principles of "Blehert's blood-and-bone" theory of modern poetics:

Formal Garden

This moonblanched algebra of stone
is so taut each touch of starlight
sings too shrill for a dog's hearing,
deafens the dumb marrow, hollowing
bones, shattering the blood
to jagged-edged rending bits.

In this light the bone-white grapes
look blue. An ashen angel crouches,
perched on the edge of a fluted birdbath.
He plucks a grape and bites it in half,
dribbling bluewhite blood on ash.

How is it we can still walk, bloodless.
What holds us erect? The angel doesn't
notice us.

206

Our feet grow heavy, cold. We cannot bend
to see them. We harden to white marble.
No one has ever thought
a thought like molten gold.

Can stone think? We are the thought.
Even the stars move. Faster now — they begin
to blur. I could move if I could choose
a movement, but after such stillness
every way is good — I want to move all ways
at once, but cannot, so remain still.

Each motion is only itself. We are traces
of motion, oscilloscope curves diligently charted,
paths of solidity, negative wormholes in time.
Let our stillness in time teach space,
teach even flatness: Let us become points,
already pointless.

There — now that's GOT to be profound. I have no idea what Parelli is talking about, and I created him! (I exaggerate — I'm sure I could figure it all out, and would, if I thought the poet were speaking to me.) If you think that's fine poetry, have I got a bargain for you! It's a bridge in Brooklyn, you'll just need a lot of heart and a crane...[2]

I also gave Parelli a "Daddy" poem, though, strictly speaking, such poems should be by daughters. Here's Parelli's stab at it (so quietly rhyming "office" with "doff his"), in which he manages to cope with his unspeakable loss by using the obligatory numb understatement, climaxing in dingle-darkness (you'll have to ask Dylan Thomas what that means — he said "dark as a dingle") as one more formalist goes back into the closet:

My Father's Hat

My father placed his two-peaked hat
Upon a closet shelf each day.
His overcoat, his dark wool suit,
His wing-tipped shoes — all went that way.

---

[2] Referring to poet Hart Crane, who wrote "Brooklyn Bridge" before drowning himself in the Caribbean. He was an important poet: Grad students should be kept out of trouble with harmless interpretive busy work. The academic definition of poem is something said so complexly that others are willing to explain it to others who don't want to know. (Why should we study you, O bard? "Because I am big, you idiot, to be unraveled." [Because I, ambiguity, ought to be unraveled.])

I don't know where he is, but then he's
Better dressed that way. He'd doff his
Hat, then sometimes give me pennies,
Relics of the fabulous "office".

These I fondled, placed in piles
Upon the flower-patterned rug.
My father's shoes on lino tiles
Scaramphed away — I felt no tug

As through the house my father went
And out again and back again
And out and back and then...and then
Shoes, hats and coats, these feel no pain.

I never wear a hat myself.
I doff my father and go stark.
My father's on a closet shelf
As dark as any cave is dark.

Hmm — maybe this is about a poet who killed his dad for his nickels (the cheapskate only gave pennies!) and stowed the bones on a shelf and dons his dad's skin from time to time. But isn't it marvelous how, instantly, when we see a poem beginning "My father", we know that daddy's a goner! Much adieu about nothing.

What's particularly fun about *inventing* such "intimacy" is that it beards the modern fad of equating poetry with "deeply personal effusion of the unconscious." Poets are taught poetry in workshops where they are made to fill up personal "journals" with intimate thoughts. Of course, this works somewhat: It works because the best way to improve one's writing is to WRITE and because these thoughts are intended to be communicated to others (the workshop - "Dear diary and please give me a good grade, Prof., and don't be too rough on this, classmates" is implicit in every line), which does wonders for one's writing. The trouble is, the students don't realize that all writing need not be "personal" or in journals (among poets whose work was seldom personal in the "modern" sense, are Shakespeare, Chaucer, Milton, Pope...well, only a few minor poets), and that all communication need not be to people studying or teaching creative writing. What a relief to invent someone ELSE'S intimate thoughts!

I will spare you the rest of Parelli's brief meteor shower. Some other volume, perhaps, if there's a demand for it. Speaking of hats in closets, one day I spun out in my mind a whole poem on the subject (and this one is supposed to be a GOOD poem, so if you laugh at it, you're laughing AT me, not WITH me, and I'm very sensitive, so don't), after hearing that a recent

208

Nobel-winning Polish poet had written such a poem, and it all turned out to be a misheard word. Here's that poem, I hope a brief respite from all this lugubrious stuff:

Poor Hat

"I heard it on the radio, her eulogy for a friend,
but from the viewpoint of her friend's HAT..."
(How clever, I thought) "...how it waits for her,
listens for her footsteps..."

(Yes, I thought, the hat thinking, please, come
clippity-creak down the hall's wooden floor, open
this closet, lift me out, don me, let me hug that
familiar gray hair, go with you into sunlight,
bob down the streets, bask in colors, cool down
in drizzle — where are you? It is dark and dusty
here where I become a discarded rag and begin
to wonder how I could ever have dreamt
of making you smart, chic, bold, complete —
how anyone could ever have cherished a sweaty,
worn-shiny thing like me, paraded me before mirrors,
taken me everywhere, panicked to have lost me until
I crept coyly from your overcoat sleeve —
such relief!

So long have we lived together, I've become part
of you, maybe all, so that anyone seeing me
pertly perched — even if only on shelf or hat rack —
would instantly envision YOU about to smile, speak
or make some gesture that is quintessentially
you. But that fluid magic is drying up
here in the dark, as a photograph yellows, turns
vague and quaint in the attic, as an unread book
loses its voice and, if ever opened, whispers
stilted, archaic words. When will the door
swish open, your fingers touch me, give me life,
let me give your life back to you? When...)

"...listens for her footsteps, wonders when it will
be fed..." (Fed? FED? Oh...) "Oh, you said 'CAT'!
I thought you said 'HAT'! How would one feed a hat?
Does it nibble your head?" We laugh, but I still
want the *hat's* eulogy. After all, a cat remains
a cat, and one size fits many, but what can be done
to console the old shoes, the favorite hat?

Now, back to business: Here are a few more rules for writing acceptable Twentieth Century poetry:

Thirteen More Views[3]

I

Isn't there always
something just a tad pretentious
about poems with
numbered sections?

II

Yes...yes,
I think
there is...
just a tad.

III

It's worse
when the sections
are very short.

IV

That's because short sections
could so easily be combined
into one reasonable-sized poem.

V

The old woman
twitches her black shawl
over her shoulders and creeps
up the cobblestones — a crow
with one wing broken.

---

[3] Wallace Stevens' 13 views were of a blackbird. That poem is another favorite for dissection by grad students. What is it about grad students? Look, grad guys, a poet is someone who talks real good (a definition I borrow from L.A. poet Russell Salamon) and often talks real pretty and sometimes real smart. Please endeavor to discover whether it may not, in some plausible universe, be not reasonably unlikely that you are to some degree alive.

VI

Everything depends on a
non-sequitur to enhance
the pretentiousness.

VII

Free form helps —
it makes everything feel so
chosen.

VIII

There must be a purpose
to each chastely isolated
word. See
how short these
lines are.

IX

You are invited
to register appropriate awe
lest others suspect that
you, too,
don't get the point.

X

I, too, would like to quit,
but "ten" is too significant.
One must impose oneself
(or pretend one has) upon
an arbitrary number like 17
or 13.

XI

Or eleven — eleven
would be dandy...

211

but seven
would have been quicker.[4]

XII

I can't think of another line...
but must, only one more
to go!

XIII

We've done it — we are
cool. Turn on the TV, knowing
you are immune to its charms, safe
in pseudo-precision. A culture
is how you hold your fork, the hand
with which you wipe and
what you substitute
for awareness. If your culture
were here, you'd be asleep
already.

Let me again stress the importance of using VERY SHORT LINES. It was discovered, soon after the general abandonment of rhyme and meter, that the one thing that prevents free-verse poetry from being mistaken for prose (unless you're Walt Whitman and sound like the Bible) is VERY SHORT LINES. And it makes each word so important and spares short-attention-spanned, TV-commercial-blitzed minds the need to comprehend more than a few words at a time or to grasp the sinuous syntax of complex sentences — just jab jab jab, then deliver the knockout punch (IMAGE!). Here's an example which, entered in a Bad Poem Contest, won only third prize. It must be better than I thought!

From

trail from
the day's draggled
snaggled
mouth
a thread
of vinegar

---

[4] Another tip of the hat I never wear to Ogden Nash's dandy candy and quicker liquor. Can Nash make hash of Stevens' achieven's?

take
from broken
windows
where no
one stares
all
day
the sliv-
ers
of yo-
ur son-
g.

Now for a rare treat: We now take you IN STUDIO to hear a poet in the
process of creating a poem to suit an editor who demands more voice, more
vision:

I am a Poet of Voice and Vision. Here

is my voice: Testing, one two three testing.
Mi-mi-mi-mi. lo lo Lo LO Lo lo lo (arpeggio).
This is me, Dean, speaking. Hello? Hello?
Can you hear me? [teehee...what should I say?
Shhh! No, YOU shhh...oh shit, the poem is ON...] Uh,
Hello, uh, hi, Mom, I'm a poet, and uh ah this
is my er fresh new voice, and goddamned
AUTHORITATIVE too, so knock off the wise-cracks, OK,
because this is my voice right here, and it can
TALK REAL LOUD BLEEP EEEEEEP sorry, OOPS
were going to run out of

Here is my vision: Peekaboo, I see you,
on a clear day forever. No, that's too simplistic.
I have a taut, contorted vision, a dark vision,
dark, but painfully acute. So, Peekaboo,
I see luridly detailed rotting bodies
vomiting on each other in the dying day.
Oh come ON. I see my computer screen, that's
what I see. I don't know what I see —
I don't even know if it's mine (alas, poor Ringo[5]).

---

[5] Ringo sang the lines "What do you see when you turn on the light? I don't know,
but I know it's mine." in the Lennon-McCartney song "I Get by with a Little Help
From the NEA" [From my Friends, actually] on the *Sergeant Pepper* album. An
"album" is a recording medium made from egg white (albumin) in the days before
CD-ROM. (Not to be confused with the other "Al-bum" — that is, the current vice-
presidential ass.)

No, wait, I really do have vision. For example,
if we made house doors wider, we wouldn't have
so many car-graveyards, because we could move
old cars into our living rooms and polish them and
upholster and stripe and polka-dot them and use them
for planters, love seats, play pens, etc. Or we could
cross Yeats with Frost and get Yeast. Or, wait, here's
a GOOD one, why can't we all just get along?[6]

Now I will combine my voice and my vision:
    And the lily shall lie down with the lala
    and lo, let the liar lay with his fleas,
    and even as I speak, so let it be done unto them.
No, wait, that's not it! That is not
what I meant at all. Wait wait this is going to be
really good...

––––––

We close this chapter with a few more sententious admonitions:

It's easy to find your own voice: Take the one that makes most sense when you listen with your own ears.

It kills us to think we are of no use to others. This bothers the criminal and the poet: Both fear they may be useless, but their solutions differ: The criminal teaches himself never to think that thought, while the poet thinks that thought regularly as an exercise, hoping that the act of persisting in the face of uselessness to others is useful to others.

Hunters wear bright colors lest they be mistaken for game. Poets, hunting for timeless truths, wear "fresh new voices". It works: Their poetry is seldom confused with timeless truth.

This poem is bio-degradable: Left in a landfill, the words soon break down into syllables, then consonants, vowels, then faint whispers, hints of sound and meaning, labials and glottals mingling with the bottles, maggots, mashed newsprint, coffee grounds, inarticulate, uh...uh...uh..., squirming microbes of meaning, harmless, offending nothing that lives.

---

[6] Alas, poor Rodney King (L.A. star of the video recorder, victim of "police brutality" — which is like saying "underwater fish"), we know him well. And then there's the Mickey Mouse Club answer: "Why? Because we don't LIKE you."

Section 4: The Current Scene

Chapter 7: There's Always Room to Park

A Few Minimalist Maxims

Poetry is a brave act — lighting a match in a dark strange place, hoping in its brief flare to find oneself surrounded by friends.

Speak up, poet — the ears have walls.

Have some poems. Careful! If one touches you, it's yours.

My poet friends talk about being poets like my Jewish friends talk about being Jews. Reader, how is it for you, being a reader?

What if the world ceased to be a subject for poetry, just sat there meaning itself like a kid with stage fright staring at the audience dead silent?

Nature is full of things good to look upon for grace of form or motion, elegance of hue. Even a fat drab humanoid can write a poem worth reading.

This is going to be a funny poem. Get ready to laugh:
(On second thought, why don't you just decide to laugh?)

Bad poems about pain are worse than mere pain, that, like a tired child, just wants attention. The poems want understanding as well.

Her poem begs please PLEASE don't blow up the planet, because we want to live! This is backwards; We should beg: Please want to live!

This poem is untitled,
but when it gets old, out of respect
you may address it as Sir.

A poet must create an imaginary universe with real readers in it.

And these are the two measures of hell: How much must be said that once did not need saying; how little can be said.

Chapter 7
There's Always Room to Park

Youth

Youth is poems entitled "Love" and "Spring" and "Pain" and "Youth".[1]

Easy parking, of course, is the nicest thing about poetry readings. No — an unfair statement. A good reading can be exhilarating, and good poetry, well-read, recited or performed, can thrill an audience. There, I've said it. Now no more Mr. Nice Guy. The rest of this chapter is the raw, impolite half-truth about "the poetry reading scene", so often a circuit of readings by the same small group of people to the same small group of people, designed to give the illusion that poets are part of a rich, populous culture, but exposing, instead, a few attention-starved marooned poets stringing unlit Christmas lights among the few palm trees of our desert island while we read to each other — and applaud politely (not wanting to admit futility) — the pleas for help we are about to bobble off to sea in old Perrier and cheap poetry-reading-red-wine bottles (or beer bottles for the very-small-press poets).

That perhaps describes only the readings by "established" poets (on their ankles are little tattoos: "Est. 1963" or the like). Some of these fine establishments would love to say they've provided poems for the Royal House for generations. I'm not sure how a poet becomes an established poet. Readings by the un- and disestablished, usually "open" readings (you sign up, wait your turn and fill up five or ten minutes with as much deathless verbiage as you can), and sometimes raucous poetry slams (where poets compete for audience approval in sudden-death read-offs, and the winner gets a prize) are more interesting — more likely to present a few surprises and attract a few hearers who've never been to a reading before. But even during the liveliest

---

[1] An obsolete epigraph. Youth is now poems entitled "Shit Cookies," "The Naked Turtles," and "EAT Me! KILL Me! FUCK MY FACE!" But the titles get more jaded when the kids reach middle school.

open readings, many listeners master the art of open-eyed, apparently-attentive deep sleep.[2] It is this cultivation of *open*-eyed sleep from which the term OPEN reading is derived.

What's worse than a life of quiet desperation? A life of noisy desperation — especially when no one seems to hear. Am I referring to poets or to almost everyone ELSE — left to *their* lives of noisy or quiet desperation from which poetry might offer a way out — if poets would locate and reach their audiences? We poets suffer the silences and noises we inflict on others by our failures to reach them. This is Karma: To Each His Sown. We are the tasters of all we purvey. This has been a serious paragraph. Please accept the apologies of the management.

I should define "Reading": It's a rust-belt city in Pennsylvania and a railroad you can buy in a Monopoly game. (Another Monopoly RR is the "Short Line", also popular among our poets, many of whom also suffer from B & O.) And it's what you do when the Liberty Bell cracks, to see if it's still working — you re-ding it. As for a POETRY reading, that's one of the small, generally harmless critters that slips in through the crack in the Liberty Bell (a crack called Freedom of Speech, though often confused with Cheapness of Speech).

My poems about readings are getting restive, telling me to shut the [expletive] up and let them have THEIR say. The [expletives] are coming from poems about poetry slams. OK, poems, have at it:

Open (Reading) Wider, Please

The apparition of those faces at the reading —
patients in a dentist's waiting room.[3]

Filler

There IS a place for poetry: After the Hunger Artist[4]
starves to death, there is a brief delay while his
body and filthy straw are replaced by fresh straw and

---

[2] Attentive-looking sleep is not an easily learned skill. Fortunately, several million elementary-school students are now, with the help of Ritalin and other drugs for children who do not easily suffer boredom, acquiring this skill, which will serve them well in future poetry readings, business meetings and Voodoo ceremonies.

[3] A takeoff on Ezra Pound's so-called haiku, "The apparition of those faces on the metro — /petals on a wet black bough," often cited as an example of "imagism" as in "I'm a gism, you're a gism…". Pound suffered from excessive imagismo, the image being his favorite gismo.

[4] See Franz Kafka's story "The Hunger Artist," where the hunger artist dies in his cage and is replaced by a panther. (A panther is a poet who is a member of the Pantheon.) The hunger artist starves because, he says, there's nothing worth eating. Many people are probably starving for poetry, but don't know it, nor do their feet show it.

a snarling panther. Meanwhile, to avoid dead time,
a poet is invited to read.

Since poets are upstaged by almost anyone, and a bottom-feeding comic or band will usually attract a larger audience than an "award-winning" poet, we poets get just a little desperate for attention ("Look, Mommie! I can use the F-word over and over!"), as suggested by the next three poems:

I'll Keep my Day Job

A triumph! Even my most trifling poems go over well — "BEAUTIFUL!" —
CLAP CLAP CLAPPITY CLAP — the applause led, I notice,
by the fierce-eyed gaunt man, second-row-left, who,

afterwards, heartily shakes my hand,
tells me how terrific my poems are

and that he is the reincarnation
of Jesus Christ and also Commander
in Chief of the Galactic Confederation Fleet
and other interesting revelations
too numerous to relate.

Urbane Violence

For years police have been coping
with acts of domestic poetry reading,
quietly desperate men and women
who inflict their poetry on spouses
and children. Now,

amid growing urban violence emerges
the unprovoked drive-by poetry reading:
Usually young, podium-hardened poets
screech up to the curb, lower the car window,
and scream out their poetry, tragically
striking innocent bystanders, as well as
fellow poets.

Obscene Poetry Callers

After 263 rejection slips,
he began to call strangers at 3 a.m.,
breathe heavily and
read them his poems.

219

Too many of the poets I hear at readings fully deserve their desperation:

It's All Relative

"I think you'll all be able to relate to this next poem," he said.
I guess I can — maybe as a third cousin twice removed.

Lives of the Poets

Such a racket of feelings:
Clearly this poet lost her mommy.
That one lost his daddy.
This one needs a good cry,
that one a good lay.
This one is hungry and that one
feels guilty that others are hungry.
This one likes having loved ones,
but isn't sure about always having them,
and if not, how that changes the feeling
of having them. This one is gaga
about something I never heard of
before, but it's purple, and I think
it's some sort of flower. That one
would like to break windows until
everyone (or whoever THE SYSTEM is)
knows that he is not one of THEM
and have THEM admire him for it,
but not too much. These poets
could be anyone, but significantly,
ah! *Significantly* so.

Next, a brief break from all this glib cynicism for a friendlier poem about a poetry salon (something Columbus dreamed of finding in the New World: " 'Salon!' he cried"):

Lily's Pad

To a lady who, for over eleven years, hostessed monthly poetry evenings at her apartment (on Hewitt St.)

At Lily's we sit in a circle,
For poetry has no ending.
It's your turn — read a poem: Keep it clean,
For Lily is unbending.

You can't miss her voice 'mid the ponderous
Preening of proud poetentials:
It's as sharp as the wince of an onion —
Even her cat's deferential.

It's a Friday at Lily's — no voice
Goes away unrevealed, not a face
But is opened in turn, then closed up...
Almost closed...left ajar, just a trace

In our eyes of the words we have dared:
"I brought something...It's not very good..."
"Well, here goes — never done this before..."
(Oh no! Have I been *understood*!)

If you don't have a poem, grab a book —
They spill from each table and wall.
Roll your own, cadge from Keats, borrow Frost's —
It's all life and belongs to us all.

Lily nags, scolds, chastises and frets,
Walks away at the hint of obscene —
But there's much more of Alice than malice
To this Kitty become the Red Queen.

For the table is heaped up with books
That cry "Read me!" — and if you do *that*,
You may find yourself nudging the ceiling
Or lost in the eye of the cat.

What a wonderful hole to fall into;
Gongs, a bright paper bird, brazen nude...
How slowly we fall through the evening
From poem to poem to food.

And Lily falls into our worlds:
At poems of injustice her rage
Makes her shake. A sad poem melts her eyes
So she has to keep finding her page,

And a wise witty line makes her glow.
There's a circle of listeners here,
But Lily's the heart of this giant
That has all of us for its ear.

Is this the whole truth about Lily?
When the tea, cheese and crackers are gone,
When the last guest smiles thankyousomuch,
And there's nothing but darkness 'till dawn,

Is she lonely, afraid to grow old?
Does she try not to think how she looks?
Is she bored with the cat's conversation?
Is she sick of her walls full of books?

Are all of these people her friends?
Or glib shadows that come and go...
But these lines are as trite as the Soaps!
You've already seen that show.

For this is a Friday at Lily's,
And this is the truth she has made;
For here one may call bosoms pigeons
Or even a spade...a spade;

Here your best and your worst poems find friends;
Here it's safe to be playful and tender,
Be outraged, despairing or weird,
Be yourself or be Auden or Spender,

Be as young or as old as you dream,
For of poetry there's no end...
Is that why we sit in a circle?
Is that what you intend,

Lady Lily, who asked me over
To join in the magic ring,
To sit on the couch and nosh peanuts
And try to make words sing?

Are the Friday nights all over?
Has the sparkle all gone flat?
Will we never more do it on Hewitt?
Is this goodbye to all that?

Ah, Lily, we are poets,
And what is poetry for
But to make of Goodbyes Hellos —
Nothing more.

222

The "Alice" above is, of course, she of Wonderland. If "goodbye to all that" sounds familiar, that may be because it's the title of a book by Robert Graves, which bids goodbye to the world before WWI. Lily is still around and active as I write this. Hello, Lily.

The next poem is only very indirectly about readings. It deals with the reluctance of most poets to think of their poems as products that, like any products, require marketing. Our readings and small presses with their very limited reach to larger audiences (I think our Moms must have taken Thalidomide,[5] so out-reach-challenged are we) are our "solutions" to our unwillingness to discover what is needed and wanted by larger audiences and to deliver it and promote it. Or so the following poem argues. It is also a take-off on a T. S. Eliot riff in one of his "Four Quartets" where we all go "…down down into the darkness" (as merrily we roll along).

The Market

King and peasant, artist and engineer,
they all go down into the market,
Master and slave, farmer, dancer,
all, all must go down into the market,
for each has or is being a product,
and each product must be exchanged,
must go down, down into the market.
Each must sell what he or she is
or does or has; each must sell himself
out of the cell of himself; all, all
must go down into the market,
even the poet who "just writes
for himself", how pleased to be
praised, how he blushes, tries
to get you, pretty pleaser, to
go home with him so that he can collect
his commission, for all, all
must go down into the market.
All, all must sell, beauty
and crone, saint and bawd, each
becomes the one pattern of patter, the
good impression, the pitch, the close:
for goods, service, values, admiration,
booty, permission to survive, charm,

---

[5] That's the sedative withdrawn from the market when it turned out that pregnant women, taking it, produced babies minus arms between hands and shoulders, an early disarmament effort perhaps.

the pleasure of knowing one is there,
influence — even help, the toughest
pitch of all: persuading slaves to dare
to go free, the desperate (wildly wary)
that proffered help is no trap.
Yes, even the selfless must sell:
The martyr must market the meaning
of his martyrdom as professionally
as priests package, position and peddle
their gods, as coyly as penitents simper
propitiation. Pouting poet parades
sullen pride, as winning as huckster's
smile. In car pools, at bus stops, each
campaigns for his opinions. Marriages
falter when spouse ceases to sell, lets
loins and limbs take over the account,
forgets the other is a customer, forgets
to maintain that competitive edge, like
salesmen who neglect first names and that
special warm handshake, expecting
old accounts always to be there out of
loyalty. O demean not humble sales, nor
mock the market nor think yourself above
tawdry buy and sell, for all, all shall
mundane mingle there; all must go down,
all, all must go down into the market.

Poets complain that no one buys poetry. Who MARKETS it? Poets complain that publishers won't. Hell, if I wanted to sell clothing or cooked meals, I'd probably work my ass off earning money and learning the trade, then go into debt a hundred thousand dollars or more and remain in debt for a year or two while I worked 60-hour weeks trying to get my business out of the red — and as often as not I'd fail. What poet has invested thus in the marketing of his poetry? Either we have just proven that clothing and cooked meals don't sell or that hoping to be "discovered" (by whom? A talent scout for the big leagues!) at a poetry reading or on the pages of *Hot Flashes Review* or *Hangeden Quarterly* is not an adequate marketing plan.

Blaque Market

Looking for ways to market poems:
On plaques? (What if they prove
implaquable?) With pictures?
On greeting cards? Sneaky:

Such contrivances — and even books
are pieces of light furniture
or decorative driftwood. When you see them
on wall or table, they are simply
where they have always been,

so one needn't notice that they came
from someone somewhere. Thus the poet
hopes to skirt the Laws against living
and communicating.

The next three poemlets deal with the settings for poetry readings:

The Editorial Wee Wee

Poetry reading: Just outside the loo,
A line of poets squirming in their shoes.
Inside, no doubt, there sits an editor who
Is holding onto it for future use.

Alimentary, Watson!

What tells me the reading
Will be a drag?
On the back of each chair
A small white bag.

A Bit Of Cutty Sarkasm[6]

Though poetry readings aren't exactly a lark —
And in poetry even larks aren't larks, being blithe spirits that never
    birds wert, anymore than of yore you could hear the
    Nicean bark[7] —
Yet seldom to the announcement of a reading do I fail to hark,
For where else is there always lots and lots of room to park?

---

[6] That is, cutting sarcasm, also a relation to "cutty sark," Scottish for a short shirt (and we give poetry short shrift), a name for whisky, a poem by Burns and one more rhyme for "park" ("sark"), but I don't recall what, if anything, all this has to do with the poem. (Don't ask me - I just write the things!)

[7] "Hail to thee, blythe spirit — for bird thou never wert" — that's Shelley's sky lark (Is there also an earth lark?). "Those Nicean barks of yore" (not my, but yore) are in Poe's "To Helen." The bark is not a bow-wow, but a boat, and a boat is secured by a bight (a loop of rope) attached to its bow (Wow!), so don't waste a good rope to secure a rotten boat, or your (yore) bark will be worse than your bight. I don't know

Come in — no, *please* come in, plenty of chairs, and we have some *very* STRONG poets today. Have a seat. Here's what you may hear:

Re Verse

Here I sit at an Open Mike,
Noticing how all the crazy things in the world I'd hoped poetry would
    change are what most of the poetry I hear sounds just like.

The Peter Principle

Some passionate male poets recite epics that stretch from April to
    December
About the beauty, strength and prowess of each his member.
Now I don't object to a little masculine self-esteem —
Even a precious poet as acned as hackneyed whose penis is no
    mightier than his pen is and his pen is a leaky Bic — even such
    poets should dream
A little — aye, a little, there's the nub:
One member maketh not a club
To beat us ceaselessly over the head with;
Nor is it something one would want — except, perchance, to sleep —
    to go to bed with.
I would not have these poets stricken dumb,
But I do propose a rule of, shall we say, thumb:
Let epic perorations swell and paeans painfully dwell on the might and
    the height of it
And the empurpled ivory-shafted glory of the sight of it,
But permit the poet eruditely to endite on it
Only as many words as with a pen (preferably felt) he can write *on* it,
Which should keep it down to one however trite sonnet,
Perhaps only a very slight sonnet,
And even that's assuming he can keep his, shall we say, interest up
Long enough, but not **too** up, lest the poem come to an abrupt
Shall we say, end. But how long
For self-love's old sweet song
Is long enough?
Of such stuff,
O brave and genital poet
With pale cheeks and eyes inchoate,
However much they want to like you,
Even the politest audience will forsike you
(Perchance to sleep) if you exceed a haiku.

---

if the Niceans are from Nice (northwest of the Canneans of Cannes) or Nicaea, home
of the Nicene Creed. Nor do I know if ignoble Niceans are Ignitions or just not nice.

But no matter if this self-advertising poem is of epic proportions, our poet will receive polite applause. Some cultures may have customs more conducive to enthusiastic audience participation:

Poetry to Die For

The new rage sweeping the planet (begun in a shabby
Baghdad coffeehouse): poetry slams in which the losing poets
are bloodily executed by the audience. At last we've found a format
that should bring poets the attention they deserve! How refreshing
to face real knives and real pain after decades of sterile slaughter
by executioners whose only tools are words like "puerile" and
    "simplistic" or
just silence. America, you should hang a poet now and again
just to show the rest you really care.

Which is why academic poets seldom risk their dignity in poetry slams, preferring death by frozen faces:

We Rest On Their Laurels

One more poet laureate reads a poem.
By brief polite clap-clapping shall ye know 'em.

And yet, some habitués of "serious" poetry readings consider them almost a religious experience. After all, if dreams contain clues to our deepest, innermost[8] selves, what could be more religious than an activity that induces sleep?

Q. E. D.

Poetry readings are a great spiritual comfort,
there being no better argument for the necessity
of God's existence than a poetry reading:

Readings support many activities besides listening.
One may, for example, doze or think about what one
plans to read or whether one's own poems went over
well earlier. One may notice the poet's clothing,
delivery, affectation. One may suppress a cough,
anticipate cheap wine and brie, set one's ears

---

[8] Why "innermost?" Why not "innerest?" That would make boring inert introversion inneresting, and we could all use the inner rest. We could even take innerest in our inner nest, if we were in earnest.

on auto-alarm to go off only at clichés, wonder
why one goes to such things....

Thus the question must arise, if a poem falls
from a poet during a poetry reading and no one
is there to listen, does the poem have any meaning?
For what meaning can there be apart from the act
of comprehension in the mind of a listener?

Unless one is willing to conclude (bizarre thought!)
that most poems are devoid of meaning, one must
posit an omni-audient God who listens
to all these poems to which no one else — not even
their authors (and based on internal evidence
of the poems, one may safely say <u>least of all</u>
the authors) — to which no one ever listens.

Thus, fidgeting here, one's attention bouncing off
the opaque walls of poem after poem, how
can one not but know that there is a God?

Poetry readings offer an additional enticement, especially for those
who are nostalgic about their school days: Readings offer excellent opportu-
nities for familiarizing oneself with chairs, walls, coffee in styrofoam cups,
clocks, windows and other staples of life as we know it:

The Yoga of Poetry Reading
or The Malaise of Reading Gaol[9]

Notice the chair you are sitting in,
its pressure against your bottom,
your bottom's pressure against it.
Notice the poet at the podium;
notice where the words are going:
To the podium? The ceiling? Past you or
not quite up to where you are?
Notice the walls, the floor, the ceiling,
the shape of the space they contain.
Notice the poet's voice appearing
and disappearing, the shape of the space

---

[9] Since the poem depicts the audience imprisoned by a voice, the allusion to Reading
Gaol (jail) seems appropriate — that's where Oscar Wilde was imprisoned. He wrote
"The Ballad of Reading Gaol", which says we always kill the thing we love. Nearly
every poet loves an audience.

it fills. Notice whether your head
is located in the same space where
it is. Notice that the poet at the podium
is still reading the same poem.
Notice the person on your left,
on your right. What are they
doing with their hands? Their faces?
Why does everyone remind you of someone else?
Are you that old?
Notice your lower back against the chair's back.
Get the idea you love the poet...HATE
the poet...feel sorry for the poet.
Now get the idea the poet hates you,
loves YOU. Get the idea the poet is
a thousand different poets in succession,
a new one jolting into view with each syllable
and that you, too, are a thousand listeners,
a new one for each syllable.
Scowl. Smile. Chuckle. Get the idea
no one in the room is paying attention
to the poet — they are all watching YOU.
Why is it that your weight presses harder
upon the floor, the chair, the ceiling?
Is it the air in the room pressing upon you?
Try to feel the words in the room,
changing things.
Get the idea that you and this poem
have been here forever, will be here forever.
Cough. Notice if others cough.
The wall begins to look patient,
companionable. The wall is leaning
on the poetry. If you didn't know
that the other listeners were
listening to poetry, based on their
facial expressions and body positions,
what would you think they were experiencing?
What is the wall experiencing?

Someone should write a book about language and walls and furniture:
Millions of words fill up rooms, litter the floors, coat the chairs. How does
this change their meanings? How often can rooms play host to even the most
abstract words (vast, agony, ecstasy, God, truth) before the words take on the
bitterness of stale coffee, the dinginess of dust-streaked acoustic tile, the
cool gray sheen of folding metal chairs? What excuse will our words give us

when they can no longer evoke anything fresh? They'll say, "We got involved with the wrong crowd." Welcome, readers, to the wrong crowd.

The next poem explains how, at an open reading, I discovered the timelessness of poetry — and I hope this poem won't give immortality a bad name:

The Silence of the Iambs

Borges[10] tells of time stopping for a year
as a man faces the firing squad, bullets
paused in flight while he, in his mind,
completes his masterpiece, a long drama in an
elaborate verse form...and then time
resumes. Time stopped for me during an open-mike
poetry reading. There, just after the words
"...touched the soft silence of your..." — soul?
heart? left ear lobe? But the poet was still there,
mouth open, her eyes in their sudden rigor, oddly
calculating; the other faces I could see were all
frozen in polite introspection, as if each,
if it spoke, would say, "I think I had too much
coffee" or "Did anyone notice my fart?" Nothing
moved. The water held its slope in the glass
I'd been lifting to my lips. Threads of cigarette
smoke hung in frayed silken twists. A petrified
ribbon of coffee bridged from lip of pot to cup,
as a waiter waited for someone never to say "NOW."
For a long time (so to speak), the interrupted poem,
too, hung there. I spent — it seemed hours —
trying to think of a next word that could save
the line from banality. In vain. For hours more
I memorized the gleam of her teeth, the contours
of paralyzed smoke. I composed letters to several
editors on various burning issues. I composed limericks
that began "The soft silence of..." — for example:

> The soft silence of fleecy white lambs
> Can't compare to the silence of clams
> (Clams, unshelled, you should touch

---

[10] This poem is based on a Jorge Luis Borges short story, "The Secret Miracle." I'm not sure which of us wrote this poem... [Refers to another Borges work, "Borges and I."]

230

Very gently, not much...)
Or free verse: Silence of the Iambs![11]

I had a long eloquent argument with my dead mother
about the importance of being a poet. I thought up
brilliant ways to make money from poetry. I tried,
again — again in vain — to redeem the poetus
interruptus or at least to predict what, if anything,
would come next, and, suddenly, I noticed
that the smoke was moving, twining, winnowing
the light, a lovely translucent creature...
Ah, time had resumed, and...I forgot to notice
how the line or the poem concluded. It must
have done so, because I found myself applauding
mechanically, trying to recall my money-making schemes...
but all my hours — days! — of contemplation
had blurred like last night's dreams, only
a few scraps of limerick remaining.

The greatest pleasure of poetry readings is observing the professionalism of the performers:

Traveling Light

My turn to read:
I tug the wrong folder
from my bulky tote bag
(stuffed with stuff), cram
it back, grab another,
stand, trip over the bag,
squeeze between knees and chairs,
stumble to the podium,
spill fifty pages of poetry
on the floor as I riffle through the folder,
gather them up any old way and
shuffle more pages,
find it, find I brought along
the old version, not the latest revision
I'd intended to read,
find something else readable...
Remember when I thought it would be
nice to be a poet so I could
travel light?

---

[11] Since "iambs" are the most common metrical feet in formal English poetry, free verse, or the absence of meter, might be called the silence of the iambs. Besides, it rhyambs.

This sounds very unprofessional of me, but for the audience it was the most entertaining part of the evening — poor Dean at the podium sans per diem. Fortunately it was an indoor reading (no wind other than my lunch), or I might still be pursuing runaway poems across the park.

An Unanswerable Argument in Favor of Immortality

Each of us will die. This will be a significant event in our lives.
I believe we shall live again. I can't accept never getting to write poems
about so significant an event. I can't unhear myself at a poetry reading
saying, "I died recently, and my next poem was inspired by that experience..."

Forgive me, but as some poets drone on, I can't help but wish they might be inspired by that experience soon.

Someone Please Tell Eliot to Wind it Up

"Today", says the Humanities Professor, "we're going to hear
        T. S.Eliot read
The Wasteland." We wait tolerantly, for the scrazzle-frazzle
of the phonograph needle to become a famous poet becoming the voice
of someone talking to whomever he's talking to (surely not us).
After hours or only seconds of scratching, a deep dry voice emerges:
"The **WASTE** LA-Aaa
        aa
          aan$_{nnn...}$ "

and sinks, never to return, since the Professor can't get the phonograph
working again,[12] so that is all I've heard of T.S.Eliot reading *The*
        Wasteland on earth
and all I need to hear.

Here's a medley of poems, each as short as I wish the subjects of these poems had been:

---

[12] The title refers to Eliot winding it up. Long ago (1940s and earlier) phonographs required winding — you cranked a handle; the phonograph would unwind as it played and suddenly slow (with sounds deepening, then dying) until rewound. Phonographs...remember? Before CD players? (No, a phonograph is not a photograph with a head cold or a harelip.) (To anyone with a harelip who is insulted by that last remark, I feel your pain: It must be awful to lack a sense of humor.) (I'm just compiling silliness about poetry. If you have a harelip, feel free to mock me. Do it in a palindrome: **Harelip, mock compiler...Ah!**)

Observations from a Poetry Reading Junkie

"I hope this poem won't offend anyone."
Hey, who listens?

———

Young poet aglow in polite applause,
being persuaded he's a great lover
by feigned orgasms.

———

Reading of battles, thousands butchered,
I think, "Why can't we just talk?"
Listening to some poets reading poems,
I think the same thing.

———

"Bear with me," says the poet,
 wishing we could be as bare as he.

———

After the reading, tired listeners stumble to the door,
feet encumbered by poor lost fragments of thought,
yipping to follow someone home.

———

Look at that audience, so quiet, perhaps even attentive —
poetry readings renew my faith in human
politeness.

———

The new game is Poetical Chairs: When the poetry stops,
you try to find a chair with someone still in it.

———

For those of you who have just tuned in, do not be alarmed:
This is only a simulation; you are listening to serious poetry.
No actual live communication to real persons, living or dead, is
intended.

———

As she introduces her next poem, the man sitting in front of me
nods, agreeing, nods so rapidly it appears he agrees,
not only with each word she speaks, but each syllable.
I think he just agreed with an "s"!

———

The angry young poet reads about fat middle-class women at a picnic
with spoiled children, while, in Africa, big-eyed children with toothpick limbs
and swollen stomachs are too weak to move or even brush away clouds
of flies. This makes me feel sorry for the fat middle-class women,
because the young poet hates them so.

———

233

He pours his words into the mike, hoping if he pours in enough,
it will overflow into our ears, then overflow them,
a few drops reaching our hearts, but the microphone
is bottomless.

———

PRRMS (Poetry Reading Repetitive Motion Syndrome):
My hands paralyzed
from polite applause.

———

Her poem had a dull refrain: Each time she got to it,
I wished she would.

———

Is it a yearning — after so many words — for the solidity of flesh
that makes so many in the audience glance at their left wrists?

———

Singers sing, dancers dance to a rapt, swaying audience.
A poet begins to read, a baby cries...

———

Poets reading in Spanish — sounds great, but I don't
understand a word of it — a vast improvement
over most English poetry.

———

His poems are all turgid sunsets and naked dawns.
Listening to them, I feel utterly alone,
as if I were an idea that woke up to find itself
in one of his poems.

———

Incessant monotonous grief, no matter what
white words spit off the tips of gray waves.

———

A petite long-haired lady poet chants, "I want you inside me!"
and in the audience twenty men try to squeeze into a
single narrow pronoun.

———

Open Reading Poet, your poems give me hope:
The few years left to me are a generous portion
if five minutes can take so long.

———

None of these poets are talking to me. I must have
done something awful. Poet after poet gets up
and speaks poetry — why won't they talk to me?
Maybe I'm not really here or I'm invisible or
people would whisper "That poet said something
to that guy in a poem and he understood — how
vulgar!" No, these are good poets, "fresh new

234

voices". It must be that I've done something
terrible, and they know.

———

Maybe it's not the poets. Maybe I'm just tired. Or maybe
tiredness has <u>always</u> been from poets, or from the
emptiness where poetry should be.

———

Listening to poets who must have written very fast,
I wish I could listen even faster.

———

Listening to an old poet,
a young poet leans forward
straining the leash.

———

The microphone isn't working. I, at the back of the room,
can hear only sporadic words: "Misty...radiant...flesh...
thrust...throb..." — probably I've heard enough.

———

He reads on and on, past many good stopping points.
The stopping points get better and better.

———

It's like listening to Wagner — I keep wondering
what will he think of last?

———

Poetry reading. Everyone in this room is dying.
This is the way we gently go, gently go, gently
go; this is the way we gently go — taking as
long as we can.

———

Outdoor reading at dusk. Fireflies glow
with our poetry.

———

The poet reads; somewhere a dog howls: mutual critics.

We've suffered with the audience. Is it more comfortable at the po-
dium? (Don't believe the griping that follows. It's *much* more fun at the po-
dium, with my public putty in my poetic paws!)

Views From the Podium (on No Per Diem)

Come to the poetry reading. My poems are much better out loud —
you get to see my mustache wiggle up and down
with the tip of my nose.

———

Today, knowing my reading will be televised, I find myself
putting on my best underwear, as if for a striptease or a car accident.

―――

I hate doing poetry readings during thunderstorms:
If I flicker, everyone will know I'm virtual.

―――

"Down, Tolstoy! DOWN!" Oh — it's just the lady in the back row
controlling her elegant Russian wolf hound.

―――

In the audience — someone who's NOT a poet!
Thank God! A reading full of poets is like
a pool full of sharks — nothing to feed on
until one of us is wounded.

―――

Light, tight, elastic — LOOKS like a tennis ball, FEELS
like a tennis ball: Hurled at the sidewalk, it strikes
with a SHPLOCH! and sticks there, not a bounce, not a
quiver. Sometimes an audience does that with one's
brightest, bounciest poems.

That's My Last Reader Hanging on the Wall

She smiles so brightly at my poems!...and at the silly stuff
the next guy reads...and the next... I feel like giving orders so that
all smiles stop.[13]

We've had an audience eye-view and a performer's. Now the emcee[14] of an open reading speaks. Poor emcee — it's his/her job to cut a poet off in mid-torrent if he's exceeded his time and others are getting restless, knowing that ever after the cut-off poet will despise him/her as brutal and insensitive. To some poets, getting cut off a few pages short of *finis* is akin to having one's baby cut in two. (But what mother would hold her bloated baby

---

[13] A rip-off from Browning's "My Last Duchess." My only fame as a scholar occurred in 1968, when a professor with whom I shared an office during my brief stint in academia footnoted my remark to him that the Duchess ("That's my last duchess hanging on the wall") was the Duke's "hang-up." To return the favor, let me say here that I am indebted for that footnote to W. David Shaw. Do you still pace the groves of academe, W. David? (Will you buy thousands of copies of this book to hide them from your colleagues, lest they see your name here?) And to Browning, so willing to hang a duchess, I say, "Put up your Dukes!"

[14] Emcee means master of ceremonies — cere being the wax used to wrap mummies; also master of sermony (restraining poets from same) and perhaps — since the emcee has no idea what the next poet will say or do, master of *che sera* sere-mony. Since we're dealing with poetry, the "mony" part has more to do with serious moan than serious money. But ultimately, it's the poet's job to make *'em see.*

up before an audience of butchers?) This next poem concerns a more gratifying aspect of emceeing:

How Poets are Made (The Emcee as Magician)

I'd seen the list of names — no one I'd ever met.
Now they are called up, one at a time, to read their poems,
each name becoming a person, a whole package of person!
It's magic! — makes me think I can create names,
write them down, say, "Is Grocken Flixenbugel here? Grocken
Flixenbugel? Do I have that right? Grocken..." — and from a
back seat someone will rise up, someone completely —
INEVITABLY — Grocken Flixenbugel!

Remember, before poetry readings, when people used to read books? Here's how it used to be:

A Private Reading:

I must tell you how much I enjoy your reading my poetry.
I get a warm, almost ticklish sensation as your eyes
pass over my words. (Did you know the mind is an erogenous zone?)
Your smiles send little shivers up my pen.
(O! Don't stop reading! Don't stop!)

That's right, reader — I *know* when you are reading my words...for Christ's sake! Stop picking your nose! Disgusting...

Captive Audience[15]

"Have you ever tried bondage?"
"No," she giggled —
"It might be fun!"
When I had her tied snugly
to the bed, naked, spread-eagled,
barely able to squirm, I took out
my... "No!" she cried out,
"Not that! Please!"—
but unrelenting, I took out
my poems and began
to read aloud.

---

[15] This poem was written and first printed years before a similar scene appeared in the *Bull Durham* movie, so how much should I sue for?

Applause:

When the hands that would reach out and touch you
(as you have touched others),
because you are beyond their reach,
touch each other.

Section 4: The Current Scene

Chapter 8: On the Care and Feeding of Fresh Authoritative New Voices

A Few Witty Schisms and Zweet Zingers[1]

A brand new poet — how the blurb rejoices!
So are they all, all fresh important voices.

A poetry editor is someone who helps a poet mail his poetry to himself.

So many books of poems, so few matches![2]

Academic poetry: An imaginary garden with real toadies.[3]

Endemic, epidemic, academic...

Where culture's a vulture, what's read is dead.

I'm a promising poet — I give you my word!

"Behind your cleverness, I sense tenderness." Yes, I use the tender to fuel the engine, you witty critic.[4]

Tired of defending your poems? Put them in a book, where they can stand for themselves, no longer spineless.

What's a fair exchange for poetry? I've been told that my ideas are worth their weight in gold.

You're reading, and suddenly you realize there's no such thing as poetry, but someone is talking to YOU — would you answer?

Beware: Breathtaking poetry ahead. Do not exhale.

"I don't know if it's poetry, but I love your stuff." Such stuff, I hope, as dreams are made of.

His wit is the brevity of his soul.

Why do we busy ourselves with this clever chitchat while yet we have a planet to blow up?

---

[1] "Zweet Zinger" alludes to whatshername (actually, like nearly all female poets of recent centuries, she had *three* names), the rather syrupy lady known as "the Sweet Singer of Michigan," but today best remembered as whatshername.

[2] Thus we refer to a poet's works as "matchless," meaning they have thus far escaped notice or are too soggy to burn or are incapable of igniting a spark in anyone.

[3] This meddles with Marianne Moore's line about an artificial garden with real toads. Of poetry she wrote, "I too dislike it," which in her (hard) case was more iron than irony.

[4] Translation: Tender: a train car carrying coal (tender tinder) for the engine. "The engine, you witty critic" is the ingenuity, critic. For those who got it the first time, I enjoin you, witty critic, forgive me for insulting your intelligiosity.

Chapter 8
On the Care and Feeding of
Fresh Authoritative New Voices

"Schizophrenia", said the radio, "means hearing
voices that aren't there" — like book reviewers,
who keep hearing "fresh bold authoritative voices"
that no one else can hear?

I wonder if I'm an authentic new voice?
Do I strike you as an authentic new voice?
Did you listen to my words
with authentic new ears?

"Feminist poet", "academic poet", "poet laureate", "modern poet",
"underground poet", "poetaster"—funny
how anything added to "poet" lessens it.

If you're in the restaurant business, you pay attention to some of the restaurant critics, but more attention to the customers. You produce food to be eaten, enjoyed and paid for. People eat or don't eat your food, and that makes or breaks you, so you find out what they like and provide it.

Poets, too, produce dishes for consumption. To understand the relationship between restauranteurs and poets, imagine a world in which no one ever comes to a restaurant except restaurant critics, based on whose published opinions, restaurants are or are not funded by grants, or the owners are or are not given jobs teaching cooking at colleges to help pay their bills.

In the absence of a paying public, poets begin to mistake critics and editors for their intended audience — and writing for critics and editors is a sure way to make certain there will never BE a paying public. This is particularly the case where poets write to please the more prestigious publications, since these choose poems by committee, so that only works safe enough to offend none of the editors gets published. Thus, poetry circles become vicious, as a few jaded voices proclaim to a few jaded ears that voices carefully attuned to those ears (trained in creative writing courses taught by the jaded ones) are fresh new voices. And since the proclaimers are, themselves, usually poets, one day the fresh new voice returns the favor — sits on a grant committee and votes awards to the jaded ones.

All these poelitics (politics of poetics — unlike poeleptics, which are drugs that cause fits of wanting to pine away by the bedsides of cadaverous damsels while at the window a raven croaks) wouldn't bother me so much if these people were at least having FUN doing it, but they seem a grim lot. Most of their poetry is concerned with the beautiful sadness of occupying a doomed body. My response, when I want to be politer than "So what?" is "Thank you for telling me that. I hope you feel better now." I wish someone would have the stomach to kiss them where it hurts and make them go away.

Is this sour grapes? If someone gave me a Guggenheim or a MacArthur or a Nobel Prize or a National Book Award or a Major New York Publisher, would I shut up and busy myself writing "real" poetry? YES! YES YES YES! I confess all! It's all sour grapes! So give me a Nobel Prize — quick! — and I'll be a GOOD poet and I'll never say another nasty thing...

I'm waiting...

Sorry, your time is up. This hurts me almost as much as it hurts you. It's a dirty job, but someone's got to do it: This chapter deals with the cloud of arbitrary opinion that surrounds poetry.

I Have a Problem With the Heart
(to my poetry-workshop buddies)

I dream they tire of critiquing my poems and begin to critique me:

"I like Dean, but I think he'd have more impact if his excesses were cropped."

"Really what we have here is a mishmash of several Dean Bleherts. The head, for example, would be quite complete on its own, and really, those slim ankles have little to do with that paunch..."

"I find the beard pretentious."

"I like the beard — keep the beard."

"Maybe it should be trimmed?"

"I think this is one of the best Dean Bleherts I've seen. The only change I'd make is, maybe, the body odor..."

"I'd prefer if he didn't have a penis, an anus, etc. I know I'm old-fashioned, but I'm so tired of people these days having all these intimate dirty parts."

"The breathing is excellent, the heartbeat very serious — but that silly smile trivializes the body's struggle to survive."

"Don't touch a thing. You're fine as you are!"

242

"Just a bit overdone..."

"What is this spirit stuff? I don't see a soul here! Make me SEE it!"

"C'mon, he's worried that he hasn't done anything worthwhile. That's so trite..."

"It's so fresh, most of it, but it ends in death — that's been done to death."

"No, no, death doesn't end it, you're missing the point!"

"Well, I like it just the way it is — the eyes twinkle, and I like the way, when you say 'How are you?' it always answers."

"He's well enough made, I suppose, but I don't understand WHY he was made."

"OK, OK, guys, we've got five billion more to look at, could we move on please!"

How rough is the poetry business? Here's part of a recent cover letter I sent off and the rejection slip I received:

"Dear Satan,
I am an unknown poet. I will gladly sell you my soul
(submitted herewith along with SASE[5]) in exchange for fame,
readers, huge book sales and critical raves. I have been published
previously in...."

"Dear Poet,
Thank you for considering us, but, alas, we already have
far more souls of poets than we can hope to use in the foreseeable
future (and we can see forever). We wish you best of luck elsewhere
and do hope to see you here eventually.

Cordially,
Infernal Editorial Staff

Young poets take rejection slips personally. I never take things personally. I'm a man — I take them manly. (To hell with these politically correct "person" words!)

Maybe He Should See Someone About That

"Sorry, but I cannot use your poem
at this time." Don't feel bad.
The editor was hungry
and couldn't eat your poem.

---

[5] SASE means Self-Addressed-Stamped-Envelope. Most poetry is, alas, self-addressed.

Or he was horny and couldn't screw it
(though your manuscript may look
as if he gave it the old college try).
Maybe he wanted to reach the top shelf,
but standing on your poem didn't help.
Maybe the editor needed a good cry,
but your poem cheered him up.
Or he wanted to play with *himself*,
but you were someone else.
Your poem wasn't bad,
but at this time the editor
couldn't use it.

There are times when I wish the editors had printed their rejection slips on toilet paper. (Editors probably wish poets would print poems on same, but would the post office deliver the returned poems?) Would it work better if all editors were mothers of small children? "Dear poet, Oh MY! This is WONderful! Thank you SO much for showing it too me! I WISH I could publish it for you, but alas...". That's better than having mothers of small children become editors: "You say you made it in school? Let's see. Hmmm. Thank you for sharing it with us. We regret that it does not suit our current needs. We hope you will try us again NEXT Mother's Day."

Almost Infinite

Hosts of weary editors cry in chorus:
"Poets, stem thy myriad plethoras!"

The reference here is not only to the myriad poems, mostly bad, that editors must read, but to the overuse in that same poetry of "infinite", "myriad", "plethora", etc. I actually heard a poem in which there was "a plethora of myriad..." (I don't recall myriad WHAT) — you know, just oodles and scads.

Now we move from editors to professors, a *very* short trip. Wouldn't it be fun if editors sent your poems back with phrases circled in red and labeled "AWK!" or "NO!" (or "Not unlikely").

Purely Academic

Twinkle twinkle, little professor
At your own humor, quite the lesser
Of two evils, for when serious,
Uncategorically you weary us.

Twinkle twinkle, little prof.
No one laughs; did someone cough?

How I wonder from afar
If it's not unlikely that you are?

English 101 (Lost, Oh Lost):

The "apathetic fallacy" or fallacy of attribution
of no feeling to that which cannot but feel
is endemic in Twentieth Century Literary Criticism.[6]
Here is a common example: A young man
goes strolling after the first spring shower,
feels in every vibrant budding tree,
each whistling robin, each droplet on each petal,
in each salvo of tender and fiery greens —

feels a surging joy as vivid as his own
and writes a poem that says so. A critic who,
with little life of his own, is unable to feel
the life that surrounds him (only enough
to suspect it may be disruptive) — a critic
long sequestered in theories of biochemical
mechanics that comfortably anaesthetize
lacerations he's inflicted on himself and others —
and to whom even the young man's joy
is a possibly contagious rash,

such a critic, reading the young man's poem,
proclaims (as student pens wag busily),
"See how the poet attributes his emotion
to birds, trees and flowers? That
is the PATHETIC FALLACY!" (Students
circle these words for the next quiz.)

The critic's proclamation is a perfect example
of the Apathetic Fallacy: Feeling nothing himself,
he ascribes his absence of feeling
to all life. He assumes, for example,
that birds and leaves cannot feel joy
and that the young poet cannot feel
the joy of others. He does not say

---

[6] For those of you fortunate enough to have eluded college English courses, a poet who attributes his own feelings to nature (e.g., the "...somber yew weeps in the rain") is guilty of the "pathetic fallacy." A poet who plays with himself in the bathtub is committing the bathetic phallicy. Putting your head in the oven and turning on the unlit gas exemplifies the Plathetic folly, see?

(but cherishes the secret thought)
that even the young man's *own* joy
is brain circuits on the fritz
or good digestion.

But this is unfair, calling it a fallacy,
for after the lecture, the critic
walks to his mud-spattered car
past dull grey-green bushes,
mite-ridden sparrows that jitter and hop
like wind-up toys — he is right:
it is a joyless world.

Plenary Indulgence

Plenaria are tiny worms. A researcher found he could teach them
simple responses: first he chopped up the educated worms
(for learning is not respected in our time).
Then he fed them to ignorant worms
(for the ignorant ever devour the learned).
Result: the ignorant worms were found to be educated
(for the punishment must be suited to the crime).

On this principle, our teachers chop up poets and force-feed them
to students, who will ever after, it is hoped, vomit poetry.

I should mention that I have been (briefly) a professor and an editor
and am a poet and a critic, which makes my saying all these nasty things the
act of a hypocritical, masochistic malcontent. Well, maybe I should *not* mention it. Since I've given away my own academic background (Assistant Professor at Cornhole You! — I mean Cornell U., 1967-69, before I took up cab
driving in order to feel I was moving people from one place to another), I
may as well show off my scholarly chops:

A Short History of Poetry

We envision civilization arising from savagery in a straight line,
Much as grapes become sour grapes or wine,
But I contend that history is cyclical,
Not perpendiclical,
New savageries arising from the fall of older civilizations we know
    nothing about,
Because the savages (who even go so far as to end sentences with
    prepositions) wiped all traces of them out.
Now in the early pre-tribal stages of savagery —

Periods of burning libraries, stomping on school teachers, being politically
    incorrect, rapery and ravagery —

A few poets survive (as dazed as lost pets) from civilized times,

But they are soft, neurotic and (being remnants of decadence) too snooty
    to use rhymes.

Those who aren't minced by axe or pulverized by hammer

For correcting some hairy warlord's grammar

And who aren't impaled on a spear

While gazing at Noble Savage with romantic leer

Or aren't (if they dismiss old Rousseau

As trite) speared while staring at ruined fallen golden arches and
    muttering "I told you so!" —

Those who survive these homicides and don't become suicides

Are fat and juicy and also soft-skinned, so are slaughtered for their sweet
    suets and besides suets, hides.

Being rather oily to primitive taste, they are best baked, so are called
    "bakers"

(Much as the first priests are called "friers") — and they try to stay alive
    by entertaining with verse, but find no takers,

For in those first wild times, poetry is a luxury;

I mean, if you were tenderizing an old poet in a pot and it chanted at you
    "HI YI YI Let us go then, you and I, HI YI YI when the evening is
    spread out against the sky HO YO TA HO like a patient etherized
    upon a table HOI YOI — OUCH!..." — would you extinguish the
    flames or would you simply add to the pot onion, carrots and — if
    you could get the cork unstuck — sherry?

Some poets are so fat they are called "lards".

Their shrill cluckings while being stewed are called "poultry". (Those
    savages are cards!)

A few poets are kept around for laughs

And learn to sing ribald songs between the campfire quaffs, while
    restraining their compulsion to correct syntactical gaffes,

And eventually during the Great Bowel Movement (which, after the
    Great Consonantal Divide, becomes known as the Great Vowel
    Shift),

"Bakers" become "Makers", "Lard" becomes "Bard" (except "Lard
    Myron" became "Lord Byron") and "Poultry" becomes "Poetry",
    and at the same time, pretentious bullshit, hitherto given short
    shrift, as society ripens, is given longer and longer and longer
    shrift,

And that's the real reason why we now think of poets as Makers,

Except when we can't be troubled with poetry because we are all
    stuffed up with a head cold, so the wriders of boembs begub once
    agaid "Bakers".

I don't know why we need critics, professors and editors when, as the next poem suggests, the poets themselves are so capable of pomposity:

The Little Blue Poet[7]

"No!" said the little blue poet
(not noticing that no one had said "I will!" in answer to his question).
"I took the workshops; I sucked up to the establishment poets;
I polished the imagery; I heightened the emotions; I included
the acceptable social themes; I wrote the poems;
I got the poems accepted by prestigious journals;
I got a publisher to do a book; and now I'm going to read it
all myself!"

I-I, Sir

"I" is a word overused in poems. Actually *words* are overused in poems.
Many poems could be improved by removal of their words
    (verbotomy),
especially when every word screams "I! I! I! I!" or, like an eager pupil
who knows the answer, "me me me me me!" And even their utter pouty
silence would be (like the "you understood" of commands) "I under
    stood" —
or MISunderstood.

Can Poultry Mutter? or Rhyme Does Not Play
or Fire in the Foyer!

Within the modern poetry arena
Where use of rhyme can get you a subpoena,
For you to cry out plainly, Dana Gioia,
That poetry may die for lack of meter
And rhyme is much like crying loudly "FIOIA!"
Inside an almost empty movie theter.

Note: Poet Dana Gioia wrote an article and book, both entitled *Can Poetry Matter*[8], which call for a return to traditional forms. Mr. Gioia is to be commended for changing his name, recently, to Dan Gi, so that the no-longer-

---

[7] Based on "The Little Red Hen," a nursery rhyme all about how Communism laid an egg in Russia, so that the people grew apathetic, and the commissars had to do it all themselves.

[8] No relationship to "Can Poultry Mutter" (a chauvinistic study of angry feminist poetry) or the deconstructionist babble — I mean Bible — *Canned Potty Matter*, excerpted in the intro to this very volume. Other works *not* written by Dana Gioia include a biography of Dylan Thomas (*Keen Portly Martyr*), a study of *Finnegan's*

needed vowels could be donated to the Committee to Save the Children of Brn and Other Vowel-Depleted Balkan Communities From Congestive Consonant Failure (or CSCBOVDBCFCCF). As you can see, the committee itself has donated all the vowels it could spare from its acronym. It is hoped that other inconsonant public figures will follow Mr. Gi's example.[9] We are particularly grateful to our 50th state, now called Haw, for it's generous response to our pleas.

Gioia — I mean Gi — and the other "formalists" are obviously influencing the way we write. Even personal correspondence is now written in poetic meter so often that most post offices have a separate mail box for "metered mail". Alas, it's plain to see, they've no effect on me.

Rhyme and meter have their advantages: For one thing, they slow poets down, which is a blessing for those of us who try to keep up with the stuff. That is, they slow SOME poets down. Others accelerate, the time required for finding rhyme words and keeping the beat more than made up for by no longer having to see anything freshly or come up with insights, when you can make anything poetic simply by adding rhyme and meter (or so some assume):

Phrygian Phrigidity [Phrygia: Kingdom of Midas]

He thought himself a poet,
For everything he touched
Turned to rhyme —
So sublime! —
Until one day he touched
A loved one and — you know it! —
There she froze
In chiming prose.

Actually, the "formalists" don't write that way. On the contrary, most of the poems published in *The Formalist* go out of the way to DISGUISE the fact that they are written in rhyme and meter by using lots of enjambment[10] and other evasions. This is the dark dirty secret of many formalists: They are still a bit ashamed of rhyme and meter. Or perhaps the idea is that NOTHING wins its way into the hearts(?) of academics that is not modulated and deadened (all that muffling ivy, you know). Not all "academic" poets are in

---

Wake (*Coin Motley Patter*), a study of Whistler's obsession (*Can Portray Mater!*) and a condemnation of doggerel (*Corn: Paltry Meter*).

[9] You can hear the screams of disem-vowelment: "AEIOU!" And sometimes "Y!"

[10] Enjambment: Run-on lines, where there's no pause or end of thought at the end of a line. This de-emphasizes the rhyme and sometimes the meter. In the last poem, "Until one day he touched/ A loved one..." is enjambment. Lately there's been a run on run-ons.

academia. It's a question of whom you're writing FOR. Writing formal poems that could be mistaken for elegant prose is a bid for respect.

Personally, when I rhymes, I RHYMES! My poems include rhymes long enough in syllable count to be poems, for example, from a poem lamenting the threatened extinction of frogs, where I wonder, if someone MUST vanish...:

> O limberly leaping amphibians,
> Why O why can't it be those grim surly creeping damn Libyans...?[11]

There — that's a nine-syllable rhyme (make it "SO grim..." for ten!). Eat your hearts out, formalists! Here's one (nine syllables) from a poem about the creation by Justinian of his encyclopedic compendium — or "Pandect" — of laws (the poem's punch line is the crowds cheering or caroling, "Here come Pandect Laws! Here come Pandect Laws!") which begins:

> Roman emperors ruled by fiat — arbitrary, inconstant, ignoble,
> Until one day Justinian said to his secretary in Constantinople...

Here's a mere-six-syllable rhyme (with meter this time) — as you can see, from 9 to 6, we're going down:

> Where you've no sun tan I tarry:
> Love is low, unsanitary!

Or drop one syllable for "Rapt in sin, unsanitary!" — worth the shorter rhyme for the sun/sin/san and the rapt/wrapped pun.

Meter, too, can be more or less disguised. (The academic game is indirection: Nothing is to be confronted directly; nothing of value can be simple; the un-excruciatingly-self-conscious life is not worth living; no statement — or, they would prefer to say, ALMOST no statement — goes unqualified; complexity is God; semi-colons are better than periods; and exclamation points are taboo except as high camp!) Modulation of meter depends on how big a difference there is between stressed and unstressed syllables. You won't find many Kiplingesque lilts or Hopkinian back flips among the formalists. Oddly enough, most formalists and most of the free-verse poets of academia all produce an identical sound: They read with an extremely stretched-out, modulated high-priestly intonation. The difference is that the faint, blues-notey upward lift of the chant comes at the end of each line for the free-verse poets (the whole line held in a gusty monotonic suspension for that final tiny lift) while the formalists put the lift at the end of each poetic foot. (At the end of

---

[11] I just did it for the poetical correctness, honest! Some of my best fiends — I mean friends — are Libyans...

250

the last line or foot, the same "melody" repeats, but the final lift is pitched several notes lower. Ending on a rueful blues note, it doesn't resolve — leaves you hanging. Hey, did you realize poetry had a melody?)

Formalist, schmormalist — most of you are still sacrificing virgins, guys. Please come down off the altar and talk to us. The preceding has been an unpaid, unsolicited message from a poet who tries his damndest not to sound like Digger O'Dell, the friendly undertaker on the old show, "The Life of Riley," whose farewell, in a deep, lugubriously juicy voice, sinking deeper for the last quiet words, was always, "Well, Riley, I guess I'd better be...shoveling off". Pappy always said, don't pull out your rhyme or meter unless you mean to USE 'em.

On Slams, Rap Poems, & Other Popularizations

I say it's poetry and I say to hell with it![12]

In the next two poems, books critique readers, hoping to make their unevaluated lives worth living:

You Just Can't Put Me Down

A book wasted a whole day on me, found me shallow,
but kept going to find out how I'd come out.

Reader Appreciation 101

Across the living room
she's reading Vladimir Nabokov.
She likes it. She has a dictionary
on her lap. We had a spat
when I tried to make sure
she didn't miss the main points,
so you'll have to take care of yourself,
Vladimir — and watch out!
She's a very tricky reader:
Sometimes she doesn't understand
the way she *seems* to understand
and other times she only plays dumb.
Actually she's rather a complex reader
operating on several levels at once,

---

[12] Refers to a classic *New Yorker* cartoon whose caption is identical, except that the word "poetry" here replaces the word "spinach" in the cartoon — of a cajoled child refusing to eat the stuff. Poetry has become the spinach of the arts. We need a Popeye who, overwhumped by a bullying world, reads (TADA!) poetry and acquires the spiritual biceps needed to make the world cower before him.

which lends her a rich resonance
(for who expects a bleached-blonde fox
to enjoy *Invitation to a Beheading*?),
but, to the uninitiated, may appear coy,
so she may put you off at first,
but once you get into her, Vladie,
I'm sure you'll love her
as much as I do.

Obviously the above was written from the viewpoint of an unenlightened soon-to-be-dead probably-white male trying to be funny. (He's probably of Jewish extraction. If you grow up Jewish, blondes have the lure of the barbaric forbidden, like bacon.) If I have offended any bleached-blonde foxes, I can only say, in all humility, GET A LIFE! (Note: The preceding text was a simulation. No actual feminists or females were destroyed in the production of these poems.) Here are four pieces on that exact subject (keeping in mind that I disclaim all responsibility for any thoughts found in my poems — the *muse* did it!):

The Tail Obtusities

The bearded poet smirks as he reads
his raunchiest wit.
In front three women shake their heads
and frown and knit.[13]

How Grimly They Bare It

Feminist poets, though often graphic,
Are seldom, if ever, the least bit laughic,
Not even when they're gay; in fact, the gay are the least gay and the
    most graphic,
Though hardly priaphic;
They milk their one theme, The Importance Of Being Ernestine,
As if it were a Jersey or a Hereford or a Guernestine.
Though a Hereford is not for milking, but for meat,
But I guess you can milk a meat cow or any cow on which you can
    grab hold of a teat.
Anyway, let's not be so literal, but get back to my subject, which is
    the literately clitoral
Or, portmanteaued, the litoral,

---

[13] Alluding to the ladies knitting at the foot of the French Guillotine during the French Reign of Terror. My three women are probably knitting their brows, but heads will roll!

Which sounds like "littoral", meaning "of the shore or beach",
As in "Once more into the beach..." — but my grasp has just been
    exceeded by my reach;
So I'd better quit or what I
Write hereafter will be torn to Orphean shreds[14] by the Clitorati.

Poetical Correctness

The Committee to Rehabilitate All Great Literature Of the Past by Injecting Sensitivity Into Dead And/or White Males (CRAGLOPISIDAWM) is making progress. Here are two examples from the sensitization of James Joyce: From his most famous short story (previously called "The Dead"): "...as the snow fell upon the living and the living-impaired..." And from the last page of *Ulysses*, here's an example of how Molly Bloom's soliloquy has been aligned with the Antioch College dating codes: "Yes I said yes I will yes...but I MEANT no."

Sensitization will accelerate as soon as a few key points are resolved. For example, should the words "Praise Him in the highest" in the psalms become "Praise him", "Praise Her", "Praise Him/Her", "Praise Her/Him", "To heck with Him"? Currently favored: "Praise Her and/or Him [ordered alphabetically] in the highest", though some contend that the dualism of highest versus lowest is, itself, sexist and heightest, implying, for example, that a height-challenged person (for example, most womyn compared to most men) is less Godly than a height-endowed person. Absent a term of exaltation suggesting "most level" or horizontalist, it has been suggested that we shift from "Praise Him in the highest" to "Praise Her and/or Him [ordered alphabetically] in the most correct and sensitive way."

Great progress, meanwhile, is being made with old — or rather with SENIOR adages: For example "to call a spade a spade" is now "to call an African American male an African American male". (An Argentine contingent insist it should be "African-United-Statsian".) A particularly energetic campaign is underway to stop male chauvinists from sniggering at pornography. Henceforth male chauvinists will safricanamerican at pornography (a few older sniggerers insist that they will snegro). Also, to pacify a contingent of Harlem prostitutes (pardon me, other-moraled commercial-sex providers), Markham's poem, "Man With a Hoe" will henceforth be called "Man With a Garden Digging Implement".

Elsewhere in poetry, formalists, who have long been inveighing against excessive use of the first person in poetry, will now inveigh against excessive use of the first persyn. This was not an easy decision. Initially it was proposed that perdaughter be substituted for person (just as "woman" became "woperson", then "woperdaughter" and, at last, "womyn"). Formalist

---

[14] The ladies of Lesbos tore Orpheus apart, and the pieces floated downstream, singing. (The bits bobbed palindromically to the sea: Bobbittibobbittibob!)

critics are ecstatic because, as one of them puts it, "Most of this confessional rant is by hysterical metrically-challenged bitches anyway, so let's leave 'person' out of it." A few object that the word "persyn" should be reserved for cloned humans (or SYNthesized persons). But a large persyntage of those present doubt that humyns will ever be cloned, because, they say, there is nothing new under the syn.

Finally, discussions are now underway to determine the proper pronunciation of s/he. Favored is a "she-he" pronunciation to rhyme with a titter (teehee), as in Chaucer's "Teehee, she cried, and clapped the window to" (which many argue should become "Tees/hee, she cried..."). But, objected some, what right has a word like "titter" to infest our language? (Several beer-bellied bearded bards in attendance begged, at this point, to be put out of their Msery, glumly predicting the end of HIS-story.)

We must complete this great work in time to salvage our children from millennia of language-forged shackles. Help us save the children. Remember, in the words that William Wordsworth would never have been able to write without continual support and nurturing from his flagrantly suppressed (and flag ranting is a particularly chauvinist activity) and unsung sister Dorothy: "The child is parent of the persyn" or, since some contend that "parent" should be "ma/pa-rent", to avoid suggesting the existence of a Ma/Pa rental agency, shall we say, "The child is pyrent of the persyn"?[15]

The Sexist Critic's Dictionary

Poultice: "A hot, soft, moist mass...applied to an inflamed body part."
Poetess: Often a variant spelling of poultice.

What's the difference between a poetess and a poultice?
In theory, the poetess can inflame one's breast
without lying against it.

If a poetess produces poetry, does a poultice produce poultry?

There IS some mysterious link between Poetesses and poultry. For example, there's that famous statement made to Emily Dickinson when she staked her poultry in a contest and won a pullet, sir! Her friend said to her, "We have bet the hen, Emmy, and she is ours!"

---

[15] A political correction of a line from Wordsworth's "My Heart Leaps Up": "The Child is father of the Man," which raises many questions: Who or what is mother of the man, father of the woman, mother of the woman? Upon whom does the child beget the man? Does the child include both male and female parts of this metaphor, like an earth worm?

Feminist critics reply that there is a similar link between "poets" and "putz"[16] and that, in theory, poets (unlike putzes) can penetrate passionately without peril of herpes, AIDS or gonorrhea.

Next — another poem I don't quite agree with, but can't take back, either. Most of the editors of little poetry magazines do their best to get the best poetry they can find to an audience, and hooray for them. And yet... — when a system isn't working, one is tempted to take it ALL down, the well-meaning and intelligent along with the obnoxious boors, just slash and burn everything and hope something better will arise from the ashes. This poem is of that "Down with the whole damned system" philosophy. Is it MY philosophy? Sometimes.

Go, Little Mag...

I wish all the magazines and little magazines
and minuscule magazines and microscopic magazines
that print poetry that no one reads
except the authors (who read it twice, once in each
of the issues they get free) and every friend
the authors can lay both hands on (who read or
pretend to) — and also each author reads
a few other poems in the same issue,
feeling magnanimous momentarily —
I wish all these magazines would stop
puling poetry and preserving the pretense
that the stuff is being read by readers
who read it because they love to read it,
which encourages poets to keep writing this odd stuff
that no one reads except as an onerous duty
or with pleasure derived from doing something
considered onerous by nearly everyone else,
even the hundreds of thousands who read
the New Yorker — all but a few — skipping
from cartoon to cartoon, only occasionally
glancing at one of the poems before they realize
what their glazing-over eyes are doing).
O, stop, please stop, big & little mags,
being the uninvited martyrs of this

---

[16] "Putz" is Yiddish for prick (penis, derrogatorily), or for anything similarly inserted, as in, "Ya putz yer right foot in...". What do you do with your putz, alienated poet? You pull it, sir. Thus each year some poet gets a Pullitzer for playing with him/herself. ("How do I get service around here?" "Pull it, sir?" "But there's No bell!") When I win my Pullitzer, I'll deny I ever said this stuff. Who writes these footnotes, anyway?!

phony battle for a phantom culture,
so that, having no editors to cling to,
we poets will find our readers again,
find out what they need and want to hear,
learn, again, to slip what's needed
into the form of what's wanted, reach
those who need to be reached, who are starved
for live communication, who mutter and swarm
at the foot of the walls we've erected
between us and them, between us and us,
these walls pretending to be doors,
these thick, heavy doors,
frozen shut on rusty hinges, these magazines
and colleges, these bastions of the fortress-culture
that with all its intricate imitations of live communication
protects us from the shock
of me being here talking to you.

While we're on the subject of poems I don't quite believe in, but can't bear to bury, here's one that's so sour and cry-babyish, I wish it didn't contain such clever puns (on incubi and succubi in the last stanza), for the sake of which I inflict it upon you:

Ghost Writing, An Exorcise in Sour Gapes
(On Making It With Incubi and Succubi)

In poetry, too, it isn't whom
you screw; it's who you let screw youm.
No point in pushing at that door;
The sign says "**PULL**" — in plain French: Whore!

Your paper, pens and ink aren't steep;
A beard is free, and words are cheap;
But sucking up to a big-name poet
Costs you dear before you know it:

Bucks to hear them read, then buy
Their books and get them signed and try
To shine — say something fresh and witty
In hopes they'll let you feed the kitty

To worship at the Master's Workshop,
Learn what rap makes his knee jerk; lop
Lines and crop and chop and tighten
Up your poems and belt and lighten

Wallet, for you've yet to woo
The editors: It just won't do
To send them poems and not subscribe —
You mustn't think that it's a bribe!

You've redone all your poems to please 'em,
These Gods in whose bright imagism
You're remade. For this you owe 'em.
Pay the price! *Submit*...your poem!

O ink is cheap and words come easy;
Pay your dues and don't feel queasy.
Perhaps it's *not* who diddles you,
But who *you* have to do it TO:

See how your stroking makes them moan?
A little praise, and they're your own!
You won't be drained by *ink you buy*;
It's *suck you buy* will drink you dry.

Most women and some men go on shopping binges. Poets (workaholics, apparently) go on workshopping binges, some in hopes of improving their poetry, *all* in hopes of improving their connections. The first thing you learn in most workshops is that all your poems are too long, that you should break them up on the page and use skinnier lines and cut the poems in half...

To Critics Who Insist On Very Skinny Poems
With Very Short Stanzas

"Give your readers more space," "...more stanza breaks," "...not so many poems per page," — the reader needs space, space, space stop filling up the poor reader's space with all these words! Space, SPACE, give the goddamned reader some S-P-A-C-E! Don't crowd so, give us space to digest, to catch up, to sleep, to think; and give us shorter lines, too, not such a clutter of curlicues, I just can't take so much thought, so much print! Do you realize that at the current rate of the word explosion, soon there will be no room for blank space on the page? In fact, we'll have to start writing between the lines of our old books, even filling in the open O's with tiny words. We'll have to start writing up and down the margins, encoding surplus words in blades of grass, genetic DNA, structures of crystals. But words produce more words. Short of deverbalizing people and machines, there's no solution in the offing. We can no longer afford the luxury of stanza breaks, one short poem on an entire page, blank end pages, margins, short-lined haiku, no, every one of your stanza breaks could have provided a home for dozens of abandoned words, that's the way it is, and you should know it, reader: You're jammed full of words, they trickle from your seams, you can't take in the least preposition without a jostling of words, you vomit words. If I left space on the page, how would you even see it? Here, here's a bit of white space. Put it to good use:

Coals to Newcastle — or Insulting the Reader's Intelligence

I'm considering footnoting my poems, not to make them more accessible,
but to insult the intelligence of those who already understand them.
But it's hard work writing footnotes: I confuse *op. cit.* with *loc. cit.*
Wouldn't it be simpler just to insult your intelligence? (Not **you**, nothing
personal, just your intelligence.) I'll try it: Your intelligence is a
smart-assed, nit-picking snob! Your intelligence couldn't tie your shoes or
pick your nose without your fingers! Your intelligence is too artsy-fartsy
to stomach an exclamation point! Your intelligence can't laugh, can't
cry, can't even fart without a body! Your intelligence doesn't know
that you are, much less who or what! Your intelligence's mother wears
CIA boots. Your intelligence...well, you get the idea, but if you want,
I'll explain it to your intelligence.[17]

It's true, many poets I know favor filling their poems with obscure allusions, but are afraid people will feel "insulted" if they explain these allusions in any way. This absence of explanation makes me feel I'm reading the work of some aloof, austere, insouciant intellect, so that it's a surprise to hear the same poet, in a public reading, eager to explain the subtle points of his poems before reading them, more like a cocker spaniel puppy than an inscrutable poohbah. Apparently these never-named people who will feel insulted aren't anyone one is likely to find in the audience at a reading. (Is it you, Harold Blum or you, Helen Vendler — or lesser critics who act the way they wrongly (?) imagine you would? But you aren't reading *this*, are you?)

"Serious" poets and critics are also, typically, allergic to exclamation points, and many proclaim that parentheses, the word "perhaps" and dashes should be purged from the poetic hardware shelves. Some would exclude ALL punctuation. Most manage to exclude nearly all readers. Personally, I'm one of those fools who will break these "rules" to make my meaning clear (and just by claiming to HAVE a "meaning," I give myself away). After all, fools are made to betoken.

---

[17] *Ibid., passim,* Amen.

258

Stop Squirming!

I'm trying to write articulately.
Does my art tickle you lately?

Poetichism[18]

I like to say things neatly,
Not wordily or repeatly;
Lines reasoned and grammatical,
Not run-on-automatical;
Sharp-witted, but not serious —
To make you light, not tearious;
But nothing rude or limericky
Nor Nashiously gimmericky;
For I've too much ambitiousness
For trivial gambitiousness.
Last, let each poem be finished —
I'm for anti-fragmentarianism!
Let all the world be dinnished
With my anti-fragment Clarionism![19]

A Toke of my Steam

For one who can't be poet without pot:
It cannot give you what you have not got.
"A thing of beauty is a joy forever" —
But made by YOU — it's not a JOINT endeavor.

Poetry would be more readable and lively if poets didn't so frequently mistake booze and drugs for the muse, or, persuaded by Shrink-of-the-month fads, swallow the myth that genius derives from insanity. All that the existence of insane geniuses (genii?) proves is that genius can be strong enough to override insanity...and perhaps that many people fear geniuses and work hard to get close to them and "help" them by tearing them down in covert ways, which boosts the number of mad geniuses. After all, if you made a good living pushing pseudo-science and intellectual pap designed to enslave people, you wouldn't welcome people able to see, think and disagree. Psychiatrists have shown particular skill in drugging, invalidating and shocking poets, who then kill themselves or curl up in little literately stammering balls and then are used as poster boys and girls for the psychiatric-pharmaceutical-government-industrial complex, which has always used its

---

[18] That is, a poetic catechism, though it's all answers, no questions. The world of poetic politics abounds with catty schisms.
[19] Life has its clarion: Carry on, carrion!

failures to argue for increased funding of "mental health" — funding of the foxes who so avidly guard our hen houses.

Being sane requires hard work. No one comes by it naturally these days. It has nothing to do with normality. It's important, therefore, to let poets and artists know that it's OK to be sane. You can still get the girls or guys. People have even been known to experience happiness without loss of their ability to write poems. Someone should explain this to poets. (I plan to do so, as soon as I'm sane enough.)

Hello...Hello...Helloooooo...

The poet meets poetic justice:
Having sought a peaceful profession
that could harm no one
(what harm in mere words?),
he now complains that words
don't change the world.

The voice in the poet's mind,
cracking out thunderous words
that whisper dryly on the page
is like a ghost freshly freed
of body in battle, not yet aware
he's lost his flesh,

savagely slashing at foemen
with insubstantial sword,
wondering why they do not fall asunder,
but go on untouched,
as if he were not there at all.

I'm certainly guilty of such ghost-writing. In my mind, I have, in this book, strewn the poetry world with gore and laughter and punctured pomposity, but all around me, no doubt, the well-oiled wheels of academia turn, unimpeded; the workshops and creative writing course assembly lines roll out the latest models; the little magazines groan with cloned submissions; and no one notices me flailing about in the dark with my imaginary sword, scarcely able to make a leaf quiver.

"Hot Enough for You?"

Language grows too old to take care of. We put language
in a Home. We visit faithfully, but it's not the same.
Language begins to confuse us with our parents, tells us
the same stories over and over. Language is looking very frail.
It won't be long now.

And like the children of such a parent, we begin to wish ("for its own sake") that language would just die. We think forbidden thoughts (Hi Ho, Hi Ho, It's off to Kevork'[20] we go!). If only there were those among us who could give the language new life...like maybe by using language to say something? But it gets even grimmer in the next three poems:

No Fuel Like an Old Fuel

To help us break our dependency on OPEC oil, we have developed the book burner. It runs best on poetry chapbooks and little magazines, which, like oil, consist mainly of compressed, refined fossils. Plenty of fuel. But we must proceed cautiously and not commit ourselves to this energy source until we've established contingency plans for containing potential spillage of raw poetry into the community, contaminating our children with literacy.

Serial Poetry

The serial killer would arrange his victims in grisly tableaus:
Dead children at apparent play, a man's slashed body on top of a woman's —
telling himself a story he didn't want to end.
Much poetry reminds me of this: Anything that once lived
must be killed, then arranged in charades of extravagant metaphorical life.
Branches and leaves patched with plaster and canvas gesticulate and moan,
stuffed birds rejoice in seasons bright with funeral-home paint jobs,
eerie puppets pose for "Despair" and "Obsession".
If you are alive and stumble upon this scene, instantly
you know you should not be there.

Poetry should be words used to make words more usable. Some talk uses up words. If words are pipelines for communication, such talk leaves the pipes clogged with gunk. Live communication is a solvent that clears the pipes. Love, God, Mother, Country — clogged pipes. And those are just the obvious ones. (Pause for cartoon showing my new secret ingredient leaving your pipes sparkling.) Where poetry itself takes more from language than it gives, language ceases to work, and we each become so alone that we can scarcely be said (nothing can be said) to exist.

The Verbs Go First

The verbs go first, crumbling to adverbs
while nouns fade from specific to generic,

---

[20] That is, Kevorkian, the Michigan doctor who is an expert on kids in China — that is euthanasia.

transitions vanish, slipping through black abstract chasms
and promiscuous metaphors free-associate as all,
all our poetry, sonnets, haiku, odes, free verse, all poems
left too long on shelves, like generations of mongrels
breeding true to produce litters of German Shepherds,
metamorphose into, not quite noise, but surreal
imagistic concrete language poems, all (by whomever) in the same
fresh unique authentic individual voice.

So much for the life of poetry. The next poem deals with *past* lives. I
don't mean to denigrate memories of past lives, only the self-glorifying specu-
lations that pass for memory among those who make eerie Twilight-Zone
mystery out of such things, as if the memory of a bowl on a table 3000 years
ago is more wonderous than the memory of such a bowl ten or two years ago
or the *sight* of one now.

Memory is memory. Many people (most psychoanalysts, for ex-
ample) can't recall anything before age five, so assume that no one else can
either. (Some weirdos claim to have had childhoods and infancies, though
they look nothing like babies!)

The next poem mocks especially those who give past-life memories
a bad name by claiming all the good names — the glamorous ones. SOME-
ONE must have been a stableboy or a cleaning lady in 1812, else how could
the 100,000 Napoleons have tolerated the reek and filth that would have
piled up around them? (Do you live again? Of course! Do you think we'd
trust you where we can't see you?)

Trade ya Two Swinburnes for a Browning

It's first come, first serve now in the distribution of past lifetimes:
Here's a list of more-or-less-famous poets still eligible
for you to have been.

Thomas Hood? No, sorry, he's been taken — only this morning.
Yes, I realize he's only a very minor poet, but we've had such a run
on famous names lately — whenever people feel degraded,
they become preoccupied with their real or fancied past glories.
It's easier to say, "I was once King around here,"
than to pull oneself out of the ditch and find a job.

And many poets feel degraded these days. All the big names
are gone now. The right to have been Shakespeare is distributed
among a consortium of unknown poets on a time-sharing basis,
but the last available 5-minute slot was filled months ago.
You should have come to us sooner. However, we do have an opening for...
let's see...how about Colly Cibber? No, you wouldn't have written

262

anything anyone would read today (except for a line on the tag
of a Good Earth herbal teabag), but you'd have been savaged in verse
by no less than Mr. Alexander Pope.

No, I'm terribly sorry, but Mr. McKuen is still alive.
Besides, how could you have been one
who is so seldom himself? Yes,
after years underground, Bukowski, at last,
has been buried. But he has a long waiting-list
of beer-swilling bards who couldn't even wait for his death
to begin to imagine they were he.
Would you consider Southey? Leigh Hunt? Joyce Kilmer?
Who? Ashbery, Merwin, the *New Yorker* crowd? —
no, none of them are available. You're laboring
under a common misconception: They're not dead yet,
they're only academic.

I spoke (can you hear me?) earlier of the poet slashing at foes, not real-
izing he's a ghost with a ghost sword that just won't cut it. For critics, often,
the reverse occurs: Feeling he is "just talking," expounding an idea, mere
words, nothing that could harm anyone, the critic is disturbed (or in some
cases pleased) to discover that his imaginary sword is sharp steel, when some
young poet's bloody head plops at his feet.

Oops

I tore her poem apart. Inside was a little naked creature
twisted up in tight sullen silence. I stroked it,
apologized, but it wouldn't speak, only shivered.
I pulled the tatters of poem back about it modestly,
smoothed them back in place as best I could —
almost like new, said "There — please tell me again,"
but the poem wouldn't speak to me ever again.

"Constructive Criticism"

I open my mouth and emit
red, yellow, blue, orange and purple
balloons. As fast as they emerge,
before they can soar, a little man
with a needle pricks each one, and
out of each, with a sigh,
falls a word.

The constructive critic here can be a snide friend or the poet himself picking apart his own thoughts, finding nothing worthy of ink. Since, with poetry as with conversation, a free flow of words *precedes* creativity, when we (or others) use criticism to stop that flow before it starts, the rest is silence. Which, after he's read too much precious stuff, may strike the critic as a good idea.

But we are too hard on the critics. Think what they suffer when, though they think it (as do most of us, kicking ourselves for thinking it), they cannot bring themselves to say what their integrity demands, like loving mothers loathe to shatter a child's pleasure. For example, here is an oft-thought, but seldom expressed bit of criticism:

> Yes, it is hard to face up
> to the murder of 6,000,000 Jews.
> I do not think it in good taste
> to mention in the same poem
> the difficulty of facing up to
> 6,000,000 Holocaust poems.

How many times can you shock the muscles of a dead frog and get a twitch? How many times (sounds like "The answer is blowing in the wind") can you make us shiver by mentioning lampshades made of human skin and gas in the showers? It can become a kind of consumer's fad, like skin piercing or tattoos. "Holocaust" is like "love" or "infinity": They are not machines for producing poetry easily (and if used that way, will soon lose their power); they are difficulties to be overcome by any poet who would make poetry of them, raw lumps in the oatmeal.

Many Holocaust poems stress that the Holocaust is unconfrontable, that no one can conceive of or confront 6,000,000 deaths. Actually, 6,000,000 people more or less like us managed, at least, to experience these deaths. Probably 6,000,000 deaths are easier for 6,000,000 people to conceive of than for just the one of me or you (unless you can recall having died 6,000,000 times), but it's not so easy to comprehend 6,000,000 people brushing their teeth or mailing a letter or even breathing (though several billion are doing that right now).

I mean to scold, not the 6,000,000 (who could?[21]), but the tens of thousands of poets who tell us what we can or cannot imagine. After all, it is our job as poets to stretch imaginations, not curl up in apathy at the foot of a wall of rotting bodies. The people who designed and ran the Holocaust[22] had no imagination at all, not even enough to realize they were dealing with people,

---

[21] Actually, I could. Shame on you guys for getting killed! Man, what I could do with 6,000,000 readers with senses of humor intact...

[22] You think you know who I mean, but you don't. Read a book called *The Men Behind Hitler* for a detailed view of the designers. Some of these eugenicists survived the war (in which they proto-typed and designed the death camps and provided

not cockroaches. Hell, to a poet, not even cockroaches are *mere* cockroaches. Possibly the point of poetry is that nothing is *merely* anything.

Something else too few critics are willing to say (though I'm sure many would love to, if they dared) is that there's nothing particularly glorious about being a victim, nor need happiness equate to blissful ignorance:

It's YOUR Fault, Reader

While you read or listen to these words, people are dying,
being born, making love, making history — statistics do not lie.
While you read these words — and one day you will have to explain
why, at a time like this, you were reading these words —
someone is bribing an official, tormenting a child,
rooting in the garbage for scraps, saying "O! I love you! O!"
You are reading these words at a very significant time.
Why are you reading these words?

Some poets are just too "Whilely." Speaking of which, the following was written in answer to a poem by a prominent poet, Jos. Brodsky, read (by the poet himself, recorded) over public radio just after his death:

Mean While

On the radio a distinguished extinguished poet reads a poem
that says while you & I drink our beers or scratch our crotches,
in Bosnia people are dying, which makes sense,
not that we shouldn't be scratching or drinking,
but maybe what we see on the news seems to occur
in some other world, but if we get that it's right now,
maybe we'll get that it's this world, the same one
where we are now — I see that, yet I tire of this trick
of simultaneity: While you laugh, a child starves; while you sleep
in a soft safe bed, a homeless man freezes on a grate. What's so sacred
about time? Or misery? Why not, while you read this poem,
the Nazis slaughter millions and the Romans
crucify Christ and an entire inhabited planet
turns cinder as its sun goes nova?
Or why not tell the dying, look,
it's not so bad; while you writhe in agony,

---

the rationale for them) to create and run the World Mental Health Organization and all its offshoots. Today their disciples run the Government/pharmaceutical/Mental-Health complex, which is senior to the military/industrial complex (we aim to conquer MINDS). Fortunately, the new complex can cure all our complexes, if you don't mind a few side-effects, like a drugged and dying civilization. Many esteemed poets don't seem to mind; why should you?

elsewhere lovers are lost in each other,
elsewhere someone enjoys a sunset
or a snowfall or a cool drink, elsewhere
Christ rises from the dead?
Should we stop scratching our crotches
and get on a plane to Bosnia (would we be allowed
to go there?), and once there do what? Get killed, I suppose,
to earn the right to have previously scratched
and guzzled. Perhaps there is something
I can do for Bosnia, someone to whom I can give money
that will be used well, someone I should vote for —
but the best I can do that I KNOW will help is
do the best I can for myself and others
as I see it to do. If — in honor of the existence of agony anywhere ever —
we were all to cringe away from joys (simple or exotic),
we and all children in Bosnia or Sudan may as well be dead.
The killers (who could be us) kill because they can't imagine anything
better to do. While they kill let us use our imaginations well.
While they (who could be us, our friends, parents, children) die,
let us live enough for us and them too.

I've heard many poets say, in SO many words, "While you guzzle booze and watch bad TV, elsewhere children are being bayoneted and starved...". I keep waiting for these poets to continue, "While I relish writing angry poems, while I stand here being RIGHT and making you WRONG, elsewhere children...". They never do. (By the way, Brodsky, what business to you have being dead while I'm writing such clever stuff? What a pill!)

A Riff for Poets, Editors and Critics
[meaning I'm too lazy to title each one]

I don't like to leave blank lines on a page; who knows what filth others may imagine there!

———

"He wouldn't know a true poem if he stepped in one!"

———

This...is your mind.
This...is a pun.
This...is your mind on puns.
Say NO to puns. (Especially
frying puns.)[23]

———

Academics — amazing! To be that way must take years of study.

---

[23] And to defeat ignorance, just say know!

266

I'm a man of principle: When money talks
I pretend I'm listening
only to critique the style.

———

It's a feminist masterpiece...I mean mspiece.

———

Fad after fad passes me by. I try to catch a crest,
but I'm too far out; each new wave slips beneath me
and rolls off to shatter on the beach.

———

"How many poets are needed to change
a light bulb?" "Thank you for inquiring,
but we are unable at this time to use ANY poets
for changing light bulbs. Please try us again
in a few years."

———

"Do you think I should send this poem to the *Atlantic*?"
"Try the Pacific — it's bigger."

———

Literary magazines should have warnings on their front covers:
"To insure freshness, open before..." — usually last decade.

———

"This poem has a haunting quality" — yes, it reminds me
of something that was once alive.

———

"Good poem, but needs cutting..." "...some unneeded words..." —
poetry now is prose in a too-tight girdle. I miss language
with fat bold bouncing cheeks.

———

"The universe is random," says a poet who,
in some other universe, carefully chooses his words.

———

Here come the ideas: THUMP! THUMP! THUMP!...

———

"Visions are given" she says "to the broken, the ravaged, those
who lay sanity aside." Yes, for those who are whole
take no handouts, but create their own visions.

———

"Who is this 'you' addressed by this 'I' in your poems?"
I is what I am. If the you fits, wear it.

———

Sad poems about the end of the world...why sad?
Wasn't it a good world? Didn't you enjoy it?

A Tut-Tutter's Stutter

I have a speech impediment:
I speak in rhyme and sentiment;
I always stammer in iambs
And praise your free verse with faint dambs.

When one of my poems isn't working, I leave it on a shelf long
enough for all the sentiments to settle out — a slow, sedimental journey,
resulting from a failure to mean exactly what I said I meant [sediment].

A Poem Should Be Mean

This poem is great — it knocks me out!
You too? I hope so — poetry
Should link us, lout to clouted lout:
A poem should not bean but me.

Note: Someone or other (MacLeish — it's become a Macliché) decreed
that a poem should not MEAN, but BE, and since someone or other said it, it
is passed on to poets as truth. To me it suggests a bumper sticker: POETS
DON'T DO IT, BUT **ARE** IT. The above poemlet is intended to suggest that
it don't mean a thing if it ain't got that wing that carries it across from poet to
reader — you know, communication? And meaning is part of that. He who
does not mean, but only Be's will not bean me. The speaker in the poem (me)
hopes that his poem knocks out someone besides himself. I think my poem
shall never be an object lovely as a tree.

Re Critical Schools (e.g. Psychoanalytic):

Landing on the surface of the sun —
Kids in an esoteric candy store
("Look! a symbol! Can this be a pun!") —
Lighting their way with candles, they explore.

I'm kind of dumb (you may have noticed): I went through decades
of college, grad school, teaching and writing without ever understanding why
something is more profound or universal or interesting for being mythic or a
symbol, why it's better not to look at what's in front of one's face, but rather
to get a hint of it via a Rube Goldberg conglommeration of allusions and
indirections, or why congealed masses of old pain and grief about as pro-
found as being hit over the head repeatedly with a mallet should be consid-
ered deep and significant by virtue of their being far away in time or space.

Frankly, I think the stars are watching US to see what we'll do next, so that they can set their galactic orbits accordingly, and I suspect that my penis is a symbol (as St. Paul says, a *tinkling* symbol) of Sigmund Freud. As for the cave of the Delphic Oracle, I think it's a foreshadowing of T. S. Eliot's mouth.

Emfunctioning the Dyspowerful

Minds mediocre think alike, O
Culture rife with babble psycho!

Like poets and editors, critics suffer from swarm syndrome. 90% of "critical thought" consists of assigning to poems and poets the favored adjectives of the day. If you're not hip to the latest adjectives, you find yourself reading a review and wondering if "hard-edged," "acid," "nervous," and "mythic" indicate a rave or a pan.

The Vision Thing

Dog poets are smellinaries. They stand in a field,
sniffing the future, detect it, trot up to it and lightly deposit
a perfect poem. Then they go home and sniff telesmell.

Dog critics, squinting, scuttling, nose to the ground,
are also sniffers, not seers. When a poem appears,
they sniff it to see if it already has their scent.
If not, they piss on it, unless it has a rival's scent.
Then they go nuts and tear it to shreds.

Toss a poet in heat among a swarm of critics,
and instantly they are squirming each other aside
to sniff its ass. "Lacks vision! Lacks voice!" they yelp,
peeing on it, nipping at it, or, delighted to find their familiar
smell ("so fresh! so unique! so savvy beyond its years!
so authoritative!"), they try to mount it. When,
exhausted, it slips away from them, for a long time,
where it piddled, ardently they roll in the stink.

Of course, not all poets and critics are dogs. There are plenty of cats as well. So how come all these tame critters are trying to put everyone *else* to sleep?

Tanka, But No Tanka[24]

He sends me his poems.
They are bad. What can I say?
Say I grow old and
lies are not true. Say I'm a
fool; teach me how to teach you.

This is the Poem

This is the poem that the modern poet wrote.

This is the corn that sprouted in the poem that the modern poet wrote.

This is the reader who gobbled up the corn that sprouted in the poem that the modern poet wrote.

This is the complex image that haunted the reader who gobbled up the corn that sprouted in the poem that the modern poet wrote.

This is the symbol the author had no intention of putting into the complex image that haunted the reader who gobbled up the corn that sprouted in the poem that the modern poet wrote.

This is the critic who "discovered" the symbol the author had no intention of putting into the complex image that haunted the reader who gobbled up the corn that sprouted in the poem that the modern poet wrote.

This is the word misunderstood by the critic who "discovered" the symbol the author had no intention of putting into the complex image that haunted the reader who gobbled up the corn that sprouted in the poem that the modern poet wrote.

---

[24] A tanka is a Japanese form (this poem is one — or tries to be) or a ship used to transport oil.

This is the meaning that needs the word misunderstood by the critic who "discovered" the symbol the author had no intention of putting into the complex image that haunted the reader who gobbled up the corn that sprouted in the poem that the modern poet wrote.

This is the universe full of tenderness and beauty unlocked by the meaning that needs the word misunderstood by the critic who "discovered" the symbol the author had no intention of putting into the complex image that haunted the reader who gobbled up the corn that sprouted in the poem that the modern poet wrote.

This is the modern poet locked up all alone in the universe full of tenderness and beauty unlocked by the meaning that needs the word misunderstood by the critic who "discovered" the symbol the author had no intention of putting into the complex image that haunted the reader who gobbled up the corn that sprouted in the poem that the modern poet wrote.

This is the psychiatrist who guards the cell of the modern poet locked up all alone in the universe full of tenderness and beauty unlocked by the meaning that needs the word misunderstood by the critic who "discovered" the symbol the author had no intention of putting into the complex image that haunted the reader who gobbled up the corn that sprouted in the poem that the modern poet wrote.

This is the fancy label (*Para-Pseudo-Schizo-Bullshitus-Syndrome*) used by the psychiatrist who guards the cell of the modern poet locked up all alone in the universe full of tenderness and beauty unlocked by the meaning that needs the word misunderstood by the critic who "discovered" the symbol the author had no intention of putting into the

271

complex image that haunted the reader who gobbled up the corn that sprouted in the poem that the modern poet wrote.

This is the physical universe whose solidity is protected by the fancy label (*Para-Pseudo-Schizo-Bullshitus-Syndrome*) used by the psychiatrist who guards the cell of the modern poet locked up all alone in the universe full of tenderness and beauty unlocked by the meaning that needs the word misunderstood by the critic who "discovered" the symbol the author had no intention of putting into the complex image that haunted the reader who gobbled up the corn that sprouted in the poem that the modern poet wrote.

This is a simple poem written in simple language to blast a gap in the walls of the physical universe whose solidity is protected by the fancy label (*Para-Pseudo-Schizo-Bullshitus-Syndrome*) used by the psychiatrist who guards the cell of the modern poet locked up all alone in the universe full of tenderness and beauty unlocked by the meaning that needs the word misunderstood by the critic who "discovered" the symbol the author had no intention of putting into the complex image that haunted the reader who gobbled up the corn that sprouted in the poem that the modern poet wrote.

****

15 years after writing the preceding (since performed breathlessly at many readings), I rewrote it to make it rhyme, as does its inspiration, "This is the House That Jack Built" — and my wife shrieked "NO! You shouldn't have changed it," joined in her alarms by two poet friends (believe it or not, some poets dare to be my friends). I yield to "my public" — all three of it. But here's the last stanza of my rhyming revision, for you rhyme-and-meter buffs and because *I* rather like it. (Poetry, by the way, is not "Jack-Built," but Jerry-rigged.)

This is a poem
To point the way home
From the trap of the physical,
Where all fall to HIS sickle —

Why? Don't be quizzical!
Just read the tome
(*Para-Pseudo-Schizo-Bullshitus Syndrome*)
In itself, quite a poem! —
Used by Herr Doktor
Who guards the locked door
Of the modern poet
Pent up all inchoate,
Alone in his world
With lustrous tears pearled,
Unlocked by the meaning,
Discarded gleaning,
That needs the word —
And this is absurd! —
Misunderstood by the critic,
QUITE analytic,
Who discovered the theme
The author couldn't dream
Would animate the image,
Murk for a dim age,
That haunted the reader,
Desultory speeder,
Who gobbled up the corn
That sprouted one morn
In the poem of note
That the modern poet wrote.

So you see, as heroes of corny Existentialist dramas would say to their eager-to-be-accused-of ANYthing-if -it-makes-them-feel-deeper-and-hipper (that is, hip-deep in it), *you are ALL guilty!* — poets, readers, critics, shrinks — you are ALL guilty of the death of civilization. So there! I'm sure glad I'M pure of heart. My book's length is as the length of ten because my art is spur — I hope a sharp spur.[25]

---

[25] It's Tennyson's Sir Galahad (in "Idylls of the King"?) who says "My strength is as the strength of ten/ Because my heart is pure." As Galahad later explained, "That's what I said to every gal I had." Hey, a good line is a good line.

And Now, From my Latest Work, a Few Natural Selections...

"Nature red in tooth & claw."
Poetry read in booth and closet.
Fellow poets, let us posit
Poetry read in truth and awe.   [Awe? Shucks!]

Section 5: Aspirations

Chapter 9: I'll Make You Talk Purty, Poet!

A Few Lines For Picking Up the Single Reader

Please, Reader, keep our illicit activity a secret, lest I be charged with use of the language with intent to communicate; you with contributing to the delinquency of a minor poet.

I could incorporate. Would you read a poem by Ink, Inc.?[1]

Poet moves among words and phrases, peers, sniffs, rejects — Diogenes looking for an honest line.

I want to make the world, not a nice place to live, but a nice place to visit.

We lack, not heroes, but poets. We have plenty of knights eager to save the day if only someone would create it.

Poets Who Give Their Poems To Strangers: Next On Oprah![2]

"Parents! Teach your children: 'If a stranger tries to talk to you, RUN AWAY!'" No wonder no one listens to poets.

Sign at the front desk: "THE LIBRARY DOES NOT MAKE CHANGE" — alas.

Poetry is a communication devoutly to bewitched.

Poetry is the who entering into and impregnating the whom with a loud WE!

I try to be alive to the world in hopes that, one day, seeing a three-year-old child look, touch and laugh, I'll be able to say, "That's nothing! My sixty-year-old poet can do as well as that!"

*How many poets does it take to change the sun?
One good one.*

---

[1] That's too good. I'll bet some damned corporation already uses that name. ("I work for I.I., sir.") A company that prints pornography could be Inking Kink Inc. If it's a subsidiary of King Features, it might be King Inking Kink Inc. (Say it fast and it's almost like delivering milk bottles.) Speaking of company names, I'd like to start a company called "A Major New York Publisher" to publish my books.

[2] "Oprah" — a drama where everyone sings or Harpo spelled backwards. Oprah sometimes gains weight rapidly, at which times signs in the studio warn, palindromically: HARPOON NO OPRAH!

Chapter 9
I'll *Make* You Talk Purty, Poet!

"You there, writer, there's a poem in my soup!"
"Sorry, Sir...there!" (plucking it out between fingertips delicately,
*   shaking off golden droplets), "Good as new!"*
"Take it back, you imbecile! I can't eat that soup now!"
"Yessir, sorry, sir" (And thank you for finding my poem).

> *There are a few other poets on this planet,*
> *but I'm the main one. When, at full moon,*
> *a stake is driven through my shriveled heart,*
> *all the others will be cured.*

After hearing from many readers that they were tired of hearing poems about poets and would prefer poems about "real life," I became puzzled. I always assumed that everyone knew what a fascinating adventure the life of a poet is. After all, no one pays the poet for poeting. Why pay a guy for having fun? But now, learning that poems about poets are boring, I have to think of a new reason for not being paid for poetry. (Because you can't eat it? We could write on rice paper.) Or else I could reveal to all you Philistines the incredibly diverse lives we poets lead. Critical literature tends to class poets as academic or underground (which is more or less the same thing — the academics are buried in fancier coffins) or by nationality or race or sex or use of traditional forms, but what about the samurai poet, the private-eye poet, the vampire poet, the used-car-salesman poet, the terrorist poet and poems written by multi-national corporations?

Apparently most critics mistake poets for grown-ups — and perhaps too many poets do too. Personally, I don't see the point in being a poet if I have to grow up anyway. After all, children are rather inarticulate. If we poets don't speak for them, who will? I once heard someone say "What a mystery! I wonder what these babies are thinking?" I replied, "Why don't we teach one to talk and then ask it?" Alas, it seems that in learning to talk, most of us forget. Few of the graces of childhood can survive English irregular verbs.

Those of us who *can* acquire a reasonable mastery of the language without growing up...(excuse me, my diaper needs changing — ah, that's better!)...yes, those of us who survive here in NevermoreNevermoreland are the poets. We live in a world free of critics, so Wendy your way to the land where pans peter out along with the punctuation. In this chapter, we discuss a few of the games poets play when they assume no one else is looking (because no one reads poetry, thank God!). Now let us spy upon the inner life (I mean besides their digestive systems, etc.) of the Poet! Watching a plump, balding poet scribbling in a notebook or pitter-patting a keyboard, who would suspect he was in the presence of (TADA!) (pocketa pocketa) the...

Samurai![3]

Hey gunslinger, Hey samurai —
watch me handle those words!
They saunter & strut — a pack of bullies.
Now they notice me. I move up to them
almost without moving. I look straight at them
as if they aren't there. Something
In my stillness stills them.
No one can be that still, that
silent. Noisily they overcome their fears. "Look here, boys —
a poet!" "Ah ha ha ho ho har!"
Knee slapping. I am still. My eyes —
You have seen such eyes in dreams. My hand,
my pen yet unseen. "Hey, boys —
Poet here is gonna make us into a poem!"
"Ah har har har!" My silence becomes audible
in their heartbeats. They stop laughing; swelling their vowels,
standing tall, the big words nudge near:
"Better move on...POET!" They spit the last word.
I am still.
"Show him who's boss!" "Break his pen!"
"Let's cut poet up & teach him to talk
purty." "Say something purty, poet —
I'll MAKE you talk purty!" A Hand moves...
Where was stillness, Lightning flashes! Instantly
my style is everywhere — at each cutting stroke, words shriek
and fall in place. A second later, all is still except
the last groans of a mortally maimed cliché.

---

[3] This poem steals a scene from the movie *Yojimbo*, a Blaxploitation flick in which the hero's buddies greet him, "Yo! Jimbo!"

The street is strewn with corpses: the excessive adjectives,
the cute words, the earnest words,
mercilessly, even a few of my own pet words
grown too big for their own good.
I show no sign of remorse nor pleasure.
I look briefly at what I have wrought.
It will do.
Suddenly my pen is sheathed. Sharply
I turn my back on the bloody poem and
stride quietly down the page, casting a long shadow.
Cowed words scurry behind doors and windows as I pass.
No one dreams of crossing my path.

Thank you, Toshiro, my funny bard.[4] Equally hard to spot behind his outwardly meek, vaguely disheveled demeanor is Phillip Marlowe or Sam Spade — but isn't poetry *The Big Sleep*?

Private Eye

He was nervous — they always are,
the new ideas, fidgeting in front of my big desk.
I didn't have to ask what he wanted. I'd seen it all before:
The threadbare concept, the vague, tired image,
bathed in unearthly light. "Look," I said,
"Why don't you go to the press?
They can find words for anything,
fast and cheap." "You don't understand —
I'm a very private thought. You
are a private poet, aren't you?"
"You bet." (Three cob-webbed file cabinets full
of private poetry.) "But I don't handle
love poems. They're nothing but trouble.
Make a bum out of you every time."
I cracked my knuckles. His cigarette ashes missed the tray.
"But you're my last hope! I've tried greeting card writers, novelists,
    cartoonists —
I even begged a whole English Lit. and American Studies Department!
No one would help me. I simply *must* have a Poet!"
His eyes were as bloodshot and chaotic as my own.
But what the hell, I'd had nothing else to say lately,
and there was a strangled eloquence about him,
just the hint of a new angle. If I'd known then

---

[4] *Yojimbo* stars the late great Toshiro Mifune, who speaks the great line, "Better if all these poets were dead," though since he mutters it to his *sake* (rice wine), it sounds like "people," not "poets."

where it would lead me — tangling with six rough drafts,
getting tied up in a sestina, fighting off a mob
of sentiments, the blood-chilling message from Mr. Big
("...indeed sorry...cannot use your work..."), and most of all
HER, Muse, sweet, sad Muse, those big dumb eyes pleading
with mine to go on, find the missing words somehow —
Ah, Muse, what did I get you into!... Had I known,
I wonder, would I still have returned his feverish stare
(He *had* to be expressed, see — it takes some of them
that way) and said so nonchalantly "Okey dokey, I'll give it
a whirl...."

Samurai? Private Eye? These, at least, are possibilities. But some
poets even dream of being desperately needed, like famous surgeons or drug
dealers:

Two CCs of 1% Lyricism — STAT!

It was a good party. I was on my third martini
when I saw the haggard wild-eyed man staring
in the doorway and thought, "Not another one!"
As I'd feared — "Please! Please!" he cried out
(the music stopped) — "Is there a POET in the house?
There's a man out here who *badly* needs a poet!"
I was tempted to slip away into the kitchen, but
after all, I AM a poet, and duty is duty...

We all know that monsters are just heroes who have been abused. In
a world where so many are blind to the heroism of writing poetry, the embit-
tered bard may give up on being heroic and become King Kong or Godzilla.
(Fortunately for the poet, no one notices.)

Return of the Poet

The eons-old ice thaws from around a monstrous prehistoric
poet. He lies pallid in the sun, looking almost alive...Look!
His pen hand! Did it twitch! OMYGOD! It's...It's
ALIVE! Men, women children (the usual lot)
run screaming down Fifth Avenue,
but not fast enough: With his pen he captures them all.
Tiny cars scuttle under his monstrous metrical foot,
honking, swerving — here, reader, have a crumpled car...

(Later we discover the poet isn't really a monster,
but was misunderstood, was trying to save Fay Wray
from a giant machine or to say something important;
the surviving helicopters and F16s are called off
and he comes down from Mt. Everest's peak
to tiptoe among the midget earthlings and nourish them
with songs — whispered so as not to deafen them —
and make light of their walls until they can grow to his size
and play.)

Son Of King Kong Meets The Poet

A kid in a gorilla mask runs up making shrill sounds to be scary.
I'm trying to write. Kid, stop trying to impress me
with your mask. I'm busy trying to impress readers with mine.

"Fierce" masks look painful.
It must hurt to be a monster.

The kid stumbles near my chair, then says
"It's hard to see with this mask on."
I tell him, "It's dangerous work
being a monster." "Yeah," he says,
"They get stepped on and crunched
by dinosaurs." "What happens
to the dinosaurs?" "They get
frozen. THAT'S what happens to dinosaurs!"

SLURRRP!
Sorry, Kid, you interrupted my writing,
so into the poem you go, gorilla,
dinosaurs and all. Whatever stops
my poems, sticks to them. (The Poet
That Ate Chicago!)

Yes! There are monsters among us!...why is no mob running from us, screaming? Oh well, we can look to the future for recognition, if not as art, then as artifact, scraps of scribble found in 20th-Century kitchen (or more likely bathroom) middens — from the days when people used to read and write:

Artifact

These are letters and words, my children;
Long ago they meant something.
You stare for a long moment,
wondering what sort of a thing is this?
A diagram? The cardiagraph of an ancient heart?
Part of some ancient ritual? You leave
the museum. Perhaps you'll never know
I was talking to you.

Sometimes we create role models for both reader *and* poet. When my dignity is sufficiently frayed by lack of recognition from friendly idiots (or, worse, by recognition of idiots who aren't me!), I play Hardy to your Laurel, reader; but more often, I play Laurel to your perplexed, bullying, know-it-all Hardy:

da DUMP da DUMP, da DUMP da DUMP...

"Now see what a fine mesh you've gotten us into!"
says thick Hardy reader to subtle Laureled poet.

"You see, it's the deacon struck
my sub-Texans in a fresh new vice[5] — OUCH!"

"Explain every word of this, poet," fumes reader,
fumbling with his tie, "or it's Oliver between us!"

"I didn't mean anything," whimpers poet, pulling
at his long hair, "but the words must Stan."

"ooooOOOOOOO!" cries reader, and kicks poet square
in his posterity!

Poet, looking hurt, picks himself up,
dusts himself off, then, with a sudden
flat-footed flurry of smug cunning,
clobbers reader with an ironic allusion.

---

[5] I know you already got that "deacon struck my sub-Texans in a fresh new vice" is "deconstruct my sub-texts in a fresh new voice," but I'm putting it here anyway, because YOU, my brilliant Sir or Madam, are one of the very few among my (almost as few) readers who got it. I congratulate you on not needing this footnote — which I sincerely hope you are NOT reading, and thank you for not smoking while this book is open — I can't take it.

"OOF!" Reader glares at poet and, with meticulous intention
(eyed the while by fascinated poet), yanks the funding
out from beneath the poet — Ollie...**OOP!** —

not realizing that in doing so...

Moments or decades later, thinking nothing more can be left
to collapse in upon them, Hardy reader and Laureled poet
protrude pained heads out of the heap of their shattered language,

exchange a long sad look
(having   nothing   to   say)
and are beaned — each of them —
(PLINK! PLONK!)
by two final falling clichés.

"ooo...**OO!**"
"Whimper whimper..."

But it's futile to bully and crush and devour. I want *living, servile*
readers who love everything I write. If only I were a dictator or Gestapo
officer or a school principal, *then* I could get all the readers:

The Management Regrets...

Dear Reader,
I am not a hard poet to get along with, and I deplore
unnecessary violence, but there are times
when the sweetest of tempers is strained.
Be warned. I expect and have every right to expect that
our next batch of poems will be the finest poems
ever written, and with your co-operation and a big push from
all concerned, that's just what they'll be, so snap to it, and
let's not hear any more whining and grouching, shall
we? Or matters may become serious.

Dear Reader,
I have been asked by my superiors
to inform you of our new policy: Any
readers found laughing or otherwise
misreacting to serious poetry or simply
skipping the poems to get to the
cartoons will be dealt with accordingly.
You are being watched.
                    Best,

Your Author

Let's be civilized about this —
Guards, take the readers out behind the barn
and shoot them.

Cameos

I try to give myself to poetry,
but poetry straight-arms me, saying,
"When I want you,
I'll take you."

———

I offer myself to poetry,
who shrugs and says "Thanks,"
politely, long used to having heaps
of embarrassing, unexchangeable gifts
gather cobwebs in the attic.

———

Don't blame me for my poetry:
The muse made me do it.

———

"Feed me!" grunts my notebook — "More words! More cleverness!
More juicy words! Feed me!" Daily I ransack the language
for fresh victims, lest my notebook, grown ravenous,
leave me speechless.

———

"READ me! READ me!" growls the man-eating poem.
Furtively the poet haunts workshops and readings,
scavenging for readers, lest he himself be swallowed
by his insatiable poem.

———

What did the grotesque idea from inner space say
to the poet? "Take me to your reader!"

———

The physical universe rambles on,
Satisfied that I am attentive
because I pretend to take notes,
while actually I scribble this gossip
to pass around to my classmates.

———

Into the crowded room bristling with
guitars, I walk with my pen.

———

284

"Tell us what gave you the courage
To plunge 300 feet off the bridge into
An icy river to save that man's life?"
"Well — I'm a poet. I thought:
What if he's a reader?"

———

No, don't thank me, Reader —
It's my job.

———

"Ahm warnin' yuh — stay away from them
poems. A lotta good men have gone into them poems,
but ain't nobody never come back."

———

You can be the hero of my poems.
I'll be the comic sidekick.

———

Look at that poet jumping up and down
and wagging his tongue — Reader,
I think he's trying to tell us something!

———

Someday, my Reader,
all these poems will be yours!

———

Do you turn away and smoke a cigarette
after reading my poems, Reader?

———

You laughed at the wrong place!
Go, Reader! And never darken my page again!

———

There are aliens among us: Even now, two gleaming balls of jelly,
each with a dark opening in front, make quick movements to scan
these lines.

———

I challenge you to a duel: Poems at two centuries!

———

I'm not sure how to classify the next role — the poet as Mr. Magoo? It
amazes me how blatantly some of the most militantly "environmental" po-
ets waste trees with their scribbling. (What do they think — that trees grow
on trees!?)

Will Anyone be Here to Hear

Perhaps as the ecological spiral
tightens to a point, the world's last
great poet will stroll down the world's

last corridor of giant trees, while,
at a discreet distance behind him
(not to distract him), the world's last
lumberjacks hack down the trees
to make the pulp to make the paper
for the book (the world's last
great book of poetry) that the poet
is being inspired to write.

It would be more elegant if we could eliminate the lumberjacks and
have the sheer creative vision of the poet (like a laser beam) causing the
instant vanishment of everything he thus perceives: POOF! That's a more
hopeful vision, too, because someone that creative could put the trees back
again — fresh new versatile trees.

The poet in the next poem has a line — and I don't mean a line of
poetry, but a LINE, like "What's a reader like you doing in a poem like this?"
or "Dear Reader, your place or mine?" (Dream on, poet — whoever heard of
a place for poetry?)

To His Shy Reader

We fumble for each other...
Is this your first time too?
As I try clumsily to reach around you
and undo your snug attitudes,
the kiss of my most serious thought
bumps into the teeth of your unready smile.

You have never been touched
by words before? You are afraid
it will hurt? And I —

I too find it hard baring to you thoughts
I seldom share with my own mirror.

Reader, we are green in these matters.
Let us be gentle with one another.
It will take humor too to unsnap and unlace
the elaborate girdles of everyday uses of language
that bind us in silence.

Let me touch you...don't be ashamed.
Already in your modest gesture
of drawing back from my personal
pronouns, I catch a glimpse

of what you are and find that —
without your body — you are
ravishing.

Almost heroic (thank God I'm no longer a teen-ager. Heroism of that sort is exhausting), this exploration of *terra incognito* — the reader! The next two poems continue this theme with Ulysses Poet and Christopher Columbus Poet:

While Penelope Stalls a Horde of Fresh New Voices...

Navigating the frail hour I've chosen
to spend writing poems, veering to avoid
the nagging Scylla clutch of undone dishes,
unanswered letters..., then slewing to
windward to dodge the sucking Charybdis
vortex of TV set, newspaper, refrigerator.

C'mon, a few of you need to look up Scylla and Charybdis. Here's a hint: Scylla is that great big dictionary with the teensy print and definitions that force you to look up *other* definitions. Charybdis is what happens to your mind if you don't use that dictionary. Penelope (in the title) is the reader, staving off (as Penelope did the false suitors while waiting for her hubby, Ulysses, to come reeling back from the sack of Troy) mobs of boring poets while "I" (Ulysses) navigate dangerous seas to bring her some live communication. (Sure, Dean, sure.)

Discovering the Reader

"The world is flat!" sages allege:
"Your words will hurtle off the edge!"

No. I believe the world is round.
I set sail, rend my voice with urging
Sullen words to make them sound:
"Sail on! Sail on! Beyond this surging
Sea of hacks, illiteracy
And editors who run in herds
Awaits a New World where I'll be
Refashioned from my golden words."

I find a world, but not the one I sought:
Vast realms, new gods, but nothing I am not.

He must have had no women aboard. If they'd heard "Sale on!" they'd have milled about him screaming "Where! Where!" (A Columbus Day Sale, no doubt.)[6]

Here come some roles for character actors, offering work to poets too old to play heroes, too urbane to play monsters:

Beware of Hello

I've created a poetry virus: It takes advantage
of a little-known weakness in human isolation
called the Live Communication utility, uses it to
penetrate the system, and proliferates itself
at readings, in creative writing courses and in magazines,
clogging the lines, making it almost impossible
for anyone to even *think* of writing SERIOUS poetry.

She's Never Forgiven Me

Poetry doesn't come easily to me.
I drag her in, kicking and screaming:
"No! Not without all my pretty
adjectives! O! My complexity! You...
you you PIG! What have you done to my
best symbols! My GOD! No! Stop! People
will see me like this and get the idea
I'm talking to them! Wait! Noooo...!"

Ever since my falling out with this academic muse, she pretends she doesn't know me. "This is really funny stuff," said a reader. "Are you sure it's poetry?"

My muse is Urania, Muse of Astronomy: I want to be a star. Has Urania been helping me? To put it palindromically: "Start, Urania! In a rut? Rats!" (Actually, as a satirist addressing my fellow poets, my muse is Uranus, which is where I advise you to "submit" [place under or stick up] your poems.)

Used Word Dealer

I try to return these words to use. Nothing fancy here:
The words I refurbish don't have that new-word smell,
you won't be dazzled blind by polished adjectives.

---

[6] Actually, Columbus cried "Ceylon! Ceylon!" He thought he was heading for Asia.

288

But my words will carry you somewhere. There are posh,
chrome-shiny words that break down just outside
the used-word lot. Mine will get you home.

———

Special deal on simple words: Easy terms!

Brace Yourself

The education of a poet is like a trip
To the dentist: Young poet opens wide,
And into his mouth are stuffed wads
Of cotton, tubes, clamps — all the
Bric-a-brac of 20th Century Poetry.
At last, mouth agape with surreal
Drains and cutting imagery, muffled
With obscure allusions, the poet
Is ready to speak ("How's it feel?
OK?" asks the dentist): "Mmphrgypxt"
Mumbles the patient/poet to his
Admiring, uncomprehending audience.

(And you thought it was *your* fault you couldn't understand poetry?
No, it's just all that impacted wisdom and maybe some insipid canines —
responsible for doggerel.)

Audition

They know I'm coming. I hear the whisper in the grass:
"Get ready! The poet is coming!" I feel the million
quaking hearts about me. This is *my* production. I can make
or break them. Tremulous, they audition for my next poem:
"Very good, old tree, nice toss of leaves, nice patchwork
shadow. I'll call on you when I need you, thank you. No,
sorry, little staring cat, not quite what I need.
Ah! That soot-speck cloud of starlings!
Get their name!"

Alas, it's true, the props and ideas must fight to get into my poems.
And almost always, when someone tells me, "You'll probably put that in a
poem," it's the last thing I care to use. (People usually say that about some-
thing "poetic" or, better, something that is already a poem and needs no help
from me.) So if you've been dreaming, as so many do, of running away from
home to make THE BIG TIME by starring in one of my poems, be warned
that you will probably end up with nearly all the other wannabe muses (women,
heroic figures, trees, squares of sidewalk half-pink and half mauve in the

setting sun...), standing on dark street corners, trying to flag down weekend poetasters and poetastresses and pretentious journalists in hopes of being used. And even if you *do* make it into a poem, you may be cut in the umpteenth revision. It's a rough life...

The Undead

"Inspire": Breathe into. The inspirer fills one with breath,
which one then exhales. It's like mouth-to-mouth resuscitation:
Breath of the dead, living, stirs me rhythmically
with such vigor that it becomes, at last, my own breath,
and I rise, as undead as they, a poet, a voice, thing of air
no mirror can see, and go forth in search of the dying
to make them live.

Which makes us vampires in reverse? Can the living dead make the living live? Then why do so many people say that poetry *sucks*? Oh well, what do they know? The same people call sucking a "blowjob" (maybe they mean "belowjob"). (Our spell checker wants to convert "Blehert" to "blowhard" or "blurt.")

...So Here We Are

"Hello", I say in sign language, "noble natives of the physical universe!
I come bearing many pretty trinkets: Happy poems, sad poems, silly poems
to trade with you for your sleek, supple bodies, glowing planets, shiny stars
and other produce." Alas, I must return empty-handed; there *are* no
natives here, just hordes of roaming visitors like me who refuse or are
unable to trade what they insist they do not own, and I lost all my poems
at a perilous crossing. Let's see...which way did I come in? Oops!

I suspect that in this universe, not even the rocks are natives. They're visitors like us who've been failing to get out for so long that they're frozen in apathy. Listen...you can just barely hear them muttering to themselves.

Enough with the explorers already. I've just cut (ouch) my "Stanley and Livingston" poem ("Dear Reader, I presume.") I'm tired of being in de Nile.

Thank God No One's Listening!

In this country a man can walk from town to town,
unarmed, unescorted, carrying manuscripts

full of priceless poetry and not be robbed;
can write any bloody awful subversive thing
and not be hanged nor jailed nor noticed.
This is a safe country for poets,
a dangerous country for poetry.

"He Read a Poem and Disappeared"

Poets, join our light-winged life squad! We mail
life threats to those deadly folk who never disagree,
and if they persist in their reasonableness,
we drag them from their dark rooms and animate them.
Usually their bodies are not heard from again.

But their voices live on? Is that a good thing, all these living voices?
Are the media happy media? (Or as Keats would say, "O happy happy media!") More often *Medea* is a tragedy. In the next poem it's tragi-cosmic:

All Things Belabored

Poet, John Keats, announced in London yesterday that beauty
is truth and truth beauty. That, said Mr. Keats to reporters
at the annual Grecian Urn Gala, is all ye know on earth
and, in fact, all ye need to know. As of this morning
there has been no official response from either Moscow
or Washington, but spokesmen from the Administration
confirm an atmosphere of cautious optimism. How
is this announcement likely to impact the English language?
We have with us in the studio Professor Quincy Wimpus
of Rhomboid University to discuss the latest developments.
Professor Wimpus, is this just more rhetorical posturing,
or does Keats really mean it this time, and if he does,
will the critics stand for it? "Well, Scott, it's hard to *say*.
Keats *is* young, but he *does* have a certain *following...*"

We end this chapter on a note of the much-despised reality. So much throbbingly bad poetry is excused as being "deeply personal," that it is logical to seek a definition of the poet's role in the Personals Column:

ISO-lated Poet ISO U

Fat, arguably funny, if not crude, 55-year-old MWP (married white poet), non-smoker, enjoys verbs, nouns and occasional adjectives, relishes pronouns, likes to twist syntax, and prepositions with respect to has a real thing about, ISO several million S/M/D W/B/Y/R M/F Rs (single/married/divorced white/black/yellow/red male/female readers) who share his exotic tastes; for long-term commitment only. Send picture, preferably Lincoln, Hamilton, Jackson or Franklin, but Washington will be considered.

Section 5: Aspirations

Chapter 10: Or At Least Less Fat

In the Beginning Were Just a Few Words

If everyone else were dead, I would be THE poet! But do not drive me to such measures, Reader: Read me!

In the words of a famous poet, "of," "the," "and," "to" and "if."

When I can feel joy and sorrow more intense than man has known, I'll be a great poet or a dog.

These are the people: kind, sad, funny, worried, angry, sour, clever, dense... — these, there are no other; if you wait for the RIGHT people, you will become a great waiter, for THESE are the people of whose agreement any greatness you achieve must consist.

To crave fame is to crave memories of having had high hopes.

Immortality? What we engrave in stone is written in future sand that, polished to glass, will reveal only the ancient explosions of stars.

Live forever in my poetry? A tempting offer. But will you live here with me?

Immortality — can't live with it, can't live without it...

Every poet's goal: To strike the world one day with a notable silence.

You find me hard to take? I find me hard to give.

When a poet dies unknown, part of each person who never read those poems dies unknown.

That which comes after one, posterity or posterior — you must be able to tell the difference, if you want to know what you can do with your poems.

Posterity, my ass!

When I'm famous, I'll be all over the place — but will I be able to recognize me?

Are we great, good or just meaty jokers?[1]

This is the present. The next line
was the future. This line
is now the past, and the next line will be
the present — and has been for some time now.

No beauty is lost for a poet:
When you goodbye it, hello it.

---

[1] For the pun-impaired, meaty jokers puns "mediocres" — and describes mortals (flesh). Humans are the only meat that dresses itself.

Chapter 10
Or At Least Less Fat

Tubby or not tubby, that is the questing.

Fame has not changed me,
  though I daily bask in the applause
of future readers.

> *Please, Lord, make me a great*
>   *and famous poet or at least*
>   *less fat.*

This chapter deals with a mirage called greatness and with a few of its lures, for example, fame and immortality. These are among the goads and banes of a poet's (especially a young — like under 100 years old — poet's) existence. For one thing, no one pays you to do your poetry, so you have to justify doing it, and how better to justify it than by telling yourself (and a few privileged friends) that you are not merely a poet, but a GREAT poet — this at a stage in your writing when you should be concentrating on writing lots and lots of poems and wasting them as fast as you can. Instead, having to be GREAT, you go about in a daze for months at a time waiting to be lofted by a gust of inspiration that will wane after seven poems and drop you in a field of stony puns and stunted metaphors.

Then there's the exhilaration of creation — ANY creation. It's easy to confuse this with greatness, because, in a way, it IS greatness. It's you, the poet, becoming aware of yourself as a joyous god in your own universe — a universe where, when you say "Let there be light!" there is light. For *you*, there is light. Whether any reader is capable of seeing your light — that is another matter. Some of the worst art ever created (for example, the movie *Plan Nine From Outer Space*) was created by artists in the full throes of joyous inspiration. They LOVED what they were doing! They were riding a wave of their own greatness. Only they lacked the tools of their trade — for example, taste, technique, awareness of any audience other than themselves. They couldn't make others see the light. Their greatness grated.

This is fine if you don't care whether anyone else knows about your greatness and if you can ignore the jeers and be fooled by the admiration of those who dutifully dote on you. But most of us soon become aware of a deafening silence out there where thunderous applause should be. And there we are — KNOWING we are great, but not knowing how to break the news to others. Nor is it easy to see what pleases others. We hang out with other poets, but can learn little from them because, somehow, great must mean greatEST. One stands alone! The greatness of any other than a few long dead poets (who, one imagines, would endorse one's status) diminishes ONE'S greatness.

And from this lonely summit of greatness, the last thing we are apt to think of is that the next step is something as humble as learning the tools of the trade, learning how to talk in poetry as a baby learns how to talk in words, so that, as the child learns words so well that he can use them to communicate without paying attention to the fact that he is using words, similarly the poet learns the devices of poetry (for example, rhythm, sounds and connotations of words, syntax, metrics) so well that the use of them doesn't impede communication — and then?...

Then am I great? Am I great yet? Aha! We're still suckers for mirages. It is hard to attain something as ill-defined as "greatness" and hard to write anything at all when working towards a goal for which (we don't realize) we have no clear definition. Each word must be a gem. A capricious, arbitrary censor sits in one's head judging each tentative line "not quite right — not what I want at all." And will I still respect it in 300 years?

No, poet, you've mastered the tools. You can point and shoot — choose an effect and create it. Now you're GOOD. You've got professional quality. Now do some good with it. Help create a richer culture. Do something you and others will value. (Say something nice.) But no, that's too simple. So we define greatness — how? By looking at poets considered great and trying to emulate them — which produces very mixed blessings, hordes of miniature Shakespeares, Shelleys, Eliots, Bukowskis...OK, so there's no end of folly. Blake says "If the fool would persist in his folly, he would become wise." And occasionally one emulates one's idol into a dark alley, does away with him and goes one's own way.

(Yes, Reader, I'm aware I switched from 2nd person to first to third to... — Hey, we're all friends here.)

Sure, there's such a thing as greatness: It's when you are widely considered to be great. Alas, I am now greatly wide and inconsiderate, but my greatness is just over the next editor. Here are some poems about "The Great Poet":

I Said SIT DOWN!

I am the world's greatest poet.
The next time I am called up to read
at an open reading with a 5-minute time limit,
I'm going to reach the end of my 5 minutes and
go on reading, poem after poem, like a filibuster,
ignoring audience hemming, the emcee's attempts
to be polite, chairs scraping, legs crossing and
uncrossing, the desperate fidgeting of poets who have
not yet read — I'll go on reading, and when the emcee rises
to take my arm, I'll pull out my poetry-reading special
and shoot him in the gut and go on reading. At first
the audience will think it's a gag, try to laugh.
The bravest will approach or edge toward the door.
I'll make them all sit down, shoot a few if necessary,
and go on reading. I have many poems
no one has ever heard.
I am the world's greatest poet.

It is indeed odd how politely we treat the poets who bore us. Perhaps audiences propitiate poets to make up for having failed to buy and read poetry. Mainly, I think audiences forget that poetry is, first and foremost, communication; just because we're "an audience" is no reason to stand (or sit) for stuff we wouldn't stomach from a drunk sharing our bus stop. Or perhaps we're just very nice, polite people and should be highly commended, like people too kind to pull weeds. Or perhaps we weren't listening.

All Poems Great and Small

I want to be so famous that in the distant future
all my friends will argue over having been me.

———

I'm a modest poet. I'd rather not discuss or even hint
about whether I am a great or unimportant poet. I leave
such unbecoming considerations to my millions of readers,
critics and scholars in the coming centuries.

———

Some are born great. All the rest are waiting to be born.

———

I wear glasses when I drive in hopes that police will mistake me
for someone mild-mannered and incapable of flight.

——

I am a Modern Poet: just a minuscule futile speck (on a tiny planet
in a minor galaxy in a universe that is an endless mindless explosion)
with a strong, fresh, unique, authoritative voice.

——

"Someday the world will recognize my genius" —
thus, we poets live not in past, present or future,
but in a future's past, aiming not at what we hope
to be, but what we hope we shall now have been.

Yes, a poet's life is a tense situation — but *what* tense? Future sub-
junctive past perfect? Or perhaps, we live in eternal timelessness, PRE-tense!
Whatever it is, it excuses us from touching down in the despised present
more than a few minutes each day. Here is a poet's daydream as he drifts
lazily just out of reach of a pile of backlogged mail and rejection slips:

Good to Be Here, Jay or Dave[2] as the Case may Be

If I were famous, I could be shockingly modest or immodest;
I could reward with notoriety all my loyal
opinions about things; I could joke about the teachers
who thought I was hopeless; I would spectate bemusedly as
whoever people *think* I am would become famous
for whatever they think I *do*; I'd become a household word:
"Honey, where'd you put the Dean Blehert?"
"It's in the kitchen under the Elvis Presley."
People will want to know, am I a Republican great poet
or a Democrat great poet. I'll be able to do commercials:
Robert Frost trims his eyebrows with a Gillette
out in the woods (mirror on a tree), Lord Byron in
L'eggs panty hose, Blehert with a Gold Card:
"Do you recognize me?" Hollywood will buy the rights
to my poems, Dean Blehert to be played by Marlon Travolta,
the reader by a cast of zillions; I'll be on all the talk shows.
"It's good to have you with us", Jay or Dave will say,

---

[2] That is, Jay Leno or Dave Letterman on the very late shows:
       Do you stay up for Koppel, late,
       Or go to bed and copulate?
       Wait up for Leno, Letterman?
       She'll fall asleep — don't let her, man!
       (Go get her, man; you'd better, man.)
       Another week of watching Leno
       While she sleeps — next stop is Reno.
(Or, palindromically put, Evade Dave!)

298

drolly. "It's good to be here, Jay or Dave," I'll reply wittily —
"London and Paris were fantastic as always, but
it's good to be back." Perhaps people will even
read my poems, if only to know about the eating habits,
sex life, etc., of someone as famous as Shakespeare and
General Motors, but more intimate. (The relief,
after so many years of stripping in this crowded public place,
when finally someone notices and yells, "Look! He's NAKED!").
AND I'll get all the girls!...but there's no such thing
as a famous living poet. If there were, he'd be famous.

Achieving fame is a challenge in any field, but at least, in most fields, you have role models: Famous actors, dancers, singers, etc. In poetry, fame is harder to visualize. If I ask anyone other than a poet to name a great poet, he or she will name someone dead. Probably this was not always the case. For example, in the late 19th Century, most literate and semi-literate speakers of English could have told you who Tennyson and Browning were and even quoted you a few passages from their works. Now poetry itself is marginalized (you can write it in the margins of this book); consequently, to become a famous poet, you would first need to make poetry itself famous.

To become a famous actor, you would simply have to dig and scramble yourself out of the deep hole called obscurity, learning all the necessary skills in the process. To become a famous poet, you would have to do the same thing, except when you'd climbed out of your personal hole, you'd discover that you were now known to a few hundred or thousand readers of poetry, and that the personal hole you'd climbed out of was, itself, at the bottom of a deep wide crater (the hole that poetry itself is in), so that a much greater climb awaits you before your work can be broadly known.

The next poem (in which the poet digs himself, but doesn't get out of any holes) suggests a motto for many off-beat poets: "If you can't join the pantheon, beat off. (Then put your underpanth and Pantheon again.)

Portrait of the Artist   (circa 1976)
or The Joyce of Pounding

Seeing a book of Ezra Pound's letters
to James Joyce, instantly I wonder
will my friends save my letters?
I forget to wonder which of my friends
will be James Joyce.
In case my friends lose my letters
before the world realizes
I am as good a writer as Pound or Joyce
and smarter and happier too,
I will save all these letters to myself.

If that sounds immodest,
consider the circumstances:
I'm sprawling in a tepid tub of water
long past my bedtime, not exactly
horny, but for some reason
(like the mountain, it's there)
contemplating self-abuse, putting off
the decision to take myself in hand
while I milk the night for a poem
that isn't merely clever.

I'm at an age where this was once
the future, so now I have to do the future
all over again and I'm not sure I can.
The night gives me only car muttering.
Almost no one has ever heard of me.
Modesty is a luxury I can ill afford.

I'd rather be Joyce than
Pound — but not if I have to read
Pound's letters.

The next two poems harken back to the days when "poetry" meant
long arguments (always the same arguments with the same two or three po-
ets) over endless cups of coffee (with an occasional patty-melt-fries-pecan-
pie excuse for taking up a table and being a smart-ass to the waitress) in a
Denny's or other all-night haunt. I've out-grown that sort of thing now —
meaning I'm no longer young enough to stay up all night and work the next
day.

With Poets At Denny's

Days of whine and ruses.
My friends across the table
ponder ponder ponder the precepts of poetry.
I sit in the paraplegic ward and ponder
(over my third free refill)
the first laws of dribble
(the Golden Drool?)
Can it be there are rules of art?
Like who will feed me today?
Like put the right me
in the right here and now?
Like never point yer pen at someone
less'n ya mean ta use it?

300

Like if you write with a Bic,
you can use the pen cap
to pick your teeth and clean your ears (in that order)?
Like keep writing?

They're talking about will it last
and does it fly and who says. How often
have I said and heard all this?
The best proof of my immortality.

I hope we ALL turn out to be immortal.
We deserve each other forever,
saying such scathing witty things
to each other that we can afford
to abandon Hope — and Crosby too.

They begin to insult each other
as usual. If I don't leave,
I'll have to order a piece of pie.
Ala mode.

I can hear myself getting fat.

For those of you who are calendarically impaired (that is, too young to remember), Hope (Bob) and Crosby (Bing) made movies together long ago in a far distant galaxy.

Being fat is a matter of taste: I keep tasting things. A poetaster, says my dictionary, is "an inferior poet." (But a disaster is not an inferior dis.) In cannibal societies (like academia) the penalty for inferior poetry is to be eaten, but since bad poets can be toxic, first the poet-taster must sample the meat. The next poem tells how poets become talk-sick:

Poet Tasters

Poets get fat in coffee shops.
If we keep food on our plates,
we don't have to look at each other.
It would be easier to look at each other
if we weren't fat. Perhaps we would be fat
anyway, if we weren't in coffee shops or if we weren't
poets or even if we weren't poets in coffee shops,
but what if we weren't in coffee shops because we had
no other place to be poets?

[Note: The shape of the last poem mocks my profile.]

301

Maybe if I lost weight, *then* I'd be immortal. Speaking of which, the next three poems tackle the nitty gritty of immortality. Immortality isn't all cakes and ale, you know. It's rather like mortality, but it takes longer.

It's 10,000 AD — Do You Know Where Your Immortality Is Tonight?

His work is quite the rage...and then it's not,
As themes and humors, irony and plot
And character and poetry and passion,
Like bows and bangs go in and out of fashion.
The poet, recognized, has barely time
To say, "I told you so!" (in stately rhyme —
Alas, who but the meanest or the rashest
Now dare to write in forms so foully fascist![3]),
And he who dreams of gloating from his grave,
Reveling in a universal rave,
Must know that on the farther side of glory —
However distant — starts another story.

Joe's Famous Burgers, Dean's Famous Universe

We write this stuff and hope someday
it will be famous, but even if it is —
even if 200 years from now you're
"the greatest poet who ever lived"
and you know about it, though haunting
another body now, only dimly remembering
this was you, not quite understanding
your feeling of triumph at this acknowledged
greatness — even so, 100 years after that
all the smart revisionist critics scorn
the benighted generations who valued your work,
and a thousand years after that,
no one's heard of you or of any of those critics,
and 10,000 years later
(when you put your hope in the future,
you get more future than you bargained for) —
10,000 years later you're part of the anonymous
pre-history of whatever culture gropes upwards

---

[3] There are indeed critics who reject the use of rhyme and meter as unfashionably "fascist." After all, we refer to rhyme schemes — why not fascist schemes? That's why for decades, in many poetry journals, we did Nazi rhymes. (That's "did not see rhymes," O pun-repellent ones.)

from the debris of yours (including fragments
of the lost language in which you wrote).

So maybe fame is a fancy wastebasket;
maybe sending poems to magazines — even when
they're accepted, even when you win
the Nobel prize — is only an elegant way
to throw them away, and maybe that's the
fun of it, these elaborate flourishes
of century-long abandon, and maybe, too,
funny things happen on the way to oblivion,

like you read a poem in a bar and someone,
hearing it, sees differently (walls
become windows) and paints or composes
something that reaches millions, some of whom,
seeing or hearing it, become wiser, tenderer,
more attentive, freer — and so forth,
the unravelment of your one communication
traceable (if only by God or the godlike)
long after your name and poems are lost
(but they're not, then, are they?) — hell,

maybe you don't have to read the poem
to anybody or even write it down; maybe
just that instant of twinkling in mind's eye
changes the universe, makes it a bit more
your own and everyone else's forever.

The last two poems treat mortality as a barrier to immortality. The
next one suggests that mortality is a form of irresponsibility among immor-
tals: Whee! I get to die, and that ends all that — someone else can clean up
my affairs, pay my debts, organize my poems and get them published! But
how does it feel to be immortal? It feels just like this...if we are. That is, if
you're immortal, you're immortal right now. So how does it feel? Geez,
sorry...it's as bad as asking a happy two-year-old how it feels to be mortal.
(And after a million years of being here and knowing it, could you not still
ask, "Am I immortal yet?" Immortality is, perhaps, inseparable from an in-
stantaneous awareness of what one is, a quality, not a quantity. But how we
do go on here....)

When You Die, I Want Royalties

Death was, I think, an invention
of the finest artists and poets:

Always, no matter how advanced their work,
in endless time, fame caught up to them
and barraged them with attention,
leaving them little time
to create new work and coating them in layers
of stiffening expectation to limit
what they might acceptably create.

Death solved all this: A poet could write
great stuff, complaining the while
that no one cared a bean for his work,
that only dead poets get respect;

then he'd die, become someone else,
a new name, new body, and go on writing
great stuff (bitching louder than ever
about not getting attention), leaving
his old work — a decoy — to bear the brunt
of adulation, reading his old work
(in school anthologies, perhaps)
with twinges of memory

(just twinges, for the penalty for using
their aesthetic abilities to sell the populace
on the merits of death — "a fresh start,
all debts canceled, no bad memories" —
was that artists, too, learned to forget,
as ALL liars always become the dupes
of their own lies in time)

at once admiring, basking in and rejecting
his own earlier work, life after life,
having and eating and regurgitating
and having and eating his
sweet sweet cake.

Does all this fuss about immortality sound just a bit childish? Yes, that is its *redeeming* quality:

The Future of our Culture Sat Here

Kids on swings, pumping, gasping:
"Pan Am[4] taking off!" "Zap! Bam! —

---

[4] Pan Am was once an airline. Airlines keep vanishing, sometimes with people aboard. Poetry is the only way to fly. (I, a critical *pan, am* the only way to fry.)

Shot down Darth Vader!"[5] Poet on a
bench, watching, writing ("I'm a
Great poet! Millions of future readers
are in tears of laughter! They're
renaming this park after me!
There's a plaque on this bench!...")

The odd thing about these cravings is that most poets scorn (or claim to) the "cheap" notoriety of tabloid headlines and what Joyce calls "the nightmare of history." And yet, it is not easy to disentangle in our daydreaming the values we associate with greatness from the craving for notoriety. After all, we want to be REAL. We want the world to tell us that we are "really something!" What a contradiction! — asking the gray average of opinion to tell us that our own vivid worlds are real. Thus confused, we don't become famous in the media; we make the media famous in our own worlds, which then turn gray.

Fame is a Goddess who swallows dreams and shits headlines. Those who want to go down in History (Fame's sister) may find History going down on them — she gives great headlines!

Fame sounds awful. But I'll chance it — a poet's got to do what a poet's got to do.

Slice of Life

I read the *L.A. Times* tonight.
It contained an immense amount of data.
This is a very real universe. The paper
was richly grained and discolored.

I too am real: My thoughts fester with useless life. My desires
are as disordered as the want ads. My prosy days are pricked out
with headlines:

POET PICKS NOSE. WIFE CALLS FOR
SANCTIONS.

POET CONSIDERS AND REJECTS
PROPOSED MASTURBATION.

POET DISCARDS IMAGE, CONSIDERS
DISCARDING POEM.

---

[5] Speaking of Darth Vader: A poet without readers is just playing with himself; I've nothing but my han', solo, because you are my dearth, Reader.

OVERWEIGHT POET ORDERS DESSERT
AS AFRICAN CHILDREN STARVE.

SLEEP STRIKES MILLIONS.
POET AND WIFE BELIEVED
AMONG THE MISSING.

In the face of these and other emerging revelations, I apologize
for the deceitful simplicity of my poems, obviously the product
of some imaginary creature.

If there's a risk of confusing fame and greatness, that's a chance the
poet must take to keep himself putting out passionate poems to pile up in the
dead-letter boxes of our ears, as he "makes himself useful" to the world.

Sick Humor

The sequel to *101 Uses For A Dead Cat*
will be *101 Uses For A Living Poet*,
all hilarious. In one drawing
he's jammed behind the wheel of a taxi
to drive people from one building
to another. And here he stands
by a table in a restaurant,
watching people read menus, hungry.
In this one he goes from door to door,
knocking, entering, selling encyclopedias,
delivering police show tickets; here
he edits manuals for the Defense Dept.;
here (this is the silliest!) he stands
before a class of bored freshmen....

We're just poor poets, working our way through mortality. But some-
times immortality, or something akin to it, some rainbow ghost of it, am-
bushes us in the damndest places:

Lost and Found Pen

My laundromat jotting continues in red ink.
When I got up to put my clothes in the dryer,
I put my blue ballpoint in the pocket
with the hole in it, and when, a moment later,
I scanned the dirty linoleum for it, I saw
only one little Mexican kid looking at me
and away from me nervously.

After an intricate orchestration
of exchanged glances, I took my pen
back from him, saying, "You shouldn't do that."
He looked crushed, so I said,
"You know what this is?" (the pen).
He shook his head, no. "You want it?"
He nodded hard.

So I showed him how it makes lines
on paper and said "Here". (Can't remember
where I picked up that pen myself.)

Minutes later, his slightly older sister
tries to return it to me; I say, "It's OK — I
gave it to him."

Now he's bouncing about with it —
figured out how to clip it to his shirt pocket
with the pen hanging outside on display.

They leave — he prances out with his blue pen,
waves to me. I write about it in red ink.

Good old pens. Sometimes they take a beating, as in the next poem, where the innocent pen is thrown down in disgust. I hope it has since forgiven me.

Domestic Squabble

It's the same thing every time:
I throw down my pen in disgust
and say, "Why didn't I take
dad's advice and go into chemistry
or, anyway, teaching?" And Muse
goes into her endless shrill litany
of all the nice <u>gaunt</u> (she knows
I hate being overweight) feverish-eyed
young poets with rhymes and meters
and symbolisms and mythic allusions
she COULD have run off with, but
NO, she let herself get stuck
with a fat middle-aged crybaby
purveyor of prosy truisms
and paltry puns...

When the muse is snitty, I go to the mirror, hoping to be consoled:

Here's Looking At You

My face in the mirror —
Nice lines of character,
sharp eyes that "seem
to see right through you,"

but cool, as if
on the other side of "you",
nothing better
is to be expected.

A distinguished face,
could be some great poet's.
We'll not argue —
It's *my* mirror.

Poetus Interruptus or Graffitus Corruptus

Here I sit, broken-hearted:
Wrote one line and the thought departed

I suppose the question that should be asked is: What *kind* of immortality? The immortality of a stone monument? Or some instantaneous state of godlike self-knowledge? In our individual lives and in our cultures, we seem to descend from the latter to the former, give up on godlike and eventually settle for the beautiful sadness (memorialized in stone) of being perishable meat. It would be nice to be remembered — but best to be the one who remembers. One way or another we are doomed to persist:

...But I Regress

If we can't be magic,
We'll settle for tragic,
That failing, try comic
Till quite anatomic.

You would think that a poet — who has so often, in the throes of writer's block, been forced to sit or pace for hours while listening to endless tick-talk — you'd think a poet would be the last person to crave immortality:

Beep! Beep!

Don't knock
Writers' block:
It's how you learn if your clock
Goes tick tick or tick tock;
But it's time to break your Bic and turn on the TV or take a long wock
When you hear your digital watch going tick tick or tick tock.

I have more trouble with blocs of writers (with agendas) than with writer's block.

Warhol says we each get our 15 minutes of fame. Lord, please don't count that tiny review in a lousy local paper! I want my full 15 minutes! 15 minutes! Only 15 minutes of immortality? To put it palindromically (as is oft my wont): WARHOL — OH, RAW!

Of Fame (Offa' me!)

I've become famous. Everywhere I go, people who've never met me
catch my eyes, nod at me, sometimes say "Hi" — Oh, they know me
all right. They lower their voices or cease their chatter
as they pass me on the street; "Look!" they no doubt whisper —
"Human!" For my humanity — the way my eyes see, my ears hear,
my conscience rebukes — is famous, and with fame comes
limitation: I am expected, being human, to act the part,
so must tame my appetites and creations, wear flesh and clothes,
suffer grief, give vent to rage — not to disappoint my public.

To My A-B-A-B Baby[6]

Today our last-night's love
In poems I rehearse.
I'm good in bed, but now
I go from bed to verse.

Awesome! and Yes! [7]

I'm now an Awesome Poet — overheard:
"Who IS he?" "Aw — some poet." Spread the word!

---

[6] A-B-A-B is the rhyme scheme of this quatrain — or BABA spelled backwards, BABA being a Yiddish Grandma or farewell from a stewardess or a rum cake or Ali's last name or Scrooge's baby talk... (ABAB is Shisk's last name.)
[7] Ozymandias — Shelley's sonnet about giant stone feet in the desert without a leg

How snide can it get, this quest for fame? Hey, being a poet is a knife-too-fine job:

And Not The Rest

Please listen just to me me me
And not the rest,
At least not to the same degree,
For I'm the best,

And for this privilege, give me money
And a name —
Reader, you will be my Honey
When I score FAME!

I do it all for you, you know;
It's all from love
My words descend on you like snow
From far above.

I don't care how the money comes in —
A book advance
Or any pie I can get my thumbs in,
Prizes, grants...

I only want what I deserve;
I'm not greedy —
A summer house, cash in reserve —
Why live seedy?

But skip all that — I'll write for free
And not protest
If you will listen just to me
And not the rest.

There is little to it, or so it seems: A brilliant idea, a pen, paper...and fame! So light! So elegant! So...spiritual! But one day, stumbling among boxes of unsold chapbooks, hunting through file cabinets full of paper (po-

---

left to be stood on by. The Persian version, Ozymandarius, became a popular TV sit-com, Ozzie and Harriet, which is the question primitive peoples asked when to determine whether or not a girl-child was ready to bear children: Is she oozie and hairy yet? In our time, "Ozymandias" is the motto of the movement to illegalize automatic weapons: UZI: MAN DIES.

ems, magazines, letters), the poet finds himself surrounded by walls of very solid stuff, much of it poetry, as described in the next two poems:

Something Solid

Poetry is about making something of nothing.
You start with a wisp of idea visible to you alone,
filling no space, lighter than air.
Then you put it on paper, so that it invades
a flake of air, absorbs and reflects light,
can burden a spring breeze, slit a careless finger,
be blotched by your blood, be seen by others...
Then you commit poem after poem
to flimsy sheets of paper, pile them in pages until,
taking the pile in both hands, you cannot tear it —
there is strength in many bound as one.
Pile them higher until you have — Lo! — a brick
of poetry — you could clobber someone with it,
even kill. Then you reproduce your brick to make
many bricks and fill boxes with them, store boxes
in attic and garage — WALLS of poetry reaching
to the ceiling, heavier than a car, bowing the beams
of the attic, crowding the garage door — then warehouses
heaped with poetry, islands, continents of poetry, poetry
planets, whole poetry galaxies... Yes, you move
among mouldering boxes, knowing that you have
achieved something solid.

Suicide Doesn't Work Either

Chaos is unconfronted creation,
like the room piled and littered
with thousands of poems in all stages
of revision. Remembering one poem
is as hard as remembering the memory
I'd meant the forgotten poem to animate.
Finding a remembered poem is as hard
as it was to find the words for it
when I wrote it. There it is,

a room full of poems in disarray,
like a life full of unwritten poems,
and here I am, where I started,
but with a life full of having written lost poems
piled up between me and anything real.

Of course, as more and more poetry exists only on disks and on web sites, the solidity of all that paper may diminish, as poets find virtual fame and virtual immortality (Death, where is thy byte?), virtual greatness. But in the absence of live communication, our virtual litter of bits and bytes will weigh upon us as heavily as our cob-webbed, leather-bound tomes.

Somehow we've got to get this stuff out to appreciative readers. Probably what we need in order to become great poets is...great readers:

The Great Reader

Nothing can stop me. One day I shall be
a great reader. Go ahead — mock my
reading in bed until noon, my reading
on the toilet until my legs tingle
on the verge of numbness as a bloodless white
horseshoe brands my bottom — mock on!
mock on! You cannot thwart my mission!
Out there across the howling wildernesses
of our civilization, 100 million writers
assume agonized attitudes, dying
to find a great reader. It's true,
I read little Latin and less Greek,
but it is enough that I become
The Great American Reader. Perhaps
no one will know my work while I live,
but one day centuries hence
some lonely poet will feel,
like the touch of a loved one
or the sudden lifting of a burden,
my understanding.

Warning: I've been told by very sharp and usually reliable fellow poets that the next poem is so long and self-indulgent that it is out of place even in this long, self-indulgent book. So it probably is, but I love it, and what's the good of a huge mishmash of a book like this if I can't bury a few self-indulgences in it, like old bones to be dug up some day. (Sure, Dean, "a few," you bet.) If you're a reader who finds such things painful, please skip to the next, tighter poem, where I exdulge myself again.

The Great Winnipeg Novel
Or How I Found My True Self At The
Winnipeg Public Library Between Buses

I just finished a best-selling passionate novel
by a woman: Family sob saga, last century,

main characters composed of steel, *savoir faire*,
pain, ecstasy and warring obsessions,
plot propped up on what they don't tell each other
until the last dramatic moment.
Marriage to The Wrong Person doesn't work.
There is Only One (color him Right)
Right Person, without whom all else
moodily withers. Etc.

I choose my words here with care: Does that mean
I speak out of passionate intensity?

Twenty feet from my table, an old man squints as he reads
Psychology Today ("Study of the Soul Today"),
and behind me, a man turns from the shelves
to scold a woman eating a sandwich:
"There's a big sign that says No Food
Allowed in Here, ya know". "I d-didn't see it..."
she stammers to his sudden back.
She bolts her sandwich, leaves. One could do worse
than suffer from warring obsessions.

The old man still reads *Shrinkology Fads*
(I write fast). I can see him
age as he reads the latest in shrink-
age. A character we can grow with.

I find me believable. I *am* real life,
aren't I? — one of those characters
that steps off the page (Kerthud! Kerthud!)
fully (too fully) fleshed and cries real salt tears
and bleeds real blood, ugh. I walk! I talk!
I'm a living doll. This is real ink.

In the novel, those who've suffered enough
without complaining, get to speak for the authoress
in long wise sentences drolly or with a far-away expression
or gazing deeply or smiling serenely, etc.
The authoress smiles from a real live
photograph inside the front cover.
She looks young enough to use lush imagery.
She knows names of fauna and flora
(There should be a third vaudeville-act sister:
Fatima?), geography, scads of history.
Her book is *Gone With The Thorns* — or is it

Coming With the Birds? I'm just a middle-class
Mid-Western boy from a middling city.
Passionate characters are from the Deep South
or Russia or Australia or Ireland or Hollywood
or somewhere where people have Destinies to pursue
instead of buses and are made eloquent,
not dull and petulant, by fever.

Though I do go on jotting in notebooks — food
for fervid fiction: "As the years passed,
he seemed to withdraw from the world
into the intimacy of his notebook..." or
"Once you've sat in the Winnipeg Public Library,
nothing will ever again be the same."
(It's not a peak over the Pacific, but then
Valley of the Thorns isn't Chapman's Homer.)[8]

"But somewhere along the thorny way,
I've grown obsessed with my own
inscrutably bland voice. It is, at least,
my own — who else would have it?"
Big deal, self meets self, loses self, finds self...

I keep wanting this poem to end up
with me passionate after all.
Ok, Ok! If I insist (obsessively):
"I (poet) have never told Dean Blehert,
the real person who goes with me
(not wanting to deflect him from his passionately banal
quest for truth, clarity, and the Great American
Publisher, and besides, feeling somewhat
to blame for it all), that he isn't
Dean Blehert after all, but was mistakenly
exchanged in his cradle for a gypsy
fragment of my imagination who,
in some wrong-turn universe, has become
a gaunt, pale, high-cheek-boned, slender-but-steel-sinewed
(eat your heart out, plump poetaster!)
Passionate Poet with Flaming Red Hair,
sardonic laugh and Deep Burning Green Eyes.

---

[8] Keats, in his sonnet on first reading Chapman's translation of Homer (*not* a chap-book), compares the experience to the discovery of the Pacific Ocean. John Donne compares his lover's body to "My America, my new-found land!" To date, no poet has reported on the experience of making love while reading Chapman's Homer, nor has Chapman's Homer been tested or approved for long-term use.

Unable to stand it any more, at last
I tell all. Pseudo-Dean-Blehert
stares blankly, then turns away
to heave one ragged sob

maybe because once in a besotted brawl
he parodied his gloriously drunken
brother to death, not knowing..."[9]

There, I'm passionate already, so can this damned poem end?
Why not? There's always tomorrow, and frankly, my Dear
Reader, I don't give a damn.

There — did you read the whole thing? Then you're probably me,
in which case I congratulate you on your good taste. (You taste just like the
inside of my mouth.)

The next poem suggests that a poet whose poems all leap from his
or her high, feverish, pale brow won't have no bawdy to call his or her own:

"What Inspires Your Poems?"

Where's that old magic — fully formed poems
poised to leap from my forehead?
Perhaps the poems are there,
but afraid to jump. There they stand, naked,
knees knocking, hugging themselves, trembling
at brink of brow (they look like
Woody Allen), clinging as the Muse urges
"Go, be brave, it won't hurt much."
The poems stammer, "It's a looong way
to that pa-a-age". My own solution has been
to let poems leap from less lofty portions
of my anatomy, springy bits, better designed
for jumping off of. But somehow
the magic isn't the same.

But as I age, the springy bit will lose its spring. The poems will have
to high-dive off the tip of my nose.

The next poem wonders whether the world happens to a poet or vice
versa. (We've given up on poems ever happening to readers.)

---

[9] Passionate clichés never die; they just fade away in ellipses…

Branching Out

Reaching out of himself,
groping for mystery,
the poet entered into
and became a tree,
the most interesting thing
that ever happened
to that tree.

When too much world happens to us (or vice versa), the ensuing dispersal and forgetting may lead us to — if not fame — the trappings of fame:

Fame and Senility

I begin to forget names. They say "Hi, Dean," and I say
"Hi" as if I knew them, just like senility — or fame,
which is lots of people you don't know feeling they know you,
you aren't sure you recognize your best friends, and
when you come home, you think you must have
walked into the wrong house, because the family there
still thinks you're just you. If you can't get yourself known
by lots of people, you can get almost the same thrill
just by forgetting those who already know you.

But perhaps greatness has little to do with fame:

What is Greatness?

Perhaps the sun imagines himself invisible
because no matter how hard he shines,
no one ever looks right at him.
Though you never seem to see me,
I must be content if, in my light,
you can see one another.

A funny thing or two happened to me on the way to immortality:

316

Strolling

Here I go walking down the street,
Pushing the sidewalk past my feet;
Lawns, children, leaves and sun —
These will go on when Dean is done.

Streets are just lines from me to you;
Cars find your door and poems too.
Lawnmowers, cats that watch me pass —
Curls of dream, dreamt by the grass.

Here I go walking down the street,
Passing Dobermans on their beat.
"WOOF!" Do they think I'm good to eat?
"WOOF!" they reply and "WOOF!" repeat.

I move on. The jagged barking goes
Away; the wounds of silence close
(Motors rumble, birds go tweet —
I am the silence on this street).

Softly strolling down the walk,
But my head is full of talk;
See, the cats all stop and gawk:
"Don't think so loud — you'll spoil my stalk!"

There's the front page blowing down the street:
It's your whole world, all incomplete.[10]
The headlines shrill: **HEY! HEY! WE'RE HERE!**
THE END OF EVERYTHING MAY BE NEAR!

The cat won't even twitch an ear;
Is she pretending not to hear?
Reliable sources hsst! and mutter,
Quietly blowing down the gutter.

---

[10]When this poem was written, the *L. A. Times* ad campaign slogan was "It's Your Whole World" — a depressing prospect. If the *L. A. Times* were my whole world, given what it's mainly good for, I'd soon be living in *The World According to Garbage.*

Dreaming and dreaming down the street...
"Try," says the sidewalk, "to be concrete."
Leaves with my notions of leafdom meet:
"Try," say the leaves, "to be discrete."

Dressed up in wind and sun and stars —
"Look! He's all naked!" squeal the cars.
Here's a dead end, but I'll go on
From me to you after streets are gone.

Section 5: Aspirations

Chapter 11: Diary of a Working Poet
or
Will I Still Respect It in the Morning

A Few Aphorisms for the Half-Arisen (Yawn)

Daily the sparrows speed-read our lawn, pausing now and then to pluck and savor a moral.

I write at night in a dark room by full moon, my ideas bright, but light-years away and not yet discovered.

"Now," said I to the world, "is the time for poetry!"
"Not now," said the world, "I have a splitting headache."

There's something I want to tell you...I forget what. Wanting to tell you doesn't go away as easily as knowing.

If I dial the right number and you're home, you'll answer. Why else do you have a phone? And so I keep writing, thinking, why else do they have a language?

Perhaps when I say "you", I mean myself. All the more reason to hope for an answer.

Kids taught to write poetry by being made to keep personal journals may become Hamlet, but never Shakespeare.

I try to write living lines (while bumping into deadlines) to throw to the world as life lines. If you catch one of my lines, attach a tin can to your end, and let me know.

Strange how my pen knows I have nothing to say long before my mouth finds out.

I said my say long ago. There's more to be said, but someone else must say it. I must become someone else.

I keep my poetry very simple lately, because I'm trying to understand what I'm saying.

If only the open notebook could attract poems as easily as it attracts the cat.

Something for nothing is a dangerous bargain. That's why I give you my poems: It's the best way I can think of to pay back whoever gave them to me.

Fascinating how much I know, that I don't know I know until someone else's readiness to hear lets me say it.

Love, I would write poems to you were you not, wherever I am, the space wherein I write.

WHERE POETRY WENT WRONG: Surprise! It didn't! Here we are at last!

Open me, O pen.

Chapter 11
Diary of a Working Poet
or Will I Still Respect It in the Morning?

This chapter turns down the volume of farce. It consists of poems/ jottings by a poet (me) about being a poet, addressed to (I hope) you. No more prose interjections — the poems are prosy enough; they can speak for themselves. I hope you can hear for yourself.

Midnight — Wow! Just finished a GREAT poem!...
but will I still respect it in the morning?

———

It's drizzling, but the leaves overhead catch nearly all
the drops, having more use for them than does this
notebook page.

———

Agents of rain follow me inside,
concealed about my person —
Aha! One of them drops from my hair,
narrowly missing this notebook.

———

Hard to write in the laundromat
with half my attention on what
the machines are doing to my clothes.
How can a quiet poet hope to compete
with professional agitators?

———

This spring day I with my pen, my neighbor pounding and
    that lark waste time.
No one pays me to write. Lark, do you sing on breaks
    from selling used worms?

If I sing like a lark, will you, lark, tell the world
    how sweetly I sing?

———

Today I had many plans, but first I took a hot bath,
thinking to soak and read for 15 minutes.
Two hours later I found it was five hours later,
my body, wrinkled as a prune, beached in water
gone cold. A man could die of erosion in a bathtub
by thus underestimating Homer's *Odyssey*.

———

It's nearly 1 a.m. — welcome to the Late Poem.

———

Ah, reader, you give good ear!

———

Poems, poems, poems — always I have to write more poems!
Reader, do you think I'm MADE of poetry?

———

I'm the finest poet that money won't buy.

———

Could I write such insouciant stuff
If caught up in the lures of prestige?
The French put it aptly enough:
Nobelist oblige.[1]

———

Now that I have your attention, what would you like me to do with it?

———

Like a boy going off to war, I promise myself I'll write everyday,
But once again my notebook lies unopened nearly a week;
meanwhile, back home, like an anxious mother,
I take up trivial tasks in fits and starts, watch TV, read magazines...
anything to keep me from wondering: What's happened to me?
Why don't I write?

———

What's a nice reader like you doing in a poem like this?

———

I write little; I earn little by writing or by any means. My wife
looks askance. At forty-two I too find it hard to tell the difference
between a heroic, long-struggling artist and a man who hasn't
made much of himself.

———

As my wife reads my poems, I put my arm around her shoulders,
cheating.

———

[1] That is, *noblesse oblige* — nobility obligates, as does winning a Nobel prize; prestige can create ham-stringing expectations. But I'm willing to chance it...

322

Pray for me, reader; after all, I've been praying
for readers long enough.

———

My poetry is very personal — don't peek!

———

Every now and then a lyrical line enters my thoughts —
seeking martyrdom.

———

I write rapidly, and yet several people have died
while I've written these lines. Some people have
no courtesy.

———

I am finding out what it will take to earn a living as a poet.
Did you know that paper and carbons and envelopes and typing and
    postage
cost *money*? I write great poems — the rest should take care of itself, no?
NOTHING takes care of itself in this lazy apathetic good-for-nothing
universe! You have to wipe its ass for it. I don't know why we put up
with a lousy universe like this.

———

I've snared no poems today. Maybe I'm not using the right bait.
Can it be that poems are not attracted to hopes, fears and worries?

———

I'll write you if you'll sit for a poem.

———

I'm writing so slowly lately — would you please read faster?

———

Nowadays a poet is no one, so when no one cares about you,
that's me.

———

(I'm a safe poet in a storm.)

———

When I stop writing, I'm dead, so bury me —
no matter what I say.

———

Monday morning is what happens to Prufrock's "evening spread out
like a patient etherized upon a table" when they run out of ether.

———

The world is crowded...but my poems are very thin.

———

I have no children. Here, read some of my poems,
and don't hurt yourself.

———

Here are some nice fresh words...
DON'T make that face at me!

Eat every noun and verb,
or you'll get no adjectives!
And stop playing with the punctuation!

———

Most of the time I stare at the blank page while my mind wanders.
A poem is a homecoming celebration.

———

I try to work on my poems. My friend's kids keep bugging me
with questions, showing me things...SCRAM! I say. At last,
I can work. The proper place for children is in a poem about
how loveable they are.

———

Words, come on, say something,
or I'll run away with a piano.

———

I don't have to do anything to get my poems out except write them.
You are reading them tomorrow or some tomorrow, so someone
must have sold them, promoted, marketed and distributed them.
Apparently, simply by writing these poems (since you are reading them)
I must have taken care of everything, including
the survival of intelligent life on earth.

———

Across the room she reads my poems; I say something;
she makes a shush at me with her hand: "Don't bother me,
I'm reading!" I am jealous of the me that wrote the poems.

———

After reading my poems, she says: "I just want to know,
do you have a lover? And do you talk that way to her?"
"No," I say, "and yes."

———

"And you a grown man!" she moaned. Of course — every punster is a
groan-man.

———

I read my poems to my friends. At another table, a lady,
not listening, eats supper. When I get to the slightly indecent
punch line, not listening, she sputters her soup, chokes, laughs.
Live communication exposes all the communication
already swarming in an indivisible ecology around our charade
of separate tables.

———

"You don't need that dessert!" True, but I must set
an example for all the readers who don't need my poetry.

———

I spent the night arguing about "Poetry" with a poet.

Father, deliver me from this peanut butter[2] I call
myself. Life is a fart of long duration. Amen.

———

When I let myself get used to pleasant chat with nobody
changing, we begin to seem to be all that we should be,
amiable and preferring nice things to not-nice things.
I can't, between pecan pie and coffee, quite grasp
what it is I'm supposed to want of us, why I should
write poetry.

———

Slowly I become the person who writes my best poems.

———

For years I tried to be myself so as to be worthy of the right woman
or able to write great poems. But I cannot be myself for any "reason",
since I must be myself before I can have reasons of my own.

———

"I wish you'd close the door," she says from the next room,
"if you're going to write such loud poems."

———

On a bench by the bay, I decide to write a poem.
Nothing comes. The heron reposed on one stick-leg
atop that pier loses patience with me
and puts the other foot down.

———

Two crows wheel and land above me, and there — a squirrel scampers.
The crows are leading two to one. In second place we have a
one-to-one tie between squirrel and poet...

———

I hear there's pro-life legislation in the works. Does that mean
my poems will be published?

———

Poetry notebook: my ledger-de-main.[3]

———

If you know this next poem, sing along.

———

Mao Tse Tung's *Little Red Book* —
Phooey! I've published *five* little-read books!

———

My poems follow well-defined sequences. For example,
those written in Chinese restaurants are closely followed
by those written sitting on toilets.

---

[2] Why peanut butter? All that arguing about poetry over hamburgers and sundaes —
I was getting chunky.
[3] That is, *leger de main*, or magic — sleight of hand. Some idiots say that poetry is
purely a leger activity.

I ponder lonely as a crowd:
Someone spilled buttered popcorn
all over this apple-green bench,
a stream of winking gold on emerald,
like Wordsworth's daffodils perhaps.
(A pigeon just pecked up a daffodil.)
And little know I now
how in quiet moments among ancient oaks,
far from L.A.'s low fever,
my visionary brain will overflow
with a scraggly mob of dirty yellow popcorn.[4]

———

Be stingy, reader. I'll just spend it all on poetry —
the cheap strong stuff.

———

As when walking the dog I carry a pooper-scooper,
so, when walking alone, I carry a pen and notebook,
in case a poem happens on public property.

———

Poetry says turn off that TV and spend some time with me.
I say look, watching TV is all I can do with this cat
on my belly, poking her paw gently into my beard
to remind me I've neglected to continue to scratch
her head. Poetry says if you cared for me at all,
you'd shoo the cat and turn off the TV. I say Shhh!

———

I read them a poem from, I guess,
the heart, then sit down in a sweat,
the heart not used to such exercise.

———

Photo of me before I grew this beard and belly, like a mirror
that no longer moves when I move, a lost reflection.
I keep losing images to the frozen mirror. Someday this body
will not move when I move, but these words
will go on moving when you move.

———

Vegie chili — like bits of cardboard. I switch to Texas-style — poor
cows —
at least none of them readers.

---

[4] Alludes to Wordsworth's "I wandered lonely as a cloud," where, coming upon daffodils, he thinks of how, long afterwards, his vision of the flowers will return to him to comfort him amid less serene scenes. No one has yet written the poem in which the daffodils describe their encounter with Wordsworth ("I pandered, golden, in a crowd…").

Letters to answer. Nothing clever to say,
so I write greetings, then attach a poem,
like a ventriloquist giving the punch line
to his smart-assed puppet.

Time to run diagnostics: Pen, working, hand...operational,
wrist, elbow, shoulder...all check out 100%; head ticking away — but nothing
comes out on paper! Must be the software.

Blank sheet: fly-paper for flitting thoughts.

Yours is the loveliest face on earth.
Why isn't that great poetry? It's true,
isn't it? Yes! And truth is beauty,
right? You bet your ass! Speaking of which...
but you wouldn't think that was poetry either.
That's all YOU know on earth.[5]

From where I sit, I hear traffic.
If I opened the door and yelled,
none would hear me. If anyone heard,
what could I say that would change
my neighbor's life? "Hello, how're ya
doin'?" What mania makes me dream
the words I write here change the world?

"You're so prolific!" Not pro-choicic?

Out for a walk — good way to write, because there is such wealth
of grass blades, chirpings, changing tree patterns, houses as neat
as pieces of candy in their endless variety of flavors, all this
to fill me back up as I empty myself, not by what I write, but by
the mental debris I discard in my search for, not words,
but speaker and hearer.

Some were paid in beauty, some in strength, some in jewels.
I got poetry. Now that a billion poems won't buy a loaf of bread,
I choke on poetry while others starve on bread.

When I was a kid, we called
the miserable old lady on the corner

---

[5] Yet another allusion to the famous Keats poem that is NOT entitled "Odor of Greasy Urine."

a witch because she'd shoo us off her lawn
and call the cops about our "gang"
for running across the yard
she bent double over every day
battling weeds. Now I am 55 years old
and a poet, shabby, but gentle.
What would you do
if you looked out your kitchen window
and saw me playing in your backyard?

———

Love letter from a reader who's amazed at the ideas we share,
she and I...and you.

———

All my lovers tell me I'm very good in
print.

———

The dog peers up at me, dabbing at air with his vivid tongue.
"I'll bet you want another bone," I say, and
my friend, across the table behind a pile of my poems, says
"Not now — I've read enough today."

———

Downstairs Pam paints. I write.
Across the room, the dog on his sofa,
the cat on her chair sleep or feign sleep.
Outside our house the world (like a giggle
of children up very early on April first)
prepares surprises for us, and we, pretending
to sleep, will pretend to be startled awake, will
gasp appreciation (I in a poem, Pam in a painting)
and go on writing, painting, preparing our surprises
for the world outside that sleeps or feigns sleep.

———

After I read, one person approaches to say
my poems were wonderful — speaking, I feel,
for everyone.

———

I'm old enough to have kids old enough to tell me
I don't make sense or ignore me. Lacking them,
I send my poems out to editors.

———

Nightly rituals: The cat licks herself. The dog scratches himself.
The notebook rubs against my pen point.

———

The cat sours with age, demanding nothing we can give her,
but demanding it loudly. And yet she is someone.

328

She is to live until she chooses not to — or is usurped
by some force that leaves us guilt-free. Why do we bother?
Millions of cats are put to death in pounds each year,
some of them surely very nice cats. But THIS one
came to us and asked to be taken in.
I should teach my poems to do the same: So much worthy poetry —
why should anyone care for mine? But if my poems look
right at you and say "Take me home!" — decades later
from your bookshelves, they'll nag you, "Pay attention to me!"

———

How long will these poems last? Hell, by the time you read this,
you may be dead.

———

My name is Dean Blehert. Do you have another name?
Or am I rereading this myself ten years from now?
Or is it centuries later, and I have another name and don't
remember writing this, and if I did, my friends would smirk
if I said, "In the late-twentieth century, I was Dean Blehert."
Sure, Sam, sure.

———

"I have this neat image," I tell my wife: "I'm working at the computer,
revising poems, surrounded by piles of paper — on the desk, the floor,
all over, towering over me, piles of poems, thousands in every stage of
incompleteness, and suddenly I'm drifting away, I'm above looking down
at this room full of papers; now I'm moving away faster, the room
gets tinier and tinier, years ago, centuries ago, lost forgotten room full of
poems..." "Oh no you don't!" she screeches — "You're not leaving ME
with all your poems!"

———

"Get a life, writer!" Good idea — then I could write my autobiography.

———

15 minutes of fame? — How *much* fame? Could I have
just a *teensy bit* of fame for an hour?

———

If I write slowly enough,
the spots on the page where I dripped my iced tea
will be dry enough to write on.

———

If I stop trying to communicate to others, my imagination shuts off.
Without imagination, it is easier not to care what happens to others,
easier to read the news. Right now I cannot imagine any of my neighbors
being helped by anything I could say or do, nor can I imagine
others elsewhere being different from my neighbors. But if I keep talking
here to you, perhaps my neighbors will change. My numb imagination
begins to itch.

329

"Dean's the father of us all," said a young poet,
introducing me to his friend at a reading.
I hadn't realized. But I've been having
one-nighters with strange minds for so long,
I shouldn't be surprised to bump into kids
I didn't know I'd fathered.

———

Once again I've written the date on the page, a small commitment.

———

She left me — my loss and poetry's: By the time I felt I could write about it,
I'd lost interest.

———

Working on a proposal: After two days of "leading reseller of micro-
computers in the federal marketplace..." and "seamless integration", I hear
someone outside my cubbyhole proclaim "Wow! THIS is a terrific sentence!"
I leap from my computer to admire this terrific sentence, not having seen
even a mediocre sentence for, it seems, years — or anyway two days. "Let's
see!" I say. He shows me. Alas, it's only one of mine.

———

Some poets just can't get beyond narcissism.
Every poem's about I — I want, I feel, I need.
I, more versatile, write two kinds of poems:
 "I" poems about my feelings *and* "He" poems,
also about my feelings — the ones my wife
wouldn't let me print if I said "I".

———

I used to be able to write poems during the commercials —
DAMN these clever commercials!

———

There's the notebook. Nothing to say to it.
I take a long walk, brush up on the sun's coming out
from a cloud to make light of things, how green and
shadow greens construe a tree, how paths wind and
narrow out of view, how birds and cars fill in the chinks
of space with their noises, how a spider thread flashes,
vanishes ahead, how flutterings tease the periphery of
vision — nothing here to write about, just refamiliarizing
myself with my alphabet.

———

This alien hand forms words. The pronouns
catch at me.

———

Different people have different talents. I'm good at writing poems
that I think are great.

These famous poets are not Dean.
Can they see me turning green?

———

A poet I know just got a second date after his name,
just like the poets we had to read in school.
I am still "1942 —". Viva la dash!

———

Oh! Ah! Ohh!!!!!! Exclamation points (zingPOP)
are cheap. But mine aren't: What few I have left
I've borne through jungles of ridicule, across oceans
of apathy, over mountains of drudgery! And when
will the professors learn that question marks
(FIZZLEpoof) are even cheaper?
(Cheaper by the dozen????????????)[6]

———

His sign reads "WILL TRADE POEM FOR RIDE."
After standing in roadside dust and fumes for hours,
he writes a new sign — "WILL LISTEN TO YOUR
POEM" — gets a ride immediately.

———

I am among fellow poets. Reader, where are you?

———

Slam poets, academic poets...I'm a slackademic.

———

You're IN when they publish your collected works.
I want to be among the Poetically Collect!

———

A Pithy Thought

Today I wash my clothes.
My days creep by in prothes.

———

Thank you for not reading this line.

———

Sleep, says the clock, but the poems I have not written
are windows in the night spilling drifting threads
of piano plinkings, laughter, light.

———

Each page I fill
lightens one of my burdens

---

[6] The last line I swiped from a comment on the previous lines by Arlington, VA poet, Hilary Tham.

and adds to another.[7]

Library. Shh — you can
just hear thousands of books
mumbling to themselves.[8]

———

Two people come up
to say they love my poems. (I
still don't like parties.)

———

Out of my tub, spider!
I'm not poet enough
To skip my shower.

———

From that window,
typing sounds. Who will read it?
Be moved? Me? You?

———

Walking — I stop before a house to jot down a poem,
and some fool dog starts barking, realizing I am about to
pilfer everything of value.

———

Her head, eyes closed, on
one leg, notebook on the other —
lightly, my pen.

———

You catch me staring hungrily at you — I was just mentally
stripping off your opinions, wondering if you'd be any
good in poetry.

———

Many years ago my hands left my shoulders, going somewhere.
Arms grew. Hopeful hands groped and grabbed, higher and higher:
The forbidden counter-tops, the dresser, the kitchen cupboards..
At last they noticed they'd reached all they could reach.
They complained to my forehead, my chin, my nose —
restlessly cupping, scratching, picking and rubbing.
So I busied them with pen and paper, taught them to reach out
by writing, and, perhaps, fooled them into thinking
they are getting somewhere.

———

---

[7] One interpretation of which is, I got the ideas on paper; now how do I get them to,
Dear Reader, you?
[8] Left unread for decades, the books become increasingly demented and incoherent.
The sound they make as they drool and twiddle their pages is "B-B-B-Biblio...".

If I hold my head high and straight
as I walk and think up poems, the poems
try to come out noble.

———

Tonight I died a little for poetry: broke my healthy diet
to order a greasy meal, out of courtesy to the cafe
holding the poetry reading; then, for the sake of
starving children everywhere, I ate every bit of it.

———

There go those actions again, speaking louder than words.
Shh! You're disturbing the words in the next room!

———

In a shopping mall, I watch people and write.
That girl...oops, she's looking right at me —
I can't write. She's more than a she and less
than a you. There's no suitable pronoun for a
stranger whose eyes are meeting my eyes. I'm
supposed to be invisible here and fluid enough
to osmose into your world. Reader, if that's you,
please look away. When you notice me,
I grow solid.[9]

———

Reader... Reader?... READER!...
Oh, you're here! Thank goodness! For a moment
I thought I was alone. It's hard when you're old like me
and can't see very well without your eyes.

---

[9] Or, as the wizard said to Dorothy, pay no attention to the man behind the curtain.

Section 6: The Management Humbly Suggests...

Chapter 12: A Poet Amateur among the Prose
or A Tome Without Pithy

A Few Short Sentences for Good Behavior

Death is contagious. If there's life in you, impart it, or you'll catch your death from those you fail to animate.

New Years — a dram of death poetry is refreshing after celebrating the passing of a year: Hair of the bitch that dogs you.

This is just poetry; it won't save you, but may locate you, so that a rescue party can be sent out.

Someone called poetry "a fine frenzy". Yes, we make our fine friends see.

Dreams don't "come true". It's like any art: You dream it and you dream it again until you dream it right.

I do not try, in my poems, to give people hope, but to give them what they've been hoping for.

"When there are no more walls, I'll have nowhere to write," said the Graffiti-writer.
"When there are no more walls, I'll have no need to write," said the poet.

Most of the world goes to bed hungry, lacks time and energy to write poems or read them. We are privileged. We owe it to these unfortunates to write and read well.

Why is a poem a poem? To get to the other side.

After you go past a word you've misunderstood, you live in a universe that is no longer what it seems.

"But that's not what I meant at all" — yet here we live, in what we said.

"CONSERVE WATER — OUR MOST PRECIOUS RESOURCE"
No, language is our most precious resource. Words like "precious"
have been wasted to the point where it is almost impossible
to tell you how much you mean to me.

Don't blow up the planet
Just to make each other wrong.
Why clutch the world so tightly?
You can have it for a song.

This is all just my imagination...but what are you doing here — in my imagination?

Chapter 12
A Poet Amateur Among the Prose
or **A Tome Without Pithy**

Note: "Amateur" means lover. Poets, seldom paid for their work, write, perforce, for the love of it (or, in the parlance of the tennis racket, for nothing [love]). Being unpaid, poets cannot be PROs. But in this chapter, I lose myself in prose, thus extending my long-winded volume — just to show you what a tome without pithy can do.[1]

To atone for the previous chapter, all prosy poems with no commentary, here's a chapter that is all prosy commentary without poems.

Every other month I publish (and have published since August, 1984) a subscription poetry letter called "Deanotations", containing my own poems, illustrated by my wife, Pam. The name "Deanotations" is, of course, eponymous. (Eponymous is smaller than a horse mouse.) Most of the following remarks are extracts from the opening letters to various issues of "Deanotations," printed here because I couldn't get them ALL into the "Introduction," and I hate to waste anything. (If I could stand to waste things, I'd never bother to write down any poetry.)

Reports in the tabloids that I've been spotted alive in sundry super-markets and bowling alleys are fatuous. I wouldn't be caught dead being spotted. Anyway, as you probably realized long ago, it is inconceiv-

---

[1] "Tome without pithy" refers to a 1961 movie and hit song, "Town Without Pity." The last line of the song refers to the terrible things that "…a town without pity can do." Personally, I get more pithed off by a tome without pithy (that is, failing to mind its own pithiness).

able that all these poems could have been written by an individual. Dean Blehert is, of course, the *nom de plume* for a large group of distinguished academic poets who wouldn't be caught dead printing things like this in their own names and who, in their own names, write serious poetry that, alas, has been caught dead.

Now that you know who *I* really am, we can begin to deal with who *you* really are. It's half past adulthood: Do you know where your childhood is tonight?

I lied. I'm only a small group. No matter how quickly I invent new selves, I remain one of the few living poets who doesn't out-number his audience (I hope...are you there?). That's encouraging. I used to have to get new readers by marrying them. It's much less expensive to give away my poems.

———

Here's some more poetry. More dazzling wit, stirring insights, and moments of truth. I know, it's an awful bore, but I just can't help it. I'm trying to stop, really I am — I even belong to Humanoids Anonymous (or HA!): Whenever I feel that terrible urge to be alive and communicate, I phone a fellow member, and his answering machine tries to talk me out of it.

But sometimes I can't stop myself. I know it looks to you as if I *want* to do these things, but you don't see my struggles. Poetry is not a crime, but a sickness. I don't inflict this stuff on you because I want to. I'm a fellow victim. It's all glandular. That's why I urge you to send me your contributions, not simply because it costs me twice what I receive to maintain this vicious habit, but because, while millions are spent to relieve the misery of alcoholics and drug addicts, not a penny is spent to stem the poetry epidemic that even now ravages our streets and literature. Our innocent children are threatened by lurking double meanings right in the school library!

This blight on our cities must be exposed! Send me the addresses of your friends! Advice from the National Anustoot of Sentimental Health (NA-SH!): Do you respond to words; are you sensitive to patterns, obsessive about honesty; do you sometimes find humor or beauty in scenes that others pass without notice; do you notice yourself getting younger instead of older? If you suffer from one or more of these symptoms, you may be EXPANDING and should see a shrink (POP!) without delay. Meanwhile, send your dollars TODAY to *DON'T EXPRESS ANYTHING NEW* (OR D.E.A.N.). And remember, when it comes to poetry, just say KNOW.

———

Recently I lost touch with you; could you tell? I could: It got harder to write. I'd probably read too many newspapers. They sap my affinity for living. I have to remind myself that I, not newspapers, create you, my readers, just as you, not newspapers, create me. Anyway, I'm over that now. (Hope you don't mind passing through my new metal detector before entering my poems.)

338

When I read the "news" I feel old. I feel my poems aren't doing enough, that no poems can do enough. This makes it hard to write poems. It's easier to turn on the news. My solution is to keep writing. I keep writing and keep writing, and eventually you and I become real to me again and I see that my poems are of use, that somewhere years from now someone about to give up remembers a line from a poem and keeps going (VIOLINS!), that somewhere even now someone reading a poem realizes that he is being spoken to and that he IS and WHO he is and makes his own acquaintance for the first time in eons as if waking from a bad dream, from the Daily News to a new day, from hopelessness to opalescence.

It's important that I and other poets see this, or one day, finding us stuck and despairing of ever creating anything fine again, psychiatrists will declare us suffering from the mental illness of the month (maybe Clinical Deep Russians or Washington-Post-Minstrel's Tindrum) and drug us to cure us for life of this uncomfortable itch to create, no doubt a brain — or is it bran? — imbalance. No, no, bran goes with raisin, not reason. This is too sad. Quick, take me to the clinics so I can blow my knows! Somewhere over the brain woe...

'Ti*s not* Klinics that poets must find; tissUE! Gesundheit.

———

The world is a huge, stony echo-ridden vault. When I have no readers, I am assailed endlessly by fragments of my poems bouncing off the walls, which distracts me from writing new work. Readers are the best absorbers (like thick drapes or acoustic tiles) for poems. If I can just coat the world with readers, become a well-furnished poet with lush wall-to-wall readers, I can eliminate the echoes.

———

It's remarkable that I can make marks on paper and have them talk to you this way (they are, aren't they?), that we have agreed on all these meanings, that when I say "you" (like a magician pulling rabbits from a hat), presto! You are here (hello?), and when I say "We" (abracadabra), here we are. (Where are we?)

Saying "hello" is a daring leap of the imagination. It's me saying to something out there, "Hey, I know there's a you there that's 'I' to itself, that someone is helping me create this game." That's a fraction of what hello says. I don't know how we do it. If it weren't so simple that I can do it without thinking, I don't know how I'd ever learn to do it. I practically have to BE you to say hello to you. It would be much easier to kick or shoot you.

Such a fuss is made about saying "I love you"! We create this crazy rich language, traipse about in these knobby, touchable bodies, slave away at these cute personalities to keep the game interesting — of *course* we love each other.

339

I suppose we forget; louse up language with lies; lose track of someone there to be touched or talked to; caress or kick or shoot a few bodies to trick them into revealing that there's someone there — and *still* they won't talk to us. For one coming out of such blindness and finding someone else there, "I love you" would be worth saying.

———

Some days all I see seems only what I've seen before. In theory all these strange faces in a crowd are new, the odds of total DNA replication infinitesimal, and even then a smile or frown or leaf shadow makes all the difference. In theory that cloud (the one you just thought of) is unlike any other cloud ever. But variation among sets of random clouds or numbers is hardly the newness poets push.

Why is it that so often the OLD become new for us — for example, visiting after long decades away the house where one grew up? Because THEN we saw newly. We were children, unable to fill in the blanks in what we saw with hand-me-down ideas, so having to create: WE made things new.

If worlds or words refuse to be new, make **yourself** new. I do it by talking to you, here. This is a place where I must talk from where I am new (my newness-ence or noon essence). If I don't, it's painfully obvious, like a bad hairpiece. If I do, you are tempted to contribute your own newness to my words. A poem will startle like a too familiar street, drenched, suddenly, with some tint or scent of almost forgotten childhood. What startles you is you. You-ness.

———

Do you feel imagined? After all, you haven't read this yet, but here you are! (I hope!) That's a goooood reader! "You" is truly a "u", a hook, baited with attention. Sentence by sentence we grab the hook and are hauled in ("we", indeed). We do it to ourselves with "I". Pronouns: Holes in the sentence through which we thrust our heads; the camera flashes; and we find we are the faces of cardboard heroes and monsters in circus scenes. And heads themselves (into which we've thrust ourselves) are pronouns in the grammar of planet earth. You can't tell the players without a head. It's essential to get a head!

———

A living language gets taken for granted — like air — and is as vital. Words go dead from misuse. Many people (lawyers, politicians, advertising agencies, spin-doctors, spin-bin doctors, journalists, etc.) do this for a living — do little else but misuse words. Languages are as rich and complex in development as forests and, for most of us, as endangered.

Every time we use a word to communicate well, we revive that word just a bit, make it more alive for others, reverse the clear-cutting of language by those who use words as push-buttons to elicit mechanical responses. Each time we use a word well, hey, we're Johnny Appleseed!

It is not quite kosher to do this. Much of modern poetics is based on the notion that communication is impossible. After all, who can prove that you're getting what I'm saying (or that you ARE anything other than neurochemical reactions)? What if the forest falls and nobody is there to hear? ("What if the forest FALL!" insists an ancient subjunctive god of the English forest.)

But I'm here and you're here to hear, and something goes from here to here and on rare occasions, on my own face I feel you smiling from ear to ear — HERE HERE! Reader dear — and there ain't no body here!

———

We exhaust words (politicians, Madison Ave., psychobabblists and bad poets do it best) and refresh them. Some poets try to jump-start language with weird positionings of words, but thereby deaden the little words. "The trigonometry of summer spurns this quagmire of desire" — fun to see gawky trigonometry strutting in drag with the girls, but what does this do to "the" and "of"? Whores them to anyone's whim, poor jaded unloved words that do all the work.

Each time a salesman sings "I really think you'll love this one — it's YOU!", not only the words "I", "you" and "really", but our ability to know ourselves and each other diminishes. Having left us no words to fill them, poets and politicians corrupt even our silences by pausing portentously after each impoverished line — MY FRIENDS...AND FELLOW AMERICANS...THE TIME..HAS COME...FOR A NEW.... We fill the gaps with screams and claps.

Poetsmust,then,revitalizethespacesbetweenwordsaswellasthewords. And the punctuation marks!!!!? Poor pooped language. Its exploiters should pay royalties each time they use words dear to the language — pay them to "the people", if some great poet would rediscover the people for us. Are you the people? Am I? "The People" — words worn to transparency — just right for tabloid headlines: POWER TO THE PEEPHOLE!

Of! Dammit! Of! Of!

The trick of much recent poetry is to booby-trap the innocent logic of syntax with nonsense — not a stream of gibberish like "bubble rats sour oyster foul snot pits blood summer", but "A bubble of rats bursts the sour oyster of our foul snot in deepest pits of blood summer" or "the calculus of winter" or "in the frayed easy chairs of incontinent autumn" or "a calculus of rats bursts the snot moon of..." (or even "...snots the burst moon of...") — it MUST make sense, because the power of syntax (A [noun] of [plural noun] [verb]s the [adj.] [noun] of our [adj.] [noun]...) carries it along, as heedless of its cargo as a speeding train, which, whether carrying vacationers, business-men, potatoes or corpses, gets where it's going.

Not much wrong with this: Millennia of sheer plod cut these logical grooves into our language, dry beds for flow of even gibberish. Why NOT use them to make us know bubbles of rats, the bursting of sour oysters, or even the ubiquitous "corridors of your mind"? We read such lines as if blind-folded and asked to touch whatever is put before us. Logical syntax is our inviter's confident glibness that lures us to plunge our hands into the bowl of moist, warm spaghetti (worms? Bleeding guts?) — at worst an adventure.

But what of the sapping of syntax, the cheapening of sentence position, the edges of our delicate diamond-tipped tools — Of, the, a, our, in, to — dulled like knives used to slice up old cardboard? How often can we treat the ancient aristocracy of articles, prepositions, pronouns and conjunctions as pimps for the perverse rompings of jaded, ill-assorted, ostentatious, nouveau-riche words, before our plain words, unwilling go-betweens, sicken from the shame of it, look for ways to lighten their load by cheating us, lose meaning — and then, without our razor-edged "the", our handy-dandy slicer/masher/ricer/dicer "of", our whole tool chest full of elaborately defined and compartmented "if", "to", "and", "on", "as", "with", "in" — Oh how shall we talk to one another!

—

Remember the good old days (I'm old enough now to have to hope that something old can be good) when comparisons via simile or metaphor were tools of communication? Now poets use the sounds of communication (ritualistic grunts of "as" and "like" and "of") mainly for two purposes: First, to string together incongruities (the evening sky like a patient on a table, your eyes like screams, the sky howled blue locomotive wails) or, among the posher poets, to compare something you've never seen or heard of before with something you've never seen or heard of before, the eye of some exotic species of frog being as orange as the petal of some exotic flower; this is supposed to show a surgically fine eye and a poet (usually poetesss) who really SEES the world, gosh, she's sensitive! - and who knows MUCH more than we do. (And who can read an encyclopedia.) But the effect is Jabberwockian: The mome raths outgrabe JUST LIKE the gyring of wimbles in the wabe.

Oh do not ask "What is it?" Ours to praise, not to inquisite.[2]

—

Dear Reader,

I hope I am inventing you to your satisfaction. Saying things re-quires inventing me to say them and you to hear them. Odd idea that a poet

---

[2] A reference to "Prufrock": "Oh, do not ask 'What is it?'/ Let us go and make our visit." Is there such a verb as "inquisite?" Oh, do not ask, don't quiz it.

sits there talking to himself. No, we invent our hearers. Not really you, of course, but "you." Just as a young wanna-be lover carries about a "you" to whom he/she addresses dreams, hoping someone will be lured by the admiration lavished on "you" to become it, so I dangle before you an assortment of "you's" and hope you'll bite, eager to become someone addressed so urbanely, subtly, toughly, seriously, playfully or whatever.

Occasionally I hear that a reader has ceased to be or never was "you" ("Dear Dean, I never did 'get' your poems…"), as disconcerting as hearing one's lover say, "It never felt good. I faked it." A poet, too, is a lover hiding boredom when he tires of being the "I" he's invented to address "you." Much of poetry is like an old bad marriage, a poet concealing his weariness with being his own invention so as not to disappoint the reader that his readers pretend to enjoy being — from habit or because it's what they were taught they should enjoy being.

When we have me and you invented well, the rest is easy: We easily find eloquent things to say to each other when we are here for each other.

If you can be all the various "you's" addressed in my poems, you're a chameleon (and being a biped, you're a stand-up chameleon). But that's my game, tempting you to be a greater variety of "you's" than you can possibly be without becoming very limber about being. What is cruelty but an inability to be someone, a fear of becoming stuck in what one pities?

"Be yourself." I'll be the one who decides to be. I hope you will too.

If the you fits, wear it.

———

I work long hours: If each lifetime is a life sentence, I hope to serve several concurrently. What then? Parole — which means "word" — back to the beginning. Perhaps I can become a *household* word. Now I am a word of few men, though hardly a man of few words. I can barely get my words into the culture edgewise, though I do get my edge in, wordwise, and perhaps will get wise in edged words.

———

Marvelous books: The pages consist of crushed tree pulp, compressed to sheets so fine that 80 or more, superimposed on one another, are only a fraction of an inch thick. And because the poems are impressed on separate edge-bound sheets, they are accessible to either sequential or random access. Each book contains thousands of different words, all comprised of only 26 characters and a few punctuation marks. Essentially, each book is a slab of wood sliced into laminations so that it can be loaded with data, then glued back together. Buy your very own read-only multi-media small-footprint optical storage device!

———

Art is a childish thing. Mom seems to love us simply for being ourselves — all the excitement about our smiles, burps and garbled words. So we toddle off into the world, expecting it to treasure us. Surprise! "Dean WHO?"

Most of us respond by becoming what we hope the world will pay us to be. A few (or most, beneath the worldly mask) remain infants and pretend the world is Mama. The artist tries to transmute what he is (I say "he" and not "He/she" because it's nearly autumn, & I hate fall slashes[3] [false lashes]) into gold, failing when he insists it's the world's job to admire him — or when he redefines self to propitiate the world. He succeeds when he smuggles his dream into the world, and it becomes the world's dream. Quite criminal, dream smuggling.

Art is a great leader. The young artist dedicates himself to the Cause, expecting to be "utilized": "I'm a song-writer; take my songs!" "I'm a comic; use my jokes!" The leader uses what little he can of this raw stuff, leaves the rest to ripen, and the new disciple scrubs latrines. By giving himself away, he thought he'd dumped on the leader the job of getting himself utilized, but finds himself still with his life to cultivate so that it will bear fruit. Yes, art is a way to remain a child (one who owns a world), but only for a child who knows his world is no less a world for not being the only world. By the way, what are YOU doing here? You're not my Mommy! (You're much too cute.)

———

Are my poems immortal? I have a wait-and-see attitude about that. Time will tell. Of course, all the poetry in this book is immortal — so far. Actually, I plan to outlive my poetry, but I hope it takes a long long time. Then I'll write new poems.

These poems consist of excerpts from my preposthumorously[4] collected works. Although I'm not yet famous, I've heard rumors that I've been seen alive in supermarkets, etc., which is pretty good, considering I'm not dead yet — not lately. Well, actually, I AM dead. That is, if this stuff is really durable, chances are that by the time you read this, Dean Blehert is dead. If you're one of the few people who read this while Dean Blehert was still alive, then, hey! — you're dead too!

So here we are, dead. Not so bad, huh? I'll bet you didn't think it would be like this. (What IS this like? Is immortality endlessly talking to oneself? One had better learn to talk well. And listen well.)

What a dirty trick! Just because you read some poems in 1998, you have to be dead in, say, 2098. How could I have done this to you! I've doomed you all! Even now my poetry is killing you! (That's the trouble with thinking you're a body: The future is fatal.)

---

[3] That is, the slash in "he/she," also called a "virgule" (tiny rod), which is a fine thing to come between a he and a she.

[4] "Preposthumorously" — that is, pre-posthumous (I'm still alive), preposterously, humorously and, in my more bawdy moods, prepuce-humorously.

Now it's 1998. Now it's 2098. You're alive. You're dead. An immortal poem can think such thoughts. Or a child: BANG! You're dead! (No! YOU'RE dead!)

Of course, if my poems can take you with them, you, readers, share in any immortality you've helped give them. But it seems a shame, those bright eyes that once twinkled over these pages, shed tears on them (or is that oil and vinegar?) now foom for words! Or form for wombs?[5] Something like that.

I'm just kidding. You're not dead. Neither am I. But you knew that all along, didn't you! I can barely remember when I was last not at all. I'm glad we ARE. It's rather nice — space around us, stunning 3D effects, much we can touch, see, others like us (like us enough to answer when we speak), colors, sounds, tastes, a universe, such a deal! — we must have worked hard for this. Hey! Careful what you touch! This is MY universe! Reader...don't touch that apple...

———

I figure I deserve to be a rich poet. I don't get any of the other perks of being a poet: I don't like booze, I'm monogamous, I'm not wild and crazy, mysterious, angry, insanely passionate, a drug addict, a chain smoker, or even a professor. I don't get to have any fun. I'd thought, at least as a poet I can be a slob and pass it off as Bohemian, to save me from having to use hair oil, which my Mom wanted me to use, because my hair wouldn't stay down, but now I have to make a living in an office and comb my hair and wear clean clothes, so I don't even get to be Bohemian, just nondescript. So I may as well get rich. So send money to help make the world safe for Dean Blehert never again to have to wear a tie.

Don't worry — even when I'm fabulously rich and famous, I won't forget you, my loyal readers, who made it all possible. I promise to have my private secretary *personally* respond to all requests for autographs.

But will fame spoil my lean, hungry poetry? No! It is said that great art is born of suffering. Bowed down beneath that burden of wealth, hounded by IRS auditors, distracted by invitations to appear on TV shows ("Good to be here, Johnny!") and endorse Bic pens ("I am Bic Pen, Tammy, Dear" [iambic pentameter]), don't you think I'd suffer? Ah! The misery, the *poetry* of it!

———

Deanotations now goes to 2000 readers, and I am increasingly asked, what are my criteria for submissions? I will consider poetry written in any form, either serious or humorous, of any length on any subject. I only require that it be written by Dean Blehert. This may seem unfair to all the Seymore

---

[5] That is, "food for worms." But I'm sure there's compensation. Maybe when *they* die, *we* get to eat the *worms!* That'll show 'em! And simultaneously turn both the tables and our stomachs.

Kermerschweigers and Nataly Grimbowskis and other non-Dean Bleherts of the world, but I feel it's time the Dean Bleherts of the world had their forum. There are magazines dedicated to the poetry of militant women, Blacks, radicals, conservatives, imagists, haiku poets, militant Black lesbian radical haiku poets, etc., but nowhere else is there a publication dedicated to the works of Dean Bleherts. If you are, yourself, a Dean Blehert, rest assured that here, if nowhere else, your work will be given friendly consideration. Don't thank me. It's a dirty job, but somebody etc.

―――

SEND ME MONEY. I'LL USE IT TO PUBLISH POEMS. You may not yet have realized that a contribution of $10,000.00 to help me keep the language alive for our descendants (so that they'll be able to cuss us out expressively while paying off the national debt), will cost you less than $1.00 a day for the next 30 years and less than a penny a day over the next 300 years — that's far less than the cost of a pack of cigarettes, a newspaper, a movie, none of which are good for you anyway. You could just send me a penny a day for the next 300 years, but think of the postage!

If 10,000 is too much, I'll take any odd thousand, even hundreds, I'm not proud. There's a certain charm to unfolding a letter and having a check slide out with the smug boldness of a public official who gets to wear a uniform. Cash is okay too. Nothing like having Abe Lincoln, Al Hamilton or Andy Jackson join in admiration of my poems. (Apparently Ben Franklin doesn't read poetry. No wonder — he was a newspaper editor.)

O, send me your rumpled green, the rolled-up refuse of your teeming billfold, yearning to be mine!

Now and then someone says, "I like the poems, but you shouldn't ask people for money — it looks bad." Is not the belaborer worthy of his hire? "But they didn't hire you. It was your idea to send out the poems." You're right. The blame is mine. The buck stops here (all too briefly). I would repent if I had time. Pass me some bucks, and I'll repent all the way to the bank.

―――

Dear Reader,

I find I am grievously misunderstood. Some of my poems make facetious mention of my future fame. A few readers take this to show lack of humility. I assure you that I fully realize that I am only a very minor poet, one small voice among millions, and even if I were one of the better ones, I'm sure there are thousands more skilled than I —and even if I turn out to be the best of the lot, my lifetime is but a moment among the centuries of great poets. And even if I AM the greatest poet earth has ever known, the earth is just one planet among millions with intelligent life, including some whose least literate clods would view our greatest poets as quaint juggling apes. And even if I do happen to be the greatest poet ever in the entire universe, this universe may be only a pimple on the nose of a giant peering at himself

346

in a bathroom mirror. And even if I'm a spiritual being, capable of being nothing at all or being any conceivable size (my nose is itching), in fact, unlimited...is that something to be proud of? So what if this whole universe with its zillions of infinitesimally squeaky Shakespeares is a pimple on my nose? Has this gone to My head? No! We remain Our old loveable Self. We will continue to answer letters, nor will We look down Our Infinite Nose at monetary contributions. We welcome kind words from readers. And best of all, We welcome company. Greatness like Ours is not an easy thing to live with. For millennia of your time, We have sought out a Mate of Our magnitude. Recently We found...HER. Alas, she said she couldn't take seriously someone with a pimple on the tip of His Nose. Reader, nothing personal, but I may need to have your universe surgically removed!

———

I've lost 30 pounds in the past few months. (Will my poems be less jolly?) If you see the pounds I've lost, don't return them. There's no reward. My lost weight is trying to get on with its own life and needs no painful reminders. After all, it's lost me, too. I plan to lose 20 pounds more. Someday my lost weight will be big enough to buy my books.

Weight loss is part of my plan to live forever. To achieve immortality, I must simply lose ALL my weight. That will lessen the strain for any heart I live on in. I don't know why one would want to live in someone's heart, but it's all the rage. No one wants to live on in the kidneys or bladders of mankind.

I worry about living forever — is it too late to start? How long must one live before one can be sure one is living forever? What if I already lived forever? What if, after starting, I decide I don't like it — can I stop? Immortality is not a decision to be made lightly.

Or rather, it's the lightest decision there is: to eliminate time from the diet — but hard, for we're used to munching our minutes-chips, as we watch the big game. After all, we can't have endless time and eat it too.

The easiest way to have time is to create it. Art does that. Bach makes trees sway to it and walls wall to it, putting the universe in its place, not music happening in time, but time happening in music. Each poem I write creates a future in which you read it, where "now when I say this" is also "now when YOU say this" (reading it, getting it), one now, not a physical universe now (Dean Blehert may be dead when you read this), but simultaneity in a time we now create. Art is a cleansing fast that gives you a chance (while not eating time) to digest the old encrusted time (mostly pain and grief) that clogs your system. Here's some fresh poetry juice — it's GOOD for you!

———

The president has just announced that poetry will, henceforth, be the only legal tender, though poems will be exchangeable for dollars for one year, to give people a chance to get rid of their outmoded cash. This will greatly simplify the economy: It will solve inflation, since money will have something behind it (a poet's understood and shared experience). The poetry standard will be safer than the gold standard, since there's no scarcity of poetry. On the other hand, there's no way a government official or banker will be able to turn the stuff out in inflationary trillions on demand. Any poetry created by the U. S. Treasury will be instantly spotted as counterfeit by any grade-school child (though not necessarily by editors, critics and literature professors, who are inclined to assume that anything from a good press deserves consideration). Now the rich will get richer by giving away their wealth, no productive poet will go hungry, and critics will become economists (no one will notice the difference). Hooray for the legally tender!

———

Most people only value what they're told it's OK to value. Value is created for them by anonymous authority hidden in tangles of complexity, the way green bits of paper acquire value from everyone's agreement and from the difficulty of determining where it comes from or who decides what it's worth. (If you can explain what the Federal Reserve is and how it works, you are more dangerous to the economy than the deficit is. Expect no thanks from naked emperors.)

Poetry, too, is valued because "they say" it's worthy. One doesn't simply sell poems to readers. That's too simple. One's poetry must go through the tangled guts of editors and reviewers. Readers know it is permitted to praise a poem when the right editor has printed it and when a critic who is respected (by someone who is respected?) says that the poet is a fresh and important "voice", perhaps "a cross between Ginsberg and Bukowski" (just one more cross for poetry to bear). Before accepting a poem, many editors ask "Where else have you been published?"

My approach, by comparison, has been giddily simple: Poet sends poems to people and says "If you like these, subscribe." Poor people, they feel terribly exposed! "Where are the editors? Where's the list of awards? The critics? How rude? How am I supposed to know what I like!"

Especially when they are expected to PAY for it — give up incredibly complex, hard-to-duplicate bits of paper for such simplicity. So, my readers, I commend your willingness to value what you value.

I commend myself too: Not only do I value what I do, but even when I stare at a poem and can't see what I ever saw in it, I keep writing, as if building a nest to attract that mythical bird, value, which always at last alights, a light indeed.

———

They tell me I'm getting to be quite famous in the future. I even get critical reviews. I hear that in about a hundred years I'll be a fresh new voice. You're doing well too. "Blehert's reader is sensitive, responsive, and gener-

348

ous, yet discriminating. I heartily recommend him or her to any poet looking for an exciting weekend audience." (That's from a review 30 years from now, when they'll be giving reviews of readers equal time in the book review section. The same issue has a scathing review of T. S. Eliot's readers: "Stale...myopic....")

———

Well, the phones are ringing off the hook, and here are the names of new members...We interrupt this fund-raising effort to bring you. Here, have some you. That's one thing art does: Gives you viewpoints to view from. Which is what a "you" is, unless you happen to be the one who's viewing from the viewpoint, in which case, welcome home! Some art gives you sticky viewpoints: You put your head through the hole in the cardboard (to be photographed as, say, a human), and you find yourself glued to the scene. That'll fix you! But my viewpoints are guaranteed slippery.

———

1989, A Note of Irani: I have hinted that we engage in a dangerous conspiracy by entering into live communication this way. It's almost suicidal to talk to each other — like lemmings, but more fulfilling: like the Salmon's Rush-to-die. So when the Poetry Police knock at your door to check out reports you're dealing in poetry that says something, just remember: Ayatola so! Ayatola and Ayatola! Khoumeni times Ayatola?![6]

———

Dear Reader,

When for long periods I spend my days talking to poets about poetry, I begin to forget who you are. You are akin to an imaginary being to whom a small child talks, at first freely, then (after being mocked by an amused adult) secretly or not at all. My reader, like the child's invisible companion, is someone to whom I can say anything — often more than I knew I knew to say — and be understood.

I don't mean that you, reader, are "merely" imaginary. Anything, to become real, must first be imagined, and once real, it must be imagined continuously to remain real, or else, like a marriage grown habitual, it withers into unreality. (When did we stop dreaming America?) I am one of those fortunate children (like Calvin with Hobbes) who has imagined persistently

---

[6] Originally printed shortly after Iran's Ayatola Khoumeni (cleric and dictator) ordered devout Muslims to kill writer Salmon Rushdie for blasphemy. I hope the Ayatola got a cut of Rushdie's royalties (though Khoumeni, having just overthrown the Shah, opposed ties to anything royal; "Royalties, Oh Shah!" scoffed the Ayatola): nothing like a "hit" order in the headlines to increase readership. Odd how willing our newspapers were to make sure the Ayatola's order reached everyone. Thus far, both Rushdie and Islam have survived the Ayatola's insanity. ("What!" shrieks Khoumeni — "Ayatolacerate you!")

enough to have some "real" readers. I even do it in public. It's like playing house: "This time YOU be the Daddy and I'll be the Mommy!" I step into my roles (all the things I can be here) and offer you all the other roles. If they suit you, you fill them up with your world, perhaps discovering in the process that you can be more than you knew.

The news tells us that all over the world people labor bloodily to tell us what we CANNOT be and MUST be. Some say, "You can't be Bosnian" (or Black, Jewish, Armenian...), others, "You should be ashamed" (or law-abiding or heterosexual or respectful or modest or...). That, too, is a way to have a game. Remember when the big kids would tell the little kids exactly what to do and never let them be the hero or the head bad guy, only the unnamed extras who get shot in the first scene?

Poetry, I think, is about being able to choose to be, an invitation to try out new voices, new ears. I think of a child's ease with his secret companion, the way they reason together and change, instantly, all the rules again and again without ceasing their play. I think of play. But when for long periods I spend my days talking to poets about poetry, I forget who you are. Good old reader. (Don't tell the grown-ups.)

———

Here are my latest attempts to say what everyone thinks and thinks he alone thinks. Who is Everyone? Sorry, I've been asked not to disclose the true identity of Everyone, lest Everyone be subject to reprisals by Them, for daring to think what Everyone thinks. I myself am not responsible for these thoughts — the muse did it! My unconscious did it!

Odd notion that everything must come from something else: If something appears to arise "magically," we assume it cannot have come from such as we. Some god or freak of indigestion must have given it to us. Once admit we can't create and **off we go:**

> If we can't be magic,
> We'll settle for tragic;
> That failing, try comic,
> Till quite anatomic.

This must be true; how can such nifty rhymes be coincidence?

Not that we ever stop creating. But when we deny we dream, we dream nightmares, our creating done behind a black velvet curtain with much wizardly hocus pocus to persuade ourselves that we have no control over what our own hands do behind the veil. And here come our creations, swarming over us, as brutal as broomsticks spawned by the ignorant magic of the Sorcerer's Apprentice.

If we poets dream only nightmares for this culture, it will try to drug itself into a dreamless sleep. It's getting late; do you know where your culture is tonight?

350

———

These poems are printed entirely on paper from trees that died natural deaths and use only recycled words (long ago I had to eat them). I don't know what the ink comes from, but the ideas expressed, no matter how meaty they seem, are all made from tofu (*soy dissant*[7]). Despite any appearances of maimed, twisted words, none were injured in the making of these poems, all of which were constructed entirely of American material by an American poet.

———

Fame might ruin me. That's how I've long explained things to myself. (So ruin me already.)

Do you explain things to yourself? Have you noticed how, once you have a good explanation, you're stuck with it? Explanations must be incredibly rare and precious: We would rather endure stale distasteful lives, illness, even death, than give up a single lame explanation. Any explanation is better than none. For many years no one understood me — I made sure of it — because I'd decided that no one understood me. It explained so much! It made sad victories of my greatest failures, for had I not survived their failures to understand me? And that's a FINE explanation for a poet — "They don't understand me!"

I can't become famous, because fame would ruin me — I'd be too busy touring the talk shows to get any poems written, I'd be mobbed by admirers, exploited, flattered into mediocrity, yes, of course, that's why I'm not famous. And you, too, probably fear my fame. After all, if I were a famous poet, you would become my famous readers. Great readers make great poets. And greatness, experts claim, is nigh unto (if not a form of) madness. (We can believe this because all the experts who insist on it are safely mediocre.) Besides, if we were famous, we'd be doomed to eventual oblivion, and we'd know it was coming. We're doomed to eventual oblivion anyway (at least our current names and faces are), but that's OK because we're not famous. The unfamous life is sort of an instant oblivion.

Or maybe we ARE famous. Every restaurant has its "famous secret sauce". You can be "Dean's Famous Reader" if I can be your famous poet. (It helps when you send me one of your famous checks.)

———

My wife tells me, "Your poems aren't just funny — they're really about vital human issues." Yes, I reply, they are about using up trees so that we can see where we're going. In the words of Joyce Killmore, "We MUST pulp more trees!" They harbor wood ticks and other diseased creatures. They make

---

[7] That is, *soi dissant* — "so to speak," as the so-distant French would say it.

it hard to see the forest — or the freeway. They have rough dry skin. They could fall down on us at any moment. They don't like us much: They are many-tentacled monsters trying to fool us into thinking they are harmless by standing still...waiting for their chance. They are hard to read. BUY BOOKS! Help stamp out trees so that we poets can write sad poems about extinct birds.

Actually some of my best friends are trees, and all my poems are printed on paper from spare branches donated by contented trees. So don't be like the illiterate race car driver who said, "I think that I shall never see a tome as lovely as a prix." There was also a sports surgeon who said, "I think that I shall sever knee..." and Hemingway's buddy who, deciding to buy a Ford, said, "I think that I sell Chev, Ernie".

These opening letters serve as proems (brief intros) to my poetry letters, though it would be nicer to serve tea — for there's no proem lovely as a tea (or, said a golfer, any tee lovelier than a Pro-Am). I am grateful to my wife for groaning dutifully at each of the above atrocities. She's priceless. I think that I sell never she.

———

Few realize how important it is that poetry be kept SERIOUS or how hard poets (mostly jolly folks who must struggle to repress their laughter) work at keeping their poetry moistly morose. We'd LOVE to make the world aware of how silly most of it is, but the danger is too great, for there is little that is sillier than sex, these two mostly water-filled cylindrical bags pressing their orifices against each other and squirming and feeling grandiose. There is an absurdity to this activity that only a poet could fully communicate — which would set off a pandemic of laughter that, once begun, could not be stopped. The least reference to sex, after the initial spasms had been controlled, would set them off again. And any attempt, thereafter, to indulge in sex would turn the lovers to quaking jelly. No erection, not even one bolstered by Viagra, can sustain such laughter. And later attempts, schooled by fore-attempts, would more wildly guffaw. The generation that learns to laugh will be the last generation, the end of man. Occasionally even now some tiny sparks of laughter escape into the tinder of our culture, but they are quickly extinguished by the great mass of morbidly lugubrious poetry that keeps wetting down the fuel. But once let poetry become joyous and riotous, and we are lost — unless, by then, we can be cloned (or clowned) in a laboratory.

———

FLASH: Scientists are now able to clone a mature poet from one of his earlier poems. It will do no good to burn my poems now that I can be cloned from just the presence of one of my poems in the mind of a single reader.

Actually, this process has been known to a selected few for years and explains how "I" (we) have managed to keep these issues filled with poems,

352

all by "Dean Blehert" (and whoever heard of a *person* with a name like that?). Here come the clones.

———

Please note: These words may not be reprinted wholly or in part without the author's written consent. The author retains all rights to movie, stage and other versions (e.g., pantomime). Do not reproduce these words on paper, film **or as mental image,** *not even in your dreams!* Do not READ these words without the author's written consent (which consent you MAY, of course, read, so long as you have ascertained, before you begin to read, that what you are about to read is, indeed, the author's written consent). If you have read thus far without express written consent from the author, you will be hearing from the author's lawyer. (Now, where did I put that lawyer?)

———

What the hell are you doing! "Reading"? Weird!

Or so it must have seemed back when literature was word of mouth: Stories round the campfire, priestly chants, as social as tea, and even when written down (to the chagrin of bards and scholars who feared writing would be the death of memory and bemoaned the crude substitute, script, as now writers lament the inroads of television) — even then words were read aloud, father to children, cleric to flock, statesman to populace, lover to lover, so that when first a man was found alone in his private room, gazing upon his bird-tracked parchment and shown to be reading, yet not speaking aloud nor even moving his lips, he was, no doubt, killed or worshiped or both for his witchery.

The nice thing about reading silently is you can make the voice in your head sound the way you wish you sounded. When I first read a poem aloud, my voice seems puny to me, because my inner voice is deep and resonant. What sort of voice are YOU giving me right now? How do you hear it, by the way — with what ears? And who is it that hears your thought when you hear it? Dumb question? No, not dumb, but spoken clearly (neither mute nor moot). How odd! Why are you talking to yourself, and why are you using MY words to do it?

And what about ME? Why do I crave little silent voices all over the world speaking these words to...whom? I am a mind-snatcher! Fall asleep next to this book, and my words will take over your inner voice! Oho! BE-WARE OF THE POETRY! Stay awake!

[Beware: The next and last chapter is serious. If you don't stop reading here, I refuse to be held responsible for unhealthy mental excitation or chemical imbalances that may result from encounters with serious ideas. If you DO read the next chapter, please remain inside the tour bus throughout. Do NOT try to feed or pet the ideas, no matter how tame they may appear. No flashbulbs, please...]

Section 6: The Management Humbly Suggests...

Chapter 13: A Few Words from the Bully Pulpit

A Few Epigiraffes (To Stretch a Point)

Art: A lie for a lie, a truth for a truth.

So many officials speak on our behalf. We object to representation without representation. Perhaps a poet can speak on our be-whole.

Some poets are in love with death — or addicted: They depend on the old bogy to give life an aura of meaning they fear they can no longer create themselves.

Death is a trick for pretending to start over. If you can't make things new, you die. Poets make things new. If we did our job, who'd need death? We'd still trade in bodies on new models now and again. And occasionally we'd lose touch, but only for the fun of finding each other again.

Beautiful sadness is not my cup of tears.

Is it poetry? Do we glisten as we listen?

We have moved apart in order to be able to play catch.

The depth of death exceeds the breadth of breath, but not the width of with.

Many poems I can't write yet — there are so many words for which we have no things.

The poems you are about to read are true. Things have been changed to words to protect their solidity. Any lessening of solidity while reading these poems is purely coincidental.

It is easy for me to get confused with the poet who wrote me: We both speak the same words. But I, the poem, have a much clearer understanding of what I'm saying.

History exhausts words; when our needs revive them, words are blind, dazed, incoherent as newborn babes. Poets teach them to talk.

*What's a poet to do? There are only so many ways to say hello...
so many ways...*

The politics of poetry are simple: Be light-winged or bereft-winged.

If you lived in this line, you'd be home already.

Who taught these words to speak with your voice?

Chapter 13
A Few Words from the Bully Pulpit

WARNING WARNING WARNING (sirens, bells, whistles): The poems you are about to read (I hope you'll read them) are NOT INTENDED TO BE FUNNY AND REALLY DON'T BELONG IN THIS SILLY BOOK, but I know you've been saying, well, smarty-pants, if you're so good at trashing others, let's see what YOU can do, so here's your chance to find me simplistic, wordy, vague, abstract, self-indulgent and all that good stuff.

Some would say, "You've written a silly book. You should save these serious poems for a separate book." Ah, but what better place for them than here, where I can't lose: If you call them lousy, I can say, "Well, but this is a book of parodies. Apparently the parody in the last chapter was too subtle for you. It was all a joke."

Again, be warned, anything in the following poems that you find funny is from YOU. I am dead...I mean dead serious. Well, not serious, just willing to play the straight man for a chapter full of poems about poetry and being a poet — which is one of those subjects poets are taught to avoid in their poetry. "Write about LIFE!" I hope I've written about both poetry and life, and that I can remove the lampshade from my head without ceasing to be the life of the poetry.

The Promiscuity of Poetry

You see, poised in the headlights,
a deer, graceful beyond words.
You try to *say* it — the words
trip over themselves,
so you tuck it away, hoping
to find use for that beauty someday.

Later you meet a girl
whose kiss has a lightness
you can't describe. The words
are heavy on the tongue.
You tuck it away in the same bag,
where it gets jumbled around
until kiss encounters deer, and suddenly
her lips touch you and,
like a deer (whose vanishing lingers on the highway
like the vanishment of the touch of lips),
Leap away.

Doing Our Best

Around me in this park parents, children,
dogs, trees are being the best parents,
children, dogs and trees they can.
Conscientious joggers jiggling, swans swanning away
in spite of floating garbage,
swings — despite rusty squeaks — swinging,
the sky skying vastly overhead,
even a building with rooms for MEN and WOMEN
holds its bricks together dutifully
as it has for decades, and inside it
my body takes a long good piss.

The world is trying hard to be a good world.
I must try to be a good poet.

You Could Write a Poem

People think poems are about things.
They say, "Look at this! You could write
a poem about it" or "You write poems?
What about?" (Do you suffer from poetry
of the trees? Have you had any good
psychological nuances lately? Did you
major in broad social issues with a
minor in angst?) No one ever says,
"Look at this! You could bring it up
at the dinner table" or "You talk
on telephones? What about?" or

358

"You're alive? What about?"
Here's a poem. Why don't I
write it down.

Power Outage

We keep using words that we're told
don't work anymore — beauty, heart,
truth, love — using them because
we *want* them to work.

                    Keats held
truth near beauty, and an arc of
brilliance leapt the gap
to illuminate his century.
Yeats had to give birth to a *terrible*
beauty to ignite us.

                These simple sparks,
like stars hazed over by city lights,
now are blanched by billboards blazoning
the truth of True Cigarettes,
the beauty of beautiful shampoo,
the breakfast cereal you'll love
and the politician you know is right
in your heart.

            Can one ashamed
to say "I love you" love?

                    We try
to heighten love and truth and beauty,
add garish auras with "diseased," "hectic,"
"skeletal beauty," "the rictus of love,"
"the bruised apples of truth left to us,"
"the algebra of the unknown heart" —

but we cannot further overload
these circuits; the fuses blew out
decades ago. Yet we stand here
in the abandoned house, flicking
the dusty light switches on, off,
on, off — because it is all we know

on earth, but not all we need to know —
hoping for light.

Water From Stone

Language, in dead mouths,
turns to stone. This explains
why poets hack and hammer words
into unfamiliar forms: to
surprise language into hectic life:

If you strike the rock, you get water,
but you never get to enter
the promised land. We are commanded
to speak to the rock simply.
It is alive and will respond.

A Poet Needs to be Strong-Winded

He wants to be a free-soaring radiance
or, like Pegasus, to bear heroic force
or to give it wings and be borne aloft by it
or at least towed along behind,
blinking back tears in the starry wind,
but he ends up thudding down the beach,
tugging at a long string, struggling
to keep the pretty thing off the ground
a few minutes more.

"Poet": From the Greek Word for Maker

We are the makers.
When there is nothing left to say,
we make something to say.
When there is no language left to say it in,
we make a language.
When none will listen,
we make them listen.
When there is no one left to listen,
we make listeners.

There's No One Here

I was talking with my friend; he made
his usual gestures and phrases;
suddenly I couldn't see my friend.

I was making love to my lover; her eyes
widened, shiny with — it could have been
passion or fear or the bathroom light
reflected; my body kept going,
but I couldn't find my lover.

I was writing a poem of yearning
beneath the cold moon and felt
the reader's "Ah, yes, that
cold-moon-yearning!" — and suddenly
I was irritated with my reader
for wanting no more than that.

Continuing to write, I noticed
the reader had vanished, my words
disappearing in darkness, like pebbles
dropped into a bottomless well —
I listened in vain for a splash.

I began to talk to myself
and heard my words echoing
before I could think them
and knew that the space I filled
had no one in it.

Empty, I put myself
where I chose to be,
put my reader where I was writing to,
put my lover, my friend
where now I notice you are
here with me,

and these, my creations, recognize
me in return, creating me
from nothing anew.

Our emptiness overfloweth.

After Hearing our Finest Poets Read and Deciding Finally That My Distress was not Just Envy[1]

I object to poetry that uses death
like tits and ass to give us a hard-on
about being human, to wring the last
gooey drop of preciousness
from whatever we think we should cherish,

a device so overused that now
one need not mention death:
It is enough to speak of anything dear
(the softness of a child's cheek,
an unexpected memory of a smile, a ladybug),
and instantly "soon gone forever and
all who cared for it as well"
pops up as pat as a patriot's pride.

Eloquent never-more-ing is no more spiritual
than lucrative lust, both of which reward us
(like a lollipop given a child who keeps quiet
and doesn't touch anything) for being
good little mortal bodies. Who would remember
himself immortal at risk of losing
the preciousness with which our certain
impending loss of whatever we love or are
endows each detail of our lives?
As the setting sun underscores each pebble
with long shadows; as the chill night
strews pearls of dew on each blade of grass;
so, we are told, death endows dearness—

but we could not, generation after generation,
keep pumping up these glad funereal tears
were it not that it is WE who endow dearness,
limitlessly. As you don't have to be Jewish
to love Levy's Jewish Rye Bread, so you don't have to be
dying to have fun.

---

[1] I wrote this rant the day after hearing eleven "chancelors" of the American Academy of Poetry read at the Library of Congress. These poets (among them Kunitz, Merwin, Wilbur, Ashbury, Hecht)) varied immensely in style, craft, theme, wit, etc., yet in one respect, seemed to me to be of one depressing voice: They all seemed to have themselves confused with dying bodies, referring to "spirit," if at all, as a vague and fashionable symbol or yearning or a glorious lost cause or chemical figment, which is one hell of a degradation from what I am and you are.

362

The game, of course, is to create effects
(and poets, who create effects with words alone,
should best know what we are not). But this stuff
that passes for fine poetry is unsporting,
like shooting ducks in a barrel: First persuade
the reader/targets that they are little things
who can't be or have much matter or take up
much space and who lease an even tinier allotment
of time. Then puff up this tiny skin balloon
with the full spiritual afflatus, all that
only an immortal being could feel, yearn, know,
until — to keep from bursting — the reader sheds
a radiant tear, O lovely lovely sadness!

Pin us down and spread our glorious useless wings.
Shrink 'em and pink 'em.

It is not our pleasure in the pure tang
of loss I reject — or in lust either,
but our fear these will be diminished if we know
who plays these games. And, too,
as an immortal being, I could be a challenging target
for effects that would shatter these frail
human vessels — if our poets dared aim
at other than a sitting duck.

And as poet, I wish YOU, my Reader, would be more
than the merely human beautifully sad sot
these poets glorify, so that I could give you
an immortal hello (I know I'd remember how,
if I ever met one who could respond)
without having to fret about the resultant odor
of charred meat.

Becoming Biographies

A living room full of poets and
poetry, we are lifting the earth
with our lightness

when I notice one of us
is dozing (is it that late?)
and kids in the room fidget

or sprawl on rug or couch
in frozen zigzag disco-twisting sleep.

We poets, too, are parents, eaters,
sleepers, a living room full of
the faces in a photograph
of poets in their younger
(am I younger?) days.

As animation ebbs, we look alien —
pictures in a biography
of the long-dead or snowy-locked
bard with face as rugged as rock
or history —

back when he had a black beard,
worried vulnerable eyes,
a self-conscious grin and
(claims the text) would trade poems
with a few poet friends

when he could take the time
from delivering police association
show tickets.

Poets go both ways,

from rosy cheeks to skulls,
from skulls to new buds, just like
"Where have all the flowers gone,"
not the direction, but the play's
the point, not that we say sweet things,
but that there's sweetness in the saying,
in the willingness to play at bones
(one die, two dice) or words.

Even the deadliest all-is-death poet
moves (if only a fraction of an inch)
from broken piece towards player
just by speaking, though his intention be
to win for his despair our company; still
to do so he must turn, face the game.

364

Where the Politically Correct Go Wrong

isn't on propriety: Who knows?
Maybe the world *would* be a better place
if Blacks were Afro-Americans, the deaf
hearing-impaired, etc. What bothers me
is the excessive importance given
my favorite playthings, words. Why
must my toys be converted to unpinned
hand grenades? And why must humanity
be abased by drumming into its (his and
hers or hers and his) poor brain that we
are frail creatures, damaged by these wisps
of air, these words? This frail paper
will not burn up with words that, supposedly,
char you to a crisp. Sticks and stones
are physiologically incorrect, but words
can never hurt me —unless I've been taught
to be a victim of words. My upbringing's Jewish.
If you call me a kike, I'll think you don't like Jews.
That will be your problem. If you teach me
how traumatic it is to be misnamed and
what a crime it is to misname others —
you give me a life lived in terror.
This is not a pipe, a gun, a knife, a penis.
I am not anything you can name me.
Words have the power we give them
to harm, to please. Words communicate
an intention. They become useless
for communication once we are taught
to blind ourselves to intention
as separate from words. I recognize
the good intentions of the politically
correct, thanks, but no thanks: In a world
where words are whips, to speak
is to enslave. The rest is silence.

Roots

Seeing how our neatly sequestered words
are linked in fecund embrace at their roots
(from one seed both hang & hanker sprout;
from another shimmer & squirrel; from another
leek, locket & luxury; and bursting from another

both mother and matter[2]), I realize I'm not needed:
In time the language makes its own poetry.

To Posterity

I

I used to be a poet;
Now I am a poem.
You used to be a stranger,
Now my only home.
Time is done with verbs:
I was, you are, we'll be.
And we're a trick of pronouns:
I'm you and you are me.
Now I touch my forehead.
(I used to have a face.)
Can you feel my finger?
Can words create a space?
If you reach out and touch me,
I'll feel it...felt it — how?
If we think my words together,
Who's listening to us now?

II

I look to the future
To give me what's mine.
I give myself to it
In line after line.
The days of my present
Are your days of yore.
When my days are o'er, mine
My days for your ore.
Your pain has not happened,
But I feel your ache:
I knew you too well,
Alas, poor Yorick!
The daze of your present
Is my daze, of yore:
"Is this all in your mind?"

---

[2] And here's a plum for the maternally militant: Father and perpetrate are from the same root.

366

Yes and no, either/or.[3]
I remain yours most truly,
And you will be mine.
You give yourself to me
In line after line.
Now we're both in a poem
And we'll end in 6 lines.
This way to the future!
Just follow the signs—>
Four lines more and, Dear Reader,
We'll both be the past —
If you think that the maker
Must stick to his last.

III

I used to am.
Now I was.
You used to will be.
Now you...was.
When you say "now",
For me it's then.
We're here together,
but when?

Why I Am Not an Important Poet

Because I don't remind you of Neruda or Lorca or anyone vivid,
 feverish and Latin,

Because I don't remind you of Miles or 'Trane or Billie or anyone
 blue, black and strung out,

Because I don't remind you of Buk or Dylan (either Dylan) or
 anyone boozy, brassy and barfy and kind of canny,

Because I don't remind you of Ginsberg or Corso or anyone beat
 or beatifically blowzy,

Because I don't remind you of TSE or W.St. or Wm. C. W. or

---

[3] Originally this line was "Asks our old ether/or," but no one understood it: That the
ether that sedates us in the sleep we call present time (everyone's agreed-upon world)
is the notion that what we create is "*mere*" imagination, not real.

Ezra P. or Robert L. or Sylvia P

or anyone one might encounter in College English,

Because I don't remind you of Walt W. washing over you
        with his murky waves or Emily D.

showing you her whatnot shelves wedged tight with delicate china
        figurines (webbed with fine cracks),

Because I don't remind you of anyone — not that there's no one I
        might remind you of, but

no one that you'd remember —

So, no, I don't remind you of anyone, so I am not
anyone that anyone would ever hear of, not memorable,
because to be memorable, one must be, already,
a memory.

Perhaps years from now, when I am forgotten
(it won't take long),
someone will remind you of me, and then
I will have become a memory.

Even then, I won't be important,
but maybe others will be important
because they remind you of me.

Snacking

I study and study the menu
(quiz on Friday?): Everything
is unappealing or too expensive
or not good for me.

I tell myself, it must be
there is some one perfect morsel
I crave, something exquisite
I can almost taste that nothing
on this menu quite is.

It's always this way

when I'm not hungry,
just trying to give myself
a treat I haven't earned.

It's like writer's block,
searching, searching (a nervously
revolving beam — did a shadow stir?
"It's just the cat." And there?...)
for the elusive perfect thing to say

when all the things I should do
but do not or should not do
but do have cut me off

from the ability to create
a me to speak and a you
to speak to.

Putting Us On

Writing is like trying on clothes in a store:
Let's see how I look in "My life has not been
a happy one" — too plain, no, let's try "That spring
all the apples were withered and worm-eaten"—
no, that's last season's rage, passé now; well,
I'll bet I'd look great in "A white plague hovers —
the irises cannot hide us" —no, gaudy, pretentious...

So you go back to the dressing room a final time
to put on the clothes you came in wearing,
but —and here's where the simile ends —
but they're gone, maybe someone took them
to try them on, maybe you never had them,
have always been naked, but —
and here the simile gets ridiculous! —
but not only the clothes are gone;

you, too, are gone, there is no
nakedness, someone is trying you on
or maybe you never were or were only
a desire to try things on,
starting with nakedness.

Honking

He wanted to say to the man
in the car dawdling ahead,
"Excuse me, please; I'm late,
could you let me past?" But some
sorcerer had taken from him the gift
of language, and all he could say
was a sneering HONNNK! to which the other,
as bewitched as he, could respond only
with a flash of snarling face and
flick of finger, and by then
he too had mistaken for rage
his frustration at not being able
to explain and lacked only the courage
to rear-end the SOB!

Caught in the grip of a similar magic,
he wanted to say to the woman
across the red-checked tablecloth
how the world and their bodies seemed
the surface of a bright balloon
filled to buoyancy with tenderness,
but felt he could only honk "I love you"
and other borrowed noises and, ashamed
to use such second-hand charms,
said nothing, said, at last,
"Yes, it's been fun; we should
do this again sometime."

The thing is to impinge, make
an effect. When light, airy things
like love and reason won't stir
a thick brain or hide, heavy blunt
symbols will; when words won't touch,
bullets will.

There are finer tools,
but now we rely on words' worn magic.
Here we sharpen recycled words for use.
No one should have to say "I love you"
with bullets, and even hate
relishes precision and would go away
if for once it could be spoken.

370

Form and Duty

There's freedom in beginnings: I set sail
Across the ocean of an empty page,
Scudding before what wind of love or rage
I choose —toward realms of gold, in wake of whale...,
But my supply of rhymes begins to fail;
The ocean shrinks, and all the world's a stage.
Tense, leonine thoughts pace the metric cage
With barely room to turn. UNUSED RAGE FOR SALE.
Competing metaphors clamor for decisions:
Scalpel! —my muse, let's see what we can save:
It's grave —time for incisions and revisions.
You'll be precision's artist or his slave.
I chose this perilous dance out of the dust
And earned the freedom to do what I must.

Terminal High

Communication, like sugar, is an energizer
(foe of insulin —the insula that no man is)
that, over-refined, purified to bodiless,
timeless, sourceless blips on a screen,
is assimilated in a flash, creating
an instant craving for more — more
empty bytes, words and images devoid

of the roughage of clammy handshakes,
awkward lips encumbered by runny noses,
shouting over traffic noise and crowds,
tasting each other's entrees and then
each other, unruly hair that needs washing,
tired feet, body odors, laughter — not coded
in exclamation points, but laughter,
the high colloidal mineral content of tears
and long silences filled and emptied by joined
and disconnected gazes —

or even without these, the catches in the voices
of poems that must be read more than once
and cannot be answered in a second or a day,
demanding a life for a life —

the slow energizing metabolic breakdown

371

of world into world, of our being
with and without and
with each other.

Supposing

Suppose I am recognized
as the greatest poet on earth —

Does that mean the kids who mocked me
in school will repent
or that the cockroaches I've crushed
will think it worth the pain?

No, but by then the meanness
of the children and the agony
of the cockroaches
will owe their existence
to my poems.

How Tom Swift and His Magic Poem
Outsmart the Consciousness Machine

Tall, fair, fifty-ish, professorial, preparing
to read his poems, a few ah words first uh
about the um UNCONSCIOUS, its er magic, and letting
the poems say what he, himself, cannot say.

It is not enough to simply say
what one's poems say?
I want his poems to be bad,
but they are good, high-strung, but eloquent —
I can even hear him talking to me — he,
not a swamp thing coated in gleaming slime.

Now a few unmagic words about his next poem.
What talks to us now — an all-purpose handy-dandy
feeling insulator, public speaker, eye-lid
controller; can dice, peel, slice and
qualify a statement every which way,
step right up! — this must be...
CONSCIOUSNESS? Looks very much like
him to casual scrutiny. It must have taken

millennia to construct.

Now he reads a poem,
the machine is reading...fading away —
yes, it is he out of hiding, his words,
each cherished. I can still make out
the ghostly outline of machinery,
a dim reminder that the audience is real
and alien, much cannot be said, some
defense is necessary, this is the poem,
not me, I didn't do it, honest! I
am a decent man, properly buttoned and zippered,
would never communicate nakedly in public,
cry out as this poem cries out before strangers,
no, the Unconscious is doing it,
and not even MY unconscious, but
OURS, so don't blame me...

but his words — he made them himself,
he cannot deny his children, yes,
he speaks to us, alive, knows us who
know his words no strangers. We applaud,
yes, yes, it is safe, stay with us. See
how he glows as we tell him he won't
hurt us, we won't hurt him, all
is understood, all is forever forgiven!

But you've been fooled before, whispers the machine,
which has served him long enough to have
its own life and will not be put aside,
seizing first eyebrows, then mouth,
then the whole body, an erect coffined space
that excludes us. Thank you, thankyou very much
says the machine, and he is safe again
behind the furrowed brow, the bureaucracy
of ancient decisions and precedents.

He hides among mirrors, puts forth
thoughts and feelings which are seized
by machinery and processed while the mouth
makes words ("One might say...", "So to speak...",
"Moreover...", "As it were..."), the eyebrows
heave and knit, weighty shadows mass
and shift about the brow, eyes dull and, duly,
twinkle, hands rise, touch, fall,
and just an errant glancing refraction

escapes the mirror maze to find us.

Like one who gets drunk to work up nerve
to make a pass, he plunges into poetry
to solve being conscious, to say
what the machine cannot. Each face
he turns to us is a decision
he has forgotten he made to be safe
by having something else be there instead.

Proudly, though hesitantly, the machine introduces
the next poem it thinks, perhaps, it can control.
"The Unconscious", paraded before us on a leash,
feels its power, almost remembers
who made the machine, stirs, reaches,
is yanked back, subsides.

    Speak to him
afterwards, more relaxed, one on one, but
cautiously: Say you enjoyed the poems, smile,
say nothing of machines bearing gifts —
you are a stranger, and mad mirrors lurk.

Black Holes

Tight, clever, intricate, dense —
but compression has a point of no return,
the spine of elasticity snapped,
long-isolated life neither answering
nor showing it has heard, a shrunken head
that won't pretend ever to have lived:

Nothing you can give it will it own
nor can the least gleam of the layers
of luminous meaning it has attracted
and solidified into itself escape.

It has lost compression's magic:
the mimicry of life when what has been crushed
expands: Crumpled paper in the waste-basket
startles us unfolding; we smile to see a chip
of paper (just add water) become a rose; to see
a thin red cylinder (just add fire) become
a dazzling umbrella of sparks; a tiny seed (add

earth and air and sun to taste) or haiku (just add
reader and stir) flower into a world:

OH! AH!

Sharpen The Sword

A sword kills so well because it is almost
humane. A blunt instrument is an outrage:
Instantly flesh rebels. Sharpen it to a point,
and it gains easy entry. Hone it to a fine edge,
and flesh welcomes it: in and out before one knows
death has been done. Sharpen the sword
further until nothing is left
but the deadly swift essence of penetration
that comes and goes and one never knows
why everything has changed, and you have
not a sword, but a poem.

Tanka:

Poet out walking
stops here and there just looking...
"BARK! BARK! Go away!"
People who stop for nothing
make domestic dogs nervous.

I Think I'll Wag My Dog's Master,
Said The Dog's Tail's Flea

"I think I'll write a poem tonight."
This sounds like a rational thing to think,
like "I think I'll tie my shoe."

Actually it's more like "I think
I'll have rain tonight and a full moon
tomorrow." A poem is an event
in many universes, many universes
realized on the matrix of one event.

It is a voice that speaks already
from the throats of those who will ever
read it, who speak already here
and are here being created —

whole unborn populations —
to be the beings from whom this,
our voice, speaks.

Write Me

"Write me a love poem," she said.
I'm trying, but I keep wanting
just to look at you. I'll write you
later. There's no hurry:

Poems aren't snapshots of what
would otherwise be lost forever.
They record what cannot be lost,
as expendable as your smile,
made to last only by virtue
of their being so utterly given away
that they keep being given away.

July Night

My head is full of poems; how can I sleep?
I stir — you lift your dim, half-woken head.
In summer heat unwritten poems won't keep.

I count iambs; perhaps I should count sheep.
My lines and I writhe on Procrustes' bed.
My head is full of poems; how can I sleep?

At our feet this sultry night a blanket heap;
But still I sweat — what labors to be said?
In summer heat unwritten poems won't keep.

You turn...turn back; clock hands in circles creep.
Blind through the night our twisting paths we tread.
My head is full of poems; how can I sleep?

Dawn's gauzy light peeks in; did a bird peep?

376

I've tried each fitting rhyme from A to Zed.
In summer heat unwritten poems won't keep.

I watch the room in sunlight slowly steep,
My poem and I wide waking, the last sheet shed.
My head is full of poems; how can I sleep?
In summer heat unwritten poems won't keep.

The Ears Have Walls

Poet out walking asks streets, trees,
houses, men and women caught up
in the hard sunshine, everything
without voice, to sing for him
as of old, offering them
his own voice to sing with.

And everything tries to sing for him,
but it's thin, grating, far away,
like an old scratchy record.

Can't things sing sweetly anymore?
Or has the poet grown deaf with age?

Despairing of anything ever again
singing with his voice, he cries out
(or is it still the world making use
of his unretractably offered voice?):

a harsh alien cry, almost not even
a voice, surely not singing —

or have we all grown old and deaf?

Copilot To Pilot: Over And Out

After reading a poem ("Orb" by A. R. Ammons) that imagined worlds beyond human perception, then bemoaned their being merely imaginary.[4]

This obsessive dream of the physical
has become so vivid for us
that the first glimmer of waking,
squinted at through bleary eyes,
is a dim ghost of the dreams
we haven't yet let go of —
a dream itself, our waking,
getting real as slowly as we credit it
and move out into it, begin to touch
and name things, create them anew.

So it is frustrating to me when you,
half awake, take me with you on a tour
of the emptiness between swirling
scintillant galaxies or show me exactly
what the ripple of passage of the shadow
of a blackbird's wing over a strip of grass
does to the cellular hubbub inside an aphid

(putting me THERE, dimly, but definitely —)
only to lament our limits and elaborately
come to terms with our human inability
to know such things as those we have just
(hanging onto your wings) known —

all "Imagination" merely. Where do poems go
when thus they die? You, who escorted me,
how could you not have been there too?
How dismiss it as mere invention?
And if it be that, can we ever know *anything*
we do not first invent?

It's true that out among the nebulae,
I was, to most of my senses, still inhabiting
a human head, but only because

---

[4] The stupidest word of tongue or pen, Dear, is "mere." (Mere words, mere imagination…mere life and death.) Or perhaps it is merely the most misused word, though "simplistic" runs a close second. "You're merely imagining things" is simplistic. "You're imagining things" is simple.

my being a head has been so long
and so forcefully and by so many
imagined.

Vision betrayed instantly — poor ember of dawn —
goes out, as, drugged by agreement, you roll over,
clench your eyes and try to sleep,
to dream the bad dream to a bittersweet end,

leaving me alone here clinging to the grey thread
of morning light beneath the shade.

Mere Words

Where are these words so lightly labeled "mere?"
You, sirs, "of," "the" and all your common sort —
Are you mere words, no action but light sport
for idle tongues? (They stammer, for I fear
They need some whatness words.) Then "Love," I hear
That you make nothing happen. You cavort
In paper sheets — no sweat! — with your cohort,
Grim "Death," cry out (sans voice) to "God"…Oh dear!
Could all of you be merely mere? — I'll not
Believe a word of it, because one day
I said "I love you" and I did, and I
And love and you were joined — mere words besot
Us so! Yet now in silent interplay
Of merely mirrored eyes, we, wordless, lie.

Shhh! Listen!

Books speak with sub-audible voices —
I wonder, does the Shakespeare I read
speak with the same pitch and timbre
as the one you read? I, too, have my own
inner voice (at least one).

I remember the first time I heard my voice on tape,
the shock — that squeaky child's voice,
when to myself I had a deep, man's voice,
like the Lone Ranger's.

I don't much listen to myself now,

but I think gradually my inner and outer voices
are becoming friends.

I Want To Be A Library

I've had enough of being merely humanoid.
Next lifetime I want to be a library.
In mythic times appointment to be a forest
was a real plum. You'd make music
with wind and sun, nurture the big-eyed deer,
solace harassed goddesses and sorrowful shepherds,
teach savagery and shadowy music.

But forests now are thin and hectic,
numb with loss; the best of them
fill libraries. So I'll try for library,
or if that's too much for me after centuries
of being manacled in arms, I'll be
the poetry section or the mystery novels:

I'll nudge forward almost imperceptibly
the book that will give each browser
cheer and insight. Or if nothing
can allay the pangs of, for example,
star-crossed lovers who grope
for brief intimacy in my dusky stacks,

I'll metamorphose them into *Romeo and Juliet*,
or *Wuthering Heights*. More calloused flirts
who violate my hush will become Harlequin Romances
or collections of dirty limericks. Even my dust
will have a mellow, ancient smell.
I will teach savagery and shadowy music.

Good Company

The library — a choice of company.
When professors recited their notes
or rambled on, I could go to the library
and listen to Tolstoy, who, before he grew
gaunt and carping, knew everyone and spoke
so simply and deeply even wood grain in
dark library tables glowed a deeper luster

to hear him. Tolstoy, Shakespeare,
Nabokov, Kafka, Lawrence — my companions
in those headier days when I needed giant worlds
to contain safely my own burgeoning boundaries.
Later, less starved for company, I took dessert
with Chandler, Hammett, Leonard, McBain,
Grafton. A choice of company. And so
I write, hoping to give as good as I got,
hoping to be good company.

Write to Remain (The Arrest is Silence)

"Anything you say can be used against you."
Comforting to know
my every word
is of use.

I use dangerously plain words.
They don't take to strangers.
You could get hurt
trying to use my words
against me.

You don't love my words at all!
You're just using them!

"Say Yes! to life." "Just say no."
You have the right to remain silent.

"Do you deny saying 'the',
'if', 'and', 'on', and 'you'?"

No...but it was just talk!
I didn't mean anything by it!

They read you your rights.
Your wrongs you already know
by heart.

"Do you deny saying 'glimmer',
'conflagration,' 'gossamer', 'bone-white'
and 'caress'?"

Yes, those were my words, but

that's not what I meant at all.

"Where was your face before you were born?"
It went for a walk, alone, then to a movie.
"What is the sound of one hand clapping?"
I hear it often at poetry readings.

"Did you ever say 'O!', 'frail', 'geometry of winter',
'I know not what', 'flashed a smile', 'darted a glance' and
'into the night'?"

I used the words, sure, but they weren't mine,
none of them, I stole them all; always,
behind the words of others,
I was silent.

"You stole...?"

Well, borrowed, yes, but only to speak
to those with borrowed ears.
I told them what they wanted to hear.
Nothing I said can be used.
Not even against the alleged me.

"You deny being me?"

There's no proof.
Pronouns have been protected
to change the innocent.

"Read him his rights."
(Ah, write me, my readers!)
"Book him."
(Yes, book me, chapbook me, anthologize me,
page me, sentence me...)

How can I remain silent
when I have never been silent?

"You are accused of being
here and communicating!"

"Anything you say will be taken down..."

What is taken down
must be taken up.

Do you think your silence cannot be used
against you? We have ways
of making you talk:
"See the birdie! Say birdie!
Very Goood! Now, see the doggie!..."

It was only a game, I just wanted
to create an effect, I didn't mean.
"A likely story."

"Just tell me one thing:
Did you do it?" Yes, but it was
intentional.

"How do you plead?"
With all my heart.

"I'm innocent!" he cried
with conviction.

Honest, I'm just a fresh new voice,
speaking with an authority and mature vision
beyond my years and sustaining
a delicate ironic balance...

"Objection: Irrelevant, incompetent
and immaterial." "Sustained."

"S-s-stained!" stuttered the s-s-specked.

What IS the truth, the whole truth
and nothing but the truth?
(Silence in the court)

You are already sentenced to life
and death: What can be done to you?

Life without parole, that is,
life without the word, silence.

I have given you my words,
and speak them now
only if you speak them.
Your silence
is my silence.

Don't be silent; be silence:
When silence speaks,
silence listens.

I retain the right
to remain violent.
You have the silence
to remain right.
You have the right to
silent remains.
The rite has you.
Silence remains.

Don't forget to write.

Newspaper: Read Read Read, fast as I can because it's a waste of time. Read everything, trying to make it not a waste of time, read fast, trying to make it a waste of not much time. Walk out of the café, leaving gray folded paper on a table; Sun, sidewalk, sky — what does it have to do with which face in a suit got elected or who got shot, burned, disagreed with where? It does, it must (must have to do with) — the world is the world is the world without end, etc. But no, I'm looking right down the street in plain morning sunlight, old storefronts stretching their bricks in the brightness and the nothing happening here is more than all the news crammed into all the wads of gray paper in the world. Or there are two worlds or many. FLASH: NEWS NOT REAL POET CLAIMS. PRESIDENT, CONGRESS, WORLD LEADERS, SEVERAL NATIONS AND SUNDRY MOVEMENTS DISSOLVE IN LOZENGED SHADOW OF CORNER TRASH CAN WHILE SHRILLY DENYING UNREALITY.

Cloud World

This is a world of clouds, precise forms dissolving.
Our bodies are a slower sort of cloud, and slower
still the molten earth and galaxies — all pretty
swirls (whirled without end!) of star vapor.

You and I are not clouds; we are as permanent
as we are formless, but our pitter-pat-poems
(raining here) are little fuzzy cloudlets
condensing to ideas.

We, who are formless, use a dissolving form
to send a cloud memo to ourselves and our kind
here among cloud chaos to remind us
(then vanish across the sky, bright omen)

that we are the makers. Poems will not last
forever: The sky-writer's message, sharp and dense
at the fine point of creation, trails off,
spreading, unraveling at the edges, and soon

cannot be distinguished from...clouds. Bodies too —
and worlds and galaxies — are languages become noise,
messages we sent each other long ago, before we'd
mistaken ourselves for our messages to each other.

A Choice of Dreams

When I sit down to write again
I find that you have changed —
You are ready to hear
new things, as changed from the reader
I once knew as is an adult from a child —
all head, huge eyes and quick tumbling about
like a bounce-up doll, hardly the same species,
one would think.

Now I must change
to be able to say
what you are ready to hear.

It is as if you sleep
and the world's noise will wake you
if I cannot concoct quick enough
dream reasons to make dream sense
of the newest noises.

Only in shared dreams are we together.

This sleep is our waking
to each other. But old dreams,
old reasons lose their magic and become
part of the noise, like litter
of old newspapers.

It's not that you have changed, no more
than I have. It's the noise that's changed —
it has captured more of our dreams,
the better to masquerade as waking.
the waking that would mock us
with gargoyled distortions of old dreams
clung to too long.

There is no waking, no sleep, only the dreamer
and a choice of dreams.

Angels

"Angel" translates a Hebrew word
meaning "Messenger". We each
came here with a message
for all the others,
could not speak each other's languages
(each had his own),
garbled each others messages
in desperate attempts to translate,
to understand...
gave up, forgot.

Hence this hell
full of fallen angels.

When any man rediscovers
what he has to say,
he can no longer remain
merely human.

The remembering alone
makes an angel, the saying
a poet.

Index of Subjects and Authors

387

Index of Titles and First Lines

397

About the Author

"The Author" — Wow! Solemn music, please!

With a name like "Dean Blehert," I must be real. And various magazines have published my poems, so I must be a real poet. (The standard thing at this point is to list all but two of the magazines so that I can end the list with "...and many others.")

If not demonstrably real, I am at least virtual, which you can verify by visiting www.blehert.com, where you'll find photos of me and Pam, more of my stuff and some of Pam's paintings and poems. Since my first name is Maurice (pronounced Morris — Dean's my middle name), I can claim to be both virtual and Morous (if not ethicacious).

Pam Coulter Blehert, my artist wife, is at least as real as I am. I touch her as often as I can, just to make sure. (Here comes our ancient cat, whining "make me real too!") In case you're not me (if you're reading this, the odds are you *are* me, but I hope a few others get this far), you'll have to trust me on this, unless you're one of Pam's old boyfriends. (Warning, if anything in this book touches you, then you too may be afflicted with reality.)

We live in Reston, with our zero sons and zero daughters, all brilliant.

This is my 6th book — I hope I got it right this time. My 15-year-old subscription poetry letter, "Deanotations" (my poems, Pam's drawings) goes out every two months. My two most recent books are:

I Swear He Was Laughing: Poems About Dogs (Mostly) Who Only THINK They Are People, But Aren't, So Can't Read This Book, So Will You Please Read It for Them? (ISBN 0-9644857-4-5)
and
No Cats Have Been Maimed or Mutilated During the Making of This Book ...But Some of Them Are Disappointed — DEEPLY Disappointed — in Me (ISBN 0-9644857-5-3)*

I am probably a great poet, but if not, I love me anyway just for being me. "How I Learned to Live with my own Greatness," (soon to be a Movie-of-the-Week!)

---

*[Order from any book store or online from Amazon.com or BarnesandNoble.com.]

402